Rethinking Development in East Asia

From Illusory Miracle to Economic Crisis

Edited by Pietro P. Masina

CURZON

Nordic Institute of Asian Studies
Studies in Asian Topics Series, No. 29

First published in 2002
by Curzon Press
Richmond, Surrey

Typesetting by the Nordic Institute of Asian Studies
Printed and bound in Great Britain by
TJ International Limited, Padstow, Cornwall

Publication of this book was assisted by a grant from RUF (the Danish Council for Development Research).

British Library Cataloguing in Publication Data

Rethinking development in East Asia : from illusory miracle
to economic crisis. - (NIAS studies in Asian topics ; no. 29)
1.International economic relations 2.East Asia - Economic conditions
I.Masina, Pietro P. II.Nordic Institute of Asian Studies
338.9'1'095

ISBN 0-7007-1214-3

Rethinking Development in East Asia

NORDIC INSTITUTE OF ASIAN STUDIES

NIAS Studies in Asian Topics

✧✧✧✧

15. Renegotiating Local Values
Merete Lie and Ragnhild Lund
16. Leadership on Java
Hans Antlöv and Sven Cederroth (eds)
17. Vietnam in a Changing World
Irene Nørlund, Carolyn Gates and Vu Cao Dam (eds)
18. Asian Perceptions of Nature
Ole Bruun and Arne Kalland (eds)
19. Imperial Policy and Southeast Asian Nationalism
Hans Antlöv and Stein Tønnesson (eds)
20. The Village Concept in the Transformation of Rural Southeast Asia
Mason C. Hoadley and Christer Gunnarsson (eds)
21. Identity in Asian Literature
Lisbeth Littrup (ed.)
22. Mongolia in Transition
Ole Bruun and Ole Odgaard (eds)
23. Asian Forms of the Nation
Stein Tønnesson and Hans Antlöv (eds)
24. The Eternal Storyteller
Vibeke Børdahl (ed.)
25. Japanese Influences and Presences in Asia
Marie Söderberg and Ian Reader (eds)
26. Muslim Diversity
Leif Manger (ed.)
27. Women and Households in Indonesia
Juliette Koning, Marleen Nolten, Janet Rodenburg and Ratna Saptari (eds)
28. The House in Southeast Asia
Stephen Sparkes and Signe Howell (eds)
29. Rethinking Development in East Asia
Pietro P. Masina (ed.)
30. Coming of Age in South and Southeast Asia
Lenore Manderson and Pranee Liamputtong (eds)

Contents

Part I: East Asia and the International Regime

Part II: Towards a Hegemonic Crisis of 'Neoliberal' Thinking?

p.2 p.45-7
p.9 WA consensus, good quotes, - more in chs 4-5

PART III: NATIONAL MODELS AND DEVELOPMENT STRATEGIES

PART IV: SOCIO-ECONOMIC IMPLICATIONS OF EAST ASIAN DEVELOPMENT – BETWEEN MIRACLES AND CRISES

TABLES

FIGURES

ABBREVIATIONS

ADB	Asian Development Bank
AFTA	ASEAN Free Trade Area
AMF	Asian Monetary Fund
ASEAN	Association of Southeast Asian Nations
CDS	Capitalist Development State
EANIC	East Asian Newly Industrializing Country
EMR	Extended Metropolitan Region
ESAF	Enhanced Structural Adjustment Facility
EUROSEAS	European Association for Southeast Asian Studies
FDI	Foreign Direct Invesment
FINNIDA	Finnish International Development Cooperation Agency
GDCF	Gross Domestic Capital Formation
GDP	Gross Domestic Product
GSO	General Statistical Office
GSP	Generalized System of Preferences
HIPC	Highly Indebted Poor Countries
HPAE	High Performing Asian Economies
IIF	Institute for International Finance
ILO	International Labour Organization
IMF	International Monetary Fund
LTCM	Long Term Capital Management
MITI	Malaysian Ministry of International Trade and Industry
NGO	Non-Governmental Organization
NIC/E	Newly Industrialized Countries/Economies
NLIEO	Neoliberal International Economic Order
ODA	Official Development Assistance
OECD	Organization for Economic Cooperation and Development
OEM	Original Equipment Manufacturing

SAC	Structural Adjustment Credit
SAP	Structural Adjustment Programme
SOE	State-owned Enterprise
TNC	Transnational Corporation
UNCTAD	United Nations Conference on Trade and Development
UNCTC	United Nations Centre on Transnational Corporations
USTR	United States Trade Representative

CONTRIBUTORS

Bruno Amoroso, Department of Social Sciences, Roskilde University, Denmark.

Nicola Bullard, Focus on the Global South, a Bangkok-based policy research and advocacy NGO associated with the Chulalongkorn University, Thailand.

C. P. Chandrasekhar, Centre for Economic Studies and Planning, School of Social Sciences, Jawaharlal Nehru University, New Delhi.

Chang Kyung-sup, Seoul National University, South Korea.

Chris Dixon, Department of Politics and Modern History, London Guildhall University.

David Drakakis-Smith, Department of Geography, University of Liverpool, Great Britain.

Jayati Ghosh, Centre for Economic Studies and Planning, School of Social Sciences, Jawaharlal Nehru University, New Delhi.

Jacques Hersh, Research Center for Development and International Relations, Department of History and International Studies, Aalborg University, Denmark.

Andrea Kilgour, Department of Geography, University of Liverpool, Great Britain.

Pietro P. Masina, Department of Social Sciences, Roskilde University, Denmark.

Michael J. G. Parnwell, Department of Politics and Asian Studies, University of Hull, Great Britain.

James Putzel, Development Studies Institute, London School of Economics and Political Science.

Jonathan Rigg, Department of Geography, University of Durham, Great Britain.

Johannes Dragsbæk Schmidt, Research Center for Development and International Relations, Department of History and International Studies, Aalborg University, Denmark.

David Sneath, Department of Social Anthropology, University of Cambridge.

Ngai-Ling Sum, Department of Politics and International Relations, Lancaster University, Great Britain.

Li Xing, Research Center for Development and International Relations, Department of History and International Studies, Aalborg University, Denmark.

ACKNOWLEDGEMENTS

An edited volume of this magnitude (at least in terms of the number of pages, it is left up to the readers to judge the quality!) is the result of a long period of work and of the concourse of many people. Now that the volume is finally ready, it is my great pleasure to express my warm thanks to all the people who have made this publication possible.

First of all I would like to thank my co-authors – not only for the scientific value of their contributions but also for their patience in adjusting to the restrictions of an edited volume. Special thanks go to Mike Parnwell for much useful advice.

The punctual comments by two peer reviewers are thankfully acknowledged. Their remarks were of great help when revising all the texts.

Most of the chapters are based on papers originally presented in a conference at Roskilde University in October 1998, and then revised and updated several times. I would like to thank all the colleagues who contributed to that conference either by presenting papers or by participating in the debate.

The conference was supported by the Department of Social Sciences, Roskilde University, and by the Nordic Institute of Asian Studies (NIAS). My gratitude goes to the directors of the two institutions – to Bent Greve and to NIAS' director at that time, Robert Cribb, for encouragement when this research project was still in an embryonic stage. Thanks go also to the colleagues of the Federico Caffè Centre of Roskilde University and to its director, Bruno Amoroso, for backing me in this venture.

The conference was financially supported by the Danish Council for Social Sciences (SSF) and by the Danish Council for Development Research (RUF) and the Tuborg Foundation. A further grant was received from RUF for the publication of the volume. These contributions are gratefully acknowledged. The organizing of the conference would not have been possible without the tireless work of Helle Hartman, Malin Westerlund, Marianne Jølby and Wang Danyi, together with the students of the 1998–99 ESST Master course.

Last but not least, warm thanks are due to the NIAS Publishing staff for friendly and professional guidance, advice and encouragement through all the stages of the work. Sandra Jones was a very accurate and strict copy-editor, Liz Bramsen an impressive desk-editor, able to keep track of even the smallest detail. Everything was checked and rechecked, and when things seemed to be ready, the typescript was checked once again by the professional eyes of Leena Höskuldsson. Andrea Straub and Janice Leon dealt with all the administrative and legal matters, while Gerald Jackson, the commander-in-chief, extended his benevolent blessing over all of us.

PREFACE

In 1997 an economic crisis in East and Southeast Asia shattered the lives of millions of people from South Korea to Indonesia. A generation which had grown up with the promise of future prosperity as the reward for economic and political discipline awoke to the reality that the dawn of the twenty-first century would see Asia struggling with economic malaise, political uncertainty and depressed standards of living.

The crisis also shattered the comfortable assumptions of many academic observers of the region. Even though Paul Krugman and others had cast doubt on the fundamental soundness of East Asian economic growth, no serious scholar had foreseen the scale or the course of the crisis. An analytical scramble-to-explain therefore quickly began.

This scramble, however, soon took a perplexing turn. The proximate cause of the crisis was Asia's involvement in abundant but volatile global money markets. This involvement, a product of global deregulation of currency and financial markets during recent decades, encouraged massive speculative borrowing and what soon turned out to be unsustainable levels of debt, which were then punished savagely in a fickle market.

A powerful line of analysis, however, emerged to blame the crisis on what was loosely called 'crony capitalism'. This term had first emerged in critiques of the Marcos regime in the Philippines and stood for a wide range of 'special' relationships between business-owners and governments in East Asia, ranging from straightforward corruption to various forms of mutual economic support. This line of analysis was perplexing, both because cronyism in its broad sense had attracted remarkably little criticism from the global economic establishment in the boom days of the early 1990s and because the direct connection between cronyism and acute crisis seemed to be tenuous.

Not only did this analysis fail to satisfy intellectually, but it also quickly developed worrying policy implications, providing grounds for exposing battered societies and fragile national economies to indiscriminate deregulation and opportunistic Western firms. The imaginative experimentalism of remedies for the crisis which were proposed from time to time would have been more admirable if they did not appear to ignore the acute short-term suffering which they were likely to cause people in the societies involved.

In response to this unexpected development in the debate over the crisis, Roskilde University and the Nordic Institute of Asian Studies combined in 1998 to sponsor an international conference on the broader context of the Asian crisis. The conference, organized by Pietro Masina, had three aims. First, it sought to assess the meaning of Asia's economic 'miracle' before 1997 in the light of a structural analysis of the global economy and especially of the role of the state in promoting economic development. Second, it sought to explain the crisis in these terms, rather than by resort to the simple accusation of corruption. And third, it aimed to bring to the foreground the human consequences of the crisis and of poorly thought-through measures to resolve it.

This book is an outcome of that conference, its chapters thoroughly revised in the light of discussions at the conference and in the light of broader academic developments since then. The Asian economic crisis may officially be over, but its consequences for the societies of Asia's Pacific rim remain profound.

Robert Cribb

ONE

Introduction

Pietro P. Masina

At the time of presenting this volume, East Asia ('East Asia' herein refers to East and Southeast Asia) has officially recovered from the crisis. Many countries of the region – and notably China – have returned to high economic growth rates. A closer examination, however, indicates that the systemic contradictions which unfolded in 1997 in the form of a financial crisis, regarding the regional economic order and the position of East Asia within the international regime, have not been adequately addressed. The post-crisis East Asia, and in general the international economic system, are far from reaching a condition of stability. At the same time, the long-standing effects of the economic turndown are still afflicting large parts of the population of East Asia – not only in the distressed Indonesia. Even in a recovery country like Thailand, for example, ordinary people whose economic activities were squeezed at a time of expected prosperity are now drowning in debts that they cannot pay back. And South Korean industry has alternated impressive upsurge and dismaying contractions.

Recovery is proving ambiguous and not as homogeneous as the crisis itself had been for the different segments of the population. In a general frame of increased hardships for the poorest, some have suffered much less or have even gained from the crisis. At the same time a large part of the population is relatively untouched by the recovery as it had been relatively untouched by the previous phases of growth.

The impact of the economic malaise on the concrete reality of millions of people's material lives is relatively unknown, since most studies have exclusively dealt with the financial aspects of the crisis. Focusing the research attention solely on financial and macroeconomic indicators has replicated the optic distortion that the literature on the 'miracle' had produced. However, through accelerated economic growth, crisis and recovery, the need for a clearer understanding of the wider implications and nature of East Asian development has emerged. The aim of the present volume is to contribute to this understanding.

The texts presented in the following pages will provide a general overview of the debate on the crisis and on the so-called 'miracle'. However, the volume takes a clear stance on a number of issues. It will look at the structural contradictions characterizing the integration of East Asia into the global economy as the foundation of the crisis. The instability produced by a non-regulated international financial market has exposed these contradictions and provided the ground for a conflagration. Speculation against East Asian currencies has been visible. Yet this speculation should be considered against the background of the broader economic and political conflicts prevailing in the international system. The volume will present the hypothesis that the forces governing the process of 'triadic globalization'[1] might have considered an excessive growth of East Asia – and more precisely the growth of China – as a threat. Although it is difficult to prove the existence of any political plan made by Western forces to orchestrate a crisis in East Asia, the attempt to use the crisis to achieve Western strategic goals (in other words, to 'tame the tigers') has been clearly documented.

The book confutes the notion that the crisis was a result of 'crony capitalism'. Corruption and market distortions have accompanied the economic growth of many East Asian countries during the 'good years'. These market distortions are considered new only by those economists who have preferred to ignore them in the past, because they were trying to explain the 'East Asian miracle' in terms of adherence to the neoclassical doctrine. The authors of the present volume had instead argued before the crisis that East Asian development was uneven and distorted. However, they have reminded how these distortions formed part of so-called 'developmental state' strategies which have characterized the economic development not only of the East Asian Newly Industrialized Economies (NIEs), but also of the 'late-comers' of the nineteenth century such as Germany and the United States. A significant literature (see *infra*) has explained that the so-called miracle had been possible because countries like South Korea and Taiwan acted in contradiction to the prescriptions of the IMF and World Bank, i.e., operating 'price distortions' in order to achieve accelerated economic growth. However, the evidence from this crisis shows that 'developmental state' strategies are not compatible with financial liberalization and full integration into the open global economy.

Furthermore, the contribution of this volume to the debate on East Asian development and on the crisis aims at drawing attention to the local people and their material life. Ordinary people have been neglected not only by most studies on the crisis, focusing as they do principally on the financial aspects, but also by the IMF-led bailouts. The representation emerging from our research is multifaceted. People had already been enduring hardships at the time of growth and have generally faced a deterioration of their living conditions during the crisis. Traditional safety nets have provided shelter and support for many, but for many others the rhetoric of the 'return to the village' has proved to be populist propaganda. The complex geography of modernization, growth and crises still demands more systematic investigation and research.

THE RISE AND FALL OF THE 'EAST ASIAN MIRACLE'

In the late 1980s the notion of a 'Pacific Century' made popular the idea that the centre of gravity of the world economy was shifting from the Atlantic to the Pacific Basin. A group of Asian countries – the so-called 'Four Tigers' (Hong Kong,

Singapore, South Korea and Taiwan) – seemed to be replicating the Japanese economic success, and East Asia was performing as the world's most dynamic economic region. This contrasted with the relative decline of supposedly Newly Industrializing Economies of other regions (e.g., Brazil and Mexico) (Masina 1996). The impressive results achieved by a number of East Asian countries were heralded as a miracle in a controversial report released by the World Bank in 1993: *The East Asian Miracle: Economic Growth and Public Policy*. Only a few months later, however, the concept of miracle was contested by the MIT economist Paul Krugman with a famous essay in *Foreign Affairs* unambiguously entitled: 'The Myth of Asia's Miracle' (1994). The debate on the nature, dimensions and implications of Asian growth was therefore already heated well before the dramas of 2 July 1997, when Thailand relinquished the peg to the US dollar, and currency devaluation and stock market depreciation spread around the region.

In denouncing the miracle as a myth, Krugman expressed the view that East Asia could not sustain high growth rates for an extended period of time. He argued that these economies showed little increase in productivity, and that growth had been produced by an increase in inputs into the productive systems through the transition from agricultural to industrial economies. He compared East Asian economies in the 1980s to the Soviet Union in the 1950s, and concluded that the so-called miracle would soon grind to a halt. Nevertheless, as Krugman himself admitted (1998a), he did not foresee a major economic crisis but rather a deceleration in growth rates.

Krugman's scepticism did not conceal the evidence of three decades of high growth rates in East Asian economies since the 1960s, ranging from 6 to 10 per cent in the 'Four Tigers' to over 5 per cent in Thailand, Indonesia (after the 1960s) and Malaysia. The entrance of China into the ranks of the so-called High Performing Asian Economies (HPAEs), with growth rates around 10 per cent since the mid-1980s, made even more compelling the understanding of a process which many considered destined to transform the world economic and political equilibrium.

Two main interpretations were presented to explain why East Asian economies succeeded where most other developing countries had failed. 'Mainstream' scholars explained the positive economic performance with the adoption of export-oriented strategies behind which lay 'sensible' internal policies based on 'sound neoclassical principles' (Tsiang and Wu 1985: 329). This construction was also incorporated in the neoliberal discourse of the international financial institutions in support of structural adjustment policies. The World Bank and IMF asserted that there was a close relationship between countries with low levels of 'price distortion', outward-orientation and high levels of economic growth (World Bank 1983).

However, the description of the East Asian success as a mere adhesion to the neoliberal golden principle of 'getting the prices right' was contested by a group of scholars who presented an antithetic view. As one of them – Alice Amsden – polemically argued, an important element in East Asian success was rather 'getting the prices wrong' in agencies' terms (Amsden 1989). This group of scholars illustrated the rapid process of industrialization and economic development in Japan, South Korea, Taiwan and Singapore as a result of selective and successful use of high levels of state intervention (e.g., Amsden 1989; Deyo 1987; Wade 1990; White and Wade 1988). The role of the state in 'governing the market' – the title of Robert Wade's famous contribution (1990) – was considered to be the main factor in promoting development. Reconnecting to an old tradition of studies started with Friedrich List and continued with Alexander Gerschenkron, these scholars looked at the 'developmental' role of the state in promoting the catching-up of late-comers in the process of industrialization. (For a more detailed discussion of the developmental state, see Chapter 8 in this volume and *infra* in this introduction.)

The aforementioned *The East Asian Miracle* published by the World Bank in 1993 was an attempt to reinvigorate the agency's neoliberal discourse, by trying to respond to the criticisms presented by the 'statist' scholars. Thus, the slogan of 'get the prices right' was relaxed into the wider prescription of 'get the basics right', i.e., recognizing the role of the state in performing key functions but still emphasizing the need for sound macroeconomic policy and stability. (More on the evolution of the neoliberal thinking is contained in the next part of this introduction and in the second section of the volume.)

It is worth underlining here that in their attempt to confute the 'developmental state' interpretation neoliberal scholars have strongly opposed the idea that economic growth could be achieved through selective market distortions. Therefore, before the economic crisis, neoliberal scholars used to describe the HPAEs as the 'least price-distorting regime in the world' (Li, Hersh and Schmidt, Chapter 2 in this volume). It was only after the crisis unfolded that scholars and institutions (e.g., Krugman 1998b; World Bank 1997) suddenly became aware of 'cronyism' and market distortions in East Asia.

Other scholars such as Jeffrey Sachs, Director of the Harvard Institute for International Development, maintained also after the eruption of the crisis their view on East Asian countries as virtuous disciples of neoclassical sound macroeconomic policies. Sachs (1997) explained the crisis as a financial panic that had little to do with the underlying 'fundamentals'. Also, he pointed out that the currency crisis was not the result of Asian government profligacy. The crisis was instead attributed partly to fragile banking systems and partly to flaws in the global financial architecture. Although the ultimate aim of Western economists like Sachs was to amend the arrangements in the international financial system in order to push further financial liberalization, the blame towards speculation was assumed with other intents by Asian leaders like the Malaysian Prime Minister Mahathir Mohamad. As is well known, Dr Mahathir considered the crisis to be an effect of global speculative trading and accused the international financier George Soros of 'currency sabotage'. Other Asian leaders also expressed similar views, blaming hedge funds as irresponsible free-riders which were destabilizing the international markets (see Sum, Chapter 3 in this volume).

The rest of the volume contests these interpretations of the East Asian crisis as a result of national 'crony capitalism' or as the outcome of mere international currency speculation. The rise and the fall of the so-called Asian miracle is analysed by looking at geopolitics and history, the evolution of the regional and international productive system and its coherence with the financial system, the changes in national development strategies, etc. The chapters move in different directions and contain a number of original analyses. However, their combined reading provides a convergent and coherent interpretation.

History is a necessary point of departure for understanding current dynamics. The present volume starts (Chapter 2 by Li, Hersh and Schmidt) by recalling that a first wave of industrialization – involving South Korea, Taiwan, Hong Kong and Singapore – took place in the frame of the Cold War equilibrium and the American strategy of 'containment' of Chinese communism. This story is by now quite well known (e.g., Hersh 1993). The United States not only supported its Asian allies through economic aid and technology transfer, but also guaranteed these countries preferential conditions for exports to its market. Crucial for the understanding of the following events, however, is the modality through which this Cold War Asian economic order was built: i.e., through restoring a Japan-led regional productive system that was closely reminiscent of the 'Greater East Asian Co-prosperity Sphere'.

The results produced by this structuring of the regional economic order were remarkable and long-standing. The first aspect was the adoption by other Asian countries of 'developmental policies', which were inspired by the Japanese model. This model was clearly at odds with the American liberal and free-trade orthodoxy, but was tolerated in view of overall geopolitical considerations. Second, regional economic integration was based on an increasing division of labour, transfer of technology and flows of foreign direct investment (FDI). This regional economic integration – in contrast to other areas of the world – was able to activate national economic forces (i.e., national bourgeoisie and the local 'Chinese Diaspora') in an effort of industrial upgrading and catching-up (Arrighi *et al.* 1993; Masina 1996). This process has been metaphorically illustrated by Japanese authors via the image of the 'flying geese': a flock of nations linked by rounds of production relocations from the countries in the forefront to those next in the line, because of changing comparative advantage. To be sure, this idyllic image also conceals the disadvantages and weaknesses connected with such a pattern of industrialization: hierarchical exploitation and 'dependent development'. However, because of favourable geopolitical conditions and the modality of economic integration, the 'Four Tigers' and partially also other East Asian countries (such as Thailand, Indonesia and Malaysia) could benefit both from 'invitation' and from propitious conditions for 'seizing the time' (Li, Hersh and Schmidt, Chapter 2 in this volume) from within the slipstream of the leading 'geese'.

From the 1980s the traditional Cold War equilibrium was increasingly eroded and geopolitical interests concentrated more on economic matters. Western countries perceived with apprehension the increasing competition from Japan and the Asian NIEs, and the high growth rates of China. In this frame the Plaza Accord represented a turning point both in economic relations within East Asia and in the relations between East Asia and the West. The Accord signed in 1985 by the USA and Japan had the aim of relieving the American trade deficit with Japan and promoting a joint intervention in foreign exchange markets to correct trade imbalances. Thus, the Plaza Accord resulted in a sharp appreciation of the Japanese yen against the dollar, which in turn accelerated the relocation of production from Japan to other Asian countries.

On the one hand, the yen's appreciation increased the capital surplus and the need for profitable investments abroad. On the other hand, the fear of greater protectionism in Europe and the United States, uncompetitive export prices and the need for cost reduction, all motivated an expansion of Japanese foreign direct investment. This substantial increase in investment outflow led Japan to become the largest source of FDI, representing about 20 per cent of the world total in 1989. Although in quantitative terms Japanese FDI was also directed to North America and Western Europe, the investment flow to its neighbouring countries was particularly significant in that it represented the extension to the region of the Japanese multilayered subcontracting system (Masina 1996). The nature of the post-Plaza regional productive order sustained by Japanese FDI is described by Sum (Chapter 3 in this volume) as synergistic:

> Japan concentrated on high-tech and R&D; South Korea and Taiwan specialized in high-valued OEM (original equipment manufacturing) related to intermediate parts, Hong Kong and Singapore as service centres, and low-value products would come from Malaysia, Thailand and China.

Such a synergistic relationship was also characterized by competition and – in some cases – by 'leapfrogging' behaviour. However, the economies of the region remained highly dependent on Japan and its regional export-oriented productive system.

The other main feature of the post-Plaza Asian economic order, complementing the Japanese-led productive system, was an American-denominated financial regime through the pegging of most East Asian currencies to the US dollar. This financial order was financed by a high level of lending from Japanese banks and a high level of Japanese FDI to the region, and was linked – in the period 1985–95 – to a 'yen-appreciating bubble' (Sum, Chapter 3 in this volume).

From the 1990s, intrinsic contradictions started to erode the structural coherence of the post-Plaza regime, opening the way for a regional economic crisis.

The first element of contradiction can be defined as overproduction/underconsumption, which emerges in consequence of regional and international dynamics. On the one hand, the successful export growth of East Asian economies is increasingly perceived in the West as a threat and is no longer justified by Cold War motivations. Therefore, the export growth 'invites retaliatory actions from countries that are the targets of that export drive and leads to a loss of GSP (Generalized System of Preferences)' (Chandrasekhar and Ghosh, Chapter 6 in this volume). On the other hand, the tendency to overproduction is inherent to the national/regional productive regime, which is characterized by an 'investment rush' on the basis of 'unrealistic projections about future global demand and encouraged the build-up of excessive production capacities' (Sum, Chapter 3 in this volume). This 'investment rush' was also connected to the increasing flows of FDI from Japan and – since the late 1980s – from the 'Four Tigers' to the other countries in the region.

The second element of contradiction is represented by the vulnerability of the financial system. East Asian economies are characterized by a high degree of capital self-sufficiency, due to a high level of national saving. However, the catching-up dynamics of East Asian NIEs demanded high investment to sustain technological innovation. The linking of most national currencies to the American dollar stabilized East Asian import–export prices and encouraged foreign borrowing that involved no exchange risks. The 'yen-appreciating bubble' encouraged the relocation of Japanese production to the region and sustained Japanese lending and FDI outflows. After 1995, however, these productive and financial orders became unstable and, eventually, prone to crisis.

From the early 1990s the liberalization of global financial markets and the increased availability of cheap credit encouraged the underlying Asian tendency to overproduction. A further acceleration in the rush to over-investment and in the inclination to depend on short-term cheap foreign money to finance long-term domestic projects came about in 1995. A new agreement between Tokyo and Washington reversed the Plaza Accord, in order to help the two countries cope with the bursting of the 'yen-appreciating bubble'. The depreciation of the yen against the dollar increased Japan's export competitiveness and allowed Japan to export its way out of post-bubble problems. As a result, 'the value of the yen fell against the dollar by about 60 per cent between April 1995 and April 1997. The speed and the extent of the fall had a major impact upon FDI and portfolio capital' (Sum, Chapter 3 in this volume). The yen's devaluation reduced the competitiveness of those Asian countries whose currencies were pegged to the dollar, and further aggravated problems of overproduction in export sectors.

Flows of short-term investments (mostly from Japan) compensated for increasing trade deficits, allowing the financing of unprofitable industrial projects and supporting the creation of real estate speculative bubbles. Large flows of short-term capital were not discouraged by the evident unsustainability of this tendency; on the contrary, international banks and hedge funds obtained large dividends from the high interest rates connected to these risky investments. At the same time, financial liberalization imposed on East Asian countries by the international financial institutions (and the USA), combined with inadequate regulatory and control systems, prevented national authorities from intervening adequately.

As is well known, these contradictions exploded in July 1997, generating a wave of confidence crisis, speculative attacks, and eventually a crisis that involved the real economy of the countries in the region. The conflagration of the late post-Plaza regime is interestingly described in detail in the chapters by Sum, Chandrasekhar and Ghosh, and Amoroso in this volume. The modalities through which the contradictions existing in the post-Plaza productive and financial order reflected on the different countries' socioeconomic trajectories are discussed hereafter in this introduction. However, it is relevant to anticipate here the intrinsic incompatibility between the so-called 'developmental state' and the process of financial liberalization (Putzel, Chapter 8 in this volume). The loss of control over international financial transactions undermined the national state's authority to 'govern the market', and exposed these countries to a crisis which resulted from 'market failures' and private actors' profligacy.

The accusation by Dr Mahathir against Western currency speculators, although probably misplaced, raises the question of the political setting of the crisis, and more generally the question of the regional and international geoeconomic equilibrium. The question obviously involves foremost the relation between China and the West (and the United States in particular). China is one of the countries less hit by the crisis (see Sum, Chapter 3 in this volume, which also provides an analysis of the 'Greater China'), maintaining a growth rate of 7.8 per cent in the *annus horribilis* of 1998. From 1980 to 1992, the Chinese share of world trade increased from 0.9 per cent to 2.3 per cent, with the manufactured composition growing dramatically from 49.7 per cent in 1980 to 83.7 per cent in 1994 (Lardy 1995: 1074). Furthermore, in the early 1990s China became the largest recipient of FDI in Asia and the second in the world after the US, with a spectacular rise in inflows as a share of the world FDI: from 1.7 per cent in 1990 to 16.9 per cent in 1994 (Masina 1996).

This impressive growth had wide repercussions on the regional economy. China became a competitor for the other countries of the region both in attracting foreign direct investment and in the export of a large variety of products. The dimensions of the country and the different level of economic development of its provinces allowed China to integrate into the regional economic system, giving full play to its comparative advantages and to competitive cooperation with the more economically advanced East Asian countries. Li, Hersh and Schmidt write in Chapter 2 of this volume: '[W]hile the Chinese economy's compatibility with the countries of the region might globally not be pronounced, Chinese provinces might ... be able to find partners.' Therefore, the 'China factor' plays a significant role in increasing the tendency to overproduction in the post-Plaza regime, with the country participating in the manufacture of machinery and transport equipment, covering the entire spectrum from low-tech to high-tech production. However, for the country as a whole, the risks of overproduction are shielded by its growing internal market and by its large productive diversification. While the East Asian NIEs compete with one another in the export of office automation and telecoms equipment, 'China's trading strength lies in areas in which the leading East Asian traders had lost their competitiveness much earlier' (Chandrasekhar and Ghosh, Chapter 6 in this volume).

But the implications of the emergence of China as a major economic power clearly extend beyond East Asian borders. They are bound to have a world dimension. 'Accommodating first Japan and then the Asian NICs represented a challenge for the global economy. A full-scale Chinese industrialization based on export-orientation would be a destabilizing factor in the world balance of power both economically and politically' (Li, Hersh and Schmidt, Chapter 2 in this volume).

The idea that the Asian crisis could reflect also an underlying conflict to the future geoeconomic equilibrium in presented in this volume by Bruno Amoroso (in Chapter 4). Starting from Machiavelli's definition of politics as 'strategic thinking', Amoroso analyses this crisis as a 'third hurricane' – after those that hit the *socialist systems* in Eastern Europe and the *welfare systems* in Western Europe – sent forth by the forces dominating the international capitalist system. This interpretation does not impute the crisis to the conspiracy of currency speculators, but looks at dynamics characterizing the process of 'triadic globalization' which produce *economic marginalization* and *political destabilization* in developing countries (Amoroso 1998). The development trajectories of East Asian economies, and of China in particular, represented a threat for the global domain of those forces governing the process of globalization. Thus, there is reason to believe that this perceived threat might have motivated 'triadic capital' to a strategic design to impair the growth prospects of East Asia and China.

Although this interpretation is necessarily hypothetical, it is supported by the analysis of the contrasts between East Asia and the West *vis-à-vis* the organization of world trade and the functioning of the international regime. The Western insistence on financial and trade liberalization could be understood as something more than ideological intransigence. It could be explained as an attempt to 'normalize' East Asia and restore Western control over the region under the rules of an Anglo-American capitalist regime.

Interestingly, Western dissatisfaction with the economic (and political) trajectories of East Asia has been more clearly visible *ex-post*, i.e., after the crisis unfolded. US authorities and the IMF have been quite adamant in linking bail-out packages to structural changes in the economic and political organization of East Asian countries, aimed at dismantling those features of developmental states which many analysts have considered as the key element of the past 'East Asian miracle'. These considerations lead us to the next aspect of our research, regarding the role of international financial institutions in the East Asian crisis and the evolution of so-called 'neoliberal thinking'.

THE INTERNATIONAL FINANCIAL INSTITUTIONS AND THE CRISIS

The debate on an 'Asian way' to development, inspired by the Japanese example and contradicting Western neoliberal orthodoxy, assumed a more defined profile after the late 1980s. This was connected to the increasing and visible conflicts between the USA and Japan over the trade regime. At that time, Japan started more openly to seek recognition for its regional leadership, also through the representation of regional economic integration in terms of a Japan-led 'flying geese' pattern. With the Cold War rationale losing appeal, the Japanese promotion of an 'alternative' strategy was increasingly perceived as a threat by the guardians of the neoliberal orthodoxy. The confrontation between Western neoliberal forces and a (Japanese-led) 'Asian model' is discussed in this volume from two angles. The first concerns the debate in the Bretton Woods institutions leading to a reshaping of the so-called 'Washington Consensus' in development. The second concerns the disarticulation of the post-Plaza regime and the impact of globalization on East Asian economies.

Chapter 5 by Chris Dixon illustrates the undertaking by Japan since 1989 to make the Bretton Woods institutions[2] take 'more notice of the Asian experience of development'. The Japanese initiative, the criticisms of the 'Washington Consensus' from several quarters, the studies about the role of the state in successful Asian experiences, and the increased visibility of disagreements about the international trade regime, all forced a readjustment of the neoliberal discourse. However, resistance to any change that could undermine the ideology and the *modus operandi* of Bretton Woods institutions was noticeable in the high echelons of these institutions.

Once again, the famous World Bank's *East Asian Miracle* described well the existing divergences: funded by the Japanese Ministry of Finance, this study went through a series of substantial revisions and it resulted in a compromise that left its original sponsor less than pleased. However, the need for a readjustment and revitalization of the 'Washington Consensus' became increasingly evident to the World Bank until the eve of the Asian crisis, as witnessed by the 1997 *World Development Report*. This report, which is subtitled *The State in a Changing World*, emphasizes the importance of an efficient state and good governance for development, although it continues to describe the state 'in a strikingly apolitical manner which denies its social context, while stressing the importance of regulation and effective institutions' (Dixon, Chapter 5 in this volume). These antecedents help put into perspective the debate that developed after the onset of the crisis, which – as is pointed out thereafter – presented macroscopic divergences within the top management of the Bretton Woods institutions.

A latent East–West divide is also visible regarding the modalities of late post-Plaza East Asian economic organization and of regional participation in the world system. With (post-Cold War) geopolitical considerations replaced by geoeconomic motivations, East Asian countries have been forced to accommodate Western demands in order to avoid retaliations against their export-driven economies. Thus, it should come as no surprise that East Asian NIEs tended to present themselves as devoted disciples of neoclassical preaching (see White and Wade 1988: 7–8). As Chris Dixon writes in Chapter 5 of this volume:

> in general the governments of Taiwan and South Korea went to considerable lengths to hide, or even deny, the extent of their state activities and market restrictions because of the fear of dispute with the USA, the composition of countervailing tariffs and reduced access to markets.

But in order to elevate growth rates in a context characterized by overproduction in export sectors, protected trade areas and mercantilist restrictions in the EU and NAFTA, Asian leaderships feel compelled to move towards financial liberalization. Financial liberalization is undertaken in order to attract foreign capital to sustain industrialization and catching-up dynamics at a time of reduced profits. However, it is also a way to diversify out of manufacturing into services in general and financial services in particular. Thus, in the early 1990s, almost all East Asian countries chose to liberalize their financial sectors and 'allowed local corporations, banks, and non-bank financial institutions freely to access international capital markets with little commitment to earn the foreign exchange needed to service the costs of such access' (Chandrasekhar and Ghosh, Chapter 6 in this volume).

Financial liberalization, however, did not accommodate the demands of the forces leading the process of 'triadic globalization'. Once the financial crisis exploded, it was the IMF that took the lead in making evident the Western capital agenda for Asia. Very appropriately Bullard *et al.* (1998) have explained how the IMF policy – which was presented in the form of recovery packages – involved an attempt to 'tame the tigers', i.e., to subordinate East Asian economies to the control of Anglo-American capitalism. A study of the IMF-led bailout programmes for Thailand, South Korea and Indonesia, and of the attached conditionalities, indicates that these programmes reflected the long-standing agenda of the IMF's principal shareholder, the US: more liberal trade, investment and ownership rules. This IMF role has been candidly recognized by the

US authorities. In her testimony to the House Ways & Means Subcommittee, the United States Trade Representative (USTR) Charlene Barshefsky described how US interests could be furthered by the IMF: 'Many of the structural reform components of the IMF packages will contribute directly to improvements in the trade regimes in those countries. If effectively implemented, these programmes will complement and reinforce our trade policy goals' (USTR 1988).

The opposition of Washington to the Japanese proposal to establish an Asian Monetary Fund also confirms the existence of a link between IMF-led bailout packages and American interests in the region. Japan, whose banks were heavily exposed in the region and whose economy is deeply integrated with its neighbours, was willing to support a regional Fund capitalized at US$100 billion and designed to respond quickly to currency and market instability in the region. This Asian Monetary Fund was conceived as being more flexible, less doctrinaire and 'more Asian' than the IMF deal. However, this proposal was turned down due to heated opposition from the American Department of Treasury and the IMF (see Bullard, Chapter 7 in this volume; and Sum, Chapter 3 in this volume).

In the course of a few months the IMF-led policy proved unable to reverse the downward trend of those countries, like South Korea and Thailand, that had submissively accepted the prescriptions they had been requested to implement. On the contrary, the crisis extended to the real economy of Asian countries and the financial contagion spread to other regions such as Latin America and Russia. Thus, the IMF faced a significant loss of authority after the criticisms of its inability to predict the crisis. Many commentators have argued that the IMF policy has been not simply ineffective, but even damaging for the countries that have sought its aid. Although the evidence of its failure has forced the IMF successively to readjust its policy, revising the prescriptions for the Asian countries, an intense debate has resulted, which – for the first time after two decades of 'counter-revolution' in development studies and practice (Toye 1987) – has dismantled the halo of authority of the so-called Washington Consensus, and confirmed the need for a new 'consensus' on development. The IMF prescriptions for East Asian countries and their disappointing results are described in this volume specifically by Bullard (Chapter 7), and Chandrasekhar and Ghosh (Chapter 6). Dixon provides the key elements of the subsequent debate (Chapter 5).

A diffuse criticism on the IMF response to the East Asian crisis is that the Fund intervened on the basis of uniform, structural, adjustment-like prescriptions, which were inadequate for a crisis connected to excessive private sector, short-term borrowing. This macroscopic miscalculation suggests that the IMF has become seriously out of touch with the reality of Pacific Asian situation (see Dixon, Chapter 5 in this volume). Therefore, the IMF conditionalities have been likened to 'telling a victim of a road accident that regular exercise and a change in diet would be good for them' (*Far Eastern Economic Review*, 12 February 1998: 52). The IMF insisted on public sector austerity measures such as budget cuts, an increase in interest rates and taxes, which were inappropriate for the circumstances of a private sector debt crisis and which in fact deepened and accelerated the contraction of economies they were meant to be helping. This criticism has been shared also by a number of conservative scholars, including the former IMF employee Jeffrey Sachs (Sachs 1997; Radelet and Sachs 1998).

Wade and Veneroso (1998) have argued that the IMF prescriptions might have produced long-term damage, because these prescriptions neglected the specific nature of East Asian financial structures. A peculiar characteristic of the 'developmental state' in East Asia is a corporate debt/equity ratio much higher than in the West. This is the result of a high level of private saving, which is channelled through banks. Banks need to lend; and firms can easily borrow in excess of their equity value. The system allows the mobilization of large resources on the scale required to compete in export markets and continually to upgrade industrial production. But this financial structure is vulnerable to depressive shocks that could cause illiquidity, default and bankruptcy.

> Such a financial structure requires cooperation between banks and firms, and considerable government support. The trick is to buffer firms' cash flow and supply of capital against 'systemic' shocks, while not protecting firms from the consequences of bad judgement or malfeasance. Restrictions on the freedom of firms and banks to borrow abroad, and coordination of foreign borrowing by government, are necessary parts of this system. (Wade and Veneroso 1998: 7)

The analysis of Wade and Veneroso supports the criticism advanced by Chandrasekhar and Ghosh (Chapter 6 in this volume) of a key aspect of the IMF strategy for post-crisis East Asia – the insistence on financial liberalization – as responsible for the 'elusive recovery'. On the basis of their study of Thailand and South Korea, the two scholars argue that no long-term sustainable recovery can be achieved in a regime of financial liberalization; i.e., without regulating the flows of short-term capital. Although since the time of their study of South Korea and Thailand the IMF has several times relaxed its prescriptions for these countries, and growth rates indicate positive signals, the criticism seems to maintain its validity. In the case of Thailand – the showcase of the IMF intervention – not only have the social costs not been reduced, but the risk of a new financial crisis in few years is still concrete (*Far Eastern Economic Review*, 4 November 1999: 10–13).

The gradual shift on some key policy positions by the IMF since mid-1998 indicated in subsequent letters of intent with Thailand, South Korea and Indonesia, shows an attempt to cope with the deterioration of a crisis which the initial doctrinaire measures did not manage to ease. Also, this change aims at responding to the unprecedented level of criticism towards the agency. Thus, for example, the IMF gradually allowed a conspicuous easing of tight fiscal and monetary policy by allowing interest rates to slowly drop and allowing government deficits to expand.

At the same time the IMF seems to understand that if countries become dependent on foreign finance in excess of their absorptive capacity, the blame should be placed not only on governments and private agents in emergent markets but also on international financial players. However, the Bretton Woods institutions' support for the reform of the international financial architecture does not reach the necessary logical conclusion: i.e., that a complete financial liberalization undermines governments' resources for avoiding undesirable effects resulting from excessive capital inflows or outflows (Chandrasekhar and Ghosh, Chapter 6 in this volume).

The significance and spread of the debate on the role of the IMF-led intervention in the Asian crisis are effectively depicted by the author of 'Taming the tigers': in presenting her contribution to this volume, Nicola Bullard entitled it as 'Taming the IMF: How the Asian Crisis Cracked the Washington Consensus'. As she illustrates, 'the debates are wide-ranging and call into question fundamentals such as the efficacy and appropriateness of the Fund's economic advice, the way the Fund operates, and its relationship with its key shareholder, the US' (Bullard, Chapter 7 in this volume). This debate on the IMF's role is connected to an increasingly shared view on the need to overcome the so-called Washington Consensus. For the first time voices for significant change come also from within the Bretton Woods institutions themselves and from within the core of the neoliberal orthodoxy. The more outspoken proponent for a 'new consensus on development' has been the World Bank chief economist, Joseph Stiglitz. This unexpected apparent 'conversion', however, suggests some circumspection. It could be interpreted as a classic Gramscian 'passive revolution': i.e., the ruling forces incorporating some demands existing in society and guiding the process of change in order to maintain hegemony and prevent a more radical transformation. Therefore, it seems wise not to overemphasize the possible innovative outcomes of this debate, at least concerning the real intentions of the Bretton Woods institutions. Thus, the authors of this volume invite this circumspection. Bullard raises the question of what will replace the Washington Consensus. The reforms currently being carried out aim at putting the train of globalization back on track. Although many of them are absolutely necessary in the short term, they do not address the underlying weaknesses of the present system. Chandrasekhar and Ghosh (Chapter 6 in this volume) agree with this view and explain how the change in the Washington Consensus promoted by the World Bank aims at restoring concord around globalization and financial liberalization. The divergence with the IMF, therefore, does not represent a different strategic view but the consciousness that some reforms should be introduced in order to make the system more viable.

Amoroso (Chapter 4 in this volume) interprets this apparent 'conversion' by World Bank officers and the IMF's admission of 'mistakes' in dealing with the Asian crisis as an attempt to smooth social discontent and opposition to the process of globalization. Therefore, this new post-Washington Consensus will try to present a human face in order to proceed more easily on the same path of 'economic marginalization' and 'political destabilization'.

Dixon (Chapter 5) reconnects this post-Asian crisis search for a new consensus on development to the debate of the last ten years. The need to incorporate into the neoliberal discourse new issues, such the role of the state in development, has been translated into a new magic concept: 'governance'. But in the Bretton Woods agency terms, good governance consists of administrative reform, which 'denies its social basis and neglects the difficulty of changing the regulatory *form* without change in the state's social *content*'.

In other words, the cracking of the old Washington Consensus is a welcome event for the authors of this volume. The contradictions existing in the international system are increasingly visible, and they imply changes in the core of the neoliberal orthodoxy and a readjustment of the Bretton Woods institutions' role. However, the new post-Washington Consensus is likely to incorporate essentially the same inner agenda and the same objectives.

CRONY CAPITALISM AND DEVELOPMENTAL STATE

A popular interpretation of the crisis (cf. *supra*) has blamed the 'cosy' relations existing between the state, corporations and national financial institutions and has depicted East Asian countries as affected by 'crony capitalism'. The existence of political corruption, nepotism and distorted development is not denied by the authors of this volume. Several contributions recall, for example, the increasing control of Suharto's family over the most lucrative sectors of the Indonesian economy. However, the description of East Asia as ruled by 'crony capitalism' is certainly misleading for an understanding of the real motivations behind the regional economic crisis. Besides, this interpretation seems to be conceived as a neoliberal attempt to avoid the blame being put on excessive financial liberalization and to help the dismantling of the developmental state, which was perceived as a threat to the neoliberal orthodoxy.

The view presented in this volume is different. In the first part of this introduction we have already recalled the so-called 'developmental state' as a key feature – together with the particular geopolitical frame and Japanese-led regional economic integration – of East Asian economic success. We have also anticipated that we understand the crisis as largely a result of the erosion of this growth pattern and of the incompatibility between state-led development and financial liberalization.

The developmental state in East Asia was not immune to corruption among public sector officials and private entrepreneurs. In this regard, the East Asian developmental state does not differ from the experiences of Western countries in the earlier stages of capitalist development. The role of governments in controlling bank lending to firms in excess of their equity value, with up to a third of national income intermediated, made a certain level of corruption inevitable, as Wade and Veneroso (1998: 7–8) remind us. However, the distinctive feature of the East Asian developmental state is that the 'resources generated through corruption seemed to be put to productive use rather than siphoned off for private consumption' (Putzel, Chapter 8 in this volume).

Mushtaq Khan clarifies this distinctive aspect by contrasting South Asia's relatively slow-growing economies with East Asia's fast developers. In East Asia, resources were channelled to capitalists and produced a pattern of 'growth-enhancing accumulation', whereas in South Asia resources were overwhelmingly directed to non-capitalists and resulted in 'growth-retarding accumulation' (Chapter 8 in this volume). In this sense, the developmental state could be interestingly likened to the fascist corporatist state as described by Antonio Gramsci (1977): a state promoting development and modernization *against* the rent-seeking interest of backward-oriented capitalist groups, but in *the interests of the capitalist class as a whole.* The comparison is also motivated by the similar threats that pre-war fascist Italy and post-war Taiwan and South Korea were facing. In both cases the capitalist classes were forced to accept the modernization of the state in order to guarantee the survival and promotion of a system of private, property-based capitalism. In Chapter 8, Putzel indicates that the internal and external threats posed to South Korean and Taiwanese capitalism were the reason why 'those with wealth and power allowed the emergence of such *dirigiste* states and accorded importance and resources to the training of their bureaucracies'.

Proceeding along this line of analysis, Putzel discusses how some Southeast Asian states – Thailand, Malaysia and Indonesia – measured up to the experience of Japan, Taiwan and South Korea. These Southeast Asian nations present similarities to and differences from the 'classical' developmental states. In these countries the application of a pattern of 'productive corruption' changed over time, i.e., presenting a regional and temporal diversity, which has tended to be underestimated in most analyses. The study by Putzel indicates that these Southeast Asian countries can only to some extent be reconnected to the experience of Asian 'developmental state'. In fact, 'they adopted some of the characteristics of the developmental state, but by no means all of them, and there were sharp differences between the three in terms of what they chose to copy'.

The selective adaptation of the model, reflecting local conditions and the regional/international setting, helps in analysing the countries' different economic performances and their respective socioeconomic dynamics (e.g., income redistribution, balance between industrial and rural development, etc.). However, taking into consideration the necessary distinctions, the inscription of the so-called 'second tier' countries within the interpretative paradigm of the 'developmental state' maintains a certain utility also in relation to the regional economic crisis. As has already been discussed, in both groups of countries the dismantling of governmental controls in key sectors of the economy and the exposure to financial liberalization proved to be a key factor in setting the stage for the economic crisis.

East Asian countries implemented financial liberalization under external constraints and as an attempt to diversify their economies into the service sector. However, this decisive step should be understood against the background of a wider process of change in the 'developmental state' articulation. The same impressive economic achievements of the East Asian countries reduced, since the late 1980s, the legitimacy of an authoritarian and repressive 'developmental state'. The pattern of 'compressed modernization' – where people's social and economic demands were subordinated to the development of national industry – became increasingly untenable. Thus, 'the continuation of rapid growth and structural change became linked to democratization, political reform, politicization of technocratic positions and liberalization' (Dixon, Chapter 5 in this volume). In this regard, the current crisis reinforced the need for a critical reconsideration of the 'developmental state', not only in relation to its past realizations, but also as a model able to inspire the recovery and future development of East Asia.

The rethinking of development trajectories in East Asia is proposed in this volume, looking at two experiences at the extreme range of economic development: South Korea and Vietnam. In the first country the crisis forced an intensification of the process of change that was already under way, with a contradictory transition towards a neoliberal social-democratic compromise. In the case of Vietnam – less directly hit by the regional turmoil than neighbouring countries because it was less integrated into the world economy – the crisis compelled a rethinking of development strategies due to the impasse of the existing models.

The traumatic impact of the crisis on South Korea is analysed by Chang Kyung-Sup in Chapter 9, describing how this unfortunate event resulted into a turning point in the process of national sociopolitical transformation. The chapter confirms the impressive results achieved by the developmental state in producing economic growth; but attention is focused on the social implications and the long-term sustainability of such a pattern. The developmental state is described as an exploitative regime, suppressing workers' political and economic rights, supposedly for the sake of international competitiveness. The alliance between private industrialists and military-turned-political leaders was able to impose its strategy through the use of political repression and physical coercion. However, the national industrialization project was not opposed by the working class, because it resulted in increasing income (although far behind profit growth for their employers).

Income policy, as discussed by Putzel in his chapter, is a key aspect of the developmental state model, in order to maintain the stability of the system and to achieve popular consensus. Popular consensus manifested itself in South Korea in a way that Chang describes as a form of auto-hypnosis, in which people preferred to overlook the hardship of their present, emphasizing the improvements from their miserable past, and projecting their hopes on a prosperous future. And 'such a mentality induced them to go through voluntary austerity and to allocate all their financial resources to education, savings, and other future-oriented social and economic investment' (Chang in this volume). This 'auto-consolatory' attitude resulted – until the onset of the regional crisis – in a sort of *false middle-class consciousness.*

While the government played a decisive role in guiding the process of industrialization through a trade-off with the *chaebols* (for a classical discussion of the South Korean developmental state, see Amsden 1989), in social terms the successive administrations 'remained completely *laissez-faire* under the doctrine of what might be called *developmental liberalism*' (Chang, Chapter 9). The state did not implement any systematic and comprehensive welfare system, and people's only entitlement was work. Only corporate welfare provided South Koreans with some forms of social protection, such as support for housing, children's school tuition, medical protection, etc., though these measures were granted as fringe benefits and not as legal rights. However, the successful combination of political repression, moderate income policy and corporate welfare, and popular support for the national developmental ideology, became increasingly untenable during the 1980s.

The end of the military dictatorship and the advent of Roh Tae-Woo's civilian government resulted in a major change in the relations between the state and industrial capital. The government tried to avoid political confrontation with organized workers' movement, and labour matters were left to business and labour. This change resulted in increased force for the labour movement (especially in large *chaebols*) and led to higher wages and increased fringe benefits. One year before the onset of the regional crisis, South Korean trade unions also achieved a major political result, forcing the government to withdraw new legislation considered unfavourable to labour. At the same time the government, notwithstanding huge amounts of budget surplus, maintained its abstinence from social welfare, and corporate welfare remained the only significant tool for improving living conditions, at least for those workers employed in large *chaebols* (see Chang, Chapter 9 this volume). With the end of the 1980s the South Korean 'developmental state' entered into a process of transformation, with key elements of the old regime dismantled, but not replaced by a new system.

The increased capital–labour class conflict in countries that had based their growth strategies on low wages remains a relatively unexplored aspect in the post-Plaza regional equilibrium. At the end of the 1980s, wages increasing over productivity growth were an important factor behind the capital's attempt – in South Korea and Taiwan, but also in the 'second tier' countries – to move towards more value-adding industrial production and diversification into services, an attempt which resulted in the regional crisis. In other terms, working-class political militancy was a key factor in the profit squeeze suffered by Asian enterprises in order to carry on 'catching up' in an increasingly hostile environment, as has already been described earlier in this introduction.

After the regional crisis unfolded, South Korea entered into a difficult and contradictory transition towards a new social and economic order. Financial liberalization and the government's relative non-interference in the capital–labour conflict had already represented a significant departure from the developmental state model. But the IMF-led bailout aims at an even more thorough result: the dismissal of the *chaebols*' control over the national economy and complete economic liberalization. It is important to note that these requests were somehow (and contradictorily) well received from the newly-elected President Kim Dae-Jung – for decades the main opposition leader – because they converged with popular opposition against the *chaebol* owners and their political representatives. Opposition from the trade unions was also milder than might have been expected, because of a so-called trade-off: under Kim Dae-Jung the organized working movement received greater political recognition, which made the unions more ready to accept compromise (and the social costs) connected with economic recovery.

However, the management of economic restructuring, and the transition towards a different regime, resulted in a contradictory process and exposed all the shortcomings inherited from the previous regime, as described by Chang in Chapter 9. On the one hand, the vested interests of the *chaebol* system are still able to manipulate leverage within the financial sector and the public administration, often overruling the same political decisions of the Kim Dae-Jung administration. The IMF prescriptions did not solve these contradictions, and possibly aggravated them, as confirmed both by Chang and Chandrasekhar & Ghosh in this volume. On the other hand, the process of restructuring is leading to a pattern of 'development with sizeable structural unemployment', bringing severe social costs for a population not protected by any comprehensive welfare system. The crisis unveiled a situation which was already characterized by sectors of the population who were officially employed but in effect suffering from chronic unemployment (see Chang, Chapter 9 in this volume). The distress suffered by a large part of the population during the worst period of the crisis and the risk of extended massive unemployment are undermining the social consensus to the system, because it is eroding the illusory middle-class consciousness.

In this frame the Kim Dae-Jung administration – also with the advice of the IMF and the World Bank – is trying to establish 'safety nets', i.e., substituting for the obsolete corporate welfare, which is of little use in a situation of massive unemployment. In other words, while in Europe welfare systems have been achieved by the working class and the socialist movement, in South Korea a rudimental welfare system is taking shape as a 'safety net' to sustain a painful industrial restructuring and the advent of Western style neoliberalism.

This process raises new questions about post-crisis South Korea. Having achieved the status of a 'developed country' with the access to the OECD, is South Korea going to replace a 'developmental state' with the same regime of Anglo-American capitalism prevailing in the West? Is this the developmental trajectory for the other East Asian, former-miracle countries? And will South Korea be able to resume a pattern of accelerated economic growth or will it become a 'normal', 'semi-peripheral' country?

Compared to South Korea, Vietnam is at the other end of the economic development hierarchy in East Asia. Vietnam embarked on a process of economic reform in the late 1980s, and in the early 1990s it restored international relations within and beyond the region. Before the crisis Vietnam was pursuing an increased integration in the regional productive system, with the aim of replicating the economic performance of its neighbours. Chapter 10 by Masina indicates that in the mid-1990s this attempt benefited from favourable geopolitical conditions (a Western interest in reinforcing the country for a potential 'containment' policy against China), witnessed by large economic support from multilateral donors. Optimism about the economic future of this country – combined with a speculative tendency in the real-estate sector – made Vietnam a large recipient of foreign direct investment, in a proportion to the GDP much higher than in the other countries of the region. However, in the months before the regional crisis and increasingly since 1998, Vietnam came under strong pressure from international financial institutions, which asked national authorities to move further in the direction of liberalization and 'market-friendly' reforms. This pressure grew stronger as the deterioration of economic conditions gave more leverage to international organizations in linking economic aid to the implementation of a specific agenda.

Although the impact of the crisis has been less severe on Vietnam than in most of the region, the country faced a slowdown in economic growth and the government was forced to maintain a strict macroeconomic control. This involved a reduction of national investments at the time when investment flows from the region were sharply declining. In the aftermath of the crisis, the country's political leadership seems divided between, on the one hand, those supporting a furthering of reforms in the direction favoured by the international financial institutions and, on the other, those who consider that the regional crisis has confirmed the risks of a too-close integration into the world economy. The perplexity of the leadership has been evidenced by the lengthy negotiation of a trade agreement with the United States.

Masina (Chapter 10) suggests that a more careful analysis of the 'developmental state' models in the region could provide Vietnam with significant support in defining a new reform agenda, thus leading the country out of the present impasse. With a more clear prioritization in its process of industrialization, Vietnam could implement needed reforms without abandoning important elements of economic planning. At the same time, this chapter stresses the importance of looking also at the shortcomings of the 'developmental state' examples in the region, in order trying to avoid repeating the same pattern of environmental devastation, depletion of natural resources, aggressive 'modernization' and over-exploitation of the working class.

The poor and the marginal between miracles and crises

Since the East Asian economic crisis unfolded, many different analyses have been presented, resulting in an important debate and a wide range of disagreements. Most of these analyses, however, have shared a common feature: they have neglected the implications of the crisis for ordinary people. At the same time, a number of journalistic reports and investigations by NGOs, on the one hand, and navel contemplation by international development agencies on the other, have started to engage with the social impact of the crisis. But the former have indulged too often in populist representations, while the latter have substantially avoided looking at the implications of increased poverty incidence in terms of the prevailing development strategy. A central attempt of the present volume, in stark contrast, is to underline the essential link between macroeconomic strategies and people's living conditions. Our study of the East Asian crisis indicates that people's ability to cope depends very much on the long-term development dynamics that the society has been experiencing. Therefore, the present volume does not simply attempt to formulate an account of the distress and hardships suffered by ordinary people during this crisis – these, although tragic and painful, could be considered as transitory phenomena. We look instead at how people coped – or did not manage to cope – with the crisis, in order to improve our understanding of the contradictory development experiences of East Asian countries.

In this regard, the crisis shed new light on the 'uneven development' pattern of the region, which the rhetoric of the miracle had partially obfuscated (nonetheless, contributors to this volume had already discussed this uneven pattern before the crisis: e.g., Parnwell 1996; Dixon and Drakakis-Smith 1997; Schmidt *et al.* 1997; Rigg 1997). The process of 'modernization' and rapid socioeconomic transformation – which, in different measure, has interested all the countries of the region – represents the necessary background to understanding how ordinary people can resist and react to a period of severe economic distress. The high social costs and the severe impact on the local populations should be understood not as a result of an abrupt accident, but as a consequence of this 'uneven development'. In other terms, as Mike Parnwell writes in Chapter 12 of this volume, 'there is the real danger that the current hyperbolic use of the term "crisis" will serve ... to [portray] these people as victims of economic meltdown rather than of the development process itself'. Further, looking through the lenses of those who had been largely 'excluded' from the economic boom and the orthodox development process, the notion of 'crisis' becomes a relative one. For these people – victims of what Peter Bell (1996: 49) has called 'maldevelopment'

– the current crisis exacerbates the hardships they have to endure, but does not represent a qualitative change in the precarious conditions of their existence.

Chapter 9 by Chang Kyung-Sup delineates very clearly how the social costs of the crisis in South Korea were a result of a development pattern which did not make any provision to protect the population in the event of an economic downturn. In this sense, Southeast Asian countries have probably been even more exposed to risks, because of their less structured redistributive policies when compared with Northeast Asia. With the possible exception of Singapore and Brunei, Southeast Asian countries do not have substantial welfare systems which can provide an adequate safety net in the case of socioeconomic crisis. And – as is discussed before – the traditional forms of 'moral' economy have often been eroded by years of modernization. However, any assessment of the social impact of the crisis is very difficult. On the one hand, information is still sketchy and largely anecdotal. On the other hand, the impact has been very different even within regions of the same country, due to the aforementioned uneven development patterns, the different ways in which the mechanisms of inclusion and exclusion have been articulated, and the forms of resistance to and fragmentation of traditional safety nets.

Key indicators, such as poverty, real wages and unemployment, signal that East Asia has experienced a severe deterioration of living conditions. Reports by international organizations have presented a dramatic description of rising levels of absolute poverty, malnutrition, unemployment, falling school enrolment, deterioration of healthcare services, and increased crime and violence (World Bank 1998b; ILO 1998). The concrete impact of these effects on individual households, however, has been very variable. In an environment of general impoverishment, for example, families with remittances from abroad have seen the value of these remittances increase, because of the devaluation of national currencies. Similarly, devaluation has, in some cases, advantaged peasants engaged in export-oriented cash-crop cultivation.

In Chapter 11 of this volume, Jonathan Rigg discusses this diversity in terms of the impact of the crisis and patterns of response in Southeast Asia. He illustrates how they depended also on factors such as labour specialization, gender or age. For instance, young people have shown a lower propensity and ability to 'return' to rural areas and farming activities than have older people. Moreover, male-dominated construction industries have been more severely hit than women-dominated export-oriented industries. Chapter 12 by Parnwell, however, although largely convergent with that by Rigg, presents a number of interesting distinctions. A comparison of these two chapters helps in addressing crucial aspects in the post-crisis debate, concerning the extent to which modernization has eroded traditional safety nets, the interaction between rural and urban areas, and the transformations that have occurred in Southeast Asia's rural world.

Rigg presents a criticism of the rhetoric of the 'retreat to the village', as a traditional Southeast Asian response to crises. He argues that the 'back to the farm' hypothesis is based on 'two heroic assumptions': first, that most urban people have maintained a close connection with rural areas and can 'return' in case of need; second, that these 'reverse migrants' can find a space in the agricultural world they had left. But these assumptions seem to consider neither the extent of the process of agricultural modernization and social change undergone in the last two decades, nor the kind of relations often existing between 'migrants' and their rural families. On the one hand, the process of agricultural modernization in many regions has gone too far to be easily reversed. And many young people have lost the skill and the propensity to engage in farming activities.

On the other hand, many urban Southeast Asians do not have a 'home' village to return to or the possibility to exploit agriculture as a safety net. In some cases, they have maintained formal connections with the village, but the traditional 'moral' economy and corporate solidarity have been lost. In other cases, remittances from urban areas have made it possible for small landowners with 'sub-livelihood holdings' to achieve sustainability. Not only could these marginal farmers (or, even more, rural people with no access to land) not support the return of their family members who have lost their non-farming activities, but also the whole family would drawn into absolute poverty. This analysis brings Rigg to conclude that the reverse flow of migrants back to rural areas might have been less than the scale of redundancies in urban-based formal work would indicate.

In his study of 'migration reversal' in Northeast Thailand, Mike Parnwell describes a picture that partially contrasts with the one reported by Rigg. On the basis of fieldwork in 25 villages, Parnwell concludes that these villages have shown 'a remarkable capacity for absorbing and supporting returning migrants', finding little niches for them in the labour market. The network of social relations at the basis of this 'moral' economy also provided these migrants with the connections they needed for returning to the urban areas (i.e., Bangkok) as soon as new jobs were available. The long-established, functional characteristics of the migration process from this region, therefore, proved to be an important resource in coping with the crisis.

The impact of 'modernity' on people's culture – translating, for example, into young people's low propensity to re-engage in farming activities after having experienced life in urban areas, is represented by Parnwell and Rigg in different ways, although this difference is more a matter of degree than substance. Both authors maintain that 'returning' migrants would consider the retreat to the village as a temporary solution or a 'survivalist' strategy. Parnwell reports that his reverse migrants preferred to return to the village rather than endure the hardship of unemployment in Bangkok, or to attempt a difficult entrance into the urban 'informal sector'. Rigg emphasizes the endeavour by migrants to remain in town as long as they could, and not to give up the aspiration to urban life.[3] Parnwell stresses the elasticity of the rural world, and the strong connections remaining between migrants and their rural families. Rigg accentuates the transformations undergone in rural areas, and the irreversibility of processes such as mechanization and cultural change.

The two chapters, however, agree in reporting that 'reverse migration' would not imply a permanent return to farming. In the villages visited by Parnwell, a large number of 'returnees' had subsequently exploited social networks to go back to Bangkok, even accepting wages that they would have refused at the beginning of the crisis. In the representation provided by Rigg, the son of his fictive (but realistic) ordinary Thai family had to leave school and go back to farming, and the family withdrew into a more self-sufficient and less market-oriented agriculture: but they conceived these forced choices as 'survivalist' strategies to be reversed as soon as possible.

The two chapters also agree in describing a deterioration of traditional safety nets as a result of modernization and development. Although Parnwell reports that villages provided provisory shelter for 'reverse migrants', he underlines that there is no indicator that the current crisis has led to the renaissance of socio-economic mechanisms connected to village corporate solidarity. Thus, the differences reported by the two authors seem to result more from the angle they have adopted in looking at the same reality than from any substantial disagreement. Parnwell focuses more on the persistence of the traditional world and its contradictory adaptation to the process of modernization. Rigg looks at the emergence of new dynamics and at the rapid process of socioeconomic transformation in the region.

Kilgour and Drakakis-Smith in Chapter 13 move our attention to the urban areas of Vietnam, describing another aspect of the process of 'uneven development' in Southeast Asia. The choice to focus on the forms of marginalization and urban poverty in a country that is still predominantly agricultural, and where most poor and marginal people live in rural areas, should be understood in the context of the present volume. The country has, by contrast, been relatively less profoundly hit by the more direct effects of the regional crisis, because of the limited integration into the world economy and the non-convertibility of the national currency. However, the impact on urban areas has certainly been more visible than on rural areas, where many households still depend on self-subsistence and self-consumption. Urban areas more keenly felt the pressure from the region's economic downturn because they were more closely linked to foreign trade and investment. Like in other countries of the region, for example, the construction industry faced an abrupt halt, resulting in massive layoffs. However, in Vietnam the way in which the crisis was endured also depended on the previous conditions of integration or marginality in the development process. Paradoxically, the poorest felt the 'crisis' less because they had benefited less from the previous period of growth.

Rising unemployment and sustained migration to the major urban centres, however, are increasingly straining the ability of the 'informal sector' to accommodate new entrants in the traditional service activities on the street, such as retailing, bicycle repair or barbering. This has led to the adoption of alternative coping mechanisms, such as daily commuting from nearby villages or circular migration, which allow the use of resources from both urban and rural areas (Kilgour and Drakakis-Smith in this volume). Further, the impact of the regional crisis is reconnected to a general worsening of living conditions in urban areas (especially the two major cities of Hanoi and Ho Chi Minh City), with the degradation of the existing housing stock, problems in access to clean water and discharge of waste water, pollution and environmental degradation, etc. With economic growth forecasts reduced as a consequence of the regional crisis, national authorities will have fewer resources to address these issues. But the problems of poverty that are evident in both rural and urban areas are closely connected to serious contradictions which are associated with *doi moi.* Thus, even the return to rapid economic growth would not be a guarantee that these poverty-related issues will be addressed adequately, unless there is a significant change in the development strategy.

The notion of 'crisis' in the lives of ordinary people as a result of 'maldevelopment' is confirmed by the case of Mongolia, and its traumatic transition from planned economy to poverty. The experience of economic reform in this country, through the rapid liberalization and marketization of the national economy, presents interesting elements for reflection on 'post-crisis' East Asia. The doctrine incorporated by the 'transition' in Mongolia is based on the same assumptions of the structural adjustment programmes, which have been re-proposed by the IMF to East Asia as a way towards economic recovery. The case of Mongolia, however, also has other interesting points of contact with the analyses of the process of modernization in other East Asian countries in terms of the persistence of traditional safety nets and 'coping mechanisms' in the face of economic distress.

Contrary to the views propounded by structural adjustment theorists, Chapter 14 by David Sneath illustrates that the dismantling of socialist economic institutions and the 'transition' towards the market economy in Mongolia do not represent a 'liberation' of the economy from artificial constraints and the return to 'some timeless traditional forms of pastoralism'. On the contrary, collectives had in some ways incorporated pre-revolutionary, large-scale pastoral organizations. In the same way, the notion of division between politics and economy, which lies at the very heart of marketization and privatization programmes, does not liberate the country from an exogenous Soviet interference: the linkage between the two concepts of economy and political power is rooted in Mongolian culture and language. Thus, the process of 'transition' can be compared to a process of Western-style modernization, which resulted in a dramatic impoverishment of the population in part because of its unfamiliarity with people's cultural traditions. In this environment networks of families and friends represent the only safety net in a process of retreat to subsistence for many pastoral families.

These contributions confirm that the impact of 'miracles' and 'crises' on the lives of ordinary people can only be understood against a backdrop of the wider socioeconomic transformations that are affecting each society. Patterns of modernization and development strategies change people's means to cope with crises and economic distress. The erosion of traditional safety nets – if not replaced by alternative welfare systems – exposes the population to economic freefall. In this sense, the reality of post-crisis East Asia proves discouraging. Although a debate on new safety nets for the poor has been opened, also on the advice of international organizations such as the World Bank and the Asian Development Bank, these safety nets are conceived as tools for further implementing a 'modernization' agenda which is enforcing new forms of uneven development in the wider context of 'triadic globalization'.

THE STRUCTURE OF THE BOOK

The present volume is organized into four thematic parts, allowing a logical structure aimed at making more visible the rationale of this joint endeavour. However, it should be noted that any partition of contributions addressing complex and interlinked questions is always problematic and arbitrary. The distribution has been based on the prevalent themes that are dealt with in each chapter, while this introduction has been conceived with the aim of drawing out the links that exist between the different contributions.

Part I presents the international and regional context of the rise and the fall of the 'Asian miracle' through analyses that interweave history, economics and politics. Part II focuses on the post-crisis debate, and discusses the role of the international financial institutions and the controversy surrounding the so-called Washington Consensus. Part III discusses national strategies and development models, introducing the diversity that exist among East Asian development trajectories. Part IV moves the focus to the human dimension of both pre- and post-crisis growth strategies, discussing the impact of macroeconomic changes on the local populations' material lives.

A conference at Roskilde University at the end of October 1998 allowed an opportunity to discuss the earlier drafts of these chapters, and to benefit from the critical contribution of other colleagues, who had either presented papers or participated as discussants. Only two contributions were not previously presented in the Roskilde conference: Jonathan Rigg's chapter, which was first submitted to a conference in Singapore in December 1998; and the chapter by David Sneath, which was prepared specifically for this volume. All the contributions have subsequently been revised and updated in relation to the common debate and the editorial imperatives of moulding diverse views and perspectives into a collective publication.

This volume (and the conference at Roskilde University before it) was conceived as a joint research effort between a group of Asian and European scholars (or more accurately Europe- and Asia-based scholars) and involved a range of expertise: economics, political science, history, sociology, geography and anthropology. The interdisciplinary nature of this work aims at providing a multi-faceted account of the East Asian economic crisis – and development strategies more generally – which presents populations and countries in a manner that is far-removed from the more orthodox and sterile description of numbers and financial indexes. The variety and complexity of the themes addressed, however, motivated the authors to consider this work as a contribution to an open debate and an encouragement to initiate new research directions rather than attempt a conclusive accomplishment and definitive statement.

The volume is dedicated to the memory of David Drakakis-Smith – an important scholar, but for many of the co-authors of this volume also a good friend.

NOTES

1 The definition of 'triadic globalization' was first introduced by a *maître à penser* of the neoliberal thinking, Ohmae Keinichi (1985). This representation was confirmed a few years later by the United Nations Centre for Transnational Corporations (1991) in a report associating 'triadic globalization' with the increasing marginalization of developing countries and the dominant role in the world economy of the largest American, Western European and Japanese TNCs. Probably as a result of this report, the Centre has been put under the control of UNCTAD, several times restructured, and eventually transformed into a

more docile institution. A critical assessment of 'triadic globalization' is contained in Amoroso (1988).

2 The Bretton Woods institutions are the World Bank and the IMF.

3 It could be noted here that Mike Parnwell's methodology focused only on those migrants who had returned to the village, and thus those who had managed to struggle on in the city were not reported.

REFERENCES

Amoroso, Bruno (1998) *On Globalization.* London: Macmillan.

Amsden, A. H. (1989) *Asia's Next Giant: South Korea and Late Industrialization.* New York: Oxford University Press.

—— (2001) *The Rise of the Rest: Late Industrialization outside the North Atlantic Economies.* New York: Oxford University Press.

Arrighi, Giovanni (1994) *The Long Twentieth Century: Money, Power, and the Origins of Our Time.* London: Verso.

—— Ikeda, S. and Irwan, A. (1993) 'The rise of East Asia: one miracle or many?', in R. A. Palat (ed.), *Pacific-Asia and the Future of the World System.* Westport, CT: Greenword Press.

Bell, Peter F. (1996) 'Development or maldevelopment? The contradictions of Thailand's economic growth', in Michael J. G. Parnwell (ed.) *Uneven Development in Thailand.* Aldershot: Avebury, pp. 49–62.

Bullard, Nicola, with Walden Bello and Kamal Malhotra (1998) 'Taming the tigers: the IMF and the Asian crisis', in Jomo K. S. (ed.) *Tigers in Trouble: Financial Governance, Liberalization and Crises in East Asia.* London: Zed Books.

Deyo, F. C. (ed.) (1987) *The Political Economy of the New Asian Industrialization.* Ithaca, NY: Cornell University Press.

Dixon, C. and D. Drakakis-Smith (eds) (1997) *Uneven Development in South East Asia.* Aldershot: Ashgate.

Dornbusch, R. (1998) 'Asian crisis themes', http://web.mit.edu/rudi/www/asianc.html.

Gerschenkron, Alexander (1962) *Economic Backwardness in Historical Perspective: A Book of Essays.* Cambridge: Belknap Press of Harvard University Press.

Gramsci, Antonio (1977) *I Quaderni del Carcere* [Prison notebooks]. Edizione critica dell'Istituto Gramsci a cura di Valentino Gerratana [Annotated edition of the Gramsci Institute, edited by Valentino Gerratana]. Torino: Einaudi.

Hersh, J. (1993) *The USA and the Rise of East Asia since 1945: Dilemmas of the Postwar International Political Economy.* New York: St Martin's Press.

ILO (1998) *The Social Impact of The Asian Financial Crisis.* Technical report for discussion at the high-level tripartite meeting on social responses to the financial crisis in East and Southeast Asian countries, Bangkok (22–24 April 1998), http://www.ilo.org/public/english/bureau/intpol/bangkok/index.htm.

Krugman, Paul (1994) 'The myth of Asia's miracle', *Foreign Affairs*, 73, pp. 62–78.

—— (1998a) 'What happened to Asia?' http://web.mit.edu/krugman/www/disinter.html.

—— (1998b) 'Asia: what went wrong?', *Fortune*, 2 March.

Jomo K. S. (ed.) (1998) *Tigers in Trouble. Financial Governance, Liberalization and Crises in East Asia.* London: Zed Books.

Lardy, N. R. (1995) 'The role of foreign trade and investment in China's economic transformation', *China Quarterly*, 144.

Masina, Pietro P. (1996) *Regional and International Dynamics in the Development of East Asia: The Case of Foreign Direct Investment.* Federico Caffé Centre Research Report no. 1, Roskilde University.

Ohmae, Kenichi (1985) *Triad Power: The Coming Shape of Global Competition.* New York: Free Press.

Parnwell, Michael J. G. (ed.) (1996) *Uneven Development in Thailand.* Aldershot: Avebury.

Radelet, S. and Sachs, J. (1998) 'The East Asian financial crisis: diagnosis, remedies, prospects', Harvard Institute for International Development, April 20.

Rigg, Jonathan (1997) *Southeast Asia: The Human Landscape of Modernization and Development.* London: Routledge.

Sachs, J. (1997) 'The IMF and the Asian flu', *The American Perspective,* March–April, pp. 16–21.

Schmidt, J. D., J. Hersh and N. Fold (1997) *Social Change in Southeast Asia.* Harlow: Longman.

Toye, John (1987) *Dilemmas in Development: Reflections on the Counter Revolution in Development Theory and Policy.* Oxford: Basil Blackwell.

Tsiang, S. and Wu, R. (1985) 'Foreign trade and investment as boosters of take off: the experience of the four Asian NICs', in W. Galenson (ed.), *Foreign Trade and Investment.* Madson: University of Wisconsin Press, pp. 320–343.

United Nations Centre on Transnational Corporations (1991) *World Investment Report 1991: The Triad in Foreign Direct Investment.* Geneva: UN

USTR Website (1998) 'Testimony of Ambassador Charlene Barshefsky United States Trade Representative before the House Ways & Means Trade Subcommittee', 24 February.

Wade, Robert (1990) *Governing the Market. Economic Theory and the Role of Government in East Asian Industrialization.* Princeton, NJ: Princeton University Press.

—— (1992) 'East Asia's economic success: conflicting paradigms, partial insights, shaky evidence', *World Politics,* 44 (2), pp. 270–320.

—— (1996) 'Japan, the World Bank, and the art of paradigm maintenance: *The East Asian Miracle* in political perspective', *New Left Review,* 217, pp. 3–36.

—— and Veneroso, Frank (1998) 'The Asian Crisis: the High Debt Model Versus the Wall Street – Treasury – IMF Complex', *New Left Review,* 228, pp. 3–23.

White, G. and Wade, R. (1988) 'Developmental states and markets in East Asia: an introduction', in G. White (ed.), *The developmental State,* London: Macmillan, pp. 1–29.

World Bank (1993) *The East Asian Miracle: Economic Growth And Public Policy.* New York: Oxford University Press.

—— (1997) *World Development Report: The State in a Changing World.* New York: Oxford University Press.

—— (1998a) 'Social consequences of the East Asian financial crisis', http://www.worldbank.org/poverty/eacrisis/partners/library/socconsq/index.html.

—— (1998b) 'Responding to the crisis: backing East Asia's social and economic reforms', http://www.worldbank.org/html/extdr/asian_crisis/backingreform.html.

Part I

East Asia and the International Regime

TWO

The New 'Asian Drama'
Catching-up at the Crossroads of Neoliberalism

Li Xing, Jacques Hersh and Johannes Dragsbæk Schmidt

Introduction

Since the 1960s, the GNP in a select number of economies in East and Southeast Asia has grown more than twice as much as that of the rest of the countries in the developing world. Their growth rates have also been significant when compared to the industrial economies and the oil-rich Middle East/North African region. The four Asian NICs (Taiwan, South Korea, Hong Kong and Singapore) were joined in the past two decades by a new generation of would-be NICs (Thailand, Malaysia and Indonesia). These countries as well as the Philippines, to some degree, were said to belong to the club of High-Performing Economies of Asia (HPEA). Japan had in the mid-1980s replaced the USA as the world's largest creditor nation and become a significant foreign aid donor. China has followed the development path of the NICs since the end of 1970s. During that period, East Asia seemed to emerge economically and, to a certain extent, politically.

The rapid growth in production and international exports as well as the overall economic achievements were interpreted by some as bringing about a shift in the world's political and economic balance. In the late 1980s, the notion of a 'Pacific Century' claimed that the centre of gravity of the world economy was shifting from the Atlantic to the Pacific Basin. The term 'Pacific Century' or 'Asian Century' was widely used by academics and politicians. US President Reagan asserted in 1984: 'You cannot help but feel that the great Pacific Basin, with all its nations and all its potential for growth and development – that is the future' (*Far Eastern Economic Review*, 17 May 1984). Former Japanese Prime Minister Nakasone declared likewise in a radio speech on 20 November 1984 that 'the Pacific era is a historical inevitability'.

Perhaps because of the intense curiosity raised by this first case of rapid industrialization outside the Western cultural sphere, the East Asian economies became the object of various academic studies and interpretations. These successful examples seemed to challenge the assumptions of the core–periphery structure supported by the world system theory and dependency theory, while the implementation of a state-directed strategy did not fit into the neoclassical development model.

However, the recent crisis questions the various interpretations of the NIC model in East Asia which had to struggle with collapsing currencies and plunging stock markets. First Thailand, then Indonesia, followed by South Korea, the world's eleventh largest economy, all had to ask the IMF for emergency loans. Even Japan, the world's second largest economy after the United States, looks vulnerable and unable to offer any substantial contribution to ease its economic problems as well as those of the region.

The interpretations of the current economic crisis have gone from former praise to criticism of the East Asian development pattern, characterized by attacks on the Asian social and political systems. Traditional debates between neoliberals and statists over the relationship between market and state, 'free' and 'governed' market as well as democracy versus authoritarianism are re-emerging not only among academics but also at the political level.

In disagreement with the neoliberal interpretation, some scholars argue that the current economic turmoil in East Asia does not reflect the 'meltdown' of the East Asian 'miracle' but rather reflects the decline of the US and the rise of East Asia in the world economy. In an internet debate, Gunder Frank argues that this is the *first* major recession of modern times which started in Asia and spread to other parts of the world. In contrast, as he explains, all previous postwar recessions in the world began in the United States or in Europe and Japan. This is taken to signify that the dynamo/dynamism has shifted from the US to the Asian region. In this view, the Asian crisis only represents a cyclical recession which should not be confused with a structural 'meltdown'. This position seems, however, to be influenced by economic oversimplification of the balance of forces in the international economy. As a matter of fact, it was international financial capital's volatility and its activity in East Asia that were the immediate cause of the recent events which created the greatest challenge to capitalism in the last 50 years, according to President Clinton.

Nevertheless there can be no question that a significant change was in the making. After the demise of Soviet-type socialism, what is happening in East Asia may even have consequences of greater proportion for the rest of the world. As one scholar has put it: 'Clearly, the crisis is a defining moment in the evolution of global capitalism in the post-Cold War period and a vigorous debate has begun on its origins and its implications for the global economy as well as for the regional and national economies' (Robison 1998: 5).

Debates and interpretations

In the past, there has been rather extensive research concerning the conceptualization of 'East Asian capitalism' (Wade 1990; Johnson 1982; Chen 1990; Deyo 1987), and disagreement has always been rife. However, the peak of the dispute occurred when the World Bank (1993) reluctantly released the controversial report called *The East Asian Miracle: Economic Growth and Public Policy.* This report explained East Asian high growth by pointing to limited government intervention but within the confines of microeconomic neoliberal theory.

The strongest voices in the current debate concerning the Asian crisis come from neoliberal economists, politicians as well as academics, who point to the role of the state as the culprit. In this line of thinking the current Asian crisis is taken as justifying their position on the superiority of the free market. This is not surprising for, as Jawaharlal Nehru observed in 1946, 'History is almost always written by the victors.' Steven Radelet and Jeffrey Sachs, who bring this quotation, add:

> When a financial crisis arises, it is the debtors who are asked to take the blame. This is odd, since a loan agreement invariably has two parties. The failure of a loan usually represents miscalculations of both sides of the transaction or distortions in the lending process itself. (Radelet and Sachs1998: 1)

This notwithstanding, the collapse of Asian stock markets and banking systems is considered by neoliberalists to be evidence that intervention strategies do not work and that protectionism is a route to economic disaster. The argument is that state-led economic development, i.e. government control of credit allocation, encourages inefficiency and corruption. The implication is that what has happened in Asia is proof that unless the free market mechanism prevails, developing countries are bound to experience crises, tensions and adjustments.

Moreover, according to this argument, the Asian disease is not only a matter of policy failure: the problem is to be found in the developmental state itself. The true lesson to be drawn is that the 'model' entails complacency, authoritarian/semi-authoritarian cronyism and corruption, as the state is politically isolated from the public while bankers and businessmen are economically insulated from market mechanisms. With no democratic public supervision system in control of the iron triangle of bureaucrats–businessmen–bankers, decisions are said to be based on personal relations rather than a response to the price mechanism. Accordingly, the Asian financial crisis is seen as a symptom of a much deeper defect. The social and political assumptions on which the Asian 'model' and 'values' rested are considered inappropriate in confronting the challenge of the time. The world economy in the era of globalization is far too complex for any state to function as the 'visible hand', i.e. regulating and guiding the national economy.

The free-market proponents who conclude that history is rendering its verdict on the Asian capitalist model have long denied the existence of such a model. In fact, Asian economies were regarded as examples of macroeconomic stability, market-driven pricing, and disciplined borrowing. In 1995, the Heritage Foundation released an index of economic freedom showing that four of the top seven countries were located in Asia. When the economies of South Korea and Taiwan boomed in the 1980s, Western analysis characterized them as the least price-distorting regimes in the world. Similar conclusions about the sources of Asian growth can also be found in studies of the World Bank and the International Monetary Fund.

The market-friendly interpretations of Asia's success aimed at countering the theses offered by neo-statist scholars that trade barriers, subsidized credit and strong state support for export-driven industries had been essential aspects of the economic development of East Asian countries. Thus, while free marketeers maintained that economic growth in East Asia occurred not because of, but in spite of state interventionism, their explanation of the present havoc the region is going through appears to be contradictory. As pointed out by a political economist: 'although the pure free market economists were anxious to deny any positive role to government policy in the "miracle", they were quick to blame government policies for the "collapse"' (Freeman 1998: 404).

While the neoclassical approach focuses on short-run efficient resource allocation as the key to long-term growth which is considered to be inherent to capitalism and can be applied to all societies, the statist perspective looks at late development in the context of catching-up strategies without abandoning the centrality of the market. Taking its cue from Alexander Gerschenkron (1962), the latter approach argues from a perspective of economic nationalism for a strong state to overcome market imperfections, protect the industrialization process from external economic forces and neutralize domestic social forces. Alvin Y. So and Stephen W. K. Chiu (1995: 12) point out that the statist perspective looks at the complex interactions between state, market and socio-political institutions. Such a strategy was basically followed by Germany and Japan as the two last successful examples of catching-up. Statism, which is often related to the capitalist developmental state (CDS) in East Asia, is seen as an indispensable factor behind the East Asian NIC model in which there is a congenial relationship between the government, economic policies and market principles (Johnson 1982).

To the extent that the objective is industrial capitalism, theories appeared which refined the neoclassical position in their portrayal of East Asian development. Revisionists or institutionalists, as they also came to be known, showed that these economies had been 'market guiding' and even 'market distorting' rather than 'market conforming' (Amsden 1989; Wade 1990). Seen from this perspective, the strategy entailed establishing the appropriate mix of market orientation and government interference conducive to late industrialization. Of equal importance to this perspective is the question of compatible social and political institutions within the context of the state–market relationship (Onis 1991: 110).

While the Listian approach – in the mould of traditional economic nationalism – refused free trade and favoured mercantilist state protection to promote enterprise, the success of the East Asian NICs evolved a path which can be called neo-Listian. From this angle, the strategic role of the state in neutralizing domestic and external forces and harnessing them to the national interest became the object of the 'development state' (Hoogvelt 1997: 205–206).

Within the fringe of mainstream economic thinking, a provocative interpretation comes from Paul Krugman (1994), who questioned the existence of an Asian development 'model' or 'miracle'. His argument is based on a discussion of utilization of production factors and he finds that

> Asian growth is mainly the result of the same things that drive growth everywhere: high investment rates, mainly though not entirely financed by high domestic saving; a rapidly improving level of education; and the transfer of large numbers of underemployed peasants into the modern sector. If there is anything miraculous about Asian growth, it is a matter of degree, not of kind. (Krugman 1997: 37)

In his opinion, Asia's growth rates in total production may have been high, but the growth rates in labour productivity were comparatively low. In other words, much of the growth can be ascribed to substantial input factors (labour and capital especially), but not to significant productivity increase. The importance of cheap labour has of course been recognized as the basic element behind the East Asian 'miracle' by scholars of Marxist persuasion (Arrighi 1994: 347). In the period in question, these Asian countries enjoyed high savings rates, rises in the percentage of people participating in the workforce, excellent and accessible education, and important investments in physical capital. In other words, the East Asia NICs might have done a remarkable job of mobilizing various resources, but not in an efficient way. Thus, the argument continues, what East Asia has achieved in the past decades cannot really find answers within the confines of an industrial-policy vs. free-market argument.

Another neoliberal variant within the mainstream has attempted to contribute to the understanding of the East Asian NICs by proposing the culturalist perspective. Its frame of reference is grounded in the values, attitudes and practices that exert influence in a process of development. Contrary to the modernization paradigm, which counterposes 'modernity' to 'tradition' as two opposing phenomena, the culturalist approach rejects the argument that economic backwardness can be explained principally by the survival of traditional society and culture. In the Asian context, tradition is thus seen as being beneficial to development. Departing from the Weberian perspective which considered societies in the Chinese cultural sphere as inappropriate for capitalism, the Confucian tradition is considered by the culturalist interpretation as having made a contribution (because of its emphasis on knowledge, education, diligence, self-sacrifice and delayed gratification) to social stability as well as its acceptance of bureaucratic governance at both governmental and enterprise levels. Attempting to surmount the dichotomy between 'modernization' and 'tradition', Lucien Pye suggests that the paradox was resolved after Western economic theories penetrated and were absorbed in East Asia (Pye 1988: 16).

The question of democracy in relation to cultural values has also been raised in the current debate. In the course of the economic crisis certain political opinion-makers have attacked the notion of 'Asian values' as a myth or distortion, arguing that 'Western' concepts of democracy and human rights are in fact not inimical to Asia or to economic growth. Accordingly,

> the first lesson from the Asian crisis is that a government that is not answerable to its people will not be likely to have open markets or the institutions required to impose discipline to overcome a financial crisis. A second lesson is that *guanxi* (connections), are never a substitute for the rule of law. (Lee 1998)

In this line of reasoning, what is to be learned from the Asian crisis is that,

> openness and freedom are essential not to capitalism in all its incarnations but to a specific form of capitalism. That is, democratic capitalism – the combination of a free political society and an open economic system, without control by government–business conspiracy partnership. (Rosenthal 1997)

A review of the attempts to conceptualize the evolution of East Asia displays an apparent lack of comprehensive meta-perspective. As a result, the regional and international dimension of the East Asian development as well as the interactions of the nation-states are left out. Thus, the dynamics of incorporating society into the world system is neglected (So and Chiu 1995: 21). This is especially strange to the extent that, as history has shown and the world-system analysis has pointed out, 'successful strategies of national upward mobility include "promotion by invitation", "self-reliance" and "seizing the chance"' (Hoogvelt 1997: 60).

The aim of this chapter

Many of the mentioned interpretations are confined within a narrow framework focusing on the relationship between national state and market. In contrast, the approach taken here is to propose an understanding of Asian capitalism and the current financial crisis based on exploring and analysing the dialectical relationship between the 'developmental state' and the macropolitical economy at the national and at the regional as well as at the global level.

As the point of departure we have the following cluster of questions in mind:

- Since 'catching-up' has been the basic Asian development strategic objective under specific favourable geopolitical conditions, can this dynamism persist at a time when those opportunities and conditions are diminishing?
- Can the East Asian economic and trade structures which were created to take advantage of the opportunities offered by the Cold War continue to unleash their development potentials in the current era of globalization?
- To what extent is the crisis the expression of a struggle waged by neoliberal Anglo-Saxon capitalism, supported by the Western-dominated global regulatory institutions such as the IMF, the World Bank, and the WTO to pry these economies open to external capital interests?
- What are the socioeconomic implications and will the 'developmental state' be dismantled? Notwithstanding past experience, the concept of East Asian capitalism and the notion of 'developmental state' appear to need serious rethinking.

Hence, the intention is to reconceptualize the East Asian crisis by re-analysing relationships between those elements that are said to have contributed to East Asia's economic success while taking into consideration new regional and global factors in the context of the international evolution as well as the impact and interaction between them. The analysis is divided into four parts:

1. the East Asian 'miracle' in view of the transformation in global geopolitics and the international political economy;
2. the national and intra-regional economic intercourse;
3. the China factor;
4. East Asian capitalism and the financial crisis.

THE TRANSFORMATION OF GEOPOLITICS AND THE INTERNATIONAL POLITICAL ECONOMY

Cold War geopolitics and the East Asian 'miracle'

In order to understand the rapid industrialization of Japan, South Korea, Taiwan and a few Southeast Asian countries, a number of scholars have urged the inclusion of historical and geopolitical dimensions. The fate of the Asian countries, seen in this light, was very much a function of the presence of the United States as an external superpower and its strategy aimed at preventing the expansion of communism at the time. According to this view

> the geographical location of the Newly Industrialising Countries was no mere coincidence. Indeed, the most successful NICs were to be found on the rim of the Asian mainland. In this connection it should be recalled that a component of the American geopolitical scheme after the Second World War had been to provide a hinterland for the Japanese economy while simultaneously isolating China and the other socialist countries. (Hersh 1993: 48–49)

Postwar American foreign and economic policies aimed at fostering developmentalism, authoritarianism and anti-communism. In Europe, afraid that mass poverty would eventually facilitate communist expansion, the Marshall Plan aimed to revive Western European industries within the shortest possible time. In East Asia the central theme of US postwar policy was basically the same: the revival of the Japan-centred capitalist regional economy including South Korea and Taiwan.

The objectives of US postwar policy towards East Asia were to cement strategic relations through economic dependence, to strengthen the position of pro-American political elites, and more importantly, to restore and nurture a Japan-centred East Asian economic growth in the hope that this would help immunize the region against anti-systemic movements.[1] In addition to containing communist expansion, as revisionist historians have shown, Washington pursued a course to create a capitalist world economic system – 'a global liberal economic regime' – and under the condition of its own participation in it, implicitly strove to restore a cloned 'Greater East Asian Co-prosperity Sphere' (the imperial Japanese regional economy) which had been destroyed in the Second World War (Schwarz 1996: 92–102). By providing security, economic support and military aid to Japan and other East Asian states, the US aim was consequently to control and define their roles within the American-led alliance and prevent them from embarking upon an independent political and military course.

It will be recalled that prewar Japan had tried to establish a regional division of labour in order to ensure Japanese superiority. Based on the notion developed in the 1930s by the economist Kaname Akamatsu, East and Southeast Asia were conceptualized as part of a 'flying geese' formation, with Japan as the leading goose. In world system terminology, the structure would be described as consisting of Japan as the centre, a semiperiphery (the two formal colonies of Korea and Taiwan), and the vast markets and suppliers of raw material of the rest of Asia as the periphery. In essence, a reconstruction of this pyramidical structure was the aim of US policy shortly after the war, but with the principal difference that the US was to be included as the centre and Japan as the semi-periphery, with the rest of Asia as the periphery to the American and Japanese economies.

The inclusion of the geopolitical and geoeconomic dimensions helps to explain the extensive role that the US played in the rise of East Asian capitalism. American military aid and financial assistance are documented to have been an important contributing factor in the economic development of East Asia, especially South Korea and Taiwan. According to CIA figures, American military and economic aid to South Korea totalled US$13 billion ($600 per capita) in the period 1945–79, which in the 1950s accounted for five-sixths of Korean imports. In the case of Taiwan, the comparable figure was US$5.6 billion ($425 per capita) (Cumings 1987: 44–83).

Under American protection, perceived external military threats and the internal danger of communist expansion were substantially reduced in Japan and the East Asian NICs. The burden of Japan's military expenses greatly decreased due to the American military presence in the region. US military bases have been documented to have not only protected these countries but also to have provided them with economic benefits such as indigenous employment, consumption and production. Even now, the withdrawal of American military forces would be considered to be a substantial economic loss in some of these nations.

Thanks to both the favourable geopolitical situation and postwar conditions, the export-oriented development strategy was especially successful in the 1960s and 1970s when first Japan and then the NICs could specialize in the production of labour-intensive goods with access to Western markets and advanced technology. The potential of the US market, starting with the Korean War and sustained throughout the Vietnam War, to absorb exports from this region helped the economies of Japan and the NICs grow at an unprecedented rate. After the Vietnam War, the US economy weakened but still fulfilled a vital function in providing the largest outlet for the industrial exports of East Asia.

The new constellation of geopolitics and international political economy

In this respect, the position of East Asia *vis-à-vis* the Western world was bound to undergo a change. The transformation of the post-Cold War international political economy characterized by the relative decline of the US economy, the rising protectionism in Europe and the establishment of two Western economic blocs (EU and NAFTA), indicates that reliance on Western markets by both the Asian NICs and the late-comers of Southeast Asia can no longer be taken for granted. The future of the international trading system has become uncertain. As a result, major industrial powers are facing the task of implementing structural changes. The social and political problems that arise from trade imbalances among major advanced countries are pushing them away from free trade. This world-wide tendency towards protectionism is aimed not only at Japan but also at the NICs' expansion of exports.

It is evident that the Asian crisis has a global dimension. Some analysts see it as a replay of the Mexican meltdown of 1995; others consider it to be a clear indication of the weakness of the world economy in the era of globalization.

Regardless of the variety of opinions, there is a need to rethink the political and theoretical assumptions of the conventional globalization discourse which focuses on the assumed benefits of deregulated financial markets. These are said to contribute new possibilities in the following areas:

- to quicken the pace of investment, job creation and growth;
- to allow high investment opportunities and higher returns on savings;
- to ensure efficient allocation of resources and steady world growth;
- to provide new incentives to pursue healthy macroeconomic policies and to overcome structural weaknesses that impede investment and growth. (Camdessus 1997)

This overly economistic optimism ignores the background of the new situation which calls for a re-examination of relationships such as capital-to-labour and capital-to-capital, capital-to-state in the context of the international political economy.

In the present period of global neoliberal capitalism, the three sets of relations are characterized by new transformations. First, in *capital-to-labour relations* the use or threatened use of capital mobility to relocate parts or phases of production processes in countries and regions where low wages and political control provide profitability as well as a lever of exploitation. Another bargaining advantage of transnational corporations (TNCs) is the use of modern technologies and the replacement of human labour with machines. These two effective bargaining chips contribute to the shifting of the relative balance of power between capital and labour in favour of the former also in OECD countries.

Second, in *capital-to-capital relations*, the distinctive features of TNCs are that they are not only global in what they produce and sell in many parts of the world, but are also conglomerates united under the common interest of creating a business-friendly international environment. By using high-tech communication and computerized technology, they can move operations from country to country, going anyplace where wages and taxes are lowest and profits highest. In other words, they have the capacity to make rational and precise choices of investment in order to maximize profits based on a favourable combination of local policies, labour conditions, infrastructure and a stable political climate. Moreover, as deregulated global financial markets are inherently unstable, they move in a boom–bust pattern. During a boom period, capital flows from the core to the periphery, but when a crisis emerges, it returns to its sources.

Third, in *capital-to-state relations*, the relative decline of state autonomy is an outcome of the mobility of TNCs, financial institutions and powerful investors to transfer production to countries or regions where state policies may be more pliable to their interests. It means that, through the use of global instant communications, investors can invest their money in anything – stocks, bonds, property, factories, foreign currencies – almost anywhere in the world. Thus, they are in a position to influence government policies and politics. The threat to move production and investment gives them strong leverage to win concessions and favourable policies. In other words, the relative weakening of the state is closely linked to the internationalization of production and finance.

As a result, states no longer seem to retain the capacity to act as buffers between domestic society and international economic actors. Rather, they adjust domestic policies or priorities to respond to the world economy. Consequently, states become 'transmission belts' of global economic forces penetrating local borders and markets (Cox 1993: 260). The domestic political and institutional spheres face an inherent contradiction: on the one hand, states are the custodians of society with the task of providing social peace and security and protecting national interests; on the other hand, the indisputable power of capital mobility reduces their capacity to do so. The case of South Korea offers an interesting example. After becoming a member of OECD, the regime had been under pressure from international economic forces to dismantle the 'visible hand' of the developmental state in the trade and financial sectors. This pressure was accentuated during the current crisis. According to some conventional economists, the country's ills could only be cured by fully subjecting to foreign 'dictate':

> Korea needs to open up the economy fully to outside participation. Foreign investors must take over and clean up the mess fully with a wave of uncompromising corporate and banking restructurings that are long overdue. Neither the government nor the Korean business community can do the job. A crisis such as the present one must be exploited to put in place a better-functioning economy ... Foreign lenders, the IMF, and the US and whoever else participates must settle for nothing less ... But if Korea is unwilling, a moratorium on commercial debt service will teach both the country and its markets an overdue lesson. (Dornbusch 1997: 26)

Potential misunderstandings emerged as to the causes of the crisis in East Asia and its proposed resolution by Western 'advice'. A tenet of neoliberalism has been that East Asian economic growth was the outcome of integration within a well-functioning global economy. In contrast, the present havoc is increasingly understood by the victims to be a symptom of dysfunction within the Western-driven world economy. This may have unintended results in contrast to the expectations of the decision-makers behind the 'Washington Consensus'. As two American analysts conclude: 'It is well understood across the Pacific that globalization caused the Asian crisis and cannot logically be its cure' (Auerback and Smith 1998).

But just as important, it has to be realized that the developmental state phenomenon in East Asia was *historically* determined, rather than culturally, economically or socially specific, although the latter elements involved in the interaction should also receive their due. This historical dimension, in connection to the external geopolitical environment and the favourable conjunction with a certain phase of postwar capitalism, determines the limits of the catching-up path followed by the East Asian developmental states as well as the emulation of such a model by developing countries in general.

The Economic and Trade Relations of East Asian Capitalism

The historical dimension in intra-regional economic and trade relations

In contrast to the experience of regions colonized by European powers, East Asian economic development can be described as an interlinked process between Japan and its neighbours, first and foremost South Korea and Taiwan. Without access to the region's raw materials, labour power, markets and capital outlets, Japanese industrialization would have been different. In fact, it was its poor economic endowment compared to the rest of Asia which permitted Japan to escape Western colonialism (Hersh 1993).

Consequently, imperial Japan played a central role in establishing the seeds of a regional division of labour. The East Asian style of economic development can to a certain extent be deemed a legacy of this relationship. Japan was the first country in Asia to industrialize and this was done much earlier than in the rest of the region. Its modernization initiative and programme can be dated back to the Meiji period when Japan mobilized its economy to face the danger of Western invasion and colonization. After having become a strong economic and military power, Japan set out to conquer East Asia and establish the so-called 'Greater East Asia Co-Prosperity Sphere' and force the Western powers out of the region.

The result of this strategy was conflict with both local populations and the West, i.e. the United States. After the Second World War destruction, Japan achieved the first wave industrialization in the region, based on American aid and technologies. Japan took advantage of the opportunities of the global economic restructuring and gradually transformed itself from a defeated nation into the second largest economy in the world after the United States.

The East Asian NICs (especially South Korea and Taiwan) followed in the second wave with access to US and Japanese capital and technologies. They implemented a statist model and within a few decades succeeded in achieving rapid industrialization. Three ASEAN countries (Malaysia, Thailand and Indonesia) made up the third wave by taking advantage of the opportunities offered by the outphasing of old production structures in Japan and the Asian NICs and by relying on their investments and technologies. China's economic take-off in the 1980s following its reform programme can be regarded as the fourth industrialization wave in East Asia.

The flying geese formation

According to the neoclassical interpretation, the above periodization indicates that East Asia's ladder-type intra-regional economic relations based on product cycle considerations and comparative advantages are delineated both in time and space. In terms of development level, Japan sits at the top of the ladder. With regard to economic relations, countries at the lower end of the ladder seemed willing to 'inherit' the 'left-overs' from countries higher up by overtaking their industries and importing their technologies. This kind of hierarchical intra-regional economic structure also explains why economic growth seems 'inherited' in East Asian countries.

The apparent chain-pattern of economic development in East Asia appears as the product of the interactions of the four industrialization waves. It bears certain similarities to the above-mentioned economic model put forward by Japanese economists prior to the Second World War. It mainly refers to the development levels and stages between countries in the region while the 'chain-pattern' reveals the structure of industrial production relations among countries in the region. The assumption of the 'flying geese formation' is that a group of nations in this region are flying together in layers with Japan at the forefront, the NICs at the middle and the rest at the bottom. The hypothesis of the chain pattern indicates that changes in the product cycles will result in the relocation of production in a number of countries by the leading economies, who will gradually move some of their industries or industrial sectors to the next layer of countries because of changing comparative advantage over time. However, it is necessary to point out that this scheme of economic development is largely centred on Japan and based on its production system. This regional development is described by UNCTAD in the following way:

> The 'flying geese' pattern … is based broadly on a vertical division of labor among countries at different stages of industrialization, with competitiveness in previously established export sectors continuously shifting the advantage from countries at the higher stages to those at lower ones, and with those at the higher stages continuously acquiring competitiveness in new product lines. (UNCTAD 1993: 131)

However, despite the fact that this apparent geographical division of labour emphasizes the importance of regionalization of economic activities based on comparative advantages, it also conceals potential disadvantages and weaknesses: economic activities and industrial production are conducted within hierarchical structures. This pattern of industrialization can be described as an ideal-type 'dependent development', whereby local and foreign capital together with the state create the basis for economic growth. The consequences are that

> the development of products and the location of industrial processes across Japan, the NIEs, and the ASEAN-3 are not determined according to the requirements of integrated industrial development in each country or region, but rather in line with the profit interests of Japanese capital and of subordinate NIEs and ASEAN-3 capitalist classes. Given intensive competition among peripheral, semi-peripheral, and, increasingly, core countries for the investments and technologies controlled by core transnational corporations, these hierarchical structures of product cycles and industrial diffusions provide a most uncongenial environment for integrated and sustainable national industrialization efforts and the kinds of integrated and sustainable regional and global productive structures that can serve the needs of workers and their communities in East Asia and elsewhere. (Hart-Landsberg and Burkett 1998: 91)

In addition, the current crisis of the regional neo-mercantilist model of East Asia is directly connected to the fact that the statist export-oriented strategy itself leads to an impasse. Under certain past geopolitical conditions, the model proved to be essential and workable in achieving industrialization in a world capitalist system that is not inherently conducive to export-driven development. But such a pattern doesn't create the capacity for economic autonomy. Without any other objective than integrating the global economy, these nations subjected themselves to certain risks. Their reliance on export-oriented industrialization (EOI) would, with time, increasingly confront these economies with problems connected to the evolution of global capitalism. The external forces of international capital are not the only source of the East Asian economic crisis, which is also the result of 'the entire emergent system of regionalized export-oriented accumulation and the regionalized class-exploitative relations underpinning and reproduced by it' (ibid.: 107).

The China factor

It is an irony of history that a contributing factor to the process of industrialization in East Asia was connected to the fact that the Chinese Revolution in 1949 came to dominate US foreign policy in the East Asian region. The victory of Mao Zedong made decision-makers in Washington aware that economic growth had to take place in the region in order to avoid the contagion effect. After a period of political and military interventions, the US thus became the 'godfather' of the East Asian miracle. In so doing, the region was offered opportunities not accessible to either Africa or Latin America. 'Invitation' and 'seizing the time' were at work in East Asia. Had China not 'fallen' to the communists, the evolution of the area would certainly have been different, with the US probably more interested in the Chinese economy and its market than that of other countries. To put it bluntly, it was largely a biproduct of the communist victory in China that the spread of East Asian capitalist industrialism was fostered and nurtured by both internal and external forces.

Extrapolating from past experience, it is undeniable that the future of the region will come to depend once again on future Chinese development. In this connection the case of China is interesting to the extent that the country is presently engaged in a transition from state socialism to that of market socialism. Under the former, the economy was characterized by a high degree of self-reliance. With the shift to an open-door strategy, China has shown eagerness to become a major player in the capitalist world economy, with the smaller East Asian economies beginning to suffer as compatibility between them and the Chinese economy is not self-evident.

While the Maoist period was perceived as a socialist challenge in East Asia leading to a US strategy of making the region a showcase of the superiority of capitalism, the success of authoritarianism and economic growth in the NICs in turn greatly influenced the Chinese leadership at the time of the demise of Mao. The possibility of maintaining communist party dominance while adjusting the economy to the demands of the world economy became the guiding principle in the decision-making.

China's position in the East Asian ladder-takeover-chain economic and trade relations is difficult to locate because of the country's vast size and unbalanced development levels between the different provinces. It is not easy to define clearly the status of the Chinese economy because all the different stages can be found across the country's region. Although, on the one hand, this signifies an unbalanced development of the economy, on the other hand, the advantages of a multi-level economy enable China at the same time to cooperate with countries at different stages whereby different Chinese provinces can give full play to their comparative advantages. While the Chinese economy's compatibility with the countries of the region might globally not be pronounced, Chinese provinces might thus be able to find partners.

This situation is obviously an advantage as it enables China to compete with other countries in almost all industrial sectors at various levels. Thus, China is capable of competing with Japan and the NICs in developing high-tech industries while it can inherit labour-intensive industries from them; at same time it can also export capital, intermediate products and some of its labour-intensive industries to less developed countries.

China and foreign direct investment (FDI)

It is argued by some scholars that foreign direct investment played an important role in the East Asian industrialization process, especially in the ASEAN region. In the case of the ASEAN-3 (Indonesia, Malaysia and Thailand) it is indeed recognized that one of the engines behind their growth was foreign direct investment. In the case of Malaysia, for example, FDI inflows as a percentage of domestic capital formation rose from 8.1 per cent in 1985 to 21.9 per cent in 1990, and in Thailand from 1.8 to 7.9 per cent for the same period (Yue in Hart-Landsberg and Burkett 1998: 89). The establishment of foreign investment as an important factor behind the ASEAN-3 growth is also used by neoliberal proponents to support their arguments in favour of free-market capitalism.

In recent years China has attracted far more foreign investment (productive capital) than any other developing countries: from US$916 million in 1983 to US$33,787 million in 1994 (Lardy 1995: 1066). Despite the fact that the bulk of foreign capital – up to 80 per cent of total foreign investment in China – comes from the network of overseas Chinese in Hong Kong, Taiwan, Singapore, Indonesia, etc. (Aseniero 1996), many of these investments could have gone to other East and Southeast Asian countries, had the Chinese economy not been considered hospitable, especially in terms of labour costs and preferential tax policies as well as political predictability.

According to some studies, this FDI-based growth has stimulated the postulated improvement in Chinese manufacturing productivity that was characteristic of the other high performing economies of East Asia. The dramatic rise of FDI in China has posed a challenge to the former NICs' economies and can be argued to be a factor behind the current East Asian economic difficulties. On the other hand, without the investment outlets for foreign capital in the Chinese economy, the problems of surplus capital would have been accentuated in the region.

China and foreign trade

As a result of a large amount of FDI inflows, the share of FDI-promoted exports in China's total trade growth has been rising steadily. According to statistics, the share of such exports in 1985 was about 1 per cent of China's total exports; by 1994 it had reached almost 30 per cent (Lardy 1995: 1074).

The pace of the growth of Chinese exports causes unease: its share of world trade increased from 0.9 per cent in 1980 to 2.3 per cent in 1992. It is spectacular not only because China's exports grew more rapidly than any other developing country, but also because the manufactured composition increased dramatically from 49.7 per cent of the total in 1980 to 83.7 per cent in 1994 (ibid.: 1076), posing a challenge to the East Asian countries. In the vision of market proponents both inside as well as outside China, had the state sectors gone through successful reforms resulting in enhanced productivity, this would presumably have had an even larger impact on the rest of East Asian economies.

In recent years, the fear of China as an economic competitor – which dominated East Asian perceptions at the beginning of the Chinese modernization programme – have to a certain extent proven to be justified. The rise of China is having serious repercussions on these countries. Already Mexico's 1994 peso devaluation was seen as a menace to the region's exporting economies (Radelet and Sachs 1998); the devaluation of the Chinese renminbi in 1994 with the reduction of the price of China's exports exerted a negative influence on East

Asian export-dependent economies and is viewed by some as one of the causes behind the current crisis (Caplen 1997; Aghevli 1999; Bird and Milne 1999).

As seen from a Japanese perspective, the currency crises in East Asia were caused by the weakened export competitiveness of the region's economies. This evolution was attributed to the pegging of East Asian currencies to the US dollar as well as falling demand in Japanese markets. This, however, had been acerbated by Japan's own devaluation of the yen, which declined by nearly 60 per cent against the US dollar between April 1995 and April 1997 (Johnson 1998: 658). Thus, coming on top of the devaluation of the Chinese renminbi in 1994, the depreciation of the Japanese yen translated into a serious decline of the competitiveness of East Asian exports relative to that of China and Japan (Hughes 2000: 230). Notwithstanding Japan's own responsibility, MITI placed the blame on China for the difficulties that affected East Asian economies (ibid.: 235).

This aspect of the turmoil which hit the East Asian region, while not distracting from the immediate cause of the crisis in the form of volatile capital's role, does raise the dimension of the real economy's structural crisis, which is fundamentally one of surplus capacity and excess supply, i.e. the problem of overproduction (Gill 1999: 5; Tabb 1998).

Due to the sheer size of its economy, the impact of the emergence of China is bound to have worldwide consequences. Should China succeed in becoming an economic powerhouse, this would inevitably affect the structure of the world system, which would have to deal with the enormity of such a success. Accommodating first Japan and then the Asian NICs represented a challenge for the global economy. A full-scale Chinese industrialization based on export-orientation would thus be a potentially destabilizing factor in the world balance of power both economically and politically. The reverse, i.e. the failure of modernization plunging the country into chaos and civil strife, would equally represent a menace to the stability of the region as well as to the rest of the world. As Aseniero puts it: 'Either way, it is the dragon – not the East Asian tigers or the Japanese flying goose or the American eagle – that will spell the future of the Pacific Rim' (Aseniero 1996: 193).

EAST ASIAN CAPITALISM AND THE FINANCIAL CRISIS

In the interpretation of the Asian crisis which sees the role of statism as the chief culprit, it is often forgotten that it was mostly foreign banks and financiers, not Asian governments, who lent billions of dollars to the indebted companies. While neoliberal discourse is using the Asian crisis to claim victory, it should not be forgotten that it was major Western investors themselves who showed faith in the region's equity market.

While Japanese productive and financial capital had been active in the area for some time, it was especially since the 1990s that, taking advantage of the deregulation of the financial sectors of these markets, Western volatile capital willingly invested, until 1997, in short-term transactions on Asian markets. The US government had been one of the main proponents of deregulation, which had been resisted by nationalist segments of the bureaucracies of Asian countries. In this respect it ought to be recalled that East Asian capital control was based on the realization that economies in this region had a rather high degree of capital self-sufficiency. As the world's biggest savers (35 per cent of GDP compared to the US rate of only 15 per cent), these countries did not need to draw on the savings from the outside world (Wade 1998–99: 49). As a matter of fact, the decision to open up and liberalize these economies was made by Wall Street financial leaders who, as members of the Democratic Party, in June 1991 picked presidential candidate Bill Clinton to carry the torch of trade and financial liberalization and to force East Asia to deregulate their economies (Kristof and Sanger 1999).

Therefore, if East Asia's problems are seen as systemic (i.e., the result of these countries' statist policies) then why did international capital markets fail to recognize this earlier? More importantly, unlike Latin America, the borrowing in East Asia was done, not by governments, but by private companies, to whom foreign banks should have applied traditional risk–reward analyses. The optimism of capital markets was based on the region's high growth rates, which encouraged investors to believe that the upward spiral and deregulation would continue. However, when investors suddenly decided that the trend could now only go downwards, a stampede of investment withdrawals occurred, making the spiral go downward at an ever faster rate.

The World Bank, IMF and the East Asian trajectory

The World Bank, as a component of the Bretton Woods agreement, has always occupied an important position in the design and consolidation of Western development discourses. Since its establishment, the World Bank, together with the IMF, used loans and investments as leverage to encourage 'positive and constructive' economic performance in recipient developing countries and in forcing them to accept market principles. Assuming its role as a global financial centre, the US effectively combined its global economic interests with its foreign policy. It has ever since monopolized the World Bank's think-tanks, its institutionalized forms and culture.[2]

The rapid growth of East Asian capitalism was originally interpreted by the World Bank as confirmation that privatization and liberalization created economic growth and efficiency. East Asian capitalism was also seen as a natural outgrowth of global capitalist expansion. Bela Balassa argued that countries should utilize their comparative advantage in specialization as the key engine to economic growth. This is a similar conceptualization to the Japanese 'flying geese' development master plan. According to Balassa (1988), the export-oriented development strategy formed a central and dynamic element of the comparative advantage framework which comes into play by reducing domestic constraints, undermining protectionist economic arrangement, and stimulating free competition as well as upgrading technologies.

However, since the 1980s the Bank's position on East Asian capitalism has been somewhat inconsistent. In its 1993 report the Bank pointed out that, on the one hand, rapid growth in each economy was primarily due to the application of a set of common, market-friendly economic policies; while on the other hand, it admitted that the high-performing Asian economies had carried out and benefited from implementing the right fundamentals – that is, encouraging macroeconomic stability, spreading basic education, establishing sound and solvent financial institutions, securing property rights and complementary public investments in infrastructure, and low relative prices of investment goods. Regarding the disputable point concerning the role of state intervention, the Bank softly acknowledged that 'mainly in Northeast Asia, in particular, in some instances, government interventions resulted in higher and more equal growth than otherwise would have occurred' (World Bank 1993: 6).

However, recognizing East Asian capitalism as compatible with or as part of the economic framework grounded in the Anglo-American neoliberal paradigm can be understood not only as a theoretical discrepancy but also as a political contradiction. According to Berger and Beeson, to fit the East Asian experience, based on the statist model, into the neoliberal framework would be inconsistent with the Bank's fundamental paradigm:

> In the first instance, the concessionary credit which was part of the Japanese approach to development aid undermined the attractiveness of credit provided by the World Bank. Second, the emphasis on the importance of directed credit as an instrument of industrial policy which is characteristic of the Japanese approach is at odds with the Bank's overarching focus on financial liberalisation. The upper echelons of the Bank also feared that, if they put their imprimatur on the developmental state model, it would undermine the Bank's own credit rating (and therefore borrowing and lending capacity) with the international money markets and its authority in the international economic system more generally. For the Bank to change its attitude towards the Japanese model would also represent a major challenge to the USA, which has historically used the Bank in its overall projection of power and influence. (Berger and Beeson 1998: 497)

All in all, the Bank could not accept the notion that the East Asian experience can serve as a model for the rest of the world. But what the Bank *can* acknowledge is that the role of the state in East Asia was constructive in economic development, and this could be learned by other countries. For the Bank, the East Asian 'miracle' essentially implies 'getting the basics right'.[3]

Following the rise of national and global inter-capitalist competition and the post-Cold War 'victory' of the neoliberal ideology and US pressure, the East and Southeast Asian elites liberalized and deregulated their economies in order to attract foreign financial flows. Instead of directing investments into the productive sectors, however, they stimulated investments into the short-term, speculative, high-profit sectors (real estate, stocks, etc.). Until the crisis, East Asia experienced dramatic growth in speculative capital inflows[4] – that is, almost half of total capital investments (USD 100 billion in 1996) (Guitian 1998). The consequence of this adjustment to the globalization-driven 'liberalization' process increased vulnerability of their economies to outside speculators as the developmental state lost control over key economic domains. More ironically, much of the capital flowing to Asia returned to the 'safe havens' of the US and Europe.

With regard to the current crisis, an aspect that has not really been touched upon relates to the adjustment policies of the IMF towards the crisis-affected countries in general and the East Asian nations in particular. The dictated policies which originate through cooperation between the US Treasury Department and the IMF (whose headquarters happen to be located in Washington) aim at protecting the foreign investors and speculators as well as opening the sectors of the 'real' economy to Western capital searching for investment outlets. In a situation of global over-accumulation, the possibility of buying enterprises in the productive structure as well as in the financial sector at bargain prices has the effect of putting these economies at the mercy of the core centres of world capitalism and thus reducing their autonomy. Another implication is related to the competition between members of the triad (US–Europe–Japan). The crisis has opened the door of the Japanese-dominated East Asian regional economy to the penetration of Western interests by weakening the post-Second World War arrangement which the United States had originally sponsored.

The geoeconomics of the crisis

In order to understand the course of events which East Asia has had to face since the summer of 1997, it is necessary to place the problematic within the context of the evolution of the capitalist world system. Having been 'invited', the NIC countries of the region were able to 'seize the opportunity' by retaining a certain degree of 'self-reliance' on the basis of a degree of economic nationalism. The high-growth models were a challenge to the dominant neoliberal approach as the lineage of Asian economic ideas owed more to Friedrich List than to Adam Smith.

It is paradoxical that it is this success story of capitalist development which is now exposed as a failure by neoliberalism. In fact, there was nothing intrinsically wrong with East Asian economies according to neoliberalist criteria. As Mahbub ul Haq, the founder of UNDP's *Human Development Report* writes, these economies had sound fundamentals: educated workforces (well-trained and technologically skilled); high domestic savings rates; budget deficits among the lowest; relatively open economies with low tariffs; fairly well-established economic institutions and export competitiveness respected in global markets. Therefore, he states:

> Much of the current thinking on the East Asian crisis is baffling. For a start, it is the height of intellectual dishonesty to call [it] the 'East Asian Miracle', for the last two decades and then, within a year, to start labeling it 'crony capitalism'. Nothing much has changed in East Asia's economic fundamentals'. (ul Haq 1998: 4)

What has changed, however, is located at the level of the global capitalist economy. Thus, if we are to understand 'crisis' in its dictionary definition as a critical turning point separating the future from the past, it is necessary to go beyond mainstream explanations of the world havoc which was unleashed by the devaluation of a relatively unimportant currency (the Thai baht) in the summer of 1997. To understand the 'defining moment'. We must take the Marxist-informed tradition into the analysis, especially its emphasis on geopolitical and historical-structural determinants.

The pattern of export-led industrialization in the NICs of East Asia, as well the regional division of labour under Japanese economic dominance, was inherently dependent on access to markets outside the region, first and foremost the United States. The viability of this arrangement was, however, of a conjunctural nature. As two perceptive analysts pointed out long before the crisis, 'the old strategy of high-speed, export-oriented growth will not get the NICs through the 1990s' (Bello and Rosenfeld 1992: 337).

By the late 1980s and the end of the Cold War, the United States was beginning to give more prominence to geoeconomics, whereby Washington was becoming more concerned with its own international economic position than continuing to be the custodian of a liberal trading order which was said to be undermining its productive capability. Becoming aggressively mercantilistic in its trading policies, the US was blaming Japan and the NICs for its large current account imbalance. Seen from Washington's perspective, there was no longer any need to maintain the privileged currency status of Japan and the other countries in the region or to support these authoritarian regimes politically. In the early 1990s, international pressure, including that from the US Treasury Department, began to compel East Asian countries to liberalize their financial and capital markets (Stiglitz, 2000: 56).

Related to the 'benign neglect' of the United States for the economic wellbeing of other countries – if proven to be disadvantageous to American interests – the accumulation regime in East Asia had now to confront two unyielding challenges:

> The first is the saturated markets and global overcapacity. The second is the financial bubbles that were produced when expanded productive investment opportunities could no longer be found for the vast savings these economies generated. (Tabb 1998: 32)

The overcapitalization and rush towards unproductive investments were accentuated by international volatile capital looking for profitable outlets in 'emerging markets' and who unleashed the turmoil by precipitated withdrawals.

Consequently, the problem is not exclusively located in so-called 'emerging markets'. The central problem facing global capitalism is caused by the overfinancialization of the world economy and the deregulated financial markets, which result in instability; hence the calls for a new regulatory regime, including the Tobin proposal for a tax on capital transactions. Regulation of capital movements is the gist of the neo-Keynesian discourse. Some of its proponents place the blame on the US administration for the current state of the global system. Will Hutton writes:

> Indeed, it is the interaction of market fundamentalism with the American systematic policy of benign neglect of the dollar over 25 years that lies at the heart of the crisis. The Americans have constantly run balance of trade deficits, unworried that the world has had to accept a vast pool of dollar liquidity growing up in largely unregulated offshore banking centres. (Hutton 1998: 17)

Whether the re-regulation of capital transactions would be sufficient to reestablish world economic growth is open to debate. Most interpretations of the crisis fall short because of their focus on appearances (the 'symbol economy'). However, the essence of the problem is located at the level of the global 'real economy'. Even though conventional wisdom refuses to acknowledge this fact, the world system has reverted to a situation of overproduction and overaccumulation. As Joyce Kolko put it:

> Despite overcapacity and overproduction in all sectors, competition forces the building of new capacity and the destruction of old. Rationalization, lower wages, and unemployment shrink the market. The interaction of these structural devel-

> opments in the capitalist economy is, as always, chaotic, dynamic, and dialectic. (Kolko 1988: 181)

At a time of intensive global competition in a climate of decreasing real growth rates of the world economy, the misfortune of East Asia is related to having been at the epicentre of the malfunctioning of the world system. These countries are in the process of being subjected to a new regime of accumulation which will affect their future and, in so doing, readjust their status to that of the periphery. The United States, taking advantage of the financial turmoil and its influence on the policies of the IMF, has dictated a strategy which serves its own perceived interests. As Deputy Treasury Secretary Lawrence Summers stated publicly at a conference of the Bretton Woods Committee: 'The IMF has done more to promote Americas trade and investment agenda in East Asia than 30 years of bilateral trade negotiations' (quoted in Hale 1998: 25).

The self-serving attitude of the US was evidenced when the Treasury Department, together with the IMF, vehemently opposed in August 1997 a Japanese proposal to establish an Asian Monetary Fund (AMF) in order to assist Asian economies to defend their currencies against speculation. This was considered to be potentially detrimental to US global interests. As an analyst writes:

> Some Treasury officials accordingly saw the AMF as more than just a bad idea; they interpreted it as a threat to America's influence in Asia. Not surprisingly, Washington made considerable efforts to kill Tokyo's proposal. (Altbach, quoted in Bello 1998: 436).

Should the US project succeed in putting these societies (including Japan) under its economic hegemony, this will refuel social discontent directed not only at the local elites but also at the United States, which will be seen as responsible for their misfortunes. The region has experienced a widespread growth of union organization and militancy in the last decade. The struggles that are in store for the working populations of the region are potentially explosive. Perhaps the economic and political struggles – in the form of food riots, student demonstrations for democracy, workers' strikes against redundancies – are signs of what can be expected. As will be recalled, the starting point of the East Asian 'miracle' was related to the fact that this was originally a zone of revolution. The view that 'East Asia has become the focal-point (once again, our remark) of the international class struggle', as David McNally writes (1998: 13), may be debatable; but the fallout of 'capital punishment' to which the region is being submitted has not yet run its entire course and is bound to call forth resistance.

Concluding remarks

Since the 1970s, East Asia has occupied a key position in the international debates because of its economic success and most recently because of its current crisis. The contending ideological disputes over East and Southeast Asian capitalism will surely continue. We have witnessed two positions which produced two different pictures: the optimism of the 'rise of Pacific century' in the late 1980s and early 1990s (Borthwick 1992), and the recent pessimism of the 'decline of the Asian century' (Lingle 1998). These two scenarios are being replaced by an all-encompassing vision – globalization.

The economic and financial crisis in East Asia has seemingly undermined the region's 'miracle' – a status earned in the past decades. As a result, the continuation of the debates on the 'East Asian model' has become of topical interest. With the end of the Cold War and the transformation of the international political economy, including China's re-emergence as a global economic and political player, East Asian capitalism precipitated changes in the development of global capitalism while at the same time being at the receiving end of forces within the world system.

In this chapter we have argued that the dynamic development of East Asia was originally encouraged by the geopolitics of the period, which fostered the re-emergence of a regional type division of labour under US/Japanese economic dominance. However, the Achilles' heel of this construct was its contribution to the creation of an overcapacity of means of production and a dependency on external outlets, i.e. the United States. The conjunction of these two trends coincided with a similar evolution worldwide. With the end of the Cold War, the United States became less inclined to give preferential treatment to competitors. The financial crisis – unleashed by 'hot money' – which hit East Asian countries offered corporate America, under the umbrella of the IMF, a 'window of opportunity' to gain access to bargain-basement price economic assets of the region, while reducing the validity of the 'governed market' challenge to neoliberalism.

It is not the intention to conclude that the current East Asian crisis represents the end of the East Asian trajectory. The Chinese character 'crisis' has the connotation of both 'danger' and 'opportunity'. East Asia might be able to rise again as a vibrant global economic player by taking the current crisis as an opportunity to make necessary adjustments. But the question is whether it will be able to maintain the characteristics of its previous 'revisionist' capitalism, or whether its future will be defined and confined within the dominant Anglo-American framework of neoliberal capitalism with less benefits to share.

The globalization thesis posits that the winners in the new international economic order will be those nations whose cultural and political institutions as well as populations readily adapt to the rapidly changing conditions. However, lessons from the Asian economic crisis – which involves social, ecological, cultural and political consequences – must be taken into consideration. This is because crisis in the transformation of the international political economy is closely connected to the changing domestic state–society relations. Therefore, critical theories must be expanded to question the concepts of the prevailing discourses.

In the context of the crisis in East Asia, it is interesting to note that a recent UN report shows an across-the-board recovery averaging 6.2 per cent growth for developing countries in Asia for the year 2000 and 6.4 per cent for 2001 (Fuller 2000). It seems that the recovery has not been dependent on whether countries have or have not applied IMF guidelines, nor whether they have reformed 'crony capitalism' which was considered to have been the chief reason for their collapse. The report points to rises in budget deficits (pump-priming) to restart their economies, higher growth rates of merchandise exports, and the arrival of private financial flows. Seen from a political perspective, the reason for the implementation of Keynesian deficit spending to restart economic growth at a time when neoliberal policy is the norm in the global economy could be ascribed to a certain awareness of the sociopolitical consequences of the crisis and the potential strength of opposition.

There are signs of an incipient resistance in Asian countries such as South Korea, Indonesia, Malaysia, China (Taiwan) as well as Russia, not forgetting Brazil and the rest of Latin America. Labour unrest has also been seen in China and Vietnam. Disenchantment with globalization and neoliberalism could well threaten the whole structure if it were to assume epidemic proportions. Likewise it is well known that latent protectionist tendencies in the United States itself could be fuelled if the trade balance were to deteriorate further as cheap imports from Asia surge and US exports fall. Although the American economy is diagnosed as being in good health and the main beneficiary of globalization, gathering clouds are causing anxiety at the beginning of the new century. Thus, as a strong proponent of globalization, the opinion-maker Thomas Friedman, warns: 'Imagine what will happen when we Americans have our next, inevitable recession and unemployment really rises. There could be a serious backlash against all these free-trade invitations and a real mass move to put back the walls' (Friedman 2000). As past experience has shown, the future may be difficult to predict with certainty. But one thing can be taken for granted: the end of history has not arrived!

NOTES

1 From the perspective of Washington, communist or socialist movements were regarded as anti-systemic movements (anti-capitalist system).

2 According to Berger and Beeson (1998: 493), 'At least 80 per cent of the economists working for the World Bank are trained in the UK or North America. Their approach and outlook, and that of virtually all of the remaining 20 per cent, is based on the assumptions and methodologies of Anglo-American liberalism and neoclassical economic thought.'

3 It means that the East Asian success was essentially based on market mechanism.

4 There is a difference between productive capital, such as FDI in the production of goods and financial capital in folio acquisitions, such as stock and shares. In the present context, capital inflow mainly refers to financial capital which is speculative by nature. As mentioned above, without China's absorption of capital, East Asia would have faced even a larger tension of capital inflow.

REFERENCES

Aghevli, Bijan B. (1999) 'The Asian crisis causes and remedies', *Finance & Development*, 36 (2), pp. 28–31.

Amsden, Alice H. (1989) *Asia's Next Giant: South Korea and Late Industrialization.* New York: Oxford University Press.

Arrighi, Giovanni (1994) *The Long Twentieth Century.* London: Verso.

Aseniero, George (1996) 'Asia in the World-system', in Sing C. Chew and Robert A. Denemark (eds), *The Underdevelopment of Development.* London: Sage, pp. 171–199.

Auerback, Marshall and Patrick Smith (1998) 'It's one world, ready or not? But some are not', *International Herald Tribune*, September 9, p. 8.

Balassa, Bela (1988) 'The lessons of East Asian development: an overview', *Economic Development and Cultural Change*, 36 (3) (supplement), pp. 273–290.

Bello, Walden (1998) 'East Asia: On the eve of the Great Transformation?', *Review of International Political Economy*, 5 (3), pp. 424–444.

—— and Stephanie Rosenfeld (1992) *Dragons in Distress: Asia's Miracle Economies in Crisis.* London: Penguin.

Berger, Mark T. and Mark Beeson (1998) 'Lineages of liberalism and miracles of modernisation: the World Bank, the East Asian trajectory and the international development debate', *Third World Quarterly*, 19 (3): 487–504.

Bird, Graham and Milne, Alistair (1999) 'Miracle to meltdown: A pathology of the East Asian financial crisis', *Third World Quarterly*, 20 (2): 421–437.

Borthwick, Mark (ed.) (1992) *Pacific Century: The Emergence of Modern Pacific Asia.* Boulder, CO: Westview Press.

Camdessus, Michel (1997) 'The Asian financial crisis and the opportunities of globalization'. Speech at the Second Committee of the United Nations General Assembly, New York, October 31.

Caplen, Brian (1997) 'What will go wrong next?', *Euromoney*, 344, pp. 38–42.

Chen, Steve (1990) *East Asian Dynamism.* Boulder, CO: Westview Press.

Cox, Robert W. (1993) 'Structural issues of global governance: implications for Europe', in Stephen Gill (ed.), *Gramsci, Historical Materialism and International Relations.* Cambridge: Cambridge University Press, pp. 259–289.

Cumings, Bruce (1987) 'The origins and development of the North East Asian political economy: industrial sectors, product cycles and political consequences', in Frederic C. Deyo (ed.), *The Political Economy of the New Asian Industrialism.* Ithaca, NY: Cornell University Press, pp. 44–83.

Deyo, Frederic C. (ed.) (1987) *The Political Economy of the New Asian Industrialism.* Ithaca, NY: Cornell University Press.

Dornbusch, Rudi (1997) 'A bailout won't do the trick in Korea', *Business Week*, 3556, p. 26.

Freeman, Chris (1998) 'The East Asian crisis, technical change and the world economy', *Review of International Political Economy*, 5 (3), pp. 393–409.

Friedman, Thomas (2000) 'Find the right balance on free trade and globalization', *International Herald Tribune*, May 20–21.

Fuller, Thomas (2000) 'For Asian economies, remedies all worked', *International Herald Tribune*, May 23.

Gerschenkron, Alexander (1962) *Economic Backwardness in Historical Perspective: A Book of Essays.* Cambridge: Belknap Press of Harvard University Press.

Gill, Stephen (1999) 'The geopolitics of the Asian crisis', *Monthly Review*, 50 (10), p. 1–9.

Guitian, Manuel (1998) 'The challenge of managing global capital flows', *Finance & Development*, 35 (2), pp. 14–17.

Hale, David D. (1998) 'Dodging the bullet – this time', *The Brooking Review*, 16 (3): 22–25.

Hart-Landsberg, Martin and Paul Burkett (1998) 'Contradictions of capitalist industrialization in East Asia: A critique of "flying geese" theories of development', *Economic Geography*, 74 (2), pp. 87–110.

Hersh, Jacques (1993) *The USA and the Rise of East Asia Since 1945: Dilemmas of the Postwar International Political Economy.* New York: St Martin's Press.

Hoogvelt, Ankie (1997) *Globalization and the Postcolonial World: the New Political Economy of Development.* Basingstoke: Macmillan.

Hughes, Christopher W. (2000) 'Japanese policy and the East Asian crisis: abject defeat on quiet victory', *Review of International Political Economy*, 7 (2), pp. 219–253.

Hutton, Will (1998) 'Free-market paradise spirals into chaos', *Guardian Weekly*, October 11.

Johnson, Chalmers (1982) *MITI and the Japanese Miracle. The Growth of Industrial Policy, 1925–75.* California: Stanford University Press.

—— (1998) 'Economic crisis in East Asia: the clash of capitalism', *Cambridge Journal of Economics*, 22 (6), pp. 652–662.

Kolko, Joyce (1988) *Restructuring the World Economy.* New York: Pantheon Books.

Kristof, Nicholas and David E. Sanger (1999) 'Free markets: Clinton gave a push', *International Herald Tribune*, February 16.

Krugman, Paul (1994) 'The Myth of Asia's Miracle', *Foreign Affairs*, 73 (6), pp. 62–78.

—— (1997) 'Asia's Miracle is Alive and Well? Wrong, It Never Existed'. *Time*, 150, (13), pp. 37.

Lardy, Nicholas R. (1995) 'The role of foreign trade and investment in China's economic transformation', *China Quarterly*, 144, pp. 1065–1082.

Lee, Martin (1998) 'Testing Asian Values', *The New York Times*, January 28: 17.

Lingle, Christopher (1998) *Rise and Decline of the Asian Century; False Starts on the Path to the Global Millennium.* Washington, DC: University of Washington Press.

McNally, David (1998) 'Globalization on trial: crisis and class struggle in East Asia', *Monthly Review*, 50 (4), pp. 1–14.

Onis, Ziya (1991) 'Review article: "the Logic of Developmental State"', *Comparative Politics*, 24 (1), p. 109.

Pye, Lucien W. (1988) 'The new Asian capitalism: a political portrait', in Peter L. Berger and Hsiao Hsin-huang Michael (eds), *In Search of an East Asian Developmental Model.* New Brunswick: Transaction Publishers, pp. 81–98.

Radelet, Steven and Jeffrey D. Sachs (1998) 'The East Asian financial crisis: diagnosis, remedies, prospects', *Brookings Paper on Economic Activity*, 1, pp. 1–90.

Robison, Richard (1998) 'Currency meltdown: the end of Asian capitalism?', *NIAS Nytt*, 2, pp. 5–9.

Rosenthal, Andrew (1997) 'Lessons of the Asian collapse', *The New York Times*, December 23.

Schwarz, Benjamin (1996) 'Why America thinks it has to run the world', *The Atlantic Monthly*, 277 (6), pp. 92–102.

So, Alvin Y. and Stephen W. K. Chiu (1995) *East Asia and the World Economy.* London: Sage.

Stiglitz, Joseph (2000) 'The Insider', *The New Republic*, 222 (16/17), pp. 56–60.

Tabb, William (1998) 'The East Asian crisis', *Monthly Review*, 50 (2), pp. 24–38.

ul Haq, Mahbub (1998) 'The East Asian crisis: just fix what's broken', *Choices*, 7 (3), pp. 4–5

UNCTAD (United Nations Conference on Trade and Development) (1993) *Trade and Development Report.* New York: United Nations.

Wade, Robert (1990) *Governing the Market: Economic Theory and the Role of Government in East Asian Industrialization.* Princeton, NJ: Princeton University Press.

—— (1998–99) 'The coming fight over capital flows', *Foreign Policy*, 113, pp. 41–54.

World Bank (1993) *The East Asian Miracle: Economic Growth and Public Policy.* New York: Oxford University Press.

THREE

The Material, Strategic and Discursive Dimensions of the 'Asian Crisis' and Subsequent Developments

Ngai-Ling Sum

Introduction

The so-called 'Asian Crisis' has been constructed and explained from many viewpoints: two of the most popular are the specific defects of national 'crony capitalisms' and weaknesses in the global financial architecture. This chapter offers a critique of these accounts and suggests an alternative, 'material-discursive' approach to the 'crisis' that pays careful attention to its structural, strategic, and discursive dimensions. This approach examines:

1. the structural background to the 'crisis' in terms of the material interconnections between the productive and financial orders in the context of global capitalism;
2. the conjunctural factors precipitating the 'crisis' and its implications for the current economic disorder;
3. the role of various actors in developing competing discourses to restructure the global–regional–national political economy and to remake their associated identities and interests; and
4. the subsequent interplay between these various material and discursive aspects in shaping the 'crisis' as it has developed since 1997.

In developing the first element of this approach to the 'crisis', my chapter will examine the development of the East Asian region since the Plaza Accord was signed in 1985. Structurally, this 'post-Plaza' period was characterized by, *inter alia*, a Japan-led *regional–national production order* financed by *export-oriented FDI* (foreign direct investment) and an American-dominated *dollar-bloc regime* linked

– at least as it operated during the 1985–95 period – to a *'yen-appreciating bubble'*. The relations between these two orders displayed a strong and stable 'structured coherence' (see below). Despite this coherence, the productive-financial orders were structurally liable to at least three forms of crisis: overproduction–underconsumption, overborrowing, and exchange rate weaknesses. This vulnerability was exacerbated by such conjunctural developments as the arrival of China as a major production site, the bursting of the 'property bubble' in Japan, and the joint US–Japan decision to depreciate the yen in 1995. For these developments disrupted the previous coherence within and between the two orders. This disarticulation, in conjunction with national–local circumstances, has had differential effects on economies in the region. For example, Hong Kong and China have maintained exchange rate stability against the dollar with the unintended development of becoming the first lines of defence of the US-dominated international currency order.

Given the specificities of these orders and their differential impact in the region, the so-called 'Asian crisis' cannot be resolved through the traditional 'rescue' programme preferred by the IMF. On the contrary, 'financial contagion' has led to a new domino effect that moved from Asia to Russia and thence to Brazil. This in turn leads us to the third dimension of the material-discursive approach – the struggle between actors, e.g., Japan, the USA, the IMF and 'Greater China', to establish new visions and identities relevant to the remaking of the global–regional–national political economy. The chapter concludes with some remarks on a possible research agenda on the remaking of the global–regional–national political economy.

TWO POPULAR ACCOUNTS OF THE 'CRISIS' AND THEIR CRITICISMS

The 'Asian crisis' has been represented and explained from many viewpoints, ranging from the defects of East Asian 'crony capitalism' (World Bank 1997; Krugman 1998) to the weaknesses of the global financial architecture and the destructive activities of hedge funds. Claims about 'crony capitalism' have been taken up by some global institutions and Western commentators to explain the 'crisis'. For example, the World Bank narrates the causes of the 'crisis' in terms of the 'perverse personal and shareholding connections between lenders and borrowers', inadequate bank supervision, a lack of transparency, state-directed lending, and political pressures for loans. These are held responsible for bad loans which could total as much as US$660 billion (Friedman 1997). Krugman is even more explicit when he links the 'crisis' to the

> 'fuzzy line ... between what was public and what was private; the Minister's nephew or President's son could open a bank and raise money from the domestic populace and foreign lenders, with everyone believing that their money was safe because official connections stood behind the institutions'. (Krugman 1998: 19)

Together with this alleged lack of transparency and inadequacies in the regulation of financial institutions, this government-directed investment system is also accused of having produced 'excesses' and 'errors'. The IMF also subscribes to these views and hopes thereby to justify its bailout package(s) for the East Asian NICs (hereafter EANICs) even though these involve domestic austerity programmes (e.g., high interest rates and restriction of domestic demand) and radi-cal institutional change, including further liberalization of the financial sector.

A second popular account is proposed by Jeffrey Sachs and has been echoed by some East Asian national leaders/governments. Sachs explained the 'crisis' in terms of a classic financial panic: a run on the banks and mass capital flight that was exacerbated by a mismatch between Asian banks and borrowers. This was accompanied by global speculative attacks on currencies and the collapse of asset values. Sachs claims that such attacks have little to do with the underlying 'fundamentals' in these economies. Instead he attributes the problem partly to fragile banking systems and partly to flaws in the global financial architecture (Sachs 1997). Some East Asian national leaders/governments have explicitly identified the latter flaws with the capacity of large global speculators/hedge funds to move around the world rapidly and without any regulation. One notable example of this account is Mahathir's speech delivered at the thirtieth anniversary celebration of the ASEAN in July 1997. He argued that the Malaysian 'crisis' is an effect of global speculative trading, and, more specifically, blamed the 'currency sabotage' conducted by George Soros. Similarly, in Hong Kong, the Financial Secretary, Donald Tsang, described the global hedge funds as 'crocodiles' and alleged that they had 'struck' Hong Kong for a second time in August 1998. Likewise, Ian MacFarlane, Governor of the Reserve Bank of Australia, described the hedge fund flows as the 'privileged children of the financial scene, being entitled to the benefits of free markets without any of the responsibility'.

Both accounts of the 'Asian crisis' are one-sided. The former focuses on some long-standing and essentially local/internal features of state–business links in specific East Asian countries. Indeed, these same features had previously been invoked (albeit with less pejorative language) to explain the success of the EANICs. In any case, these features can hardly explain the timing, the degrees, volatility and diverse forms of the 'crisis' in the region as a whole. Yet, as the 'crisis' has unfolded, this interpretation has been strategically appropriated by the IMF to lend moral weight to its attempts to impose its well-known and long-standing structural adjustment policies on the worst-hit East Asian countries as a condition for receiving financial support. Conversely, the second account, especially in the versions promoted by local politicians, assigns too much weight to the external factors and/or global actors. Implicit in this interpretation is a global-versus-national approach which is then used to justify nationalist policy responses by East Asian states. This approach explains neither the speed nor the varying incidence and depth of the 'crisis'. As for Sachs's argument, it highlights the healthy 'fundamentals' of the East Asian economies and relates the 'crisis' to some behavioural and speculative features of the international financial system. He interprets the 'crisis' as essentially a financial one and leaves both the 'real economy' and its interconnections with finance underexamined. In addition, in focusing on the national and/or the global level, both accounts miss the multiscalar complexities of the 'crisis'.

TOWARDS A MATERIAL-DISCURSIVE APPROACH TO THE 'CRISIS'

This chapter argues for an alternative, material-discursive approach of the 'crisis'. Due to the limitation of space, it concentrates on three key aspects. The first is the structural background to the 'crisis'. This involves examining material interconnections, rooted in the triadic nature of global capitalism and existing on different scales of economic activity, between the productive and financial orders. More specifically and with reference to the post-Plaza period, whereas the production order in East Asia was characterized by a Japan-led *regional–national regime* financed by *export-oriented FDI*; the financial order was characterized by an American-dominated *dollar-bloc regime* linked to a *'yen-appreciating bubble'*. These two orders were articulated in a reasonably complementary and stable manner. Thus, one could talk of a 'structured coherence' (Harvey 1982) among the main features of these orders on the global–regional–national scales. Despite this coherence, the productive order is structurally vulnerable to crises of overproduction/underconsumption, whereas the financial order is susceptible to overborrowing and exchange rate weaknesses.

Given such vulnerabilities, the second aspect concerns conjunctural factors that undermined the coherence with and between the two orders. These factors include the arrival of China as a low-cost, high-tech competitor; the US–Japan decision to depreciate the yen; and the bursting of the Japanese 'property bubble'. Their impact has nonetheless varied across different economies in the region.

Given the specificities of these orders and their interconnections on different scales, the so-called 'Asian crisis' cannot be resolved through the IMF's preferred 'rescue' programme. On the contrary, 'financial contagion' has led to a 'domino effect' that moved from Asia to Russia and thence to Brazil. This in turn leads us to the third aspect of the material-discursive approach – the struggle between actors, e.g., Japan, the USA, the IMF and 'Greater China', to establish new visions, identities and interests relevant to the remaking of globalities and regionalities. We begin with the first aspect.

The structural background to the 'Asian crisis': articulation between the production and financial orders

Structurally, post-Plaza Asia has developed in the context of an increasing triadization in global capitalism (Ohmae 1990). Among the factors shaping this tendency in Asia we can note:

- the increasing importance of collaboration within each part of the East Asian triad to ensure cost reduction in production, R&D, etc., and rapid cost recovery in an era of accelerating as well as increasing competition;
- the information and communication technology revolution, which allows rapid transmission of production and financial information within and across triads;
- the impact of the 1980s neoliberal turn, which introduced financial liberalization to the region;
- the end of the Cold War, which has increased the priority of multilateral geoeconomic concerns relative to bipolar geopolitical worries in this region;
- the emergence of Japan as the regional hegemony and the rise of the EANICs as major players in the global economy; and
- the growing US–Japan trade deficits and accumulating surpluses in Japan.

These developments contributed to the emergence of complementary and stable relations between the production and financial orders in East Asia. The production order was mediated by a Japan-led regime that integrated East Asia into the wider global economy. This began in 1985 when the US tried to reverse its trade deficits with Japan through the Plaza Accord. This entailed a yen–dollar accord which required joint US–Japanese intervention in foreign-exchange markets to correct trade imbalances. This resulted in the yen's appreciation against the dollar. Saddled with uncompetitive export prices, the need for cost reduction, surplus capital, and fearing greater protectionism in US and European markets, Japan recognized that it needed to transfer some of its manufacturing production to other parts of Asia. Initially this occurred through industrial and trade finance. For example, Japanese FDI in 1986 was nearly double that of 1985. By 1988, the figure had doubled again; it peaked in 1989 at US$67.5 billion. This process was mediated by a transregional class alliance articulated to the specificities of national–local capitals and conditions. Details of such alliances are beyond the scope of this chapter but Bernard (1999: 190–198) offers interesting case studies on Thailand and South Korea.

This transregional class alliance was expressed and reinforced discursively by the metaphor of a 'flying geese' region, in which Japan was portrayed as the spearhead of the flock and the four EANICs were following close behind, while the six ASEAN economies were seen as the next to take off (Li *et al.* in this volume). This image of the 'flying geese', though not uncontested, aimed to reinforce a 'synergistic' division of labour. It was seen as synergistic because Japan concentrated on high-tech and R&D; South Korea and Taiwan specialized in high-valued OEM (original equipment manufacturing) related to intermediate parts, Hong Kong and Singapore as service centres, and low-value products would come from Malaysia, Thailand and China. In this regard, the region was tightly integrated to provide semi-conductors, electronic goods, textiles and clothing, and other products mainly for the American markets.

Such synergistic intra-regional relationships were also marked by competition and 'leapfrogging' behaviour. There were well-known 'leapfrogging' cases and some firms were able to compete with their Japanese counterparts (e.g., Hyundai, Singapore Airlines and Hong Kong Bank). However, these examples are better treated as exceptions rather than the rule. Developing the capabilities to acquire and operate foreign technology did not necessarily lead, in each country, to an ability to adapt or innovate, let alone to 'leapfrog'. A study in Singapore's electronic industry showed that local firms pursued a long-term, painstaking, incremental learning path rather than leaping from one vintage of technology to the next. Their development involved a 'hard slog' rather than a 'leapfrog' (Sum 1997: 228–230). In this regard, economies in the region were highly dependent on Japan. More specifically, roughly half of total trade was intra-regional, with a high proportion of the exports from Japan to EANICs (except South Korea) comprising capital goods and sophisticated parts. These capital goods were used as inputs by Japanese or Japan-related subsidaries/subcontractors for the region's export-oriented production.

This Japan-led regional production order was complemented by the American-dominated financial order. The latter can be examined in terms of its credit and currency forms. First, regarding the credit form (concerned with the organization of credit), Japan was the major provider of industrial and trade finance. This was organized through direct lending by Japanese banks to Japanese multinationals and affiliates in the region. FDI financed a high import content of intermediate capital from Japan. Up to 1995, Japan accounted for 20 per cent of East Asian FDI. Second, regarding the money-currency form (the contradictory functions as national money and international currency), all East Asian economies have their own national currencies but most of them are externally pegged to the US dollar. This confidence in the dollar created a kind of dollar-bloc regime (or pegged-rate dollar standard) which was linked to a 'yen-appreciating bubble'. This money-currency form suited the export-oriented region in two ways. First, since most of East Asian imports and exports are/were invoiced in dollars, it reduced the currency risks involved in trading with major markets in the US or elsewhere. Second, the dollar pegs anchored their domestic monetary policies. This means that the policies of Indonesia, South Korea, Malaysia, the Philippines, Thailand, Hong Kong and Singapore were loosely tied to one another. This protected each of these economies from competitive devaluations by the others and thereby stabilized their domestic price levels from the 1980s to 1996 (McKinnon 1999: 97–99).

The important question here is not so much what constituted the credit and money-currency forms; more important is the way in which they articulated with and complemented the post-Plaza production order. Given the 'catch-up' dynamics of the region, the EANICs were strongly oriented to investing in upgrading technologies and/or innovating for niche markets. This required high investment and, given that these economies compete/cooperate to export primarily to the US market, profits for some tend to be relatively low. The combination of export-orientation, high investment and relatively low profit meant that this production order required much external trade and finance.

In terms of external trade, a dollar-bloc regime stabilized their import–export prices with little risks of competitive devaluation between the 1980s and 1996. Moreover, given that this regime was also linked to the 'yen-appreciating bubble', export competitiveness in dollar terms of the EANICs also improved relative to Japan. Under these conditions, the former not only became OEM/cheap labour sites of Japan; but export platforms could also enhance the region's external trade. As for external financing, a dollar-bloc regime under stable yen–dollar rate encouraged foreign borrowing that involved no exchange risk. In the case of Japanese lending and FDI, the 'yen-appreciating bubble' was also significant – especially once Japanese interest rates were lowered in 1987. The share of Japanese FDI going to emerging Asia and China rose from 12.1 per cent in 1985 to 46 per cent at the turn of the 1990s. In turn, such outflows, especially Japanese capital heading for the EANICs, stimulated EANIC investment flows to the ASEAN countries. This further deepened the regional production-financial order.

In short, the investment- and export-oriented Japan-led production order was highly dependent on external trade and financing. It was complemented by an American-dominated dollar-bloc regime that could enhance its external trade by stabilizing its import–export prices as well as providing external financing at no exchange risk. So complementary and stable were these features between 1985–

95 that they produced a certain 'structured coherence' between the production and financial orders (see Table 3.1).

Table 3.1: The 'structured coherence' between the production and financial orders in the post-Plaza Period, 1985–95

Post-Cold War/Post-Plaza (regionalization in Asia)	Later Bretton Woods (dollar-bloc regime)
Regional–national Production order	***Regional–global Financial order***
Production form	*Credit form*
JAPAN	— external finance
— R&D developments	— trade and industrial finance
— technology	— high import content of FDI
— component exports	
EANICs	*Money-currency form*
— OEM	— pegged-rate dollar standard
— trade and financial services	— stable yen–dollar rates
ASEAN/China	— 'yen-appreciating bubble'
— labour-intensive production	
Exports to → **USA**	→ Role of US dollar and FDI

Key: OEM = Original equipment manufacturing
EANIC = East Asian Newly Industrializing Economies

Crisis tendencies of the export-oriented production-financial orders

Despite a mutual 'structured' coherence, the production-financial orders also had certain crisis tendencies in their production, credit and currency forms. These included, respectively, risks of relative overproduction/underconsumption, excess liquidity and exchange rate vulnerability. Thus, in terms of the production order, corresponding to the 'catch-up' dynamic of the region, the allocation of domestic and Japan-related credit tended to privilege investment rather than consumption. The risk here is one of overinvestment and overproduction. Rapid expansion of (potentially excess) productive capacity in the region tends to increase land and labour costs; and the resulting expansion of production can exceed market growth and thereby trigger falling prices for the resulting goods. When costs rise and prices fall, profits are squeezed. One counter-tendency to this was the shift from higher to lower cost production sites within the region, but this intensified investment demands and problems of excess capacity as well as profit squeeze.

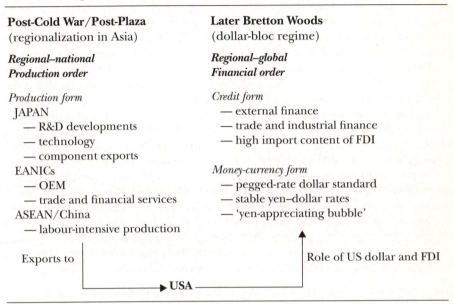

This tendency for overproduction/underconsumption and profit squeeze can be aggravated by financial liberalization and the availability of easy credit at no exchange risk. The inflow of foreign investment and credit capital may exceed the absorptive capacity of economies already prone to overproduction. This (over)supply of cheap foreign credit may enter into stock market speculation, property price inflation and even risky loans to local companies. This increases the tendency towards bad debts and even credit contraction. Speculation can make this worse by generating rapid rises in asset values (e.g., shares and property). This in turn can induce overproduction of property at mega-level prices. As speculators turn from buying to selling, the 'property bubble' bursts and banks start to call in loans and cut credit lines. This development generates non-performing loans and may even lead to potential or actual bank runs or failures.

There is no necessary link between this kind of crisis in the credit form and a currency crisis, i.e., a speculative attack on a currency that forces a sharp devaluation/depreciation (Liew 1998: 313). But this did become a problem when those Asian economies started to run balance-of-payments deficits and to over-borrow under the dollar-bloc regime. In terms of trade balance, deficits appear when export values do not keep pace with imports to enhance industrial capacity and productive real estate. Accumulating deficits make it hard for these economies to maintain their peg to the dollar. This pressure upon the pegged system was coupled with a declining quality of investment. Since governments in the region could no longer maintain the dollar peg and started to depreciate, the size of the foreign debt burden that local firms had to service rose in local currency terms. In other words, currency depreciation may raise the borrowing costs and can result in firms defaulting on their debt payments. This debt problem can then spread to more prudent banks and firms.

Some conjunctural factors behind the 'crisis': disarticulation within and between the production and financial orders

These crisis tendencies were actualized by various conjunctural developments. Regarding the production order, the tendency towards overproduction in the EANICs was intensified by the entrance of China into global–regional production. The latter's competitive edge stems from its supply of cheap skilled and unskilled labour as well the preferential conditions it offers to foreign capital. Given the PRC's strong competitive challenge, the EANICs were forced to respond by upgrading their technologies and/or by expanding their innovative capacities. This was associated with attempts to move higher up the value chain in established sectors (e.g., clothing and electronics) and/or to move into or upgrade their position in service industries. This occurred in conjunction with the relocation of Japanese industries to the region. Together they formed part of the Japan-led production order with each cooperating and struggling to climb the technological/innovation ladder. This 'catch-up' process and efforts to upgrade/innovate encouraged new rounds of investment in the region's economies. Between 1990 and 1995, gross domestic investment grew by 16.3 per cent per annum in Indonesia, 16 per cent in Malaysia, 15.3 per cent in Thailand, and 7.2 per cent in South Korea. By comparison, investment in the US grew by 4.1 per cent per annum over the same period.

This 'investment rush' occurred on the basis of unrealistic projections about future global demand and encouraged the build-up of excessive production capacities. For example, in response to a temporary shortage of 16 megabyte

Dynamic Random Access Memory chips (DRAMs), Korean *chaebols* increased their investment between 1994 and 1995. Supply shortages had disappeared by 1996, however, and excess capacity began to build up. The retail price of DRAMs dropped by 90 per cent in 1996. Similar excess capacity could be seen in the Thai property market – with 365,000 unoccupied apartment units in Bangkok in early 1997. In both cases, of course, overcapacity led to declining profit rates.

This 'investment rush' and falling profitability were also confirmed by a firm-based study (Claessens *et al.* 1998) of selected Asian economies since late 1980s. Rates of corporate investment were found to be consistently high for all economies, apart from Hong Kong (Table 3.2). This regional 'investment rush' exposed

Table 3.2: Capital investment in selected Asian economies (per cent, medians)

	1989	1991	1993	1995
Hong Kong	16.6	7.6	19.8	5.8
South Korea	13.8	19.6	11.2	12.4
Singapore	7.6	8.8	11.3	12.5
Taiwan	n.a.	14.3	8.4	11.2
Malaysia	7.6	9.6	13.4	14.6
Thailand	12.9	15.0	15.0	14.5
Indonesia	n.a.	12.4	8.6	13.8

Source: Adapted from Claessens *et al.* 1998: 8

these economies to problems of overproduction as prices of goods fell and profitability was relatively low. The same study recorded relatively low profitability rates in Hong Kong, South Korea and Singapore as compared with Taiwan, Malaysia, Thailand and Indonesia. However, in general, all six economies, except Taiwan, were experiencing declining profits in some form (Table 3.3).

These problems of overinvestment and overproduction were exacerbated by the limited potential to absorb switch export markets from the USA and/or fully to absorb any unsaleable export production within the region itself. Consumption has obviously risen in the region as economic growth has continued, but the weight and dynamic importance of export-oriented production make rapid reorientation of output very difficult. The Japanese and EANIC economies have high saving ratios and the crisis may even increase the inclination to save. This is especially clear for Japan with its aging population and decade-long stagnation. Conversely, although the Chinese market is potentially huge, the low-wage regime in China and its low per capita income (e.g., US$621 in 1998) inhibit any switch to this market of the goods produced in the region and previously exported to high-income economies.

Table 3.3: Return on assets for selected Asian economies (per cent, medians, in real local currency)

	1989	1991	1993	1995
Hong Kong	5.3	4.8	3.8	3.9
South Korea	3.9	4.0	3.6	3.6
Singapore	4.5	3.9	4.6	3.9
Taiwan	n.a.	5.1	6.5	6.5
Malaysia	5.6	6.2	6.5	6.1
Thailand	1.0	11.2	9.8	7.8
Indonesia	n.a.	9.1	7.9	6.2

Source: Adapted from Claessens *et al.* 1998: 4

These problems of overproduction/underconsumption were exaggerated by access to cheap credit and the bursting of the 'yen-appreciating bubble'. In the early 1990s, cheap credit became easily available in the global–regional contexts of: (a) the liberalization of the global financial markets; (b) the emergence of Tokyo and Hong Kong as regional financial centres; (c) the bursting of the Japanese property/stock market 'bubbles' and the emergence of bad debts therein; and (d) the resultant low interest rate in Japan (reaching half a per cent). The ample supply of portfolio capital in Japan was matched by the fortuitous bursting of the 'yen-appreciating bubble' in 1995. In that summer, the American Treasury and the Japanese Ministry of Finance agreed on a deal to help re-elect Clinton and allow Japan to continue to export its way out of its post-bubble problems. This would be achieved by depreciating the yen against the dollar (i.e., reversing the Plaza Accord) and thereby increase Japan's export competitiveness. In return, Japan would continue to supply cheap credits to the public and private sectors in America and thereby finance federal debt, domestic consumption and trade deficits (Johnson 1998: 658). The 'yen-appreciating bubble' burst and the value of the yen fell against the dollar by about 60 per cent between April 1995 and April 1997. The speed and extent of the fall had a major impact upon FDI and portfolio capital.

A fall in the value of the yen slowed down FDI flows from Japan to the EANICs. This was matched by the outflow of Japanese portfolio capital to these economies as the falling yen created arbitrage opportunities for local and overseas banks based on low interest rates in Japan. Japanese, American and European banks began to develop new offshore practices which came to be known as the 'yen carry trade'. Godement illustrated these practices by means of the following two-part example:

> Borrowing (by banks) at 1 per cent on three-month terms while the yen stands at 100 to the US dollar, and immediately lending at 6 per cent for one year in a

currency tied to the dollar is the first part of the trick. Paying back the initial loan after the dollar has climbed to 110 yen, or even better, loaning again the money while rolling over the short-term yen, is the second part. (Godement 1999: 44)

Owing to its popularity as a credit device, most Asian economies came to depend on short-term cheap money from 'offshore' to finance long-term domestic projects. In 1995–97, Japan was the single most important source of portfolio investment and provided about 31 per cent of the total in the region. For their own political and economic reasons, some Southeast Asian governments (notably Thailand and Indonesia) started to run easy credit policies to foster growth. On balance these portfolio credits tended to be short-term and many went into the property markets, speculation, infrastructural projects and corporate bonds. Thus the Japanese property/stock market bubbles were exported to other parts of Asia. In the case of Thailand, much of the portfolio investment from Japan was poured into property speculation; by 1995, an overhang of unsold buildings was leading some building firms to close down. By 1996, non-performing loans in Thailand were about 9.2 per cent of its GDP. As for South Korea, a massive rise in investment increased the volume of stockpiled goods. Faced with cash-flow problems, firms obtained more short-term loans from foreign banks. By 1996 the non-performing loans in South Korea were about 6 per cent of GDP (Sparks 1998: 25–27; Liew 1998: 306).

Two incidents occurred at the end of the first quarter of 1997 that intensified the problems of overborrowing and exchange rate vulnerabilities. Japanese banks and subsidies needed to increase their own assets towards the end of the fiscal year, and they were less willing to roll over short-term credits. This tightening of Japanese credit was coupled with a sudden rise in the yen, making short-term borrowing less attractive (Godement 1999: 45). This created a vicious spiral of illiquidity, leading possibly to insolvency and a consequent worsening of new asset positions of the Japanese creditors. In turn, this deterioration of financial intermediation abilities of Japanese banks exacerbated the domestic and regional credit crunches. This further prompted the increase in the amount of non-performing loans and encouraged some firms to sell off their products cheaply. It also led international bankers and hedge fund managers to expect that the region's currencies would soon or later depeg from the dollar and depreciate (or be allowed to float). Such depreciation would increase the size of the debt burden of local firms when measured in local currency.

Speculators first attacked the Thai baht on 5 February 1997. To defend the currency, the Bank of Thailand raised interest rates and bought billions of baht forward. This domestic credit squeeze put more pressure on weak financial institutions and forced companies to close down. By mid-1997, the Bank of Thailand had used about half of its foreign reserves in defence of the bhat. On 2 July 1997, it allowed the baht to float. Non-performing loans were estimated at 25 per cent of the total. Only two out of the 58 financial institutions that were closed have sufficient capital to reopen (Sparks 1998: 25–28). This triggered a financial contagion that quickly spread from Thailand to other parts of Asia between July and December 1997. It was estimated by Howell (1998) that US$62.2 billion of private financial capital fled the region in 1997 and monthly data for 1998 show that outflows have not halted.

Differential impact of the 'crisis' and the case of 'Greater China'

The above conjunctural developments – the arrival of China as a competitive production site, the export of the Japanese property/stock market bubbles, the US–Japan deal to lower the value of the yen, the regional credit crunch – weakened the 'structured coherence' within and between the production and financial order. They became disarticulated when the export-oriented production order overproduced from within and failed to secure cheap and exchange risk-free credits from without. Such disarticulation at the end of the 1997 did not have the same impact on all economies in the region. Data relevant to this period reveal a differential impact of the 'crisis' on then 'stronger' economic formations (such as Singapore, Taiwan and Hong Kong) and 'weaker' formations (such as the Philippines, Malaysia, South Korea, Thailand, and Indonesia) (Table 3.4).

Table 3.4: Differential impact of the 'crisis': changes in stock prices and currency (percentages measured in US$, 1 Jan.–31 Oct., 1997)

	Stocks	Currency
A) 'Stronger' Economic Formations		
Singapore	-28.7	-12.3
Taiwan	6.9	-12.1
Hong Kong	-19.5	0
B) 'Weaker' Economic Formations		
Philippines	-42.4	-33.4
Malaysia	-46.0	-32.8
South Korea	-28.0	-14.3
Thailand	-45.4	-58.0
Indonesia	-21.6	-53.0

Source: Adapted from *Fortune*, 24 Nov. 1997: 32

In this regard, it is perhaps more accurate to refer to Asian crises instead of the 'Asian crisis'. Economies in the so-called 'Greater China' region,[1] especially Taiwan, seem to have escaped the worst effects of the contagion.

This differential impact of the 'crisis' was largely related to their pre-existing strengths and embedded capacities of each economies. Relevant factors here include current account balances (Table 3.5), foreign debts and reserves (Table 3.6), degree of openness to global capital, state capacities (e.g., regulatory capacities over financial institutions) and, equally important, on the balance of economic, political and social forces with different interests. It is beyond the scope of this chapter to deal with the specificities of individual economies and

Table 3.5: Current account balances (as % of GDP)

	1995–96	1998–99
A) 'Stronger' Economic Formations		
Singapore	16.1	16.4
Taiwan	3.0	2.2
China	0.6	0.7
Hong Kong	1.4	1.1
B) 'Weaker' Economic Formations		
Philippines	-3.7	0.3
Malaysia	-7.1	-1.4
South Korea	-3.3	7.0
Thailand	-8.0	5.6
Indonesia	-3.6	2.2

Source: Adapted from J. P. Morgan, *World Financial Markets*, first quarter 1998

Table 3.6: Asian foreign debt and reserves (US$ billion), end 1997 estimates

	Total debt	Short-term debt	Reserves
A) 'Stronger' Economic Formations			
Singapore			88
Taiwan	46	29	81
China	152	42	141
Hong Kong			75
B) 'Weaker' Economic Formations			
Philippines	58	15	9
Malaysia	39	14	24
S. Korea	155	60	17
Thailand	102	32	20
Indonesia	131	27	28

Source: Adapted from J. P. Morgan, *World Financial Markets*, first quarter 1998

their diverse strategies of restructuring. A substantial body of literature has concentrated on the cases of Indonesia, Malaysia, Thailand and South Korea, with the latter two economies showing signs of economic recovery since the end of 1998. Instead, this section seeks to examine briefly some of the 'stronger' economic formations, especially those within the 'Greater China' region.
Taiwan has escaped from the devastating impact of contagion. This is attributable to its pre-existing strengths which include:

1. a flexible small- to medium-sized manufacturing system based on cost-effectiveness;
2. infrastructural and financial support to industries from the government and KMT-related economic forces;
3. its position as an exporter of capital with large reserves;
4. the associated low external debts of the government and corporations;
5. a not-yet-fully financially de-regulated system with exchange controls on foreign investment; and
6. an early devaluation of the New Taiwan Dollar (NT$) in August 1997.

Benefiting from this strong position, Taiwan was still expecting an official GDP growth rate of around 5 per cent. Given that private credit comprised 166 per cent of GDP and public credit took the total to 200 per cent, it could not entirely be sheltered from contagion. The government imposed new controls on foreign exchange, cutting off speculators' access to the local dollar by restricting trade in non-delivery forward contracts. In August 1998, the government approved a NT$193.7 billion economic stimulus package covering a range of infrastructure projects. Other 'crisis-related' symptoms began to appear in the latter part of 1998. In the corporate sector, for example, there was financial trouble at the Central Bills Finance and the Taichung Medium Business Bank, which were temporarily taken over by government-linked institutions in November 1998. Together with a series of defaults on stock payments and debts by medium-sized firms (e.g., An Feng Steel, Kuoyang Construction Company), the stock index plunged by 40 per cent between its August 1997 peak and January 1999. The KMT-led government has set up a US$8 billion Stock Stabilization Fund to prop up share prices. In the case of the property sector, falling prices also stimulated the government to introduce an NT$7 billion scheme to bail out the real estate market by offering low interest loans to home buyers. Given the local political context (especially with the challenge of the DPP), these KMT support packages involved a politics of redistribution when unemployment rate also rose to 3 per cent in the mean time.

Up to the time of writing, China has largely escaped the worst impact of the contagion because of:

1. trade surpluses and relatively large reserves;
2. limited financial liberalization in foreign banks – which can handle the yuan only in Pudong and Shenzhen;
3. a partial command-economy with exchange and credit controls;
4. a non-convertible currency that is not a good target for speculators; and
5. a domestically oriented economy with export assistance.

Despite these strengths, there was frequent talk that the Chinese yuan would devalue, especially after the devaluation of the Brazilian real and the period when the yen was weak against the dollar. The justifications for not devaluing are:

- the high import content of China's trade would cancel out the possible benefits on exports after devaluation;
- yuan devaluation would mean greater debt-servicing and this would affect the values of H-share and Red Chip companies;
- evaluation would lower the inflow of foreign direct investment;
- it would put severe pressure on Hong Kong's currency board system; and
- China was unwilling to devalue on the fiftieth anniversary of communist rule.

Instead, the Chinese government has sought remedies by fiscal stimulus and monetary easing. For example, the Chinese government has assembled a 200 billion reminbi fund aimed at financing increased public works projects. It has also raised tax rebates on exports of coal, cement, ships, textiles and steel by between 2–8 per cent. Nevertheless, the economy was faced with an export slowdown from 21 per cent in 1997 to less than 1 per cent in 1998. It has also revised expected growth rates downwards from 8 to 7 per cent. In October 1998, the collapse of Guangdong International Trust and Investment Corp (GITIC) exposed problems of the local trust and investment corporations (LTICs) which had built up total external debts of US$8.1 billion. More specifically and with reference to Gitic, its collapse sparked off not only a foreign credit crunch; but also the local–central conflict over southern 'pragmatism' and northern 'dogmatism' as well as the rivalry between Guangdong and non-Guangdong cadres. In early 1999, the central government decided not to bail out Gitic and embarked on policies that seek to reform the Chinese financial system (e.g., reducing the number of ITICs from 240 to 40).

In the case of Hong Kong, the dollar came under speculative pressure on several occasions in July, August and October 1997. The Hong Kong government intervened in the market initially by pushing up interest rates in the inter-banking sector and later by imposing penalty interest on the borrowing of the Hong Kong dollar. Hong Kong was able to maintain the pegged system because of:

1. its high foreign reserves;
2. its long-established prudent fiscal policy, which meant there was no external debt;
3. its in-built mechanism for interest rate adjustment;
4. its tight supervision of financial institutions (e.g., the use of a gross simultaneous account system among these institutions); and
5. its capacities derived from acting as an industrial, financial and commercial middleman between China and the rest of the world.

Despite these strengths, the pegged exchange rate is maintained under conditions of high interest rates, capital flight from the Hong Kong dollar, and reduced external demand. These pushed the local stock index and residential property prices down by over 50 per cent between October 1997 and June 1998. This asset depreciation, especially in the property sector, cut at the heart of Hong Kong's internal 'growth' dynamics as this had developed since the opening of China. For while Hong Kong firms move their manufacturing industries to the mainland, the service and property sectors fill the gap created by the so-called 'hollowing-out' process. More specifically, the property sector became even more dominant. It comprised banks (in the form of credit), construction companies (in the form of property assets), the government (in the form of land and revenue), and the middle classes (in the form of wealth). The bursting of the 'property bubble' has given rise to fear among this property-related bloc about further asset depreciation.

In order to prevent the assets from further depreciating, the government stopped land sales and refunded rates to local residents. The Hong Kong dollar came under further attack in August 1998 when the yen depreciated against the dollar, with hedge funds selling the Hong Kong stock market short in the expectation that the index would fall as interest rates rose. Speculative attacks propelled significant amounts of capital outflow as some people believed that this might also force a yuan devaluation. This time the government reacted by: (a) drawing on its reserves to buy US$15 billion worth of selected Hong Kong shares (60 per cent of these were property related – higher than the weight of this sector in the stock market); and (b) introducing a package of technical measures to strengthen the transparency and operation of the linked exchange rate system (e.g., a rediscount facility to reduce interest rate volatility). The pegged system was once again maintained but at the expense of high interest rates, weak domestic demand and rising unemployment. Hong Kong's GDP fell 5 per cent and the unemployment rate had reached 6 per cent by the beginning of 1999. However, wages and rents are still high. At the beginning of 1999, the government announced that it would resume land sales in April. This continual support of the property sector was further reinforced in the 1999 budget in which the two 'kisses for life' (i.e., the building of a 'cyberport'[2] and a possible Disneyland theme park) are overwhelmingly property-related projects. In much the same situation as Taiwan, the Hong Kong government's support packages for the property sector involved a regressive politics of redistribution that was challenged by the Democratic Party as the unemployment rate rose to 5.8 per cent in the same period.

Compared with most East Asian economies, Hong Kong and China emerged as the two non-devaluing economies. The two governments coordinated actions to maintain Hong Kong's pegged system and insulate the 'Greater China' (sub)region from currency decline. China participated by providing foreign exchange market expertise and stand-by funds to defend the Hong Kong dollar. This is because a devaluation of the Hong Kong dollar would affect the value of HKD-denominated investment and prices of Chinese H-share and red-chip corporations. It would also increase their debt-burden in the Hong Kong currency, and, perhaps, lead to higher interest charges and the possibility of non-performing loans. Conversely, a yuan devaluation might not benefit China and could trigger a devaluation of the Hong Kong dollar. Through the non-devaluation of the two currencies, the Hong Kong dollar and the Chinese yuan were seen by the US and IMF as crucial (sub)regional nodes in maintaining the stability of the later BrettonWoods system. Despite disputes with the US over trade and human rights issues, Beijing was being constructed as the US's possible 'number-one ally' in the region. As for Hong Kong, its 'currency board system' pegged to the US dollar was hailed by the IMF as a possible 'cure' for monetary problems (Enoch and Gulde 1999: 40). As an unintended development, the Chinese yuan and the Hong Kong dollar came to assume the 'first line of defence' of the American-dominated international currency order.[3]

STRUGGLES BETWEEN ACTORS IN THE REMAKING OF REGIONALITIES AND GLOBALITIES

Given the specificities of the 'crisis' and the differential impact/responses in the region, it is hardly surprising that actors would agree on strategies to remake the region. This leads us to the third aspect of the material-discursive approach, i.e., the role of actors in constructing different discourses concerning possible future regionalities and globalities. Due to the vast number of actors involved, this chapter can only illustrate this approach with the cases of Japan, the US, the IMF/World Bank.

Japan's construction of regionality: the AMF idea and its containment

Given Japan's industrial and financial involvement in the region, its firms and banks were the most exposed to economic turmoil. The Ministry of Finance of Japan was eager to bail out overexposed domestic banks. At the same time the Ministry of Foreign Affairs wanted to assert a greater degree of regional leadership in the face of increasing Chinese influence. Thus Japan was interested in constructing some kind of collective mechanisms that could lessen the potential financial disturbance. As early as March 1997, Japan proposed such mechanisms in the first meeting of the regional bankers' group (EMEAP). Two novel features in this regard were that Japan's proposal concerned financial mechanisms to deal with the 'crisis' and that it was proposed in a new regional forum.

Seeking to deflect a region-centred solution to the 'crisis', the IMF began to construct the 'crisis' as a 'liquidity' problem. It also selectively appropriated the previously ignored critiques of 'crony capitalism'. This strategic appropriation placed the blame squarely on the national and 'crony-ridden' nature of the Asian government–business relations. It left unexamined the nature of the global–regional economic systems organized around the later Bretton Woods regime (e.g., the dollar-bloc regime with Japan having little control over the value of its currency). In turn, the Japan initiative for some 'financial mechanisms' was shaped into a 'Thai support fund' in August after consultation with the IMF and domestic authorities.

Given the country-specific and ad hoc nature of this support fund, it failed to stop the 'contagion' from spreading from Thailand to Indonesia, Malaysia and the Philippines. Being the most heavily affected country in the region, Japan was eager to see a quicker, more flexible and less stringent scheme of regional 'rescue'. It thus unveiled the idea of an Asian Monetary Fund (AMF) in the IMF–World Bank annual meeting in Hong Kong in September 1997. With a possible capitalization of US$100 billion, the AMF symbolized a regional source of finance which could provide quick and flexible disbursements to alleviate regional currencies in crisis, as well as to provide emergency balance-of-payments support to crisis-hit economies. In other words, the AMF idea constructed a new form of regionality that could by-pass the cumbersome decision-making procedures of the IMF and could deepen the regional cooperation under the leadership of

Japan. This idea attracted considerable interest from Malaysia, Taiwan, Thailand and South Korea. China expressed some concern over the idea but was not entirely uninterested.

Unsurprisingly, the US and IMF opposed the AMF. By constructing a new scale of lending activity, the latter was seen as threatening American national security/ economic interests (LaFalce 1998: 1) and the IMF's hegemony. This can be understood within the context of American domestic politics. Since the White House was increasingly constrained by the Congress in committing financial resources abroad, Washington was forced to use the IMF as a primary mechanism for exercising US influence on world monetary affairs (Altbach 1997: 9). Hence any challenge to the IMF would be seen as running counter to US interests. The creation of the AMF would also drive a wedge into a US-sponsored project dating from the early 1980s to construct an 'Asia Pacific' identity (Sum 2000). It would also marginalize the IMF's debt conditionalities and its regime of truth by creating an alternative site of action.

Accordingly, US and IMF officials sought to contain the AMF idea by appropriating some of its concerns into their own agenda. In the same Hong Kong meeting, IMF officials tackled the problem of stringent and inadequate funding of the IMF by calling for a 45 per cent increase in members' quotas. This suggestion partly addressed the issue of inadequate funding; but it also signalled to national actors in the region that the IMF wanted to remain sole 'international lender of last resort'. Troubled by the turmoil in the region, national actors, including Japan, reiterated the IMF's centrality in the global financial architecture. This reaffirmation could clearly be seen from the outcome of the Manila Framework Group meeting in mid-November. The Group endorsed 'the need and desirability of a framework for regional cooperation' but added that this 'arrangment ... would supplement IMF resources'. In this regard, the Manila agreement succeeded in: (a) containing, at least temporarily, the regional initiative within the IMF regime; (b) defusing the constest between the IMF and the AMF; and (c) constructing a globality that involved global–regional cooperation and supplementation. As an indication of this cooperation, they also welcomed the US$30 billion aid assistance from Japan – later known as the 'New Miyazawa Initiative'.

The new 'domino' effect and the renegotiations of IMF–World Bank's identities

Partly to regain the centre stage, the IMF extended its neoliberal regime, especially the 'conditionality' practices, to Thailand, South Korea and Indonesia (the so-called 'IMF 3') between August and December in 1997. The mechanism deployed to this end was the imposition of the blanket-type contractionary economic practices associated with the structural adjustment programmes (e.g., cutting the budget deficit by tightening of fiscal policy, restricting central bank credits to government) and an insistence on greater transparency on behalf of the banks and their Group of Seven (G7) governments.

The IMF's actions backed by the US Treasury failed to arrest the 'contagion'. Its 'domino effect' has rippled from Asia to Russia thence to Brazil. Figure 3.1 shows its route from July 1997 to September 1998. In September, the near-collapse of the Connecticut-based Long-Term Capital Management in USA also exposed the vulnerabilities of major American and European banks and hedge funds, e.g., Merrill Lynch and the Union de Banques Suisses (Graham 1998).

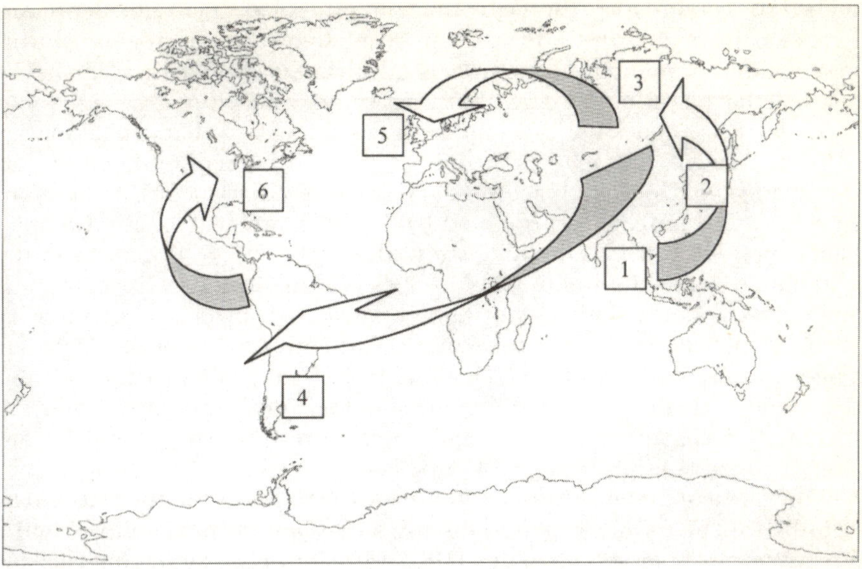

Key:
1 July 1997 – depreciation of the Thai Baht
2 December 1997 – IMF bailout of South Korea
3 1998 – collapse of the Russian rouble
4 August 1998 – tumbling of Latin American markets due to panic in the wake of Russia's default on obligations and currency devaluation
5 Late 1998 – falling oil prices weaken oil-rich Norway; Sweden and Denmark also hit
6 Late 1998 – low consumer confidence on both sides of the Atlantic; collapse of long-term capital management in the USA; dangers of a US downturn

Figure 3.1: The route of the new 'domino effect'
Source: Adapted from *The Sunday Times*, 30 August 1998

Table 3.7: The IMF's Regime of Truth since the 1970s

Identities	**'Conditionality' practices**
Neoliberalism (under the 'Washington Consensus')	Structural Adjustment Programmes (contractionary measures)
— Good governance	— Tight monetary policy
— Accountability	— Tight fiscal policy
— 'International lender of last resort' with full conditionality	— Higher taxes to eliminate deficits

The IMF's failure to arrest the 'contagion' prompted a barrage of criticisms. Even actors from the free-trade tradition began to question its regime of truth. These include prominent economists (e.g., Bhagwati, Krugman, Sachs). They deployed the pages of the *New York Times*, the *Wall Street Journal*, and the *Washington Post* to question this regime. Bhagwati argued that capital markets are by their nature unstable and require controls. Krugman outlined the case for exchange controls as a response to crisis. Bhagwati went further by noting that free capital mobility is promoted by the 'Wall Street–Treasury Complex' which equates its interests to the 'good of the world' (1998: 12). Sachs in turn focused more on the folly of the IMF's policies during the crisis. Specifically, he criticized its austerity measures of tightening money, high interest rates and tight fiscal policies under the structural adjustment programmes (SAPs) and argued that they have transformed a liquidity crisis into a financial panic in the Asian context. He proposed that the IMF should revise its standard formula for economic reform, make its decision-making more transparent, and become more accountable for the impact of its policies.

In the midst of this elite 'dissent', there were changes within the IMF and the World Bank. The former began to discuss the issue of 'capital control' and to reverse some policy targets upon the 'IMF 3' (e.g., the deficit targets for Thailand, South Korea, and Indonesia were reset to 3 per cent, 4 per cent and 8.5 per cent respectively between July and September 1998). As for the World Bank, it took steps to distance itself from IMF's structural adjustment approach. The Bank's chief economist, Joseph Stiglitz, was at the forefront of the IMF–World Bank split. He openly questioned the usefulness of the adjustment programmes at the WIDER Annual Lecture (1998). He argued for a 'Post-Washington Consensus' which should encompass a broader set of goals in designing adjustment policies in developing countries. He suggested that the new goals should move beyond the increases in GDP to the more extensive goals of sustainable, equitable and democratic development. Stiglitz's attempt to go beyond the 'Consensus' resonates with the positions of some NGOs that have been calling for an end to the IMF adjustment programmes. They also called for the IMF–World Bank to become more transparent and responsive organizations designed to address poverty reduction (see Bullard, Chapter 7 of this volume).

Partly in response to these criticisms and demands, the IMF and World Bank renamed its 'Extended Structural Adjustment Facility' to a 'Poverty Reduction and Growth Facility', and rephrased its 'conditionality' requirements in more reform-sensitive terms. Likewise, in the IMF–World Bank meeting in September 1999, the World Bank highlighted 'povery reduction' as a 'main objective' and suggested that 'debt forgiveness' should be delivered 'with participation of civil society' and 'social safety nets'. Apart from these internal renegotiations of IMF–World Bank identities, many proposals have been made concerning the future of these two identities. They include reports and rebuttals from the G24, the US congressional panel of the International Financial Institutions Advisory Commission (the Meltzer Commission), government entities under the Clinton administration (for example, the US Treasury), and Washington-based think-tanks (for example, the Institute of International Economics). A detailed discussion of these reports and their implications for globality is beyond the scope of this chapter. However, close attention needs to be paid to how the IMF–World Bank identities are being renegotiated and re-embedded within an unequal power structure, and to how these global players are seeking to legitimize a regime of economic truth that still remains grounded in orderly (as opposed to disorderly) 'liberalization, good governance, and accountability'.

Reinventing regionalities: from the AMF to the 'New Miyazawa Initiative' and beyond

Concurrent with the contestation of the IMF's regime of truth, the AMF idea was reinvented by Japan in October 1998 at a meeting of Asian finance ministers. Tactically, Japan sought to disentangle this initiative from the AMF and the latter's struggle with the IMF. It thus adopted the following strategies:

1. to give the idea a new name – the 'New Initiative to Overcome the Asian Currency Crisis' (more popularly known as the 'New Miyazawa Initiative') (see Figure 3.2);
2. to redefine it as a new aid package (and not a currency stabilization scheme) that would be part of a multilateral G7-sponsored US$ 90 billion 'contingency' facility with an Asian focus; and
3. to route the 'New Initiative' through the G7.

The US benefited from this insofar as the 'New Miyazawa Initiative' enabled it to exert quasi-scrutiny over Japan's regional initiative under the IMF–World Bank regime. At the same time the Initiative enabled Japan to install a regionally focused initiative with the support of the US and related international agencies such as the IMF and the Asian Development Bank.

For Japan, the regional space created by the 'New Miyazawa Initiative' was appropriated by the Ministry of Foreign Affairs and Ministry of Finance in the following ways:

1. as new resources to carry out financial diplomacy in the region;
2. as opportunity to bail out crisis-hit Japanese firms; and
3. as a chance to provide loans in yen which is part of an effort to 'internationalize the yen'.

First, the Initiative armed the Ministry of Foreign Affairs with extra resources to carry out its financial diplomacy. Just before the APEC Summit in Kuala Lumpur in November 1998, pressures were building up over the possible US–Japan trade deficit of US$300 billion in the year of 1999. Being a trade-oriented forum, the APEC Summit was one of the arenas in which the US pushed to open markets in the region, especially that of Japan. More specifically, this meeting saw a move to open up US$1.5 trillion in international trade in nine key sectors (the so-called Early Voluntary Sectoral Liberalization Plan). Some of these sectors (e.g., fishery and forestry products) were precisely those that Japan is eager to protect. Given their divergence and Japan's strong resistance, US officials jacked up the aid discourse on 'Japan not doing enough to help Asia', thereby constructing Japan as the 'villain'. At the same time, China was hailed as 'hero' and 'number-one ally' because it helped to maintain the stability of the dollar-bloc regime by not devaluing its currency.[4] Partly in response to the American challenge that 'Japan is not doing enough for Asia' and partly to rally support to delay APEC's trade liberalization plan, the Ministry of Foreign Affairs deployed the aid-related

Total financial support to Asian countries: US$30 billion

A. Medium- to long-term financial support: US$15 billion

i) to provide direct official financial assistance
- extending loans from Export–Import Bank
- acquiring bonds issued by Asian countries
- extending ODA yen loans

ii) to support Asian countries in raising funds from international financial markets
- using the guarantee functions of Export–Import Bank
- providing export insurance
- providing interest subsidies

iii) to co-finance with the World Bank and the Asian Development Bank

iv) to provide technical assistance on debt restructuring

B. Short-term financial support: US$15 billion

i) to facilitate trade finance

i) to take the form of swap arrangements

Figure 3.2: The objectives of the first stage of the 'New Miyazawa Initiative', 1998
Source: Ministry of Finance of Japan, 3 October 1998

'New Miyazawa Initiative' to gain support from Thailand, Indonesia, Malaysia, Taiwan and China. The Kuala Lumpur Summit thus ended with: (a) trade ministers voting to refer Early Voluntary Sector Liberalization to the World Trade Organization; (b) finance ministers calling for new measures (such as supervision of banking systems and securities markets) to be discussed in the G22; and (c) President Clinton and Prime Minister Obuchi launching a US$10 billion 'Asian Growth and Recovery Initiative' to aid bank restructuring and trade finance in the region.

Second, adopting the discourse of 'Japanese and Asian economies recovering together', the Initiative disbursed the first stage of loans to Thailand (US$1.85 billion), Malaysia (US$1.5 billion), and Philippines (US$1.4 billion) through a new global–regional network comprising the Asian Development Bank, the World Bank, and the Japan Bank for International Cooperation (created by merging Export–Import Bank of Japan (JEXIM) and Japan's Overseas Economic Cooperation Fund (OECF)). This network provided Japanese tied loans to crisis-hit countries. The nature of the tie can be seen in the Fund's guidelines, which

> prescribe that qualified proponents for identified projects be wholly-owned Japanese companies. Or if a tie-up with a counterpart exists, such as US companies, more than 50 per cent of the total man-months devoted for a specific project should be undertaken by the Japanese counterpart. This departs from the traditional approach of simply tying loans to either Japanese companies, or companies belong to any of the DAC-member countries (Palma 1999).

In this regard, the tied nature of the Initiative may have the effect of enabling the Ministry of Finance to use public funds to bail out Japanese crisis-hit private corporations (Greenfield 1999).

Third, given that the Miyazawa Initiative is not permanent, Japan sought to build a more durable regional foothold by extending it to a second stage. In December 1998, the Ministry of Finance announced the launching of an Asian yen-bond market based on the auctioning of Financing Bills and, in addition, exempting Treasury Bills and Financing Bills from a withholding tax. Together these offers represented an injection of 2 trillion yen into the proposed Asian yen-bond market. They would enable Japan to: (a) facilitate the internationalization of the yen; (b) counteract Asia's excessive dependence on the US dollar; and (c) actualize Miyazawa's idea of a tri-polar currency (the dollar, euro and yen) which originated in France. This plan to 'internationalize the yen' seemed to gain some initial support from the ASEAN countries. However, up to the time of writing, limited interest has been shown in practice from within the region for the following reasons:

- the already very high levels of public debts issued by Asian governments;
- the uncertain benefits of a possible yen-based currency system where America (and not Japan) is still the major export market for most countries in the region;
- the well-established frameworks in Asia assuming the use of the US dollar (not the yen) in international trade;
- the continuing problem of memories from the Japanese military occupation; and
- the implied requirement that Asian countries reorient their geopolitical allegiances to Japan.

Nonetheless, ideas of the AMF, EAEC and, more recently, the bilateral currency pact known as the 'Chiang Mai Initiative' are now agenda topics that are discussed in bilateral and regional/international forums. They are powerful symbols in developing future regional discursive networks that may (or may not) contribute to the building of new regional institutions.

Some Concluding Remarks: A Possible Research Agenda

The above discussion suggests that there are emerging discursive and material struggles over the new 'global–regional–national financial architectures' as the established global and (emerging) regional hegemonies (e.g., the US, Japan) engage in conflict/cooperation. Among other things, these involve struggles to establish and codify the nature and purposes of new globalities and regionalities (e.g., 'Post-Washington Consensus', AMF, 'New Miyazawa Initiative', 'Chiang Mai Initiative') and their associated identities and practices. At the time of writing, these competing discourses/practices can be constructed and appropriated by different global–regional–national networks of actors for their own purposes. Moreover, currently the US, Japan and to some extent Malaysia are building their respective discursive networks. These tendencies towards conflict/cooperation and their respective discursive codifications and otherizations of what constitutes the 'future' are crucial to any remaking of globalities and regionalities. Given that some Asian countries are caught in the vicious circle of the overproduction, falling profit, overborrowing, exchange rate vulnerability, bursting of property/stock market/currency bubbles, tight credits, and unemployment; escaping from these chains is often the target of the search by national leaders for a 'quick fix' and for scholars to reassert their preferred models of analysis (e.g., a 'developmental state' that can impose capital controls and/or neo-Keynesian measures).

This chapter argued that, as the 'crisis' involves a structural disarticulation between the regional-national production and global-regional financial orders, it is not susceptible to speedy resolution and/or uni-scalar solution. Thus my own brief intervention in terms of a material-discursive approach is concerned not only with analyses of the 'crisis' (e.g., symptoms and causes) but also with the ongoing restructuring processes. On the latter, this chapter highlights the processes that are involved in the remaking of global–regional–national political economy and its complexities. Such complexities could be translated into a possible research agenda in three interrelated ways: discourses, scales and materiality.

This chapter has demonstrated the importance of discourses in mediating the re-embedding of power relations. Much more work needs to be done on networks of actors involved in constructing and appropriating new globalities and regionalities. On this issue, there are emerging discursive networks centred upon the US, World Bank and Japan in generating new meanings of what constitute the new global–regional–national political economy (e.g., the 'Post-Washington Consensus', the 'New Miyazawa Initiative', 'internationalization of the yen' and the 'Chiang Mai Initiative'). They are jostling to generate diverse objects of globalities and regionalities in and through the (re-)construction and (re-)combination of symbols and codes. This creates a strategic field in which alternatives are constructed and alliances can be built to shape and be shaped by structural constraints that are related to the post-Plaza, the later Bretton Woods, and the 'Washington Consensus' regimes.

Second, this chapter also reveals the importance of scale in the restructuring process. It has shown that this process is marked by newly-emerging scales of action (e.g., G20, AMF, the 'New Miyazawa Initiative', the 'Chiang Mai Initiative', a free-trade zone between Japan and South Korea) that are beyond national/global-level concerns. Such emerging scales raise two issues. On the theoretical level, they question traditional arguments such as the 'development state' thesis. The latter attempts to explain economic success in terms of qualities of nation-states. In this regard, it is less equipped to explain 'crisis'/failure and restructuring that involve new scales of actions. If one is less interested in chanting the chorus to 'the model is dead, long live the model', it is an appropriate time to rethink such approaches and possibly combine them with other approaches in order to transcend the internal/external and the national/global distinctions. On the policy level, the co-existence of old and new scales of actions (e.g., IMF and the 'Chiang Mai Initiative'; G7 , G20 and G22, IMF practices and national capital controls, etc.) may pose problems of interscalar articulation and issues of the 'fit' across them. A resort to national 'quick fixes' may miss important issues regarding new scales and their articulation with the national. To help take these changes into account, this chapter calls for a shift from binary way of thinking (e.g., national and/or global, internal and/or external) to a more multiscalar level of analysis both theoretically and in terms of policy consideration.

Third, this chapter has demonstrated the articulation and disarticulation between the production and financial orders of the post-Plaza regime. The breakdown of such complex structures raises questions beyond those of a financial 'quick fix' and social after-thought (such as microeconomic reforms or building social safety nets). Here one should rethink the materiality of the global–regional–national political economy by moving from a financial 'quick fix' to a finance/industry/trade 'fit'. The latter may be related to the following questions:

- What are the relations between industrial, financial and commercial circuits and their new linkages?
- What are their scales of activities and how are they being deepened?
- What are the social implications of such deepening?
- What structural constraints and conjunctural opportunities involved in remaking the above (e.g., power of global/regional hegemony)?
- What is being selected under the changing power relationship between old and new institutions (e.g., IMF, World Bank, G8, G22, the 'New Miyazawa Initiative')?
- What are the emerging identities and regimes of truth associated with these institutions ('orderly liberalism', 'post-Washington Consensus', national protectionism)?
- What are the power relations involved in the latter?

NOTES

1 'Greater China' here is interpreted to include Taiwan, (southern) China and Hong Kong.

2 In the 1999 budget speech, the Financial Secretary of Hong Kong proposed to develop a US$13 billion 'Cyberport' that provides the essential infrastructure to develop Hong Kong into an e-commerce hub of the region. It is expected to provide 12,000 jobs after completion in 2007.

3 In this regard, the Hong Kong dollar and Chinese yuan can be compared with the pound sterling as a first line of defence for the US dollar from the 1950s to 1970s.

4 The talk of a 'strategic partnership' between the US and China was disturbed by the mistaken bombing of the Chinese embassy in Belgrade and US/Japan proposals for a Theatre Missile Defence System with implications for China's eventual reunification with Taiwan.

REFERENCES

Altbach, E. (1997) *The Asian Monetary Fund proposal: a case study of Japanese regional leadership,* Japan Economic Institute Report 47A: 1–12.

Bernard, M. (1999) 'East Asia's tumbling dominoes: financial crises and the myth of the regional model', C. Leys, *et al.*(eds), 'Global Capitalism vs Democracy', *Socialist Register*: pp. 178–208.

Bhagwati, J. (1998) 'The Capital Myth: the Difference Between Trade in Widgets and Dollars', *Foreign Affairs,* 77, p. 7.

Claessens, S., S. Djankov and L. Lang (1998) 'East Asian corporates: growth, financing and risks over the last decade', World Bank Discussion Paper, October 27.

Cornell, A. (1999) 'Japan pushes for Asian version of IMF', *Australia Financial Review,* February 12.

Dwyer, M. (1998) 'IMF Starts to query its own ideology', *Australia Financial Review,* November 30.

Enoch, C. and Gulde, A-M. (1999), 'Are currency boards a cure for all monetary problems?', *Finance and Development*, December, pp. 40–43.

Friedman, A. (1997) 'World Bank raises alarm on East Asian economies', *International Herald Tribune*, December 9.

—— (1999) 'U.S. talks of "Crisis" in Japan trade', *International Herald Tribune*, February 4.

Godement, F. (1999) *The Downsizing of Asia*. London: Routledge.

Graham, G. (1998) 'Stark staring bankers', *Financial Times*, October 5.

Greenfield, G. (1999) 'The World Bank's bigger brother?', Alarm Update, 37, Oct.–Dec., http://is7.pacific.net.hk/amrc/alarm/AU37/993701.htm, accessed on 14 February, 1999.

Harvey, D. (1982) *Limits of Capital*. Oxford: Blackwell.

Howell, M. (1998) 'Asia's "Victorian" financial crisis', http://www.ids.ac.uk/ids/global/conf/howell.pdf, accessed on 13 March 2001.

Johnson, C. (1998) 'Economic crisis in East Asia: the clash of capitalisms', *Cambridge Journal of Economics*, 22: 653–661.

Krugman, P. (1998) 'Asia: what went wrong', *Fortune*, March 2.

Keishi, S. (1998) 'Beyond anti-Americanism', *Japan Echo*, December: 8–11.

LaFalce, J. (1998) 'The role of the US and the IMF in the Asian financial crisis'. Address given before the Institute of International Economics, Willard Hotel, Washington, January 27.

Liew, L. H. (1998) 'A political-economy analysis of the Asian Financial crisis', *Journal of the Asia Pacific Economy*, 3 (3), pp. 301–330.

McKinnon, R. I. (1999) 'Exchange rate co-ordination for surmounting the East Asian currency crises', *Journal of International Development*, 11 (1), pp. 95–106.

Ohmae, K. (1990) *Borderless World*. New York: Harper Perennial.

Palma, A. (1999) 'Miyazawa Fund: a new Japanese tied fund approach', International Market Insights, Dec., http://www.ita.gov/td/untiedaid/phil-miyazawa699.htm, accessed on 14 February, 1999.

Porter, B. and D. Saunders (1998) 'APEC bogs down at crossroads', *South China Morning Post*, November 19.

Sachs, J. (1997) 'Personal view: Jeff Sachs', *Financial Times*, July 30.

—— (1998) 'The IMF and the Asian Flu', *American Prospect*, June 1, p. 66.

Sparks, C. (1998) 'The eye of the storm', *International Socialism*, 78, pp. 3–38.

Stiglitz, J. (1998) 'More instruments and broader goals: moving toward the post Washington Consensus', WIDER Annual Lecture No 2, Helsinki, January 7.

Sum, N-L. (1997) 'The NICs and competing strategies of East Asian regionalism' in A. Gamble and A. Payne (eds), *Regionalism and the World Order*. London: Macmillan, pp. 207–246.

—— (2000) 'Three kinds of "New Orientalism": the construction of trans-border identity of the Asia-Pacific', in C. Hay and D. Marsh (eds), *Demystifying Globalization*. London: Macmillan, pp. 111–132.

World Bank (1997) 'Are financial sector weaknesses undermining the East Asian "miracle"?', News Release No. 98/1474/EASIA, http://www.worldbank.org/extdr/extme/1474.htm, accessed on 13 March 2001.

FOUR

Economy and Politics in the East Asian Crisis

Bruno Amoroso

Preliminary remarks

The East Asian crisis will be recorded as one of the least foreseen events. However, once the crisis had unfolded, a debate developed along the same lines that we have experienced with the previous crises in other regions of the world. Economists once again started to discuss the need for a 'new Global Financial Architecture', the relation between interest rates and exchange rates and their impact on devaluation. Marxists and structuralists verified the predictability of their theories on the economic cycles (the Marxian's, the Schumpeterian's or the Kondratieff's ones), while Institutionalists regained their strength by focusing on institutional and market transparency and on crony capitalism. Once again a debate blew up within the international institutions on delays, mistakes or misunderstanding that had made the crisis and their bad forecasting and policy interventions possible. This debate has also included a critique of wrong policies imposed on countries by the IMF and World Bank structural adjustment programmes (SAPs) against the warnings launched by governments and 'radical' writers. Paradoxically, even the 'authors' of these policies – the economic and political forces governing the process of globalization – have blamed the 'actors',[1] i.e., the leaders of the international institutions which have implemented policies functional to the interest of the Triad. The irony of history is that through this old-style 'organized mystification' (to change everything to leave things as they are at the present), the leaders of the old world financial system will become the leaders of the 'new Global Financial Architecture'. Perhaps some new Nobel Prizes in Economics may be awarded to scholars in charge of this readjustment of the neoliberal strategy.

It is not entirely right to say that the Asian crisis was not predicted, just as it is wrong to declare that the warnings were only partial and ideological or deprived of clear empirical evidence. In fact, it has been well analysed and demonstrated by a number of authors that the chain of financial crises since the 1970s could not be referred to traditional contradictions in capitalist economies (such as capital labour contradictions in single countries) or to the lack of capitalist modernization in other systems.

Historians such as David F. Noble (USA), sociologists such as Serge Latouche (France), and political scientists and jurists such as Pietro Barcellona (Italy) provided the theoretical ground for this understanding. They pointed out that the essentially new nature of the current stage of capitalist growth is either ignored or denied by neoclassical, institutionalist or Marxist authors. While André Gorz (1991: 9) declares that 'capitalist modernization is not at issue', Pietro Barcellona (1998) locates the problems precisely in the 'foundational traits of modernity', in the forms of its historical evolution which have turned it into a rogue spacecraft, not in any errors of implementation. Along lines that are reminiscent of David F. Noble's and Serge Latouche's thought, Barcellona observes:

> Thinking of a radical alternative means that we must, here and now, take it upon ourselves to change our way of living, beginning with our cities and our daily lives. And here in the West we must engender another culture in that we have been responsible for the one so far produced – industrialist, productionist and rooted in man's overpowering and domination of nature. (Barcellona 1998: 69)

Critical authors such as Riccardo Petrella (Club of Lisbon 1995), Susan George (1992) and myself (1998) have empirically explored the role of finance in the new form taken by capitalist accumulation since the 1970s. Their analyses outline the new and more complex relations established by capitalist globalization in the relations between the economy and politics. The answers to these kinds of problems raise complex problems of theory and methodology when dealing with specific events such as the Asian financial crisis.

The dominant current literature reduces the concept of politics to matters related to institutional building and mediation of conflicting interests within given value. To narrow down politics – and its relations to the economy – to institutional or economic engineering does not take us very far. This overturned use of the policy concept must be re-established in its original and classic form as expressed by Machiavelli: politics is not the passive reflection or adjustment to economic variables and behaviour but strategic thinking.

Capitalist globalization expresses itself via economic strategies (economic marginalization) and political strategies (political destabilization). The economy is an instrument of power, not the aim. The economy is the power instrument by which the '*pax americana*' enforces itself on societies. As a leading US political scientist – Robert Gilpin – indicates, globalization is the instrument to preserve in the US's hands the control on the world government. Would any Westerner, he asks, accept to be governed by the Chinese in 20 years time because of their prevalence in the size of population and in terms of economic results? The task of globalization is to prevent this condition, by all means.[2] The economic history of our time (the East Asian financial crisis among other things) and the accompanying political events (the NATO wars against Yugoslavia among others) indicate how this task is carried out.

The Asian crisis is not the outcome of unwanted inbalances in the economies or mistakes by international institutions and governments. On the contrary, it is the result of globalization strategies aiming to reinforce existing imbalances in the economies and to weaken the possibility of national or meso-regional resistance to them.

A DIFFERENT INTERPRETATION OF THE ASIAN CRISIS

The causes of the financial crisis are different from those stated in the dominant debate. In my opinion they are not the outcome of financial or structural stress or disarray but part of an informal regulation strategy established by globalization to maintain its economic and political control on world economies. Globalization has been in progress as early as the second half of the 1970s, with three financial hurricanes: those of 1979, 1989 and 1997–98. Therefore, I interpret the recent financial hurricane as the third unleashing of globalization.

The first had its beginnings in the election of Margaret Thatcher in Great Britain in 1979 and of Ronald Reagan in the US in 1980. In less than five years the European welfare systems were effectively undermined, precisely in those countries where this experience was born and most deeply rooted.

The second hurricane was in 1989. It had its beginnings in the fall of the Berlin Wall, and established the new *apartheid system* of globalization. In a few years the judiciary tempests which accompanied the political and financial destabilization put an end to the autonomous Italian and French plans for European development, that aimed for a European development more independent of the United States and to a different approach to the Mediterranean region. Once the risks of resistance and conflict in the Mediterranean had been, at least for now, neutralized, the remaining obstacle to the affirmation of the *global apartheid* was Asia, in particular China and India. The continuation of the strong rhythms of economic growth on this continent would render impossible the continuation of the domination of capitalistic globalization and, inevitably, would place limits on its political control.

To destabilize the strongest Asian societies became the principal objective after the liquidation of the Soviet Union. A direct attack on China on the economic front is not easy and needs to be preceded by the weakening of the phalanx of neighbouring countries, making the governments of these countries weaker towards the West and more aggressive towards China and the other countries of East Asia in general.

Therefore the financial hurricane turned towards these smaller countries of the region with the objective of weakening them economically and creating a fissure between governments and their populations. In fact the aid packages offered by globalization to these countries tend to increase the dependence of their dominant classes on the West, distancing them from their own middle classes and from the national interests of their peoples. The key lines of this strategy are to isolate China (and India), inflaming again new and old conflicts in the region (particularly in Southeast Asia).

Like the 'crisis' of the welfare systems and the 'crisis' of the Eastern European socialist systems, the East Asian crisis was not foreseen. It is peculiar that theory constructions aiming to explain societal change and transformation are only able to reflect backwards and not forwards on these events. The inability of social science to predict events is not pointed out here to express academic discontent. Rather, we want to underline the persistence among social scientists in avoiding the paths of research that might produce an improvement of the situation. This contribution is an effort in this direction. Therefore, we consider it important to situate the recent Asian crisis in a broader context, where it is analysed as the third wave in a process of economic marginalization and political destabilization which started with the welfare systems crisis (the first wave) and continued with the socialist systems crisis (the second wave).

The crisis of the welfare systems

The crisis of the welfare systems was so little foreseen by social scientists that many of them still have problems in acknowledging it. The paradox is even more remarkable because the criticisms of welfare systems have been very acute during the last 25 years, by the reformists as well as by the conservatives. But when the crisis became obvious during the 1980s, social scientists stopped talking about structural and political problems and reduced everything to a lack of 'consensus' (incomprehension by the people of the real aims and functioning of the system) and mistakes in financial management.

To avoid misunderstanding, it is of course true that the welfare systems had reached an impasse in Europe. But this was not because their aims – equality and efficiency – were accomplished or because they were wrong. The reason is that it became increasingly clear that their achievement would have required fundamental changes in the economic (capitalist) system's structure and behaviour, and this went far beyond what the European power structure could tolerate. Thus, the existing pressure for fundamental changes in society – aiming at developing further the welfare states towards the welfare societies – was oriented instead towards the destabilization and dismantling of the welfare state. Therefore the capitalist transition from the *welfare economy* to the *apartheid economy* took place. The only real example of 'implosion' of a system during this half century is the crisis of the welfare state (see Amoroso 1999).

The crisis of the socialist systems

Similar considerations can be made about the other big 'crisis' of recent decades, viz. the collapse of the socialist systems in Eastern Europe. Even the harshest detractors did not forecast their collapse. The surprise has been so great that we still lack fundamental answers to the many questions raised by this collapse. All the arguments put forward recycle prejudices and information already used and known before the crisis.

A cautious European liberal scientist, Norberto Bobbio (1989), remarked that the collapse of the two great utopias of the twentieth century – the reformist one of a 'possible civilization' and the revolutionary one of 'communism' – remain unexplained. This condition leaves us no better placed to find a solution to the same problems with which they were dealing.

The Asian crisis

Now we are facing the problem of how to interpret the Asian crisis. Once again, nobody had foreseen it. The critics had emphasized the high social costs and contradictions of the Asian model. The apologists focused on its ability to reshape and revive the virtues of the market and capitalism.

The awareness that such a crisis requires a keen analysis of the existing interplay among many factors – economy, politics and social problems – is widespread and hardly questioned. However, any attempt to conceive of the economy as something more than wrong prices, or of politics as something more than institutional gaps, or of psychology as something more than voters' and consumers' behaviour, and of social problems as an integrated element in the evaluation of events, seems disturbing to many colleagues. To integrate political strategy and economic strategy in the explanation of the events appears to be nothing less than a conspiracy theory.

As I am convinced that any form of power structure is the result of economic and political strategies, which are equally important in determining the outcome of historical events, I happily take the risk of being misinterpreted as a conspiracy theorist. I am convinced that any researcher trying to get to the core of the main events of our time, the three mentioned waves, will have to face the role of politics and political strategy. Here I define the role of politics as being determined by the leading classes and groups and by the level of social consciousness of the people in a country, conflicting with strong international political and economic forces.

THE FINANCIAL CRISIS IN ASIA

The facts are well known. The Asian crisis we are dealing with erupted during the summer of 1997 and then rapidly spread, generating economic crises and social disasters throughout East and Southeast Asian countries, with severe consequences in Indonesia, Thailand, South Korea, Malaysia, the Philippines and Japan.

Various authors had expressed doubts about the ability of these countries to maintain in the long run the high growth levels achieved during the 1980s and 1990s, but the continuation of the growth was not questioned (e.g., Krugman 1994). Other authors pointed out the weakness in the financial markets and institutions of the region, and the IMF warned Thailand in 1996 and 1997 about the risks of financial instability. But these warnings appeared more as an instrument to exert pressure on these countries for institutional and market reforms in the general drive for modernization and liberalization than as a serious warning for the stability of these countries.

Other scholars (Bello and Rosenfeld 1992; Hersh 1993) expressed more elaborate structural considerations and they certainly came closer to forecasting an economic breakdown. However, the crisis exploded not as a social and structural breakdown but as a 'financial crisis'.

The reading of the evidence about the present Asian financial crisis cannot ignore the experiences accumulated during previous currency crises in Western Europe, Eastern Europe and in Latin America. The transparency of the financial system and deteriorating 'macroeconomic fundamentals' were pointed out as the main causes of the crisis. The most recent waves of crisis in Western Europe were experienced in Scandinavia, i.e., in countries with modern and advanced production systems and the clearest and most transparent set of financial institutions. The real causes of the crisis have yet to be explained. The economic and institutional background for the crisis in Eastern Europe and in Latin America was the existence of poor 'macroeconomic fundamentals' affecting the general equilibrium of these economies and producing the establishment of the well-known 'vicious circles': large fiscal deficits – producing excess demand – deficit financing by the central bank – money supply to swell – process to spiral – trade deficit – shortage of foreign currency ...

Furthermore these countries were exposed to

1. the general trend of globalization pushing investments away from developing countries;
2. the constant political pressure made on these government by the triad capital;
3. the rapid inflow and outflow of capital resulting from the speculative character of the short-term 'productive investments'.

The resources for governments to resist such pressures are very low in Latin America and in Eastern Europe. Therefore, the measures established to counteract these phenomena were the devaluation of the local currency, the cut of the budget deficit and the tightening in monetary policy to rein in inflation.

The Asian countries' economic conditions at the outbreak of the crisis were very different. The 'macroeconomic fundamentals' received positive evaluations by the international organizations in charge of their monitoring. The reasons were always pointed out in the following way (e.g., ADB 1999: 25):

- high rates of growth;
- fiscal balance;
- low inflation;
- high rates of domestic saving;
- low current account deficit;
- high rates of investment.

During the 1990s, the high growth rate of Southeast Asian economies was stimulated by currency rates 6–7 points higher than the dollar-dominated financial instruments. The general context that made possible the persistence over time of sound 'economic fundamentals' can be explained by

1. the expansion of the market;
2. the inclusion of new countries such as China and Vietnam in the process of regional cooperation;
3. the increased consumption together with the creation of a wide middle-class (contrary to what happen in Latin America and Africa);
4. a high level of autonomy of the national leading groups.
5. a very low exchange rate risk;
6. a positive trend of FDI' inflow due mainly to overseas Chinese capital.

It is in this context that the Triad banks became the major lenders to the region's financial institutions and businesses, and many East Asian governments promoted deregulation of domestic financial markets and liberalization of cross-border capital transactions in order to attract capital inflows.

The conditions were, of course, different from country to country, and in particular from the policy strategy and the Western attitude towards countries such as China. A disturbing factor from the Triad point of view was that the capital inflow to the Western-friendly Asian countries was partly redirected towards 'communist' countries of the region. To better understand the variety of causes and effects of the crisis, it is useful to take a closer look at the events taking place during this period in the economies of Thailand, Malaysia, Korea and Indonesia.

The Thai economy, for example, enjoyed a large fund inflow, producing a steady foreign exchange reserve growth, up to the equivalent of six months' imports. But this generated a growth in domestic money supply, with strong domestic demand, import increase and export shrinkage, which accelerated inflation and the current account deficit rose to 8 per cent of GDP. Why was the financial sector the weak point from which the crisis arose? The technical explanation provided by the experts is simple. The great inflow of funds consisted mainly of 3 month to one year short-term-credit dollar-dominated loans. Normally they are rolled over. Suddenly the international banks decided that this situation could not continue and the credit was stopped. The consequences were the collapse of the financial market, a serious banking crisis and economic disorder. This same thing was repeated, with some variations, in Malaysia, South Korea and Indonesia as well as Thailand.

Three kinds of explanations are provided to justify such a sudden halt in credit flows:

1. In Thailand, the crisis was mainly provoked by a speculative bubble in real estate, where banks were involved.
2. In South Korea, the crisis was mainly due to the soaring of loans to *chaebols* and in Indonesia to 'economic conglomerates' connected to particular families.
3. In Malaysia, over-investments in some sectors (electronic, auto and petrochemicals) were pointed out.

This sudden halt in international credit to local banks, with seemingly little regard for the economic and social impact on these countries, resulted in bankruptcy, current account deficit growth, intervention by national banks, outflow of capital and the interference of speculators. Perhaps it is worth noticing that the role of the hedge funds in causing the Asian financial crisis has been used as scapegoat to divert attention away from the responsibilities of the Triad banks and institutions. Some researchers have tested the hypothesis that hedge funds were responsible for the crash in the Asian currencies in late 1997. Analyses of the changing positions of the largest ten currency funds in one currency, the Malaysian ringgit, and to a basket of Asian currencies, show that their estimated net positions were not unusual during the crash period, nor were the profits of the funds during the crisis. In conclusion the authors state that there is 'no empirical evidence to support the hypothesis that George Soros, or any other hedge fund manager was responsible for the crisis' (Brown *et al.* forthcoming).[3]

THE POLICY PROPOSALS

The crisis first struck the countries with the closest ties to Western economies and which were more advanced in terms of economic growth. However, during 1998, its effects spread out also to other areas and countries, which lean on economies that are less dependent on financial and export flows, such as China and Vietnam. The impact in terms of a rise in poverty and unemployment in Southeast Asian countries was remarkable. The dramatic effects were further amplified by the stabilization policies imposed by the IMF, which were a repetition of the fiscal austerity and tighter monetary policy imposed during the 1980s on Latin America. This was done despite the fact that these countries were already running budget surpluses, tight monetary policies and low inflation. The outcome of the implementation of the IMF recommendations was the spreading of the crisis to other East Asian countries, thereby generating new political and social crises.

The policy proposals that have emerged in order to cope with this dramatic situation have been various, but they seemed to converge on one point: the need to reform and to strengthen the existing international financial institutions. The usual jargon of democratization, transparency, participation and harmonization was used to disguise the real problems of power and contents. It might be useful at this point to make a short critical summary of these proposals and to explain why I profoundly disagree with the approach they represent.

The proposal put forward by Western political leaders such as Bill Clinton and Romano Prodi was the establishment of a world government of the economy, under the global leadership of the United States. They made this proposal despite the fact that the real cause of the crisis was the very existence of the world government of the economy led by the Triad. A nostalgia for past 'splendour' was evident. Robert MacNamara, moving very fast among different jobs – the military hawk in Vietnam, the World Bank leader and today preaching for environment – expressed his feeling about the Asian crisis by recalling the climate of the Second World War; he has been followed by those preaching for a new Bretton Woods.

The critical voices asked for the 'disarmament of finance' (Club of Lisbon 1997), as if finance and speculation were an outgrowth of globalization and not its best weapons for penetration, destabilization and domination. Rather more clearly, timely and discreet are the voices and interventions of the international organizations right at the helm of the global economy. The International Monetary Fund and the World Bank have dealt with the complexity of the growing contradiction between capitalist globalization and society with the same resoluteness and barbarity with which Alexander the Great undid 'the Gordian Knot': rending it apart with the force of the sword.

The resistance that the above-mentioned two institutions have met and are going to meet in Asian countries surprises them. What has worked very well in Latin America, in the Arab countries and even in Europe by creating *compradora* governments does not seem to work in Asia. To resolve this question, they have shown a readiness to listen to advice on the matter. All reform proposals are welcome and they seem to appeal also to critics. The problem is that the only reform necessary is the suppression of these international institutions. They are the administrative body of global apartheid and the destruction of this system entails their own destruction too.

For this reason I appreciate the careful analysis provided by Bullard (in this volume) and others of the new discussions and contradictions inside and between these institutions about their role and their future (the crisis of the Washington Consensus). But I think that the conclusions of these analyses are too optimistic.

It is true that the IMF admits to having made some 'mistakes' in the government of the crisis and that it has been criticized by the World Bank for showing scant regard for the social impact of the 'adjustment policies'. However, the IMF's and World Bank's understanding of these 'mistakes' is different from the one proposed by Bullard. They are convinced that globalization is right and must go on. They only worry about how to make this process progress more smoothly and therefore they propose to take more care in the future of how to manage the reactions produced by the impact of their policies. The management of social problems and political resistance, following the new guidelines of the IMF and World Bank, cannot be separated from the overall strategy, which is the Triad's strategy of globalization. Therefore, the international financial institutions try to impose a new Washington 'Consensus', making some formal concession to the need of 'safety nets for the poorest', but also trying to expand the scope of their intervention to new policy areas.

The World Bank has produced over the past decade reports dealing with a broad number of issues: how pension systems should be organized in the world (*Averting the Old Age Crisis,* 1994); what kind of environmental policies are compatible with globalization (*Development and the Environment,* 1992); what kind of development we need (*The Challenge of Development,* 1991), etc. These ideas have already produced disasters by their dissemination in the West and other areas of the world. Now it seems that they want to use the recent economic crisis to impose these prescriptions on East Asia, too.

The international experts provide another level of analysis and proposals. Paul Krugman (1998), among them, finds that the crisis is provoked by local government corruption ('the minister's nephew, or the president's son could open a bank'), missing responsibility ('too many people seem to have been granted privilege without responsibility'), speculation ('highly speculative real estate ventures and wild loans' to 'credulous foreign investors'). After this description, which recalls a simplified picture of Western capitalism, he concludes that the crisis became a 'downward spiral' mainly due to irrational behaviour. The answer to the complex matter of the relation between the economy and politics is solved by recourse to simplicity and rhetoric: 'But economics is not a dismal science because the economists like it that way; it is because in the end we must submit to the tyranny not just of the numbers, but of the logic they express' (Krugman 1998).

The Asian crisis is for Krugman a matter of 'implosion', a term widely used by experts to describe the crises in the Soviet Union and in Western Europe. This implies that everybody and nobody is responsible. The topic of 'government corruption' and 'family links' in business, as a deviation from sound capitalist traditions, has recurred in the debate and in the evaluations of international institutions. For this reason it might be interesting to recall old and new studies about capitalism. In his study about the origins of European capitalism, Fernand Braudel notes:

> All these great capitalists are businessmen that operate at long distances, ceaselessly, on relevant gaps between prices and between exchange rates. They need reliable persons – if not accomplices – and in any case reliable links, real guarantors. And for this purpose relatives are always the most suitable persons. The father situated in one place and the sons, the brothers or nephew, in other places along the line of the ports: all agents, travelling or residents ... Diaspora or strategic installations: two old characteristics of mercantile capitalism, which existed long before the eleventh century. (Braudel 1999: 49–51)[4]

More recent studies about the structure of national and transnational capitalism show that family relations, diaspora and lobbies are still the load-bearing structure of modern capitalism.

THE CAPACITY OF ASIAN COUNTRIES TO RESIST AND THE POSSIBLE ANSWERS

The capacity of the Asian countries to resist the financial hurricane of globalization depends on at least three factors that have always characterized Asian societies. The first is the existence of a strong national leadership not easily transformed into being consumerist (*comprador*), as has happened in Latin America and Africa in general. The key indicators of this East Asian peculiarity are the significant results achieved in poverty reduction and the process of formation of large middle classes. In these areas East Asia has proceeded along the same path that has characterized the rise of welfare states in Western Europe. In many parts of the world globalization has produced the decline of the middle classes and the rise of new poverty. During the last 20 years the tendency towards a decline of the middle class – i.e., an increasing polarization in society – has been visible in Latin America (Argentina, Brazil, Mexico, etc.), in the Arab world and increasingly also in Europe. The Asian countries, instead, have been trying to build their economic and political strategies on the rise of the middle classes – and this contradicts the overall strategy of globalization.

The second factor is the low penetration of economic, institutional and capitalistic modernization and therefore the survival of a high degree of integrity within the society, in its various values, components and functions. In this context the linkage of finance is too weak to drag the rest of the economy along with its. The market and the commodification of the production and consumption functions are an important but not a dominant factor in East Asian society. The vast network of an informal, family-based economy and its underpinning by village social relations remain difficult to penetrate and attack.

The third factor bolstering the Asian countries' capacity to resist resides in the incipient process of cooperation between these countries at the sub-regional level (China, India, ASEAN). This affords an opportunity for economic and political synergy.

The conflict between the forces of triadic globalization and the autonomous development of East Asian society has been evident, for example, in the violent economic and political aggression against Indonesia. The support given by the

Indonesian government to the strengthening of ASEAN seems to have triggered Western aversion to this country, considered in the past among its most trusted allies. It is well known that Indonesia had supported the admission of Vietnam, Cambodia, Laos and Myanmar into ASEAN, and the attempts of this organization to resist Western pressures. The crucial role played by the process of regional cooperation among East Asian countries is also demonstrated by the US opposition to the Japanese proposal at the beginning of the crisis to establish an Asian Monetary Fund.

The Malaysian reaction to the crisis by introducing tight controls on capital flows is another positive sign of a different strength compared with the weakness of Arab countries in defending their rights in their region against the US and EU intrusions. (The US intrusion takes mainly military and economic forms, while the European Union has launched a great operation of neo-colonialism under the headings of 'partnership' and 'shared wealth' in the Mediterranean. This might be considered a peculiar form of partnership, being fully managed and incorporated within the administrative structure of the European Union.)

The policy proposals to be implemented after the Asian crisis can be drawn as a natural outcome of the analysis presented in this chapter. It is necessary to transform a global apartheid system in a decentralized polycentric system of world regions. This means abandoning the colonial idea of universal principle of democracy and rights administered by the West. This also means abandoning the nightmare of the global market and the global village, which are the legacy of an old colonial way of thinking: one God, one king, one money, one market, one justice. Therefore the problem is not how to reform the international financial institutions to make them to work better. The problem is how to abolish them and allow the world regions to organize, to control and to administer their own business. The polycentric world organization based on the main world economies in the sense of Braudel (the meso-regions) is the only viable solution to a crisis that otherwise will only deteriorate and lead to further hardship for the East as well for the West.

NOTES

1 The use of these concepts is illustrated in my recent book on globalization (Amoroso 1998).

2 Yale Professor Robert Gilpin candidly admitted this reality in his intervention at a conference in Florence in the spring of 2000.

3 See also the interview with George Soros published in *Die Zeit* on 15 January 1998: 'Das ist wie ein Flächenbrand'.

4 My translation from an Italian text, not available in English.

REFERENCES

Amoroso, Bruno (1998) *On Globalization, Capitalism in the 21st Century.* London: Macmillan.

—— (1999) *L'Apartheid Globale, Globalizzazione, Marginalizzazione Economica e Destabilizzazione Politica.* Roma: Edizioni Lavoro.

Asian Development Bank (ADB) (1999) *Asian Development Outlook.* Oxford: Oxford University Press.

Barcellona, Pietro (1998) *Il declino dello stato.* Bari: Dedalo.

Bello, W. and S. Rosenfeld (1992) *Dragons in Distress: Asia's Miracle Economies in Crisis.* London: Penguin.

Bobbio, Norberto (1989) 'The upturned utopia', *New Left Review,* 179.

Braudel, Fernand (1999) *Espansione europea e capitalismo (1450–1650).* Bologna: Il Mulino.

Brown Stephen J., William N. Goetzmann and James Park (1998) 'Hedge funds and the Asian currency crisis of 1997', NBER (National Bureau of Economic Research) Working Paper, 6427.

Club of Lisbon (coord. by Riccardo Petrella) (1995) *Limits to Competition.* Cambridge, MA: MIT Press.

—— (1997) 'Disarming Finance'. Mimeo.

George, Susan (1992) *The Debt Boomerang: How Third World Debt Harms Us All.* London: Pluto Press.

Gorz, André (1991) *Métamorphoses du travail: quête du sens: critique de la raison économique.* Paris: Galilée.

Hersh, Jacques (1993) *The USA and the Rise of East Asia since 1945: Dilemmas of the Postwar International Political Economy.* New York: St Martin's Press.

Hobsbawn, Eric J. (1994) *Age of Extremes – The Short Twentieth Century 1914–1991.* London: Pantheon.

Jomo K. S. (ed.) (1998) *Tigers in Trouble. Financial Governance, Liberalisation and Crises in East Asia.* London: Zed Books.

Krugman, Paul (1994), 'The myth of Asia's miracle', *Foreign Affairs,* 73 (6), pp. 62–78.

—— (1998) 'Asia: what went wrong', *Fortune,* 2 March.

Radelet, Steven and Jeffrey Sachs (1998) 'The East Asian Financial Crisis: Diagnosis, Remedies, Prospects', *Brookings Paper,* 28 (1), pp. 1–74.

Wade, Robert (1992), 'East Asia's economic success. conflicting perspectives, partial insights, shady evidence', *World Politics,* 44 (2), pp. 270–320.

World Bank (1998) *Social Consequences of the East Asian Financial Crisis.* New York: Oxford University Press.

Part II

Towards a Hegemonic Crisis of 'Neoliberal' Thinking?

FIVE

THE DEVELOPMENTAL IMPLICATIONS OF THE PACIFIC ASIAN CRISES

Chris Dixon

INTRODUCTION

The financial crises and subsequent recession that have affected most of the Pacific Asian economies since July 1997 have brought into question most of the established interpretation of the region's pattern of growth. This is particularly apparent with respect to the international agency neoliberal-based views of the region's development. At first sight the IMF conditionalities, public statements and the way they have been reported in the Western media appear to have strengthened the neoliberal position. However, this has involved a remarkable *volte face*. Almost overnight the Pacific Asian economies ceased to be a model for other Third World countries and became a warning of what *not* to do. This, by far the most abrupt and dramatic shift in the international agency views, combined with the increasing criticism of IMF prescriptions, is leading to serious questioning of the neoliberal approach.

CHANGING NEOLIBERAL VIEWS OF PACIFIC ASIAN DEVELOPMENT

The neoliberal 'counter revolution' in development theory (Toye 1987), which emerged from the early 1980s Third World debt-related crisis, placed national policy at the centre of the development agenda.[1] From this period the World Bank replaced its focus on poverty with an emphasis on structural adjustment (Mosley *et al.* 1991: 22–23). Integral to what became termed the 'neoliberal developmental orthodoxy' and the 'Washington Consensus on development', was the view that since all countries experience the same external environments, differences in economic performance must relate to internal policies and the way in which the external environment is dealt with. Under this approach the Pacific Asian economies were presented as the product of the adoption of export-oriented strategies behind which lay 'sensible' internal policies based on 'sound neoclassical principles' (Tsiang and Wu 1985: 329). Out of this, the view began to emerge that the successful Pacific Asian economies – Hong Kong, Singapore, South Korea and Taiwan – might be presented as a 'model' for the development of Third World economies as a whole. The resultant internal policy-based model had three components: limited government intervention in the economy, low level of price distortion, and an outward oriented strategy of export promotion. Other factors in the development of these economies, which tended to set them apart from the rest of Pacific Asia and more especially the Third World as whole, were treated as residuals (for a discussion, see Cumings 1987).

During the 1980s the three components of the neoliberal model were collapsed by the agencies into one simple requirement – 'get prices right'. It was asserted that there was a close relationship between countries with low levels of 'price distortion', outward-orientation and high levels of economic growth (World Bank 1983). This view has been questioned even with respect to the evidence presented in support of the position by the World Bank (1993: 301; see in particular Amsden 1989, 1994; Jenkins 1991, 1992; Singer 1988; Gore 1996; Kiely 1998: 78). Indeed, Amsden (1989: 139–155; 1994: 630–631) has suggested that an important element in Pacific Asian success was 'getting prices wrong' in agency terms. This was only part of a much wider range of criticisms of the neoliberal position on the part of those who judged the development of the Pacific Asian economies to be the result of high levels of state intervention (see for example Amsden 1989; Deyo 1987; Wade 1990; White and Wade 1988). These broadly developmental state views were principally based on the experience of Japan, Singapore, South Korea and Taiwan and were presented in their fullest and perhaps most coherent form by Wade (1990 – see the discussion by Putzel, Chapter 8 in this volume). However, it should be stressed that there is a wide range of views concerning the nature of the variously labelled interventionist, developmental or embedded state in Pacific Asia (see discussions in Appelbaum and Henderson 1992; Clapham 1996).

During the early 1980s, when the initial neoliberal perspective on Pacific Asia was being formulated, a number of the region's economies experienced a series of major economic crises. These were very different in form and origin from those affecting the region in 1997–98. The earlier crises were rooted in escalating balance-of-payments and budget deficits, and public sector debt, which were reflections principally of international recession and the collapse of non-oil commodity prices rather than the large-scale private sector debt that characterized the 1997–98 situation (for an overview, see Dixon 1995b). The only points of similarity between the two periods of crisis are the overvaluation of currencies because of their close link to the appreciating US dollar and the prescriptions of the IMF and World Bank, which stressed austerity measures, liberalization and a reduction in the level of state intervention.

The most seriously affected economies, Thailand and the Philippines, were during 1979–81 regarded as being on the verge of economic and, perhaps, political collapse. With the benefit of hindsight it is clear that in the case of Thailand these fears were greatly exaggerated. The Philippines was, however, plunged into a period of economic and political instability from which it only appeared to be emerging during the mid-1990s. A much shorter but extremely sharp crisis affected South Korea in 1980–81, when GDP declined by 6.7 per cent. During this period South Korea, Thailand and the Philippines resorted to assistance from the international agencies and became subject to formal structural adjustment programmes.

A second wave of crises occurred during 1985–86, and these seriously affected Indonesia,[2] Malaysia and Singapore. In part these crises reflected delayed reaction to the factors responsible for the 1980–81 crises, reinforced by the fall in oil prices. Hong Kong experienced a sharp fall in growth during 1985 and only Taiwan appeared to be little affected. With the exception of the Philippines, all the Pacific Asian economies soon returned to a pattern of rapid growth. However, this has to be seen in the context of rapid recovery in the regional and international economies accompanied by a degree of regional and national economic restructuring. The latter being particularly evident in the emergence of major manufacturing export sectors in Indonesia, Malaysia and Thailand. In regional terms there was a rapid internationalization of the production based in the established Asian NIEs (newly industrialized economies). This involved relocation of labour-intensive manufacturing activities into such lower-cost locations as Indonesia, Malaysia and Thailand. As a result of these developments, these economies were able to export themselves out of their crises through the rapid establishment of export-oriented manufacturing sectors. This process was accompanied and, to a degree, facilitated by the liberalization of trade and financial regimes in both the older NIEs, such as South Korea and the newer, such as Thailand. However, the liberalization of these economies from the mid-1980s onwards owed little to the formal structural adjustment programmes (see for example Dixon 1995b: 223–225; 1999a: 111–139; 1999b; Gills 1996).

During the early 1980s the international agencies appeared to be indulging in a remarkable level of 'double-think', advocating liberalization and reduction of state activity in South Korea while maintaining the view that these were *not* features of such successful Pacific Asian economies. However, from the late 1980s in response to the volume of criticisms and the increasing evidence of continuing state intervention in the NIEs, the neoliberal interpretation of their development underwent a measure of change.[3]

Publicly, the neoliberal image of the Pacific Asian economies was becoming increasingly difficult to maintain, in view of the increasing disputes between, in particular, the USA and Japan over trade restrictions and export credits (see Schoppa 1997 for an overview). In general the governments of Taiwan and South Korea went to considerable lengths to hide, or even deny, the extent of their state activities and market restrictions because of the fear of disputes with the USA, the imposition of countervailing tariffs and reduced access to markets (White and Wade 1988: 7–8). In contrast, during the 1980s the Japanese government began to assert the virtues of the Japanese approach as an alternative to the neoliberal perspective on development (see Wade 1996: 4, 6–14). From 1989 there was a very clear push by Japan to make the World Bank[4] take more notice of the East Asian experience of development (Wade 1995: 6–9; Berger and Beeson 1998: 496). This led in 1991 to the Japanese Ministry of Finance funding a study of Pacific Asian development, published in 1993 as *The East Asian Miracle* (World Bank 1993). There is considerable evidence that the report went through a series of substantial revisions as it worked its way up through the World Bank hierarchy, and the Japanese government was less than pleased with the result (Amsden 1994: 630; Wade 1996: 20–23, 28–29; Berger and Beeson 1998: 497).

Wade (1996: 14–17) argued that many officials within the World Bank regarded the Japanese model as a threat to the Bank's position for a number of reasons. These have been summarized by Berger and Beeson (1998: 497):

> In the first instances, the concessionary credit which was part of the Japanese approach to development aid undermined the attractiveness of the credit provided by the World Bank. Second, the emphasis on the importance of direct credit as an instrument of industrial policy which is characteristic of the Japanese approach is at odds with the Bank's overarching focus on financial liberalization. The upper echelons of the bank also feared that if they put their imprimatur on the development state model, it would undermine the Bank's own credit rating ... with the international money market and its authority in the international economic system more generally. For the Bank to change its attitude towards the Japanese model would also represent a major challenge to the USA, which has historically used the Bank in its overall projection of power and influence. From the point of view of the World Bank, the Japanese model also gave legitimacy to the 'interventionist impulses'which exist amongst governments and elites of the various countries which are beholden to the World Bank. Ultimately, for those looking out on the world from the commanding heights of the World Bank, the Japanese model was a 'systematic threat' to the status quo.

As finally published, *The East Asian Miracle* was a highly compromised and politicized document which, as Amsden (1994: 615) has concluded, reflected conflicts within the World Bank. The study examined the growth of what was termed the High-Performing Asian Economies (HPAEs): these comprised Japan and the four Asian NIEs together with Indonesia, Malaysia and Thailand. As with earlier studies, the focus was on internal policy with little attention devoted to international, historical or other factors, which are dismissed in three pages (out of 389). This was particularly problematic given the profound differences between the earlier generation of Asian NIEs and the new ones in South East Asia (see discussion by Putzel, Chapter 8 in this volume).

Inevitably, given the extremely varied nature of the HPAEs, the policy prescriptions tended towards the most general common denominators. The simple slogan of 'get prices right' was replaced by a broader-based exhortation to 'get the basics right'. This stressed the need for 'sound macroeconomic policy and stability'. Thus, the World Bank (1993: 2) emphasized that 'good macroeconomic policies have paid off in East Asia, and they will pay off in Africa'.

More significant than the broadening of the agencies' key development concept and slogan was a revision of the way in which internal policy and the state were viewed. Here, as Gore (1996: 100–101) has demonstrated, there was considerable sleight of hand. Once it was no longer tenable to maintain the fiction of the non-interventionist Pacific Asian states, it was necessary to subsume the activities of the states into the neoliberal paradigm. This was achieved by describing state intervention in the HPAEs as 'market friendly'.[5] Under this conceptualization the state intervenes reluctantly when there are failures of the market and subjects the intervention 'to the discipline of the international and domestic markets' (World Bank 1991a: 5). The intervention in the HPAEs was also depicted as replicating the operation of the market by the operation of a system of rewards and penalties. Such intervention resulted in a low level of distortion of markets and prices, a marked contrast to the results of state activities elsewhere in the Third World (World Bank 1993: 351). However, as was noted above, this view has been challenged, the Pacific Asian economies in many case having higher levels of price distortion than Latin American countries labelled as 'unsuccessful' by the World Bank.

While the existence of state intervention in the HPAEs was at last recognized by the World Bank, it was still very much played down. Indeed, it was asserted that there was no evidence that state activity in any way benefited Pacific Asian economic growth and perhaps in its absence this would have been ever greater (Page 1994: 624). Further, other Third World economies were specifically warned not to use the example of Pacific Asian state activity as an excuse for resistance to market reform (World Bank 1993: 6). There is even in this revised view of the Pacific Asian economies a remarkable ability to ignore or rule out inconvenient facts that do not sit well with the neoliberal position. As Amsden (1994: 630) has stressed, the bibliography in *The East Asian Miracle* is notable for the absence of a large number of references which presented a very different view of the Pacific Asian development. What is termed the 'revisionist view' of Wade (1989, 1990) and Amsden (1989) is presented with little comment in a little over a page (World Bank 1993: 83–84). Not surprisingly the whole study was heavily criticized (see in particular Amsden 1994; Gore 1996; Kiely 1998; Wade 1996).

The production of the *The East Asian Miracle* was accompanied by other changes in the neoliberal position. From 1989 increasing reference is made to 'good governance' in World Bank, IMF and related publications and loan conditionalities (see for example: World Bank 1989; 1991b; Williams and Young 1994). Indeed, the Washington Consensus came to comprise a complex of liberal capitalism, democracy and good governance. This development served to focus increased attention on the institutions of the state as instruments of effective policy formulation and implementation.[6]

In 1994 UNCTAD (1994: 25) went very much further than the other agencies in emphasizing the positive role of the state in Third World development as a whole. While for the World Bank, Berger and Beeson (1998: 498–499) suggest that a further stage in the 'discovery of the state' and the revision of neoliberalism so as to accommodate 'the state-led development trajectory of East Asia to neoclassical economics' was marked by *The Key to the Asian Miracle* (Campos and Root 1996). While this was not a World Bank publication, José Edgardo Campos was a co-author of *The East Asian Miracle.*

Between 1993 and 1996 there appears to have been a gradual shift towards the acceptance that governments and state institutions played a positive role in the development of the Pacific Asian economies. This development, which appears to have centred on the World Bank, has to be seen in the context of the increasing difficulty of ignoring the reality of Pacific Asian development in the light of increasing American bilateral demands for liberalization (Haggard and Cheng 1989; Bello 1994; Bello and Cunningham 1994; Sender *et al.* 1997: 96), the increasing economic strength and influence of Pacific Asia, and continued Japanese pressure for recognition of the 'Asian way' (described by Wade 1996).

A decisive further stage in what Berger and Beeson (1998: 497–501) termed the World Bank's role in the 'reinvention of liberalism', was marked by the publication of the 1997 *World Development Report.* Subtitled *The State in a Changing World,* this study's central tenet was that states should be made more efficient, for 'development without an effective state is impossible' (World Bank 1997: 25). Good governance is given equal weight with correct policies in explaining Pacific Asian economic success (ibid.: 33). Much was made of the role of the state in laying the foundations for development and accelerating it at all stages, including that of the USA during the late nineteenth century (ibid.: 21, 61). However, while these views may be seen as giving highly qualified support for the Pacific Asian approach (Berger and Beeson 1998: 500), they fall well short of endorsing state-led development and the various conceptions of the developmental state. Indeed, the Bank continues to depict the state in a strikingly apolitical manner which denies its social context, while stressing the importance of regulation and effective institutions (see the comments on IMF prescriptions below).[7] Thus, in the 1998 *World Development Report: Knowledge for Development,* repeated reference is made to the role of governments in regulating, supporting and indeed directly developing and disseminating knowledge. In this context there are repeated references to governments intervening where there has been 'market failure' and filling gaps left by the private sector. The concluding section of the report states:

> Recent development thinking has been based on the assumption that markets work well enough to ensure development and alleviate poverty. Our growing understanding of information constraints suggests that markets alone are often inadequate; societies also require policies and institutions to facilitate the acquisition, adoption, and dissemination of knowledge, and to mitigate information failures, especially as they affect the poor. This view implies an expanded mandate for public action. (World Bank 1998: 156)

As neoliberal views of Pacific Asian development encompassed a combination of domestic, regional and international changes, this meant that they were being applied to a widening group of increasingly heterogeneous states. Overall, until the 1997 crises, the Pacific Asian economies proved extraordinarily difficult to fit convincingly into any neoliberal paradigm (Gills and Philip 1996: 588). Given this, why was the effort maintained for so long? In addition to the internal concerns of the World Bank outlined above and the undoubtedly similar concerns of other key institutions, there were three interrelated factors. First, there was the neoliberal imperative that successful development could only take place within the neoliberal paradigm. Second, there was a need for a clear success case in order to promote the position. Third, and perhaps most importantly, the Cold War made it desirable to demonstrate the superiority of the free market. From a neoliberal perspective, the latter point was amply demonstrated by the apparent 'collapse of socialism' and moves towards the establishment of market economies in Eastern Europe, the PRC and Vietnam. In these changed circumstances the need to continue to present the Pacific Asian economies as the product of free-market activity with limited, but market-friendly state activity, was greatly diminished. Thus, the scene was set for a radical change in the neoliberal perspective on the Pacific Asian economies:

> The Asian model is no longer the showpiece of capitalism in the developing world, but is directly at odds with the ideology and interests of the world power [the USA]. In addition, the Asian model has proved vulnerable to the speculative financial flows that have multiplied since the collapse of the Bretton Woods system. (*The Nation*, 19 August 1998: A5)

Preston goes further, placing the debate surrounding the crisis firmly in the context of 'interregional post-Cold War and post-Bretton Woods adjustment', stressing that:

> The United States has long been a key player in Asia, and is committed to the pursuit of a global liberal market political-culture project. It seems clear, therefore, that the present situation will inevitably involve the countries of Pacific Asia in conflict with the United States. (Preston 1998: 149)

With the rapid spread of financial crises from July 1997 onwards, the international agencies and the Western media rapidly promoted a view of the Pacific Asian economies which depicted them as closed to foreign ownership and riddled with corruption and 'cronyism'. Overnight it was as if the view that they were open economies characterized by low levels of market-friendly state activity and limited distortions to the market had never existed:

> Corruption and crony capitalism have weakened solid economies built on years of hard work and prudent investment. Lax, outdated banking rules had left nations unprepared to handle a flood of foreign funds. In short, a potent mixture of globalization, poor governance and greed brought about the crisis that now engulfs the region. (*Far Eastern Economic Review*, 12 February 1998: 46–47)

As a result it was necessary to 'dismantle an economic system based on collusion between state, banks and business, and the restrictive markets' (IMF Managing Director Michel Camdessus – cited in *Far Eastern Economic Review*, 18 December 1997: 64).

It is striking that 'although pure free-market economists were anxious to deny any positive role to government policy in the "miracle", they were quick to blame government policies for the collapse' (Freeman 1998: 44).

The full impact of the crisis and this remarkable *volte face* on the neoliberal view of Pacific Asia and development in general has yet to emerge. At first sight the crisis and the blame widely attached to the region's states, appeared to re-establish the credibility of the earlier neoliberal position. However, as is discussed below, the crisis and its handling are leading to a marked divergence of views between the IMF and the World Bank, and splits within the neoliberal consensus as a whole.

The liberalization of the Pacific Asian economies

The changing neoliberal perception of the nature and lessons of Pacific Asian economic growth appears to have taken place with little attention to the internal changes that affected these countries from the early 1980s onwards. Paradoxically, as the neoliberal position changed to accommodate a positive role for the state in certain of the Pacific Asian countries, the continuation of rapid growth and structural change became linked to democratization, political reform, politicization of technocratic positions and liberalization. These changes, to a degree, undermined the developmental effectiveness of, in particular, the South Korean and Thai states (see Gills 1996; Dixon 1999a: 111–139, 1999b, 2001; Economist Intelligence Unit 1998; Thomson 1996).

Pressure for liberalization came from the international agencies and principal developed world trading partners (Haggard and Cheng 1989; Bello 1994; Bello and Cunningham 1994; Sender *et al.* 1997: 96). This was part of the broad agenda for the creation of an NLIEO (Neoliberal International Economic Order) through the elimination of barriers to the movement of goods, capital and enterprise (see Gore 1996: 85). In this process the IMF, the World Bank and other international agencies played a crucial role (Bergsten 1996). From the late 1980s the Pacific Asian economies became particular targets for Western and, in particular, American government and business interests, who pushed for liberalization of trade and financial regimes. Much of this took the form of increasingly heavy bilateral pressure on individual countries to relax restrictions (Haggard and Cheng 1989). As Gills (1996: 671) has noted, concessions on the part of such states as South Korea merely resulted in new and broader demands. This international pressure was undoubtedly a major factor in the moves to liberalize the Pacific Asian economies, and was, for example, frequently cited as the key reason for such developments by South Korean economic officials (Gills 1996: 671). However, changed international and domestic circumstances also created domestic pressure for liberalization.

In South Korea liberalization became a key element in the drive for internationalization and globalization of the economy, which was seen as vital to the continuation of the countries' successful economic development by both government and major business interests (ibid.: 667). The liberalization of the financial sector was also seen as an important part of the move towards accelerated growth of the tertiary sector. In Thailand this view was reinforced by the perceived need to maintain financial inflows of funds and grandiose plans on the part of the government and the Bank of Thailand for Bangkok to became a major regional financial centre and the 'Singapore of the mainland' (Handley 1992).

Closely interlinked with the development of national policies that favoured liberalization was the emergence of similar views within elements of domestic capital. In South Korea the *chaebols* and the government came to share a similar globalizing agenda. Within Thai domestic capital, the pressure for liberalization has to be seen in terms of the overall process of democratization and rapid manufacturing-based economic growth, which from the early 1980s gave increasingly direct political power to business interests.

During the period 1980–85 the dominant interest of Thai business was served by resistance to structural adjustment and, in many cases, increased levels of protectionism.

From this period the acceleration of foreign investment-driven manufacturing and export-led growth placed increasing economic power in the hands of interests, that while often concerned about protection from foreign and domestic competition, wished to see significant liberalization, particularly of the financial sector. As a result, between 1988 and 1995, Thailand experienced a period of rapid, though highly selective, liberalization (Dixon 1999b, 2001). The interests of capital came to dominate the Thai state, politicizing key technocratic positions within the Ministry of Finance and the Bank of Thailand, which had previously imposed conservative financial management and regulated the banking system. This politicizing of the country's financial management was accompanied by the election of a series of extremely unstable coalition governments which encountered increasing difficulty in decision-making, policy formulation and implementation. Thus, from the mid-1980s there was a general undermining of the developmental effectiveness of the Thai state (Dixon 1999b, 2001).

It appears that the crisis-stricken Pacific Asian economies grew rapidly and successfully with generally high levels of state activity, controls and market distortion until liberalization undermined what they had come to do well. There is however the possibility that from the early 1980s onwards liberalization was *necessary* in order to *maintain* growth. Undoubtedly it was seen as such by national governments and elements within domestic capital. Certainly a case can be made for this in terms of the export of capital from the old NIEs and its importing into the new. If we allow this connection, then there is a very real contradiction which resulted in the economies concerned becoming more vulnerable to financial crises at a time when changes in the global economy were making these much more likely and far-reaching in their effects.

THE IMPLICATIONS OF THE IMF PRESCRIPTIONS

Prior to the crises, Indonesia, South Korea and Thailand had macroeconomic indicators which, in international agency terms, were regarded as 'sound'. Indeed, during 1996 the economic performance and macroeconomic management of all three economies had been endorsed by the IMF and/or the World Bank (see material cited in Bullard *et al.* 1998a: 506, 512, 519; Sachs 1997: 17). Little or no concern was expressed over exchange rates, private sector borrowing or declining export growth. Indeed, the IMF appears to have regarded the high levels of short-term private sector borrowing as an acceptable feature of the market (see for example citations in Chandrasekhar and Ghosh 1998; Ghosh *et al.* 1996). Thus, once the crisis hit, the IMF ignored the overborrowing of the private sector and began applying uniform structural adjustment-like prescriptions aimed at restoring macroeconomic imbalances and public sector debt.

In this respect the IMF appears to have been seriously out of touch with the reality of the Pacific Asian situation. Many doubted 'whether the IMF actually recognized the novel elements of the crisis and their implications' and persisted in applying 'old medicines for a new disease' (Jomo 1998: 19; see also Chandrasekhar and Ghosh 1998: 74–78; Bullard *et al.* 1998b: 85–96). One commentator has likened the IMF conditionalities 'to telling a victim of a road accident that regular exercise and a change in diet would be good for them' (*Far Eastern Economic Review*, 12 February 1998: 52). Others have been much more critical, suggesting that the IMF policies magnified the crises, deepening and prolonging the subsequent recessions (see for example Feldstein 1998; Sachs 1997).[8] Wade and Veneroso (1998: 5–7) go further, arguing that these critics have seriously underestimated the long-term damage that the IMF's policies have inflicted on the Pacific Asian economies.

The IMF prescriptions for Pacific Asia also went well beyond the established structural adjustment programmes. Substantial and *immediate* liberalization was required, particularly of controls over foreign ownership.[9] Here there was a marked departure from earlier conditionalities under which liberalization was seen as part of longer-term development. Additionally, there were extensive criticisms of individual regimes, drawing particular attention to corruption and 'cronyism'[10] and, in the case of Indonesia, emphasizing the need for changes in government. Overall, Feldstein (1998: 24) likened the conditions imposed on Indonesia and Thailand to the comprehensive reform programme formulated for Russia.

Cronyism and corruption became particular targets for the IMF and indeed many commentators on the crisis. However, this does not seem to be based on any analysis of what is meant by these terms in the Pacific Asian context. The link between economic crisis, cronyism and corruption has been made most of with respect to Indonesia. Here the scale of corruption and cronyism and their concentration around the Suharto family represents an extreme situation by any standards. However, it is difficult to substantiate any causal relationship between corruption and economic crisis. Having said this, many of the formal and informal linkages between business and the agencies of many (if not all) of the Pacific Asian states concerned *can* be labelled in this way. This is to overlook the often vital developmental role that such interrelationships played, particularly in the close capital regimes that characterized many of the region's economies until the late 1980s and early 1990s (see Putzel, Chapter 8 in this volume). In addition, it is worth reiterating Milton Friedman's comments on the extent of cronyism and financial malpractice and scandals in the developed economies (interview in the *Far Eastern Economic Review,* 26 May 1998: 78).

For some commentators the leading role that the IMF has taken in attempting to manage the Pacific Asian crises has resulted in it going well beyond its established terms of reference (Bullard *et al.* 1998a: 540; Unger 1996: 23; Wade and Veneroso 1998: 11–12). This has been particularly commented on with respect to making governments responsible for private sector debt, the demands for the removal of restrictions on foreign ownership, a change of government in Indonesia and the break-up of the South Korean *chaebols* (see for example Bullard *et al.* 1998a: 526–528).

Whilst during the public-sector-related debt crises of the 1980s and the 1994 Mexican crisis, emphasis was placed on the use of international funds to service commercial debts, since 1997 the IMF has expected the Pacific Asian governments to accept responsibility for private sector commitments. In earmarking funds to finance balance-of-payments deficits, the IMF was effectively ensuring that the debt service commitments would be met. Such use of IMF funds and prescriptions to protect the interests of international banks based in Europe, Japan and the USA and, to a degree, absolve them from the consequences of their unwise lending policies[11] has resulted in widespread criticism (see for example Atkinson 1998: 17; Bullard *et al.* 1998a: 527; Dixon 2000: 9–10; UNCTAD 1999: vii; Wolf 1997). However, it is important to stress that some consider that the IMF has also protected Pacific Asian governments from the full consequences of their own actions and their failure to provide adequate financial regulation (see for example Meltzer 1998). Much of this type of criticism comes from the American right, which considers that the IMF has not sufficiently promoted either liberalization or, more significantly, American interests in Pacific Asia.[12]

In both Thailand and South Korea as a direct result of agreement with the IMF, there have been moves to remove restrictions on foreign ownership and takeovers. From December 1998 foreign companies were permitted to purchase up to 55 per cent of South Korean concerns and from December 1999 they were permitted to acquire 100 per cent. Similar measures have been implemented in Thailand. Overall, the pressure for rapid liberalization of rules and restrictions on ownership, trade, finance and markets is to give Western and Japanese business the sort of access that they have long wished to gain to such economies as South Korea. These demands, when taken with the pressure for the public sector to assume responsibility for private sector debt, has led to speculation on the emergence of an IMF–Wall Street axis and the extent to which the IMF policies on opening economies to foreign ownership are linked to American and Japanese business interests (Bello *et al.* 1998: 50–51; Bullard *et al.* 1998a: 525; Wade and Veneroso 1998: 20) However, the IMF's promotion of liberalization is nothing new, and as Wade and Veneroso (1998: 20) have noted, in terms of its result there is perhaps little to choose between explanations based on conspiracy and those based on interest groups.

The IMF prescriptions for the Pacific Asian economies have been closely linked with the need to develop the necessary regulatory and decision-making processes. Indeed much was made of the need for reforms that will eliminate cronyism and corruption and implement 'the golden rule of transparency', 'good governance' and 'best practice' in financial regulation developed in the West.[13] While it is difficult to dispute the view that there *are* issues of regulation, decision-making and implementation, yet there is little clear indication of how in practice these areas will be addressed, beyond the usual reference to 'capacity building'. The development of the necessary regulatory and institutional frameworks appears to be treated by the IMF as an exercise in administrative reform. This reflects the neoliberal conceptualization of the state which denies its social basis and neglects the difficulty of changing the regulatory *form* without change in the state's social *content.* There appears to be no point of contact with even the World Bank's revised view of the role of the state in the development process outlined earlier in this chapter.

The IMF failed to predict the crisis; in fact it endorsed the economic health of the most seriously affected countries and then dramatically reversed its views:

> The IMF arrived in Thailand in July with the ostentatious declaration that all was wrong and that fundamental surgery was needed ... [when] the ink was not dry on the IMF's 1997 annual report that gave Thailand and its neighbours high marks on economic management. (Sachs 1997: 17)

This, together with the apparent initial failure of the IMF to grasp the nature of the crisis and the application of what many have seen as inappropriate policies, has led to widespread criticism and has seriously damaged the Fund's international standing. Adverse comments on the IMF's policies have come increasingly not only from its established critics and recipients of its programmes (see for example Oxfam 1998; Khor 1998), but also from within what had previously been seen as the neoliberal consensus (Bello 1998: 50; 'The fight for the fund', *The Economist*, 21 February 1998; 57–58; 'Fund under fire', *Far Eastern Economic Review*, 14 May 1998: 60–65). These have been summarized as

> including former IMF employee and director of the Harvard Institute for International development, World Bank chief economist, Joseph Stiglitz, solid, conservative journals such as *The Economist* and the *Financial Times*, Republicans and Democrats in the US Congress, and even bone-dry neoliberals such as former US President Ronald Reagan's chief economic adviser Martin Feldstein as well Milton Friedman of the Chicago School. (Bullard *et al.* 1998a: 538)

Particularly striking are the signs of increasing discord between the IMF and the World Bank over both the immediate policies imposed in Pacific Asia and the wisdom of rapid financial liberalization as witnessed, in particular, by the comments of Joseph Stiglitz (1998)[14] and the debates at the 1998 IMF/World Bank annual meeting (see Keenan and Sender 1998). In Thailand the discord between the IMF and the World Bank appears to be reflected in the latter's willingness to finance government programmes which have had their funding cut at the behest of the IMF. However, against this has to be set the World Bank's apparent agreement with the IMF over policy towards Indonesia.

The dissent over and within the neoliberal position was given added weight in September 1998 by Malaysian moves to impose stringent controls on capital movements.[15] This, as Bello (1998) has noted, resulted in the predictable criticisms from the IMF.[16] However, the Malaysian measures should be seen in the context of increasing concerns over the dangers to all countries posed by complete freedom of capital movements (UNDP 1999: 6) and the view of such persons as Joseph Stiglitz that financial markets should be controlled (cited in Bullard *et al.* 1998a: 539). There are signs of increasing pragmatism amongst policy-makers that appear to be undermining the IMF position (see for example on Thailand, *Far Eastern Economic Review*, 10 December 1998: 62).

Apart from the disagreements over the policies, questions have been raised over the extent to which the Fund has exceeded its brief, the interests that it has come to serve, and the secrecy that shrouds its activities. To be fair the Fund has admitted that in the early stages of the crisis it made mistakes, has had second thoughts on the wisdom of rapid financial liberalization (Garten 1999: 82) and has softened its approach to the stricken economies (see for example for Thailand, *Far Eastern Economic Review*, 14 May 1998: 58, and for Indonesia, *Far Eastern Economic Review*, 11 June 1998: 54).[17] However, these admissions have done little to deflect either criticisms or demands for reform of the Fund (see for example Feldstein 1998). In this respect the Fund's fortunes have undergone a dramatic change from those it enjoyed in the early stages of the crisis, when it was able to advocate that it should play a greatly enhanced role in a completely restructured international financial system (see for example the address by the IMF Director Michel Camdessus, Royal Institute of International Affairs, 7 April 1998).

CONCLUSION

The crises of the early and mid-1980s and the subsequent periods of structural adjustment indicated that the Pacific Asian economies were extremely vulnerable to economic instability. This was forgotten in the rapid recovery and subsequent rapid growth of all except the Philippines, and the spreading of the 'miracle' into Indonesia, Malaysia and Thailand during the late 1980s and into the PRC and Vietnam during the early 1990s. From the mid-1980s, continued rapid economic growth, structural change and internationalization were accompanied by democratization and liberalization of trade and financial regimes. The result, particularly in South Korea and Thailand, was to open the economies to increasingly volatile international trading and, more especially, financial conditions. At the same time the changes tended to reduce the developmental effectiveness of the South Korean and Thai states. The criticism of these countries' macroeconomic management, financial regulation, policy formulation and implementation by such agencies as the IMF seems to have taken place with no consideration of the changes that have occurred in these economies and their places in the regional and international economies. Indeed, the IMF prescriptions appear to have been formulated with little regard to the past or present realities of Pacific Asian development or the changes within neoliberal discourse.

Under prevailing international conditions, further liberalization may result in the economies concerned becoming more vulnerable to externally induced crisis and having less control over, and less ownership of, their economies. Increased foreign ownership could result in profits flowing increasingly to American, European and Japanese companies, thus further undermining the long-term basis of Pacific Asian growth. However, the reality of the state structures in the region are such that many governments will find it extremely difficult to implement fully the required reforms. Indeed, despite international pressure, the pace of reform has been slow with increasing signs of resistance from entrenched interests (see for example Dixon 2001 on Thailand). In addition, the anticipated 'firesale' of Pacific Asian assets has not developed and the expansion of foreign ownership has been limited. With respect to the implementation of reforms, the situation is very similar to that which prevailed during the structural adjustment period of the early 1980s. Then, many of the region's governments were 'caught in a bind' and unable to engage in more than a very limited degree of the required restructuring (Robison *et al.* 1987: 11–12). For the agencies, the failure to rapidly implement reforms reflects a lack of commitment to the conditionalities rather than the social context in which the governments are operating. Continued pressure, where combined with a failure of economic recovery, may precipitate political change, the direction of which will be far from certain. It is difficult to square the pious hopes of democratization with the sort of strong governance that the IMF conditions require. Indeed, such economies as Indonesia could be pushed into the sort of long-term economic and political chaos that characterized the Philippines from the 1979–81 debt-related crisis onwards.

However, as in the early 1980s, recovery could well take place in most of the economies without the full implementation of the reform programmes. Indeed, this increasingly looks to be the likely scenario. While the lives of large numbers of people in the region have been dramatically and perhaps permanently damaged, there are no signs that the crisis will form a major historical break. There is to date no evidence to suggest that despite ongoing economic and political problems, even the most seriously affected economies will revert to the Third World 'norm'. On the other hand, there is no indication that, despite the

IMF conditionalities and the continued pressure from the West in general and the USA in particular, the Pacific Asian region will be transformed into the advocated open liberal form. For while the ruling elites face considerable problems of adjustment, there are few signs of shifts in their composition or developmental ideologies. Indeed, all the indications are that liberal reforms will continue to be piecemeal and pragmatic rather than wholesale. Where major political interests are involved, liberalization will continue to be resisted.

Whatever the eventual outcomes of the 1997–98 crises, the image and understanding of Pacific Asian development will have undergone a fundamental change. However, much more significant will be the long-term impact on the neoliberal perspective on development. It may well be that the Pacific Asian crisis proves to be the catalyst for a major and long-overdue paradigm shift towards the establishment of increased national control over trade and financial regimes.

Kwon described *The East Asian Miracle* as

> almost a text book example of neo-classicists visibly confused but too proud to admit their failure – having been so quick to blame government for economic failure in the past, they are now reluctant to admit a positive role for government in a successful economy. (Kwon 1994: 635)

The changes in the neoliberal perspective and the divisions that have emerged since the publication of the *East Asian Miracle* and, more especially, with the Pacific Asian crisis, have made this disarray even more evident. Particularly significant are the split between the IMF and the World Bank[18] and the debate over the wisdom of financial liberalization. Bello has gone so far as to suggest that there will be a major shift in global development policy because:

> The Asian financial crisis has simply served to underline the fact that the theory about the net benefits of globalization has little or no empirical backing. As with all ideologies, it was faith parading as science. Indeed, history, cunning as usual, appeared to derive a perverse pleasure from contradicting at almost every turn the Benthamite pronouncements ... Those free markets and the free flow of capital would result in the greatest good for the greatest number. (Bello 1998: 50)

NOTES

1 This shift has to be seen in the context of changes in international political economy, the seemingly intractable economic problems facing North America and Europe and the related political shift marked by the elections of Margaret Thatcher and Ronald Reagan.

2 Indonesia came to an agreement with the international agencies over a funding package and a schedule of reforms that amounted to a programme of informal structural adjustment.

3 This also has to be seen in the wider context of developments and divisions within neoliberal discourse as a whole, particularly with respect to institutionalism and rational choice (see for example the discussions in Törnquist 1999: 87–103; Downing and King 1996: 116).

4 Japan was the second largest shareholder in the Bank after the USA.

5 This term had already been used by the World Bank in the 1991 *World Development Report*.

6 This has to be seen in the context of broader changes on neoliberalism (see note 10).

7 For a fuller discussion of the 1997 World Bank report, see Boer 1998 and Törnquist 1999: 99–101.
8 The 'overkill' and far from fully initial approach of the IMF towards the Indonesian, South Korean and Thai crises may well make other countries extremely reluctant to call in any of the international agencies until they feel that there is no alternative. This attitude seems to be evident in the case of Malaysia.
9 Dornbusch (1997: 26) suggested that a rapid increase in foreign participation would be vital to the processes of 'clean up' and restructuring because 'Neither the government nor the Korean business community can do the job.' However, against this has to be set the lack of any evidence that supports the view that financial and other sectors of economies become better regulated and operate more effectively for having appreciable foreign participation.
10 This term 'cronyism' has been widely and indiscriminately applied to the crisis-affected countries. It was first coined to describe the extreme situation that existed in the Philippines during the Marcos period. However, it has become generalized to apply to any instances of 'cosy' relationships between the agents of capital and politicians.
11 For views on the irresponsible nature of much of the international lending to the Pacific Asian private sectors and the forces behind it see, for example, Chandrasekhar and Ghosh 1998: 67; Krugman 1998; Persaud 1999; Raghavan 1997: 12; UNCTAD 1999: 56.
12 For a selection and summary of virulent anti-IMF statements and reports orginating in the USA see: Policy.com Issue of the Week, 2 February 1998: IMF Funding at http://www.policy.com/issuewk/98/020298d.html.
13 This overlooks both very great variety of regulatory practices and institutional frameworks found in Western economies and the increasing difficulty of regulating the rapidly globalizing financial sector. As Milton Friedman has commented, the European and American financial sectors have in recent years had a series of crises and scandals some of which can be blamed on inadequate regulation, malpractice and cronyism (interview reported in the *Far Eastern Economic Review*, 26 May1998: 78).
14 See, for example, speech in Helsinki, 7 January 1998, cited by Bullard *et al.* 1998: 539.
15 This parallels those imposed by Chile during 1994 following a serious currency crisis. The apparent success of these measures in restoring financial stability and insulating the economy from subsequent volatile international movements has been quietly ignored.
16 However, at the 1998 annual meeting of the IMF and the World Bank, the IMF did concede that national controls over financial flows could play a short-term role, provided that they were not seen as alternatives to reform (Keenan and Sender 1998: 12).
17 Against these changes has to be set the complete defence of the IMF's policies by the Funds Deputy Director Stanley Fischer (1998).
18 This has come to include policy towards the HIPC (highly indebted poor countries) and attitudes towards the levels of public expenditure (see, for example, Elliott 1999).

References

Amsden, A. H. (1989) *Asia's Next Industrial Giant: South Korea and Late Industrialization.* New York: Oxford University Press.

—— (1994) 'Why isn't the whole world experimenting with the East Asian model of development? Review of the *East Asian Miracle*', *World Development*, 22: 627–633.

Appelbaum, R. P. and J. Henderson (1992) 'Situating the state in the East Asian development process', in R. P. Appelbaum and J. Henderson (eds), *States and Development in the Asian Pacific Rim.* Newbury Park, CA: Sage, pp. 1–26.

Atkinson, M. (1998) 'No bargains for Korea in this sale', *Guardian*, 15 January: 17.

Bello, W. (1994) *Dark Victory.* London: Pluto Press.

—— (1998) 'Breaking with faith', *Far Eastern Economic Review*, 24 September, p. 50.

—— and S. Cunningham (1994) 'Trade warfare and regional integration in the Pacific: the USA, Japan, and the Asian NICs', *Third World Quarterly*, 15, pp. 435–458.

—— S. Cunningham and Li Kheng Poh (1998) *A Siamese Tragedy: Development and Disintegration in Modern Thailand.* London: Zed.

Berger, M. T. and M. Beeson (1998) 'Lineages of liberalism and miracles: the World Bank, the East Asian trajectory and the international development debate', *Third World Quarterly*, 19, pp. 487–504.

Bergsten, C. F. (1996) 'Globalising foreign trade', *Foreign Affairs*, 73, pp. 24–48.

Boer, L. (1998) 'The state in a changing world', *Third World Quarterly*, 19: 935–940.

Bullard, N., W. Bello, and K. Malhotra (1998a) 'Taming the tigers: the IMF and the Asian crisis', *Third World Quarterly*, 19, pp. 505–555.

—— (1998b) 'Taming the tigers: the IMF and the Asian crisis', in Jomo K. S. (ed.), *Tigers In Trouble: Financial Governance, Liberalization and Crises in East Asia.* London: Zed, pp. 85–132.

Campos, J. and H. L. Root (1996) *The Key to The Asian Miracle: Making Shared Growth Credible.* Washington: The Brookings Institute.

Caufield, C. (1997) *The Masters of Illusion: the World Bank and the Poverty of Nations.* London: Macmillan.

Chandrasekhar, C. P. and J. Ghosh (1998) 'Hubris, hysteria, hope: the political economy of crisis and response in Southeast Asia', in Jomo K. S. (ed.), *Tigers In Trouble: Financial Governance, Liberalization and Crises in East Asia.* London: Zed, pp. 63–84.

Chen, E. K. Y. (1979) *Hyper-Growth in Asian Economies: a Comparative Study of Hong Kong, Japan, Korea, Singapore and Taiwan.* London: Macmillan.

Clapham, C. (1996) 'Introduction', *Third World Quarterly*, 17, pp. 591–602.

Cumings, B. (1987) 'The origins and development of Northeast Asian political economy: industrial sectors, product cycles, and political consequences', in F. C. Deyo (ed.), *The Political Economy of the New Asian Industrialization.* Ithaca, NY: Cornell University Press, pp. 44–83.

Deyo, F. C. (ed.) (1987) *The Political Economy of the New Asian Industrialization.* Ithaca, NY: Cornell University Press.

Dixon, C. (1995a) 'Origins, sustainability and lessons from Thailand's economic growth', *Contemporary Southeast Asia*, 17: 38–52.

—— (1995b) 'Structural adjustment in comparative perspective: lessons from Pacific Asia', in D. Simon *et al.* (eds) *Structurally adjusted Africa.* London: Pluto, pp. 202–28.

—— (1999a) *Thailand: Uneven Development and Internationalisation.* London: Routledge.

—— (1999b) 'The Thai economic crisis: some internal causes'. Paper presented at the AAG Annual Conference, Honolulu, 23–26 March.

—— (2000) 'The Pacific Asian economic crises: private sector debt, public responsibility and the role of the IMF'. Paper presented at the Developing Areas Research Group meeting on Debt and the Developing World in the New Millennium, University of Sussex, 7 January.

—— (2001) 'The Thai economic crisis: the internal perspective', *Geoforum*, 32: pp. 47–60.

Dornbusch, R. (1997) 'A bailout won't do the trick in Korea', *Business Week*, 8 December: 26.

Downing, K. and D. King (eds) (1996) *Preferences, Institutions and Rational Choice.* Oxford: Clarendon Press,.

—— (1998) 'The custodian state and social change – creating growth without welfare', in J. Dragsbaek Schmidt, J. Hersh and N. Fold (eds*), Social Change in Southeast Asia.* Harlow: Longman, pp. 40–59.

Economist Intelligence Unit (1998) *Financing development in Thailand*, London.

Elliot, L. (1999) 'Now plan for real poverty relief', *Guardian,* 26 April, p. 21.

Feldstein, M. (1998) 'Refocusing the IMF', *Foreign Affairs*, 77, pp. 20–33.

Fischer, S. (1998a) 'In defence of the IMF', *Foreign Affairs*, 77, pp. 103–106.

—— (1998b) 'The Asian crisis: a view from the IMF'. Text of a speech given by the First Deputy Director of the International Monetary Fund at the Midwinter Conference of the Bankers' Association for Foreign Trade, 22 January, Washington, DC.

Forbes, D. (1993) 'What's in it for us? Images of Pacific Asian development', in C. Dixon and D. Drakakis-Smith (eds), *Economic and Social Development in Pacific Asia.* London: Routledge, pp. 43–62.

Freeman, C. (1998) 'The East Asian crisis, technical change and the world economy', *Review of International Political Economy*, 5 (3), pp. 393–409.

Friedman, M. and R. Friedman (1980) *Free to Choose: a Personnel Statement.* New York: Harcourt Brace Jovanovich.

Garten, J.E. (1999) 'Lessons for the next financial crisis', *Foreign Affairs*, 78, pp. 76–92.

Ghosh, J., A. Sen and C. P. Chandrasekhar (1996) 'Southeast Asian economies: miracle or meltdown?', *Economic and Political Weekly*, 12–19 October.

Gills , B. K. (1996) 'Economic liberalisation in South Korea in the 1990s: a coming of age or a case of graduation blues', *Third World Quarterly*, 17, pp. 667–688.

—— and G. Philip (1996) 'Editorial: Towards convergence in development policy? challenging the "Washington Consensus" and restoring the historicity of development trajectories', *Third World Quarterly*, 17, pp. 585–591.

Gore, C. (1996) 'Methodological nationalism and East Asian Industrialisation', *European Journal of Development Research*, 8, pp. 77–122.

Haggard, S. and T. Cheng (1989) 'The new bilateralism: East Asian NICs in American foreign economic policy', in S. Haggard and T. Cheng (eds), *Pacific Dynamics: the International Politics of Industrial Change.* Boulder, CO: Westview Press, pp. 305–330.

Handley, P. (1992) 'Banking on Bangkok', *Far Eastern Economic Review*, 16 January, pp. 34–46.

Henderson, J., B. Eccleston and G. Thompson (1998) 'Deciphering the Asian East crisis', *Renewal*, 6, pp. 73–86.

Jenkins, R. (1991) 'The political economy of industrialisation: a comparison of Latin American and East Asian newly industrialising countries', *Economic Development and Cultural Change*, 22, pp. 197–231.

—— (1992) '(Re-) interpreting Brazil and South Korea', in T. Hewitt, H. Johnson and D. Wield (eds), *Industrialisation and Development.* Oxford: Oxford University Press, pp. 167–198.

Johnson, C. (1982) *MITI and the Japanese miracle: the growth of industrial policy, 1925–1975.* Stanford: Stanford University Press.

Jomo K. S. (1998) 'Introduction: financial goverance, liberalization and crises in East Asia, in Jomo K. S. (ed.), *Tigers in Trouble: Financial Governance, Liberalization and Crises in East Asia.* London: Zed, pp. 1–23.

Keenan, F. and H. Sender (1998) 'Little help in sight', *Far Eastern Economic Review,* 15 October 1998, pp. 10–13.

Kerkvliet, B. J. Tria and D. J. Porter (1995) 'Rural Vietnam in rural Asia', in *idem* (eds), *Vietnam's Rural Transformation.* Boulder: Westview and Singapore: Institute of Southeast Asian Studies, pp. 65–96.

Khor, M. (1998) 'A poor grade for the IMF', *Far Eastern Economic Review,* 15 January: 29.

Kiely, R. (1998) 'The World Bank and development', *Capital and Class,* 64, pp. 63–88.

Koppel, B. (1997) 'Is Asia emerging or submerging? Perspectives on the future of the Asian Miracle', *NIAS nytt,* 4 (December), pp. 5–10.

Krugman, P. (1998) 'What happened in Asia?', http://web.mit.edu./krugman/www, January.

Kwan, C. H. (1994) *Economic Interdependence in Asia-Pacific: towards a Yen Bloc.* London: Routledge.

Kwon, J. (1994) 'The East Asian challenge to neoclassical orthodoxy', *World Development,* 22: 635–644

Label, L. (1998) 'The myths of the Asian crisis', *Asiaweek,* 1 April, pp. 28–29.

Lal, D. (1980) 'A liberal international economic order: the international monetary system and economic development', *Princeton Essays in Economics and Finance,* 129.

Livingston, I. (1997) 'Industrial development in Laos: new policies and new possibilities', in Myra Than and L. H. Tan (eds.), *The Challenge of Economic Transition in the 1990s.* Singapore: Institute of Southeast Asian Studies, Singapore, pp. 128–135.

Meltzer, A. H. (1998) 'Moral hazard goes global: the IMF, Mexico and Asia', *American Enterprise Institute,* January.

Montes, M. F. (1998) *The Currency Crisis in Southeast Asia.* Singapore: Institute of Southeast Asian Studies.

Mosley, P., J. Harrington and J. Toye (1991) *Aid and Power: the World Bank and Policy-Based Lending. Volume 1, Analysis and Proposals.* London: Routledge.

Oxfam International Briefing (1998) 'The real Asian crisis', April, Oxford.

Page, J. M. (1994) 'The East Asian Miracle: an introduction', *World Development,* 22, pp. 615–625.

—— and P. A. Petri (1993) 'Productivity change and strategic growth policy in the Asian miracle', World Bank Staff Paper, Washington.

Persaud, A. (1999)) 'Mechanisms for avoiding the next currency crisis'. Paper preented at the Conference on Currency Crises, 15 November. London Guildhall University.

Praipol Khoomsup (1993) 'Energy policy', in P. Warr (ed.), *The Thai Economy in Transition.* Cambridge: Cambridge University Press, pp. 296–324.

Preston, P. W. (1998) 'Reading the Asian crisis; history, culture and institutional truths', *Contemporary Southeast Asia,* 20, pp. 241–258.

Raghavan, C. (1997) 'BIS banks keep shovelling funds to Asia despite warnings', *Third World Economics,* 177, pp. 12–13.

Robison, R., R. Higgott and K. Hewison (1987) 'Crisis in economic strategy in the 1980s; the factors a work', in R. Robison, R. Higgott and K. Hewison (eds), *South*

East Asia in the 1980s: the Politics of Economic Crisis. Sydney: Allen and Unwin, pp. 1–15.

Rodan, G. (1989) *The Political Economy of Singapore's Industrialization.* London: Macmillan.

Rosenberger, L. R. (1997) 'Southeast Asia's currency crisis', *Contemporary Southeast Asian*, 19, pp. 223–251.

Sachs, J. (1997) 'The IMF and the Asian flu', *The American Perspective*, March–April, pp. 16–21.

Schmidt, J. D. (1997) 'The challenge from South East Asia: social forces between equity and growth', in C. Dixon and D. Drakakis-Smith (eds), *Uneven Development in South East Asia.* Aldershot: Ashgate, pp. 21–44.

Schoppa, L. J. (1997) *Bargaining with Japan: What American Pressure Can and Cannot Do.* New York: Columbia University Press.

Sender, H., S. Jayasankaran and J. McBeth, (1997) 'Not a happy bunch: World Bank/IMF meeting wasn't the party expected', *Far Eastern Economic Review*, 17 October, pp. 69–70.

Singer, H. (1988) 'The World Development Report 1987 on the blessing of outward orientation: a necessary correction', *Journal of Development Studies*, 24, pp. 125–136.

Stiglitz, J. (1998) 'More instruments and broader goals: moving toward the post-Washington Consensus', WIDER annual lectures, Helsinki, UNU/WIDER.

Thomson, M. (1996) 'Late industrialization, late democratization; developmental states in Asia-Pacific', *Third World Quarterly*, 17, pp. 625–647.

Thurow, L. (1992) *Head to Head. The Eoming Economic Battle between Japan, Europe and America.* New York: Morrow.

Tonelson, A. (1994) 'Beating back predatory trade', *Foreign Affairs*, 73, pp. 123–135.

Törnquist, O. (1999) *Politics and Development.* London: Sage.

Toye, J. (1987) *Dilemmas of Development.* Oxford: Blackwell.

Tsiang, S. and R. Wu (1985) 'Foreign trade and investment as boosters of take off: the experience of the four Asian NICs', in W. Galenson (ed.), *Foreign Trade and Investment.* Madison: University of Winsconsin Press, pp. 320–343.

UNCTAD (1994) *Trade and Development Report.* Geneva: UN.

—— (1999) *Trade and Development Report, 1998.* Geneva: UN.

UNDP (1998) *Human Development Report.* New York: Oxford University Press.

Unger, R. M. (1996)'The really new Bretton Woods', in M. Uzan (ed.), *The Financial System under Stress: an Architecture for the New World Economy.* London: Routledge, pp. 11–25.

Wade, R. (1989) 'What can economics learn from East Asian success?', *Annals of the American Academy of Political Science*, 505, pp. 68–79.

—— (1990) *Governing the Market; Economic Theory and the Role of Government in East Asia.* Princeton, NJ: Princeton University Press.

—— (1996) 'Japan, the World Bank, and the art of paradigm maintenance; the East Asian miracle in political perspective', *New Left Review*, 217: 3–36.

—— and F. Veneroso (1998) 'The Asian crisis; the high debt model versus the Wall Street–Treasury–IMF complex', *New Left Review*, 228, pp. 3–23.

Watkins, K. (1998) *Economic Growth with Equity.* Oxford: Oxfam.

White, G. (ed.), (1988) *The Developmental State.* London: Macmillan.

—— and R. Wade (1988) 'Developmental states and markets in East Asia: an introduction', in G. White (ed.), *The Developmental State.* London: Macmillan, pp. 1–29.

Williams, D. and T. Young 1994) 'Governance, the World Bank and liberal theory', *Political Studies*, 42, pp. 84–100.

Wolf, M. (1997) 'Foolish investors should not be bailed out', *Financial Times*, 16 December, p. 14.

World Bank (1983) *World Development Report.* New York: Oxford University Press.

—— (1989) *Sub-Saharan Africa: from Crisis to Sustainable Growth*, Washington, DC: World Bank.

—— (1991a) *World Development Report: the Challenge of Development.* New York: Oxford University Press.

—— (1991b) *Managing Development: the Governance Dimension*, Washington, DC: World Bank.

—— (1993) *The East Asian Miracle: Economic Growth and Public Policy.* New York: Oxford University Press.

—— (1997) *World Development Report: the State in a Changing World.* New York: Oxford University Press.

—— (1998) *World Development Report: Knowledge for Development.* New York: Oxford University Press.

SIX

Finance and the Elusive Recovery

Lessons for Emerging Markets from South Korea and Thailand

C. P. Chandrasekhar and Jayati Ghosh

It is now commonplace to date the economic crisis in Southeast Asia from July 1997, when the Thai baht was allowed to float and quickly depreciated against the US dollar. It is true that the financial contagion that followed led to collapsing currencies and slumping stock markets across the region, and that the real economic crisis appeared thereafter. But signs of impending problems were evident in several of these economies for some months before. In Thailand, for example, there had been speculative attacks on the currency from around August 1996, which were warded off only with great difficulty by the Thai government. Moreover the balance-of-payments imbalances, which triggered such speculative attacks were clear from early 1996 (see, for example, Ghosh *et al.* 1996). The first Thai company to miss payments on foreign debt defaulted as early as 5 February. Similarly, in South Korea there were problems evident at least from January 1997, with several *chaebols* facing difficulties in servicing some of their loans.

Seen in this light, the sheer longevity of the crisis becomes a matter of note. It was more than two years after the first clear signs of crisis, and nearly one and a half years after the full-blown financial débâcle that this article was first written. Yet, the Southeast Asian region continued to be in the throes of a recession, if not a full-fledged depression, and the subsequent partial recovery also has proved to be fragile and easily reversible once the fiscal stimulus was reduced. While the financial indicators that first signalled the crisis have now largely stabilized, the problem of severe unemployment persists. And finance remains the key to understanding both the nature of the crisis and the apparent inability to recover from it to regain a secure growth trajectory.

In this chapter, we shall examine the factors that led up to financial liberalization, the link between financial openness, and crisis and the problems that the persistence with open regimes creates for efforts to overcome the crisis. In the discussion, we shall focus on two countries that have come to symbolize the crisis in its various forms: Thailand and South Korea.

Thailand was the first country to experience a major financial crisis, and started the downward spiral through contagion in the region. South Korea's economy is entirely different in its structure, macroeconomic fundamentals and even in its degree of development, and yet its financial crisis was remarkably similar. Both countries went speedily to the IMF for assistance, and subsequently both have been exceptionally 'well-behaved' in conforming to the IMF's policy guidelines. Nevertheless, in both countries there had been sharp and continued declines in output and economic activity, and the process of contraction was overcome only when the IMF permitted a degree of reflation by repeatedly relaxing the budgetary targets it had set for them. Before that, the superficial signs of stabilization in terms of more stable currencies, slightly lower interest rates and less volatile stock markets, were generated only through a contraction that squeezed large current account surpluses out of economies in severe crisis. Overall, it appears with hindsight that the region experienced, on a smaller scale, a 'lost period' similar to the 'lost decade' experienced by Latin America in the 1980s, even though the economic processes involved were very different. This is especially ironic given the extent to which the East Asian region had been touted as the example for other developing countries, including those in Latin America and Africa (see Stein 1995 and Wade 1990, among others).

FINANCIAL OPENNESS AND ECONOMIC INSTABILITY

Why did recovery prove to be either elusive or transient across the region as well as in Thailand and Korea? For an answer to that question we first need to look more closely at the nature of the crisis and the particular manner of its unfolding. Once the spectre of a financial crisis began haunting Wall Street and the West, even mainstream international opinion, led by the World Bank, was seeing 'premature' financial liberalization in developing countries, with inadequate supervisory and regulatory institutions as a proximate cause of the crisis. This, together with global capital market imperfections that resulted in surges of capital flow in periods of prosperity and waves of panic in periods when economic fundamentals were perceived to have weakened, are even now being seen as the factors that led up to the East Asian crisis.[1] However, this tendency to adopt positions that sound similar to the more radical critiques of financial globalization that were scoffed at until recently, is accompanied by a refusal to accept at least some of the systemic influences that led up to the crisis. In particular, it is being argued that financial liberalization *per se* is acceptable so long as prudential norms and guidelines are in place; and that goods market liberalization, which requires a vibrant export sector to finance a rising import bill, is unequivocally positive. To quote the World Bank:

> The potential for all countries to gain from freer trade and from expanded flows of foreign direct investment remains as compelling and valid as ever, indeed continuing to increase with advances in transport and communications techno-

> logies. Developing countries will continue, as in the first part of the 1990s, to see the payoffs of almost two decades of economic reform and structural adjustment. (World Bank 1998)

It is to ensure the realization of those predicted payoffs that the Bank seeks to draw some lessons from recent experience, which diverge from those implicitly drawn by the IMF.

The IMF too has learnt its lessons. It has not only backed a call for 'strengthening the international financial architecture', but has also cautioned countries against hastening towards capital account convertibility, and has chosen to put on hold its call for fiscal contraction in East Asia. The explanations for this superficial change in perspective are not hard to find. First, with the near-collapse of hedge funds like Long Term Capital Management in the US, it became clear that 'lack of transparency' was not a problem typical of emerging markets but rather was and is a feature intrinsic to the liberalized and proliferating global financial system. The international banking system, in search of the high returns promised by risky investments, had lent sums to such funds that were many multiples of their capital bases, thus helping to fuel a speculative boom in both emerging markets and developed country stock markets. As the expectations on which such investments were made were belied, there was a real threat of a collapse of the speculative bubble, and even of that collapse driving the developed industrial nations into a deep recession. Second, it became clear that the restoration of at least a semblance of growth and stability in the Asian region, in the economies in transition and in Latin America, was a prerequisite for stalling a global recession, which was a real possibility. With the consequences of liberalized finance being felt closer to home, the governments of the developed countries and the international financial institutions woke up to the fact that unregulated finance creates financial and real instability.

This reality has generated a degree of unprecedented candour even on the part of the IMF, which was hitherto instrumental in pushing for financial and capital account liberalization in all the developing countries in which it had any policy influence. The IMF's *World Economic Outlook* declared:

> It would be wrong ... to attribute financial crises exclusively to policy shortcomings in the crisis countries. Financial crises of the type experienced in Asia and Russia also illustrate the difficulties that emerging market countries can experience when they suddenly become the targets for very large capital inflows. History is replete with episodes in which developing countries have experienced large-scale capital inflows in situations when rates of return in the industrial countries were relatively unattractive, for example during periods of cyclical economic weakness, or when developing countries have appeared to offer particularly promising investment opportunities ...
>
> Complications often arise for two reasons. First, because of the magnitude of the resulting capital inflows relative to the absorptive capacity of the recipient countries, the inflows may contribute to surges in property and stock market prices as well as appreciating real exchange rates – asset price bubbles that often prove unsustainable. Second, when cyclical conditions normalize in creditor countries, or when perception of countries' fundamentals change, investors and banks may no longer find the higher returns in emerging market countries worth the risk.

> Bouts of excessive optimism among international investors followed by episodes of excessive pessimism can also be a problem, as illustrated by the inadequate yield spreads on emerging market debt instruments immediately prior to the Mexican and Asian crises, and by the excessive jumps in risk premia in the wake of these crises, even for countries with relatively sound policy records. Indeed, such cycles go back hundreds of years. Through these channels, and in conjunction with weak financial systems in many emerging market countries, and other weaknesses in policies and institutions, fluctuations in the global economic and financial environment may therefore contribute to the proneness of emerging market countries to crises. (IMF 1998a: 20–21)

It cannot be denied that excessive dependence on foreign capital inflows, especially short-term debt, is an important explanatory factor for the nature and the severity of the crisis in East Asia. But a fuller explanation must touch on a related set of issues: Why did these countries, with remarkably high domestic savings and investment rates, choose to invite foreign capital flows of this magnitude? And why did capital from the ostensibly more transparent and rule-based financial systems in the more developed financial markets choose to invest sums in these countries which we know, with hindsight, were far beyond their capacities to absorb?

FINANCIAL CENTRALIZATION AND VOLATILITY

To answer the second question first, we need to examine the manner in which finance capital rose to a position of dominance in the global economy and the role that cross-border flows of capital have been playing in the process of globalization. Initially, there were specific developments outside the realm of finance itself that contributed to an increase in international liquidity, such as the surpluses generated by the oil shocks which were largely deposited with the international banking system. Subsequently, financial liberalization increased this overhang by:

a. increasing the flexibility of banking and financial institutions when creating credit and making investments, as well as permitting the proliferation of institutions like the hedge funds which unlike the banks were not subject to regulation;
b. providing the space for 'financial innovation' or the creation of a range of new financial instruments or derivatives such as swaps, options and futures that were virtually autonomously created by the financial system; and
c. increasing competition and whetting the appetite of banks to earn higher returns.

The massive increase in international liquidity that followed these developments found banks as well as other financial institutions desperately searching for means to keep their capital moving. At first, there were consumer credit and housing finance booms in the developed industrial nations. But when those opportunities petered out, a number of developing countries were discovered as the 'emerging markets' in the global financial order. Capital in the form of loans and portfolio investments began to flow into these countries, especially those that were quick to liberalize rules relating to cross-border capital flows and regulations governing the conversion of domestic into foreign currency.

Singh (1996) has documented the abnormally large reliance on outside finance for corporate investment in the more prominent newly industrializing countries, and offered some proximate explanations for this. The result of these developments was that there were a host of new financial assets from the emerging markets in the international financial system, which were characterized by higher interest rates, ostensibly because of the greater risks of investment in these areas.

There are certain features characteristic of the global financial system which evolved in this manner. Principal among these is the growing importance of unregulated financial agents, such as the so-called hedge funds, in the system. Many years back the Group of 30 had cautioned governments that these funds were a source of concern because they were prone to 'undercapitalization, faulty systems, inadequate supervision and human error'. Though hedge funds first originated immediately after the Second World War, they have grown in number and financial strength in recent times. Their number is currently placed at between 3,000 and 4,000 and they are estimated to be managing US$300–400 billion of investors' money. These investors include major international banks, which are forced by rules and regulations to avoid risky transactions promising high returns, but they use the hedge funds as a front to undertake such transactions.

The operation of the now infamous Long Term Capital Management (LTCM) illustrates one of the roles these institutions play. Operating out of the US, as most hedge funds do, LTCM managed a part of the money of leading banks, like Travellers Group and UBS of Switzerland. The fund's principal trading activity was based on exploiting the differentials in interest rates between different securities. It was to the credit of LTCM, it was argued, that it indulged in such trades by investing primarily in sovereign debts in emerging markets which were more secure, and yet garnered returns as high as 40 per cent on capital. What was less praiseworthy was the extent to which its operations were based on borrowed capital. On an equity base of a little less than US$5 billion, LTCM had borrowed enough to undertake investments valued at US$200 billion or more. This was possible because there was nothing in the regulatory mechanism to limit the exposure of these institutions relative to their capital base.

Such flows of credit to a few institutions are significant because in a world of globalized and liberalized finance, when countries are at different phases of the business cycle and characterized by differential interest rates, capital flows in the direction of high returns. Nothing illustrates this better than what the markets of the time termed the 'yen-carry trades'. According to the IMF Capital Markets Report for 1997 (IMF 1997: 98–99):

> Foreign purchases of US treasury and government agency bonds and notes reached US$ 293.7 billion in 1996, and there was a further US$78 billion of foreign purchases of US corporate bonds. Similarly strong capital inflows to US securities markets have been apparent in the first quarter of 1997: foreign purchases of government and corporate bonds during the first quarter of 1997 were slightly above the quarterly average during 1996.
>
> Particularly wide interest differentials between the United States and Japan, in conjunction with the belief that the Bank of Japan did not want the yen to strengthen in 1996–97, were viewed by some large global hedge funds as a potentially lucrative situation. These so-called yen-carry trades involved borrowing in yen,

> selling the yen for dollars, and investing the proceeds in relatively high-yielding US fixed-income securities. In hindsight, these trades turned out to be considerably more profitable than simply the interest differential, for the yen depreciated continuously over the two years from May 1995 through May 1997, which reduced the yen liability relative to the dollar investment that it financed.

The implication of these and other flows to the US was that international liquidity 'was intermediated in US financial markets and invested abroad through purchases of foreign securities by US investors ($108 billion) and by net lending abroad by US banks ($98 billion)' (IMF 1997: 100).

There are a number of points to note here. To start with, the current global financial system is obviously characterized by a high degree of centralization. With US financial institutions intermediating global capital flows, the investment decisions of a few individuals in a few institutions virtually determine the nature of the 'exposure' of the global financial system. Unfortunately, unregulated entities making huge profits on highly speculative investments are at the core of that system.

Further, once there are institutions that are free of the now-diluted regulatory system, even those that are more regulated are entangled in risky operations. They are entangled because they themselves have lent large sums in order to benefit from the large returns that the risky investments undertaken on their behalf by these institutions seem to promise. They are also entangled because the securities on which these institutions bet in a speculative manner are also securities that these banks hold as 'safe investments'. If changes in the environment force these funds to dump some of their holdings to clear claims that are made on them, the prices of securities the banks directly hold tend to fall, affecting their assets position adversely. Thus there are two consequences of the new financial scenario. First, it is difficult to judge the actual volume and riskiness of the exposure of individual financial institutions. Second, within the financial world there is a complex web of entanglement with all firms mutually exposed, but each individual firm exposed to differing degrees to any particular financial entities.

Entanglement takes other forms as well. With financial firms betting on interest rate differentials and exchange rate changes at virtually the same time, debt, stock and currency markets are increasingly integrated. Crises, when they occur, do not remain in one of these markets but quickly spread to others, unless stalled by government intervention. Finally, the rise of finance in the manner described above feeds on itself in complex ways. The explanation for the liberalization wave in the developing countries is that this pyramidal growth of finance, which increased the fragility of the system, was seen as an opportunity. Enhanced flows to developing countries, initially in the form of debt and subsequently in the form of loans and portfolio investments, led to two consequences. First, the notion of external vulnerability which underlay the interventionist strategies of the 1950s and 1960s no longer seemed relevant – after all, any current account deficit could be financed, it appeared, with capital inflows as long as such inflows were ensured. Second, growth was now easier to ensure without having to confront domestic vested interests, since international liquidity could be used not merely to finance current and capital expenditures but to ease any supply-side constraints that might dampen or bring to a halt such growth.

The financial press, the international financial institutions and large sections of the academic community argued that this created an opportunity to launch an integrationist growth strategy in the developing countries, since in any case the sums required there were seen as a small fraction of the international liquidity being created by the financial system. For Western finance, emerging markets were a hedge, and for developing countries international finance was an opportunity. A cosy relationship seemed easy to build. It appeared that all that was needed was the liberalization of finance and a monetary policy that ensured interest rates high enough to make capital inflows attractive even after adjusting for risk.

The East Asian experience

In the case of East Asia, these arguments could be dismissed on the grounds that growth was hardly a problem. However, there is reason to believe that, despite their high savings rates, the decision to liberalize finance and allow free capital inflows was in part the result of a growing inability in these countries to sustain the export-based miracle growth rates that had made them the favourites of international capital. It is now almost universally accepted that in terms of the degree of openness and the extent of intervention by the state in the functioning of markets, the East Asian countries pursued widely varying strategies. However, the common element in those strategies was the crucial role of exports in sustaining their high growth rates. Unfortunately, successful export growth has its costs, especially when it is such rapid growth that it involves continuously increasing international market shares. It invites retaliatory actions from countries that are the targets of that export drive and leads to a loss of GSP (Generalized System of Preferences), it triggers a rise in domestic wages, and it often results in infrastructural bottlenecks. All of this in fact happened, and it tended to undermine the very export competitiveness that underlay the high rates of growth in these countries.

Those who extolled the export-orientation in these countries and the associated 'flying geese' phenomenon, which saw such a strategy replicated in new countries in the region, recognized this reality. But they also presumed that the early NIEs would in response successfully diversify into more technology-intensive, high-end sectors and sustain their export drive. This was partially true. But what also happened is that intra-regional investment flows created similar capacities as those which characterized the 'early East Asian industrializers', in newer and more competitive locations. To the extent that this resulted in competition within the Asian region among those seeking the same markets abroad for the same products, older suppliers often lost out in the competitive battle that ensued.

Nothing illustrates this better than world trade in the 'office automation' and consumer electronics sectors. Most Asian countries have experienced deceleration or decline in their manufactured exports since the middle of 1995, and the causes for this sudden drop have still not been adequately explored. One factor most commonly cited is the saturation of developed country markets, particularly for the office automation & telecom equipment segment and the machinery & transport equipment category. In the case of most of these countries these accounted for an overwhelmingly large share of total exports. The slowdown of trade growth in these categories is therefore seen to have had a disproportionate effect on exports from these countries.

If we examine the relative shares of 11 product groups in total merchandise trade in 1996, we find that since 1985 these shares have varied little, with two exceptions: the share of mining products has declined from 22 to 11 per cent (due mainly to a decline in the value of trade in petroleum), while that of machinery and transport equipment has increased from 31.0 to 38.8 per cent (WTO 1997). Two items of significance within the latter category were office machines and telecom equipment and automotive products, whose share of merchandise exports stood at 12.2 and 9.2 per cent respectively in 1996. Of these two, office automation and telecom equipment constituted a major export for developing Asia, accounting for 26.3 per cent of their total merchandise trade in 1996. If the 1996 shares are compared with those for 1984, the share of office and telecommunications equipment in world merchandise trade nearly doubled over the 12 years, from 6 to just over 12 per cent. Thus, telecommunications and office equipment had made important contributions to world trade growth in the late 1980s and early 1990s, with rates of export growth that were higher than the average for all commodities. It could therefore be argued that a subsequent slump in the market for those commodities would have affected Asian trade performance quite adversely, given the importance of those commodities in East Asia's export basket.

This argument carries weight for a number of reasons:

1. If we take the six principal items of consumer electronics, office equipment and telecommunications, eight East Asian economies accounted for 46 per cent of developing country exports of these items and 9.5 per cent of world exports in 1990/91.
2. These commodities accounted for a significant share (15.4 per cent) of merchandise exports from these 8 countries.
3. Since these were the most dynamic areas in world trade growth during the 1980s and the first half of the 1990s, East Asian success in exports in these areas would have allowed them to ride the boom in this segment while being insulated from the slump in others.

This partly explains the divergence in the growth performance of these economies compared with the rest of the world during those years. However, what is perhaps more crucial is that the saturation in the market for these items had set off a competitive struggle among economies in the region, which because of intra-regional investment flows, had specialized excessively in these areas. Winners in that battle like the Philippines, or those countries that had not specialized in such products, had been the gainers. The Philippines doubled its exports of office automation and telecoms equipment in two years, from US$5,047 million in 1994 to US$10,056 million in 1996. These items therefore came to account for almost half its merchandise exports in 1996. Such growth must have triggered a price war besides slowing export growth in other Asian economies. On the other hand, China is a country in which none of these products, excepting radio broadcast receivers, featured in its list of principal exports. Its export dynamism is based on a number of traditional manufactured exports like textiles and clothing which accounted for 25 per cent of its manufactured exports in 1996. That is, China's trading strength lies in areas in which the leading East Asian traders had lost their competitiveness much earlier, forcing them gradually to vacate the markets for such exports.

Thus, the trade experience of the East Asian countries afflicted by the currency crisis had indeed been specific, inasmuch as it reflected a fall in export volume growth and unit values triggered by an excessive specialization through relocation in areas where capacity growth had come to exceed market growth. It was to deal with these problems inherent in the strategies that they were following, that many of these countries chose to diversify out of manufacturing and into services in general and financial services in particular. Both South Korea and Thailand shared ambitions of becoming the financial hub of the East, and of seeing a sharp rise in the services component of their GDP. Financial liberalization was therefore viewed as the means to achieve this end, as well as to meet the growing pressure from the developed industrial nations to open up the financial sector as a *quid pro quo* for keeping open developed-country markets for manufactured exports from the East. As a result, during the early 1990s, almost all East Asian countries liberalized their financial sectors and allowed local corporations, banks, and other financial institutions freely to access international capital markets with little commitment to earn the foreign exchange needed to service the costs of such access.

But that was not all. An appreciating real exchange rate encourages investment in non-tradable sectors, the most obvious being the property market. Given the differential in interest rates between domestic and international markets and the lack of any prudence on the part of international lenders and investors, local agents borrowed heavily abroad to invest in property and stock markets either directly or indirectly. The resulting boom generated the incomes to keep domestic demand and growth increasing at relatively high rates. This soon resulted in signs of macroeconomic imbalance, not in the form of rising fiscal deficits financed by the government mint, but by a current account deficit, reflecting the consequences of debt-financed private profligacy. It was inevitable that this would soon result in a collapse of investor confidence. When that did occur, capital was pulled out and currencies depreciated; those with dollar commitments in the offing rushed into the market to purchase dollars early and cut their losses. The spiral continued, generating a liquidity crunch and a wave of bankruptcy. (Chandrasekhar and Ghosh [1998] elaborate this argument.) This is something that is recognized by the IMF as well.

Despite such knowledge, there still appears to be no forgiveness on the part of the IMF, in terms of changing the core policies that it prescribes for developing countries facing balance-of-payments difficulties. In particular, international policy-making circles still refuse to come to terms with the link between export dependence, financial openness and instability. In Southeast Asia, even though the IMF belatedly diluted its basic remedy of high interest rates, cuts in government spending and other deflationary measures which had exacerbated the crisis, it appeared anxious to ensure that the most obvious conclusion regarding the need to regulate capital flows was not drawn, and that other developing countries did not follow Malaysia in instituting some forms of currency control.

Further, it fears that faced with inadequate capital flows, developing countries may be encouraged partially to insulate their economies, thereby creating a national space within which they could seek to spur growth with government spending. Thus, in the IMFs view, 'in all countries, it is particularly important that the difficult external environment does not lead to defensive exchange rate and trade actions with negative international consequences or to market-closing measures' (IMF 1998a: 4). All this is seen as a prerequisite for restoring foreign investor confidence and wooing back the same foreign capital which had created all the problems in the first place.

There has been widespread criticism of the IMF's East Asia strategy, not only from the World Bank but also from independent analysts (see, for example, Wade and Veneroso 1998; Bullard *et al.* 1998, and, more recently, Stiglitz, 2000) and even from those who were earlier very bullish about all forms of economic openness and globalization. Thus Radelet and Sachs (1998: 1) criticize mainstream assessments of the crisis by pointing out, just as Jawaharlal Nehru's famous remark concluded, that just as history is written by the victors, so 'financial history, it seems, is written by the creditors'. They admit that 'the crisis was not the inevitable result of an Asian capitalist model, but rather, an accident of partial financial reforms that exposed these economies more directly to the instability of international financial markets' (Radelet and Sachs 1998: 23). The implication is that continued financial openness is inimical to recovery.

Despite its unpopularity, the IMF continues to hold on to what is still in essence its earlier position. This reflects not only the structure of power within that organization, but also the persistence of its beliefs regarding how current capitalism works. The IMF obviously believes that restoration of capital inflows is the only viable route to recovery in the countries hit by the crisis, and that liberalization aimed at facilitating such flows and macroeconomic and financial policies aimed at attracting them formed the only acceptable response to the crisis in these countries. Such beliefs are based on the premise that investor confidence in a world of globalized finance is country-specific and that the 'fundamentals' that spur such confidence are not undermined by greater financial openness.

THE NATURE OF INVESTOR CONFIDENCE

Consider the argument that investor confidence is country- or region-specific. It is now clear that the all too brief period when the financial markets of some developing countries and economies in transition were seen as the favoured destination of international investors, is over for the time being. The outlook for most emerging markets is muddy if not definitively negative. According to the IMF, in 1997 total net capital flows to all developing countries declined from the previous year's levels by around US$63 billion, or around 30 per cent. Tables 6.1, 6.2 and 6.3 give more detailed estimates from the IMF for Asia, Latin America and East European economies in transition. As expected, Asia shows the most dramatic change (IMF 2000).

Data on gross private financial flows to emerging markets indicate that gross (or new) financing peaked in the second and third quarters of 1997, and that in the first half of 1998 it was running at about half of pre-crisis levels. Asia has

Table 6.1: Net capital flows to Asia (US$ bn)

	1984–89	1990–96	1994	1995	1996	1997	1998	1999
Net private capital flows	13.1	56.0	66.4	95.1	100.5	3.1	-54.9	-32.4
Net direct investments	4.5	32.9	45.2	49.8	55.1	62.6	50	40.8
Net portfolio investments	1.5	6.7	9.4	10.9	12.5	0.8	-15.3	-16.6
Other net investments	7.0	16.4	11.8	34.5	33	-60.3	-99.5	-56.5
Net official flows	7.8	8.5	5.4	4.5	10.1	28.3	28.6	4.4
Change in reserves	-2.1	-29.7	-53.8	-44.5	-56.1	8.6	-48.8	-23.6

Source: IMF (1998a)

Table 6.2: Net capital flows to Latin America (US$ bn)

	1984–89	1990–96	1994	1995	1996	1997	1998	1999
Net private capital flows	-0.2	46.1	47.5	38.3	82.0	87.3	69.0	38.3
Net direct investments	5.3	19.1	24.9	26.1	39.3	50.7	54.0	45.6
Net portfolio investments	-0.9	32.3	60.8	1.7	40.0	39.7	33.0	2.1
Other net investments	-4.6	-5.3	-38.2	10.6	2.7	-3.1	-18.1	-9.4
Net official flows	8.2	1.2	-4.1	20.6	-13.7	-7.8	1.6	2.6
Change in reserves	0.5	-18.4	4.2	-25.5	-28.3	-14.6	17.7	20.5

Source: IMF (1998a)

accounted for most of the decline in gross flows since mid-1997, but flows to other regions have also been adversely affected. In August 1998, gross financing virtually dried up, reflecting the turbulence in Russia and other emerging markets.

Table 6.3: Net capital flows to countries in transition (US$ bn)

	1984–89	1990–96	1994	1995	1996	1997	1998	1999
Net private capital flows	-1.7	10.6	18.5	42.9	15.1	25.7	13.6	23.3
Net direct investments	-0.2	6.4	5.4	13.4	13.5	18.5	17.4	17.8
Net portfolio investments	0.0	10.4	21.0	17.8	24.4	19.0	6.7	13.6
Other net investments	-1.6	-6.2	-8.0	11.7	-22.8	-11.9	-10.6	-8.1
Net official flows	0.2	1.1	-12.2	-8.5	-0.2	9.3	12.2	2.9
Change in reserves	-2.7	-5.0	-8.7	-35.8	-1.0	-5.3	-1.2	-13.5

Source: IMF (1998a; and 2000)

As a result of all this, net private capital flows in 1998 as a whole have been estimated by the IMF to be a further US$85 billion lower than in 1997, at around US$64 billion. This is less than a third of the net inflow recorded in 1996.

Table 6.4: Capital flows to developing countries/emerging markets (US$ bn)

	1995	1996	1997	1998	1999
Net private flows: IMF	147.3	190.9	131.8	87.6	104.1
Net private flows: IIF	228.1	327.9	265.7	147.8	148.7

Note: The IIF's figures relate to what it defines as 29 emerging markets.
Source: IMF (1998a) and IIF (2000)

A survey by a private agency, the Washington-based Institute for International Finance (IIF) (2000), has come up with similar indicators of a decline in finance to *emerging markets*, though the estimates of the IIF of capital flows to emerging markets are far higher than the IMF's figures for developing countries (Table 6.4). The IIF's estimate of disaggregated flows is presented in Table 6.5. The IIF report highlights the following important features of capital flows to emerging markets:

1. Net private capital flows to 29 major emerging market economies are estimated to have fallen to a little below US$150 billion in 1998 from US$266 billion in 1997 and a peak of over US$325 billion in 1996. This fall reflects both the direct impact of the financial crises in Russia and Asia and consequential effects transmitted through financial markets.

2. Lending by private creditors is estimated to have fallen to US$16.2 billion in 1998 from US$124.7 billion in 1997 and US$202.5 billion in 1996. Net lending by commercial banks is estimated at a negative US$49 billion in 1998 as net repayments by Asian economies offset positive lending to emerging market economies elsewhere.
3. Secondary market spreads on emerging market bonds widened substantially after the Russian devaluation and unilateral moratorium in mid-August 1998. The IIF believes that in many cases these spreads substantially exceeded levels that correspond to a realistic assessment of default probabilities in individual countries.
4. Direct equity investment was relatively less affected by the financial crises and at US$118 billion was estimated to account for close to four-fifths of private capital flows in 1998. Portfolio equity flows, in contrast, fell to only US$14 billion that year from US$26 billion the year before, as emerging equity markets fell steeply and inflows seen in the first half of the year were partially reversed.

Table 6.5: External financing to emerging markets (US$ bn)

	1996	1997	1998	1999
Current account balance	-96.2	-80.6	-10.1	8.3
Net external financing	335.5	304.6	200.6	160.6
Private flows, net	327.9	265.7	147.8	148.7
Equity investment	125.4	141.0	131.5	155.8
Direct	91.7	115.3	117.9	138.8
Portfolio	33.7	25.7	13.7	17.0
Private creditors	202.5	124.7	16.2	-7.1
Commercial banks	116.8	33.5	-49.0	-39.1
Non-bank	85.6	91.2	65.2	32.0
Official flows, net	7.6	38.9	52.8	11.9
International financial int.	6.6	29.0	36.4	4.0
Bilateral	-7.0	9.8	16.5	7.9
Resident lending/other	-154.7	-181.7	-148.2	-116.7
Reserves change	-84.5	-42.3	-42.2	-52.0

Source: IIF, January 2000

It is now generally accepted among observers of varying ideological and analytical persuasion, that this is not a tendency that will quickly reverse itself. Even the IMF, generally the last multilateral economic institution to accept any unpleasant reality, had conceded in its *World Economic Outlook* (1998) that there is a real risk that the panic may fail to subside for some time. This is likely to imply significant net outflows of foreign capital from many economies, as already witnessed in the Asian crisis countries and in Russia. The growing fear and insecurity among market participants, which is reflected in the large yield spreads seen recently, could become self-fulfilling and result in the prolonged disruption of international financial flows with severely depressing effects on economic activity as well as on world trade.

What is important to note here is that the crisis – in the specific form of dramatic reduction in net capital inflows – is currently attacking virtually all emerging markets, not simply those that have been identified as having specific domestic problems or which are perceived as particularly risky prospects. This is essentially a repetition of a historical pattern in international lending and portfolio investment which can be traced back more than a century, whereby problems of repayment or potential default in one recipient country have led to dramatic declines in all such inflows to all developing countries, rather than being confined to the individual transgressor. International lending to developing countries has always been characterized by such cycles, and sharp collapses in such flows consequent upon repayment problems of a small subgroup of debtors, are evident in the 1920s, 1930s and, of course, in the external debt crisis of the 1980s (Kindleberger 1986). The current talk of 'contagion' as if it were a qualitatively new market phenomenon misses this obvious historical point. It has typically been in the nature of private international capital to move in such a manner, and the current expansion of global finance has only accentuated such a tendency.

LIBERALIZATION AND INVESTOR CONFIDENCE

The second difficulty with the IMF's revised perspective is its failure to recognize that the fundamentals which may become crucial for the sustenance of investor confidence can be undermined by liberalization itself. Not surprisingly, when the crisis (which had been brewing for more than a year) first erupted with the devaluation of the Thai baht in July 1997, mainstream international opinion, influenced by the international financial institutions, argued that wrong domestic policies in the countries hit by the crisis were responsible for the crisis. The thrust of the analysis underlying that opinion was the idea that private profligacy financed by a non-transparent, state-directed financial and banking system, had fuelled a speculative boom based on capital flows from abroad. This tendency was in turn attributed to irrational and corrupt collusion between the state and private capital in these countries. The boom itself was seen to involve unwarranted expansion of overgeared productive enterprises as well as speculative investments in the property and stock markets. When developments in international trade triggered a slowdown of growth in these economies and their 'fundamentals' ostensibly came up for scrutiny, it was inevitable according to this view that a collapse steered by a loss of investor confidence would ensue.

The real change in terms of analysis is that now the situation where countries become dependent on foreign finance, in excess of their absorptive capacity, is blamed not merely on governments and private agents in emerging markets but also on the international financial players. And the conclusion that is drawn is not that countries should turn their backs on such finance and pursue a more insular strategy which discourages the use of foreign capital inflows, but that they should adopt more prudent macroeconomic strategies and that they and international investors should strive for greater transparency in the financial sector to ensure that only the best users are in a position to access capital and that such users and the international investors are not denied what are seen as market-determined profit opportunities.

In fact, one very common conclusion that has been constantly repeated since the start of the Asian crisis in mid-1997 is the importance of 'sound' macroeconomic policies, once financial flows have been liberalized. It has been suggested that countries like Thailand, South Korea and Indonesia have faced such problems because they allowed their current account deficits to become too large, reflecting an excess of private domestic investment over private savings. This belated realization is a change from the earlier obsession with government fiscal deficits as the only macroeconomic imbalance worth caring about, but it still misses the basic point. This point is that, with completely unbridled capital flows, it is no longer possible for a country to control the amount of capital inflow or outflow, and both movements can create consequences that are undesirable. If, for example, a country is suddenly chosen as a preferred site for foreign portfolio investment, it can lead to huge inflows which, in turn, cause the currency to appreciate, thus encouraging investment in non-tradables rather than tradables, and altering domestic relative prices and therefore incentives. Simultaneously, unless the inflows of capital are simply (and wastefully) stored up in the form of accumulated foreign exchange reserves, they must necessarily be associated with current account deficits. The large current deficits in Thailand and elsewhere were therefore necessary by-products of the surge in capital inflow, and that was the basic macroeconomic problem. This means that any country that does not exercise some sort of control or moderation over private capital inflows can be subject to very similar pressures. These then create the conditions for their own eventual reversal, when the current account deficits are suddenly perceived to be too large or unsustainable. In other words, what all this means is that once there are completely free capital flows and completely open access to external borrowing by private domestic agents, there can be no 'prudent' macroeconomic policy; the overall domestic balances or imbalances will change according to the behaviour of capital flows, which will themselves respond to the economic dynamics that they have set into motion.

That is not all. When this dynamic results in a crisis following a collapse in capital flows, restoring growth within an open environment of the kind that the IMF insists upon often proves near impossible. This is because the structure of an open regime (which is also open financially) is such that growth comes to depend not on exports but investments in non-tradables, particularly certain services and in asset markets, financed with capital inflows. Reversing this dependence on non-tradables and services in and of itself requires large investments, in order to restructure existing capacities and create new, internationally competitive ones. However, the economic contraction or slow growth that follows the collapse in investor confidence makes it extremely difficult to rebuild that confidence in adequate measure. One way in which the IMF has sought to deal with this problem is to relax its fiscal deficit targets in countries that accept its conditions about openness. However, since intravenous injections of money into the system within an open regime inevitably widens the current account deficit and necessitates capital inflows, there are limits to which even this strategy can be pursued, determined by the ability of the IMF to organize the necessary foreign capital. In the event, sustainable recovery in these economies proves elusive and they find themselves on a trajectory which worsens the burdens of adjustment heaped on a population ravaged by unemployment and an erosion of real earnings.

Sustainable recovery in these countries requires a different strategy. It involves a turn away from the excessive openness resulting from the mad pursuit of easily accessed foreign capital. For a time, the sheer availability of such finance, at least for a minority of highly publicized emerging markets, convinced developing countries that the problems of external vulnerability, which had warranted the earlier import-substituting industrial policies, were no longer relevant. Now, however, there is greater realization that these problems of external vulnerability have not gone away, and can be as vicious as ever. This has meant a revival in policy ideas that are based on some degree of insulation from the vagaries of international markets, particularly financial markets. While a full return to the earlier forms of import-substituting regimes is obviously not advisable, the only way in which fiscal deficits can be used to trigger growth is if there exists an 'area of control' insulated from the debilitating consequences of the free flow of capital, goods and services. Unfortunately, while the IMF is willing to relax its fiscal deficit targets, it is still completely against control and regulation over trade, exchange rates and capital flows.

To corroborate these conclusions, we examine below the consequences of the post-crisis adjustment experiences of South Korea and Thailand. The factors leading up to the crisis in these countries are essentially similar to those elaborated above, in that the liberalization of various markets played a role in creating the macroeconomic conditions for crisis. However, we do not concentrate on these, which have been described elsewhere (Chandrasekhar and Ghosh 1998; Chang 1998; Pasuk 1998; Lauridsen 1998) but on developments after the onset of the crisis in mid-1997. Thailand illustrates an instance where the pursuit of IMF-style policies has not managed to restore investor confidence, with devastating effects on the economy and especially on the poor. The South Korean case indicates that even such a restoration of investor confidence may not be enough to generate an adjustment leading to sustained recovery.

The IMF and economic depression in Thailand

In the wake of the crisis, Jayasankar Shivakumar, the World Bank's Director for Thailand, declared that 'ten years will pass before the structural reforms take effect and prosperity can be measured for the vast majority of people'. IMF and World Bank officials have never been known either for their sensitivity or for their eagerness to avoid the devastating effects their so-called 'reforms' have on the majority of the people in countries that follow their advice. Even so, this quotation is remarkable for the casual manner in which a medium-term prospect of continued economic disaster was prophesied for Thailand. It is even more remarkable given the alacrity and humility with which the Thai government has in general accepted the economic policy advice of the IMF and the World Bank in its attempt to counter the current crisis. Clearly, if the Thai people must continue to suffer for much of this decade, the blame for this must also lie with these policy advisers, who have been closely associated with the strategies that are causing such suffering.

As late as November 1996, when it was already apparent to discerning observers that the Thai economy was heading for difficulties, Michel Camdessus, Managing Director of the International Monetary Fund, publicly held up Thailand as a model of macroeconomic policy for other developing countries. In August 1997, after signing the first of a series of letters of intent with the Thai government, he once again approved of the government's proposed policies to deal with the current crisis, which he felt would 'decisively contribute to stability in financial markets in Asia'. Since then, Fund officials have continued to insist that the policy package advocated by the IMF is the only possible way to deal with the crisis, and have also accepted that the Thai government has in general followed their recommendations without demur.

Yet in the period from August 1997, the IMF has been through no less than six letters of intent with the Thai government, as continuously deteriorating economic circumstances rendered the earlier agreements irrelevant. For most disinterested observers, it is now clear that the IMF policies contributed significantly to the deterioration: rather than helping to form the solution, the IMF has definitely been a major part of the problem. The IMF approach was initially based on two broad planks of fiscal compression and tight monetary control, both of which added to recessionary tendencies in an economy whose basic initial problem was asset deflation. This real economy recession, along with constrained access to credit, had in turn meant that Thai companies faced greater difficulties in repaying loans, which has made the banks worse off, further adding to problems of the financial sector. The continuing interaction between these downward pressures led to the economic depression across Thailand.

The initial explicit aim of the IMF's strategy in Thailand, as elsewhere, was to restore foreign investor confidence, in the hope that a renewed inflow of foreign capital would allow economic growth to resume. To this end (and also as part of the overall dogma of reducing the role of government), it proposed extensive privatization of public assets, with the sales open to foreigners, as well as greater openness to foreign investment and ownership in areas such as real estate. Measures such as an expansionary fiscal strategy to counter the recession, to be financed by raising taxes, were explicitly ruled out. So the only hope of recovery rested with foreign investors who had to be enticed to come back into Thailand with large net inflows through whatever means possible. It is interesting that this revival of foreign investor confidence was hoped for in an economic context in which even domestic investor expectations were bearish in the extreme, with domestic markets shrinking and costs rising because of rising import costs and tighter credit.

It is not surprising that such a strategy failed, nor that it was associated with worsening economic conditions such that output targets had to be continually revised downwards. The recession, which really became a full-scale depression, also meant that the fiscal targets set by the IMF could not be met despite the Thai government's ruthless cuts of a whole range of necessary development and welfare expenditures.

Thailand's record of fiscal surpluses came to an abrupt halt in 1997 when the government announced a deficit of 31.15 billion baht – the first such deficit in ten years. For 1998, the government had originally promised to the IMF a budget surplus of 1 per cent of gross domestic product, or about 50 billion baht, for fiscal 1998, ending in September. This was supposedly to offset the interest costs on debt incurred through the Bank of Thailand's efforts to prop up failing financial institutions. To meet the target, the government engaged in severe budget cuts and imposed new indirect taxes.

The economic contraction in the first half of 1998 forced the government to reconsider this fiscal strategy. Maintaining the 1 per cent budget surplus became almost impossible with falling tax revenues because of recession. The third letter of intent with the IMF, signed in February 1998, conceded this. Instead of a 1 per cent of GDP surplus, the Thai government was allowed to run a deficit of up to 1.5 per cent of GDP for the central budget and 0.5 per cent for state enterprises. But even the new targets proved unreachable, as the economic recession continued to wreak havoc on tax collections in the first quarter. A new revision was necessary by May 1998 when the fourth letter of intent was drafted. In this, the overall public sector deficit target under the programme for 1997/98 was changed from 2 to 3 per cent of GDP.

The fifth letter of intent in August 1998 revised fiscal targets once more. The 1999 budget, which began October, was permitted to have a deficit target of 3 per cent of GDP, the same as the 1998 budget. This excluded the 1.5 per cent of GDP budgeted for financial restructuring costs. Monetary policies were to be maintained, especially since short-term rates in the money market had fallen from 20 per cent earlier in the year to about 10–12 per cent. However, short-term interest rates, it was argued, should be 'promptly raised to counteract speculative pressures'. The government's priorities were to be corporate debt restructuring and financial reform measures. Both were seen as 'essential to re-establish normal market relations, allow the resumption of credit flows, and support a recovery of the private sector' (Govt of Korea 1998). The sixth letter of intent of December 1998 went even further. The overall public sector deficit for 1998/99 was now targeted at about 5 per cent of GDP. In addition, the interest costs of financial restructuring were estimated at 3 per cent of GDP.

All this suggests that while the IMF may have learned something from the débâcle thus far, it was nowhere near enough for it to provide a viable way out of the crisis. That had to wait for a Thai government decision to put an end to IMF monitoring. In allowing the government to run a modest deficit, the IMF acknowledged that public spending may be one of the few ways to stimulate the economy, given the shortage of private capital available for productive investment and expansion. In fact, in an IMF press release (IMF 1998c), Michel Camdessus 'welcomed the easing of fiscal policy, and the strengthening of the social safety net[, because] these factors, along with the significant interest rate reductions that have taken place in recent months, will provide a strong foundation for economic growth next year'. However, the successive agreements lacked sufficient measures to spur the economy and ease unemployment. To start with, they failed to recognize that the growth-inducing consequences of higher deficits would be limited for two reasons: first, higher deficits did not reflect higher spending, but a fall in tax revenues far greater than in spending. Second, the new demands generated by enhanced spending could well spill over in the form of higher imports rather than higher domestic production. Further, the package focused on additional spending on corporate and financial restructuring rather than on the expansion of employment opportunities. Thai critics argued that this involved wasting hundreds of billions of baht in attempting to bail out now-defunct finance companies whose major shareholders had long since cashed in and headed into comfortable exile abroad.

The Thai growth record

The failure of the package comes through from an examination of its effect on output, employment and general living standards. As is evident from Table 6.6,

Table 6.6: Thailand: GDP growth rates (%, 1988 prices)

	Overall	Non-Agric.	Agric.
1990	11.2	14.1	-4.7
1991	8.6	8.8	7.2
1992	8.1	8.6	4.8
1993	8.5	9.8	-1.3
1994	8.9	9.4	5.3
1995	8.8	9.7	2.5
1996	5.9	6.2	3.6
1997	-1.7	-1.9	0.4
1998	-10.2	-11.2	-1.4
1999	4.2	4.2	3.9

Source: Bank of Thailand

the very high rates of growth that marked the 1980s in Thailand also continued into the 1990s. The early years of the 1990s in fact saw aggregate real GDP grow at around 10 per cent per annum, which came down to the still high rates of around 9 per cent in the middle of the decade. Given the volatility of agricultural growth, most of this increase came from industry and services. But by

1996, a deceleration was apparent, and this slowdown reflected both the deceleration in exports (which fell to zero growth in that year) as well as the saturation of domestic demand consequent upon a feverish speculative boom in real estate and financial assets. The crisis has been seen as primarily financial in nature, but of course it was closely related to real economic imbalances which were partly a creation of the financial spurt and in turn contributed to it.

Like several other developing country regimes in the early 1990s, the Thai government harboured ambitions of cashing in on the globalization of finance by attracting large amounts of capital inflow. Indeed, the Central Bank in 1993 announced its plan to develop Bangkok as a regional financial centre, taking advantage of Thailand's central location in Southeast Asia and the apparent trend of continuously rising exports. Foreign exchange controls were relaxed in the early 1990s to encourage a freer flow of capital. In 1993 the Central Bank allowed the establishment of international banking facilities to help mobilize offshore funds for domestic lending. These measures generated a heavy influx of foreign capital, the majority in the form of short-term credit seeking to exploit the higher interest rates available in the local market. Portfolio investments also increased as share prices on the Stock Exchange of Thailand jumped.

Meanwhile, however, the basket peg system introduced in the mid-1980s, which effectively fixed the baht to the US dollar, was continued. At one level, this was of course a basic requirement to become a regional financial centre and retain foreign investor confidence. But the combination of this rigid exchange rate regime and liberalized capital flows inevitably set the stage for greater macroeconomic instability in the future. It should be remembered that a flexible exchange rate regime would not have got around this problem, since the high rate of capital inflows would if anything have made the baht appreciate even faster in real terms. The source of the problem in Thailand was actually in the very feature that was being lauded by international finance and the Bretton Woods institutions at that time. Essentially it was the sudden and dramatic increase in capital inflows that can be described as the original sin that created the future macroeconomic imbalances. In the first place, the relatively high baht made exports less competitive, and also encouraged a boom in imports. This was also possible because the trade regime had been progressively liberalized by that point. Growing consumerism spurred heavy import demands, paid for in turn by capital inflows. Associated with this there was a shift in domestic investment away from tradables into non-tradables, and especially into real estate and similar sectors. Unproductive investments in property and speculative securities also led to higher costs, wages and capital good prices, further undermining the competitiveness of Thai exports.

All this also encouraged greater dependence on foreign capital than was necessary or even warranted by the domestic investment pattern. Thai companies, seeing no exchange risks under the currency peg, flocked to international markets to borrow at interest rates lower than those prevailing in the local market, despite increasing leverage ratios. Financial institutions were also beneficiaries of relatively cheap foreign funds. As the economic expansion continued, lending criteria eased as banks and finance companies competed for increasingly risky investment opportunities.

As a result, the current account deficit reached a peak of 8.2 per cent of GDP in 1995. The ratio of foreign debt to GNP reached 50.14 per cent in 1996, pointing to the country's deteriorating external position. It is wrong to attribute this solely to the fixed exchange rate, however, as the Nukul Commission appointed by the Thai government has suggested. In fact, it is really the continuous and growing dependence on large capital inflows which was responsible, since this would have led to a high level of the baht even in a floating rate regime.

The flotation and associated devaluation of the baht on 2 July 1997 was the culmination of a period during which it had become increasingly difficult for the Bank of Thailand to defend the currency in the face of speculative attacks. But it triggered a major financial and then economic crisis, into which the country sank even more deeply in the following year. Output slumped and there were major losses in employment. The domestic credit system nearly collapsed, and this magnified falls in sales, trade and working capital. Output which fell by just about half a percentage point in 1997 contracted by 8 per cent in 1998. The economic crisis had by then wiped out productive gains of the previous seven years.

Table 6.7: Thailand: trade growth rates (%)

	Exports	Imports
1996	-1.9	0.6
1997	3.8	-13.4
1998	-6.8	-33.8
1999	7.4	17.7

Source: Bank of Thailand

Meanwhile, the devaluation of the baht did less than expected to boost exports, as is evident from Table 6.7. The export decline continued in the first half of 1999, amounting to a negative growth of 2.4 per cent. Agricultural exports should have benefited greatly from the baht depreciation, but they did not.

Along with the credit squeeze which affected working capital costs for exporters, the inability of exporters to take advantage of baht depreciation has been attributed to a lack of bank financing, weak Japanese import demand, and a sharp economic contraction in Asia. The result was the closure of many small and medium-sized operations, and many more job losses, especially in the textile and garment industries.

The current account, which was transformed from a deficit to a large surplus in 1998, reflected the collapse in imports rather than any real pickup in exports. The value of imports in 1998 declined by almost 35 per cent compared with the previous year. This was reflected in the trade balance figures, shown in Table 6.8. The result was a healthy-looking current account, but a closer look reveals a sharp drop in imported raw materials for key industries such as textiles, automobiles, electronics and electrical appliances. Production for the domestic market was also fraught with difficulty. Some firms were being squeezed by a lack of credit and falling cash-flows, while others saw their markets vanish, or were making products that sold only at low prices that drastically reduced profit margins.

Table 6.8: Thailand: balance of trade (US $ bn)

1996	1997	1998	1999
-16.1	-4.6	12.2	8.9

Source: Bank of Thailand

Official figures placed unemployment at close to 2 million people in 1998, but the rise in the unemployment rate from 4.4 per cent in 1998 to more than 5 per cent in the first two quarters of 1999 suggests that this could have jumped to 3 million in the subsequent year, as corporate bankruptcies and downsizing continued. The greatest job losses have been in the industrial sector, but several services activities were also increasingly under threat.

Meanwhile, economic conditions initially worsened, even for those who still had employment because of rising inflation. However, the depth of the recession helped to steady prices. The overall rate of inflation, shown in Table 6.9, rose sharply in 1998, but declined substantially thereafter, as the economy entered a classic deflationary path.

Table 6.9: Thailand: annualized rate of inflation

1996	1997	1998	1999
5.9	5.6	8.1	0.3

Source: Bank of Thailand

Ironically, these deflationary tendencies were further reinforced by the tight monetary policy imposed as part of the IMF package. The private sector, which was already strained from higher costs and declining revenues, was further burdened by the lack of new credit and debt service costs. Small and medium-sized banks came under fierce liquidity pressure in the first quarter of 1998, as deposits moved to larger institutions and foreign banks and interbank credit lines were cut. Local banks have seen asset quality decline further because of high interest rates and recession.

Even at this writing, prospects for the banking sector in the medium-term remain bleak. The sheer scope of the bad-loan problem, coupled with poor market sentiment, have left many banks and finance houses seriously undercapitalized and facing insolvency. Bankruptcies and unemployment are expected to skyrocket, particularly with the implementation of the foreclosure law passed in October 1998, which gives creditors greater leeway to seize collateral from delinquent borrowers. The result could be a self-reinforcing downward spiral, unless active policy measures are put into place to reverse it. All this had forced several small and medium-sized banks to turn to the Central Bank's Financial Institutions Development Fund for support. But this institution simply does not have enough funds, given the enormity of the task at hand.

Thailand's experience is one that suggests that the pursuit of IMF-style macroeconomic policies does not spur investor confidence and trigger a recovery. Further, persisting recession makes it impossible to meet the IMF's fiscal targets, so that pursuing the strategy recommended becomes impossible. The result of course is a non-equalizing process of growth, the burden of which falls on the poor and the fixed income earners, who played no role to play in the debt-financed profligacy that triggered the crisis. The apparent recovery in output growth in 1999 has been based essentially on the positive fiscal stimulus provided by large fiscal deficits, in turn largely financed through Japanese money provided through the New Miyazawa Initiative in 1999.

THE SOUTH KOREAN EXPERIENCE

The Thai experience has been interpreted by the IMF and other financial market analysts as suggesting that the recovery can be elusive in East Asia because foreign investors may refuse to return. The South Korean experience contradicts that conclusion. Its has been quite a while since South Korea's banks were subjected to the first credit-rating downgrade, because of their exposure to conglomerates going through an unprecedented financial crunch. And the country which epitomized East Asia's 'rags-to-riches' story has indeed moved quite a distance from the situation that it was in even a year after it had accepted a loan from and subjected itself to conditionalities specified by the IMF. In the interim, South Korea has stabilized its balance of payments and restored a creditable rate of growth of income. As a result, the country has won credibility with the IMF. However, it must not be forgotten that this return to growth has occurred in the wake of a prolonged and painful recession, the after-effects of which are still being felt.

For example, on 24 July 1998, more than six months after the process of adjustment began, the Government of Korea in one more letter of intent to the IMF declared: 'The domestic economy ... appears to be falling further into recession and consumer and investor confidence is at a low ebb. Unemployment has increased faster than previously expected and more layoffs are expected to result from the acceleration of restructuring' (Govt of Korea 1998).

The story of this decelerating growth is reflected in Table 6.10. GDP growth, which had slowed marginally from around 8 per cent during 1994–96 to a little over 6 per cent per annum over the first three quarters of 1997, fell sharply to 3.9 per cent at the height of the crisis during the last quarter of 1997, when negotiations with both the IMF for the US$57 billion rescue package and the banks for the roll-over of short-term credits placed at close to US$100 billion were successfully concluded. But after these agreements were concluded, the process of deceleration in growth was transformed into one of contraction, with GDP falling by 3.6 per cent in the first quarter of 1998 and by a massive 6.5 per cent during the subsequent three quarters. Almost all of this contraction in growth was attributable to three sectors: construction, manufacturing and services in that order. In the event, the unemployment rate, which stood at 2.6 per cent in 1997, rose to 6.8 per cent in 1998. Despite the recovery in growth during 1999, the unemployment rate was reported to be above 5 per cent at the beginning of 2000.

Table 6.10: South Korea – quarterly growth rates (%)

	GDP	PFCE	GCF
1997 Q1	5.7	4.4	0.3
1997 Q2	6.6	5.1	0.2
1997 Q3	6.1	5.1	-3.7
1997 Q4	3.9	-0.2	-9.8
1998 Q1	-3.6	-8.4	-20.6
1998 Q2	-7.2	-9.7	-23.7
1998 Q3	-7.1	-8.9	-22.2
1998 Q4	-5.3	-5.8	-17.9
1999 Q1	4.5	5.0	-4.3
1999 Q2	9.9	7.8	4.9
1999 Q3	12.3	8.4	6.9

Source: Bank of Korea
Note: PFCE = Private final consumption expenditure; GCF = Gross capital formation

The proximate explanations for the dramatic downturn in manufacturing are not hard to find. Since the South Korean economy is characterized by a high export-to-GDP ratio, the slowdown in export growth resulting from the regional crisis should itself have contributed to slower manufacturing growth. The dollar value of exports, which fell in the first quarter of 1998, recovered only marginally thereafter and stagnated at close to that level until the fourth quarter of 1999 (Table 6.11). But were been two other important trends underlying the recession (Table 6.10). First, there was a collapse in investment reflected in a contraction in gross capital formation which in absolute magnitude fell by 10 per cent in the last quarter of 1997, 20 per cent in the first quarter of 1998 and by 24 and 22 per cent respectively in the second and third quarters of 1998. Second, there was a downturn in private final consumption expenditure, resulting from the increase in unemployment and the erosion of money incomes accompanying the recession.

This collapse of domestic demand called for a reflationary strategy, especially since the Korean crisis of 1997 was more a reflection of bank overexposure in corporations taking a beating in international and domestic markets. The IMF itself noted after concluding Article IV consultations in May 1998 that:

> In 1994–96, Korean conglomerates undertook an aggressive investment drive financed by large increases in borrowing from domestic banks, which, in turn, sharply increased short-term external borrowing. During 1997, an unprecedented number of highly leveraged conglomerates went into bankruptcy as the build-up

in capacity proved unviable, owing to the depreciation of the yen, a sharply adverse movement in Korea's terms of trade, and the slowing of domestic demand in 1996. The bankruptcies resulted in a severe deterioration in the balance sheets of Korean financial institutions. (IMF 1998b)

Table 6.11: South Korea: monthly trade performance (US$ m)

	Exports	Imports	CAB*
Avg. 1st half 97	10875.9	12402.0	-1679.3
Avg. 97 3Q	11393.9	11895.9	-487.8
Avg. 97 4Q	12242.3	11505.6	1664.6
Avg. 98 1Q	10746.1	7899.6	3649.7
Avg. 98 2Q	11265.9	7847.1	3636.3
Avg. 98 3Q	10160.4	7154.0	3205.2
Avg. 98 4Q	11574.2	8207.9	2895.4
Avg. 99 1Q	10084.6	8522.2	1989.4
Avg. 99 2Q	11914.0	9586.7	2119.1
Avg. 99 3Q	11695.9	9919.5	2249.1
Avg. 99 4Q	14200.6	11888.9	1909.2

Source: Bank of Korea
*CAB = Current account balance.

All of this was attributed to hasty capital account liberalization during 1993–96, which substantially eased controls on short-term borrowing. While this called for a combination of capital controls and a restructuring of the financial sector, some effort to stimulate demand was necessary in the interim. The principal error of the strategy worked out by the IMF for South Korea was that it equated the difficulties generated by public profligacy with those stemming from private profligacy encouraged by financial sector liberalization. So it recommended to South Korea what it imposes on countries where balance-of-payments difficulties result from excess public deficits financed directly or indirectly by borrowing from abroad, viz., deflation led by a sharp curtailment of public expenditure.

This engineered deflation was to take two forms. First, a tight monetary policy designed to push up interest rates. As the South Korean government's first letter of intent to the IMF stated:

> To demonstrate to markets the government's resolve to confront the present crisis, monetary policy will be tightened immediately to restore and sustain calm in the markets and contain the inflationary impact of the recent *won* depreciation. In line with this policy, the large liquidity injection in recent weeks will be reversed, and money market rates will be allowed to rise sufficiently and will be maintained at that level or higher as needed to stabilize markets. (Govt of Korea 1997a)

This signalled a rise in all interest rates, with the aim of halting speculative trading in the won and of attracting foreign investors back into the market so as to strengthen the currency. For South Korean firms, overgeared due to past government encouragement and adversely affected by demand conditions, the increase in the interest burden was a prescription for bankruptcy. The understanding was that an essential prerequisite to deal with the financial crisis was a restoration of capital inflows and that some bankruptcy of Korean corporations was a small price to pay in pursuit of that goal. In fact, through capital market liberalization and the substantial liberalization of restrictions on the aggregate holding by foreigners of equity in domestic corporations, bankruptcies were sought to be converted into a benefit by encouraging sales of assets to foreigners at bargain prices that would contribute to capital inflows.

The second means of engineering deflation was fiscal contraction, ensured through a surplus on the government's budget. When the IMF programme was initially adopted in December 1997, the IMF had demanded a package of tax and expenditure measures, designed to yield revenues equal to 1 per cent of GDP, which was expected to deliver a fiscal surplus (of 0.25 per cent of GDP) in 1998. Despite this, growth in 1998 was expected to remain positive at around 1 per cent, revised down from expectations of 2 per cent or more. However, by February even the IMF had to accept that a weaker growth outlook for 1998 and the impact of the exchange rate depreciation would make a fiscal deficit of around 1.5 per cent of GDP inevitable. In the updated memorandum on the Economic Programme prepared for the second quarterly review in May 1998, it was decided that 'with the updated macroeconomic projections indicating weaker growth, and ongoing structural adjustment in the economy, a larger fiscal deficit (1.75 per cent of GDP) will be permitted.'

But barely two months later in July a new economic memorandum declared: 'In order to support economic activity and to further strengthen the social safety net, the Supplementary Budget to be passed in August increases the deficit in 1998 to 4 per cent of GDP'. And the letter of intent dated 13 November 1998 stated clearly:

> The government is attempting to stem further economic contraction through a combination of stimulative fiscal policy and accommodating monetary policy. The National Assembly approved the Supplementary Budget in September to allow the fiscal deficit to expand to around 5 per cent of GDP in 1998. The draft budget for 1999 also incorporates a fiscal deficit of 5 per cent of GDP with public investment spending to be concentrated in the first half of the year. The actual application of planned spending is being monitored on a weekly basis to make sure that fiscal stimulus takes effect in a timely manner. (Govt of Korea 1998c)

Monetary policy was also eased. Call rates declined to well below pre-crisis levels, although lending rates declined less rapidly.

The reasons for this continuous flexibility with regard to the fiscal deficit and monetary policy are not hard to find. When the IMF programme began in early December 1998, the projection was that, as compared with growth in GDP of around 5.5 per cent recorded in 1997, the growth in 1998 would be around 3 per cent. To quote the first letter of intent:

> The programme is intended to narrow the external current account deficit to below 1 per cent of GDP in 1998 and 1999, contain inflation at or below 5 per

cent, and – hoping for an early return of confidence – limit the deceleration in real GDP growth to about 3 per cent in 1998, followed by a recovery towards potential in 1999. (Govt of Korea 1997a)

By February 1998 the GDP growth projection was placed at a positive 1 per cent, although zero or negative growth was seen as a possibility. By May the letter of intent projected real GDP growth at minus 1 per cent, while admitting that 'more negative growth remains possible'. Soon thereafter on July 24 the projection was changed to the objective of 'containing the decline in real GDP to 4 per cent, with recovery starting in 1999'. The Memorandum of Economic Policies prepared for the IMF in November 1998 remained silent on growth in 1998 and includes in its macroeconomic projections for 1999 the expectation of 'positive growth resuming during the year; the timing and strength of recovery will depend critically on improvements in domestic confidence and the external environment'. Very clearly the notion that larger deficits and the 'early return of confidence' would trigger a recovery had not been realized. Deficits did not work because the economy remained open and their effects did not remain in the domestic economy.

Nor did restored investor confidence seem to matter. According to the IMF Executive Board's assessment announced in May 1998, substantial progress had been made in overcoming the financial crisis. To start with, after continuous depreciation until March, the won appreciated slightly and stabilized. In November the currency stood at around 1,250 to the dollar as compared with 1,620 to the dollar in February. Second, inflation was close to zero on a month-on-month basis since March 1998 and the annualized rate at 7 per cent in August was well below the 9 per cent target set in July. Third, after the debt restructuring agreement with foreign banks reached in early April 1998, which converted private short-term debt into government guaranteed long-term debt, albeit at a high interest rate, the South Korean government successfully managed a US$4 billion bond issue. This compares with Malaysia's decision in late July 1998 to postpone a US$2 billion Eurobond issue because of poor market conditions. Fourth, as a result of the contraction in economic activity, imports of all categories of goods virtually collapsed in the last quarter of 1997 and the first quarter of 1998, so that even with exports performing poorly, the current account was in surplus from November 1997, with the surplus averaging close to US$3.8 billion a month after February 1998. Fifth, according to the IMF's assessment, there had been a significant increase in portfolio inflows. Sixth, bargain hunting by international corporations seeking to pick up assets of beleaguered South Korean firms had resulted in large inflows of capital. Finally, as a result of all this, the usable foreign reserves rose sharply from less than US$9 billion in December 1997 to over US$40 billion in August 1998, surpassing all expectations.

So the issue is not one of the persistence of a lack of confidence but of the fact that the return of such confidence had failed to spur economic recovery. This is because the kind of flows that sustained the speculative bubble of the mid-1990s could not be expected any longer. On the other hand, the IMF's 'adjustment strategy', which put South Korea on a traverse involving direct deflation through sharply curtailed capital formation, enforced bankruptcies and reduced government expenditures, had set off a cumulative decline which slightly more permissive fiscal regimes and restored investor confidence were finding too difficult to reverse. Within the IMF's framework, only a sharp turn-around in exports could have provided a new stimulus to growth. Unfortunately, exports were taking a beating as the contagion from East Asia spread to other parts of the world and began to tell on growth in the industrialized countries as well. Clearly the IMF's policies had set South Korea on a disastrous traverse which created conditions that undermine the ability of the system to realize the principal goal of the strategy: a restoration of growth with stability.

Table 6.12: Non-performing credit of South Korean banks (million won)

	Bad Credit	**Non-perf.**
1990	1.9	7.2
1991	2.1	8.3
1992	2.4	10.3
1993	2.9	12.1
1994	1.9	11.7
1995	2.3	12.5
1996	2.5	12.2
1997	10.1	22.6

Source: Bank of Korea

Further, the downward slide of the real economy was making the process of dealing with the financial crisis even more difficult. As we have mentioned, for the corporate sector the results of IMF-style deflation were disastrous. Corporate insolvencies that averaged around 3,500 companies a quarter during the first three quarters of 1997 and rose to more than 6,000 during the last quarter, touched close to 9,500 during the first quarter of 1998. This had a financial implication. Corporate insolvencies were precisely the reason for the sharp rise in the non-performing credit of the Korean banking system in 1997. The non-performing credit ratio increased sharply to 6.0 per cent at of the end of December 1997 from 3.9 per cent at the end of 1996, because of the bankruptcy of large companies such as Hanbo, Kia, Halla and Sammi, which held large outstanding credits. What emerges from Table 6.12 is that the non-performing credit ratio of the South Korean banking system actually fell from an average of around 7 per cent during 1990–93 to an average of about 5 per cent precisely during the years (1994–96) of the credit financed boom in South Korean industry. It was the subsequent reduction in growth that pushed this ratio up once again, by making it difficult for South Korean corporations both to cross-subsidise their operations and to meet their debt service commitments.

The implications are clear. The IMF's recipe for South Korea not only failed to restore growth, but also contributed to a worsening of the core financial crisis. So long as the costs of that 'error', determined by an overwhelming concern with protecting the interests of international finance and winning its confidence once again, were borne by South Korea's workers and white-collar employees, the West accepted the virtual economic genocide of a nation. But as the evidence grew that the consequences of the crisis would touch on the bottom lines of the large corporations of the West and erode the livelihood of its own population, disillusionment with the IMF increased.

CONCLUSION

It is now acknowledged by almost all observers that the late 1990s crisis in emerging markets may be more than a passing tendency or a simple cyclical downturn in the pattern of capital flows. It could mark the beginning of the end of a particular phase of international capitalism, in which deregulation and increased economic integration – the typical features that are described as 'globalization' – led to dramatic material changes as well as a much greater degree of volatility and uncertainty.

It is increasingly evident that there is very little option for greater regulation of volatile capital flows, for developing countries which need a minimum degree of stability to pursue their own developmental goals. The alternative, it is now clear, is both too uncertain and too costly in terms of the economic devastation wreaked on citizens. Thus, in the most significant 'emerging markets' – those in East and Southeast Asia, along with Russia – most domestic macroeconomic changes in the past decade have been driven by capital flows, rather than the other way around. And because these capital flows have been relatively unregulated thanks to financial liberalization, they have created domestic economic pressures which governments have been powerless to confront.

The most stark evidence of this comes from the extent of the macroeconomic adjustment which has been forced on the Southeast Asian countries in the wake of the capital outflow. In 1998, barring the Philippines which managed to keep its surplus small, the other ASEAN–4 countries and South Korea were forced to generate current account surpluses of between 3 and 13 per cent of GDP. The most dramatic changes were in South Korea and Thailand, which moved from the fairly large deficits of 1996 to relatively huge surpluses in 1998. These surpluses were squeezed out of economies that were contracting heavily, and meant declines in personal disposable income far in excess of the fall in domestic output generated. Thus, the improvement in trade balance has had to come from massive import compression in these economies, reflecting the general state of worsening depression.

The message for other developing countries is clear, and should not be allowed to disappear in the miasma of misrepresentation which the IMF and other institutions are seeking to spread, by focusing on 'crony capitalism' and other such tendencies which are clearly present in every single capitalist country, including those of the advanced West. Developing countries simply cannot afford to allow completely unregulated capital flows, and will have to rely on various different ways of controlling and regulating such flows in accordance with national priorities.

Freedom from the uncertain pattern of growth driven by capital flows, in turn implies that these countries have to ensure that vulnerability on the current account is constantly under check. What the Southeast Asian crisis suggests is that even medium-term export gains are not a guarantee that excessive trade liberalization might not lead to greater dependence on capital flows and a possible economic downturn.

NOTES

1 For a detailed elaboration of this argument, see World Bank 1998.

REFERENCES:

Bullard, Nicola, with W. Bello and K. Malhotra (1998) 'Taming the tigers: The IMF and the Asian crisis', in Jomo K. S. (ed.) *Tigers in Trouble: Financial Governance, Liberalization and Crises in East Asia.* London: Zed Books.

Chandrasekhar. C. P. and J. Ghosh (1998) 'Hubris, hysteria and hope: The political economy of crisis and response in East Asia', in Jomo K. S. (ed.) *Tigers in Trouble: Financial Governance, Liberalization and Crises in East Asia.* London: Zed Books.

Chang, Ho-Joon (1998) 'The Korean crisis: A dissenting view', *Third World Economics*, January.

Ghosh, J., Sen, A. and C. P. Chandrasekhar (1996) 'Southeast Asian economies: Miracle or meltdown?', *Economic and Political Weekly*, October.

Government of Korea (1997a) *Letter of Intent and Memorandum on the Economic Program*, Seoul. Korea, December 3. (available at IMF website, www.imf.org)

—— (1997b), *IMF Stand-By Arrangement: Summary of the Economic Program.* Seoul, Korea, 5 December. (available at IMF website, www.imf.org)

—— (1997c), *Letter of Intent.* Seoul, Korea, 24 December. (available at IMF website, www.imf.org)

—— (1998a), *Letter of Intent and Memorandum on the Economic Program.* Seoul, Korea, 7 February. (available at IMF website, www.imf.org)

—— (1998b), *Letter of Intent.* Seoul, Korea, 24 July. (available at IMF website, www.imf.org)

—— (1998c), *Letter of Intent and Memorandum on Economic Policies.* Seoul, Korea, 13 November. (available at IMF website, www.imf.org)

Government of Thailand (1998). *Letter of Intent and Memorandum on Economic Policies of the Royal Thai Government.* 24 February. (available at IMF website, www.imf.org)

Institute for International Finance (IIF) (1998) *Capital Flows to Emerging Market Economies.* Washington, DC: IIF, April.

—— (2000) *Capital Flows to Emerging Market Economies.* Washington DC: IIF, 24 January.

International Monetary Fund (1998a), *International Capital Markets: Developments, Prospects and Key Policy Issues.* Washington D.C.: IMF.

—— (1998b), 'IMF concludes Article IV consultation with Korea', Press Information Notice (PIN) No. 98/39, 19 June. (available at IMF website, www.imf.org)

—— (1998c) *World Economic Outlook.* Washington D.C.: IMF, October.

—— (1998d) *World Economic Outlook: Interim Assessment.* Washington D.C.: IMF, December.

—— (2000) *World Economic Outlook.* Washington D.C.: IMF, April.

Kindleberger, Charles P. (1986) *Keynesianism versus Monetarism and Other Essays in Financial History.* London: George Allen & Unwin.

Lauridsen, Laurids S. (1998) 'Thailand: causes, conduct, consequences' in Jomo K. S. (ed.) *Tigers in Trouble: Financial Governance, Liberalization and Crises in East Asia.* London: Zed Books.

Pasuk Phongpaichit (1998) 'The Thai economic crisis and the way forward'. Mimeo, Bangkok, Thailand.

Radelet, S. and Sachs, J. D. (1998) 'The East Asian financial crisis: Diagnosis, remedies, prospects', *Brookings Papers on Economic Activity*, 1.

Singh, Ajit (1996) 'Liberalization and globalization: financial liberalization and its implications for industrialising economies'. Paper presented to Conference on Globalization and Development, University of Malaya, Kuala Lumpur, August.

Stein, Howard (ed.) (1995) *Asian Industrialization and Africa: The Alternatives to Structural Adjustment.* London: St Martin's Press.

Stiglitz, Joseph (2000) 'Development policy at the new millennium'. Mimeo.

Veneroso, Frank and Robert Wade (1998) 'The Asian financial crisis: the unrecognized risk of the IMF's Asia package', *Public Policy*, January.

Wade, Robert (1990) *Governing the Market: Economic Theory and the Role of Government in East Asian Industrialization*, Princeton: Princeton University Press.

World Bank (1998) *Global Economic Prospects and the Developing Countries: 1998–99.* Washington, DC: World Bank (Web site, www.worldbank.org).

SEVEN

Taming the IMF
How the Asian Crisis Cracked the Washington Consensus

Nicola Bullard

Thanks to the Asian crisis, the IMF is now a household word. In Bangkok, bars offer exotic IMF cocktails, shaped like bombs with a sparkling fuse while peasants in the Thailand's Northeast have added the 'IMF Era Man' to the panoply of demons to be exorcised during the annual rocket festival. In Korea newspapers report IMF suicides, while in Malaysia they thank God that they don't have the IMF, because Mahathir in addition to the IMF would be just too much! IMF funding has, for the first time, become a topic of heated debate in the US Congress while, at the October 1998 World Bank and IMF meetings in Washington, there was a discernible unease: If you listened carefully you could almost hear the tectonic growl of the Washington Consensus shifting, heaving and cracking.

And it's about time. For too long, the IMF has gone about its business, dictating economic policy to any country unfortunate enough to need its money, without any inclination to engage in open debate about what it does, how it makes decisions, and whose interests it is serving. But all this is changed, thanks to the Asian economic crisis.

This is an important political moment but to make the most of it we need to understand what ground has been gained and what still needs to be done.

What is the Washington Consensus and why does it matter?

The Washington Consensus has dominated economic thinking for almost two decades. Firmly grounded in neoliberal economics, the doctrine preaches that the solution to under-development lies in three stages of economic transformation: stabilization, structural adjustment and export-led growth (Green 1996).

Stabilization comprises two elements: controlling inflation and reducing the supply of money by cutting government expenditure and raising interest rates.

The second phase of structural adjustment – which follows hot on the heels of stabilization – aims to establish a market economy. The main objective is to 'get the price right' by reducing 'distortions' such as tariffs and price controls, limiting the role of the state which is seen as interfering with prices and the free market, privatizing state-owned enterprises and promoting the private sector, 'reforming' the labour market to allow for flexibility such as short-term contracts and subcontracting, and reducing government deficits by cutting expenditure and increasing revenue through taxes such as VAT.

The third element of the Washington Consensus is the promotion of export-led growth, boosting exports by reducing trade barriers and encouraging foreign investment by liberalizing investment regimes.

If this all sounds remarkably familiar, it is because this programme was perfected in the era of Thatcher and Reagan and has infiltrated economic thinking in almost every corner of the world. It is the perfect preparation, or softening-up, for fully fledged global economic liberalization. However, as we have seen in Asia, the crossing from state-led capitalism via the Washington Consensus and onto the globalized free market is fraught with dangers. Simply, when bad development meets globalization, the result can be devastating.

East meets West

The Asian economies most affected by the 1997 economic crisis – Thailand, Indonesia, the Philippines, Malaysia and South Korea – each adopted various elements of the neoliberal model with various degrees of enthusiasm, adherence and coercion. The resulting combination of Washington Consensus and Asian state-led capitalism created a kind of *real economik*, in which the interests of domestic and foreign elites were protected and promoted, and then repackaged by the World Bank as the model of successful development.

Export-led growth was tremendously successful in terms of ensuring year-on-year economic growth, but this was not matched by the expansion of political participation and economic democracy, resulting in weak (and often repressive) political systems, limited accountability and poorly developed domestic markets.

In the early 1990s, as the momentum of export-led growth began to slow, these countries rapidly liberalized financial markets to attract foreign capital and to spur growth through equity markets. In response G7 banks, investors and speculators swarmed into Asia in search of higher returns because their own economies were in recession. One measure of the success of financial liberalization is the phenomenal growth of capital flows to emerging markets, doubling in just two years, from US$154 billion in 1994 to US$304 billion in 1996. Private capital flows to the Asian Five – Thailand, the Philippines, Indonesia, South Korea and Malaysia – almost tripled in three years, from US$37.9 billion in 1994 to US$97.1 billion in 1996. However, by 1997, the net flow was minus US$11.9 billion, a staggering turnaround of US$109 billion in just one year (Institute of International Finance 1998). Much of this 'hot money' was seeking a quick return and high profits and was used to finance property development and consumer credit. In many cases there was a poor match between short-term loans and long-term investments.

What was the source of the crisis?

Comparison between the five countries embroiled in the Asian economic crisis is a useful way of identifying the key causes of the Asian crisis. South Korea, Thailand, Indonesia, the Philippines and Malaysia have a number of common features: all adopted an export-oriented growth model, each had experienced relatively high and consistent economic growth for two decades (with the Philippines being a notable exception, largely due to that country's extraordinarily high debt burden accumulated during the Marcos era) and each became increasingly dependent on foreign capital at the expense of domestic capital. To finance growth, these countries embarked on a rapid but rather unsystematic process of financial liberalization from the early 1990s and provided a de facto guarantee for investors by pegging currencies to the US dollar.

But here the comparisons break down. Each country has different political, social and economic institutions, different distributions of wealth, natural resources, population size and education levels, rural-to-urban ratios, and the relative importance of industry and agriculture varies enormously. Therefore, it is likely that the shared characteristics of rapid liberalization and weak institutions, dependency on exports, and the surge in foreign speculative investment are important explanatory factors.

It is useful to focus on Thailand, the epicentre of the economic crisis. By early 1997, it was evident that Thailand's boom was about to go bust, with a slowdown in export earnings, a glut in the property sector and a growing number of shaky financial institutions. Once the market got wind of the collapse of one of the country's largest finance companies, Finance One, speculators started to attack the baht and investors took their money out with alarming speed. The Thai government threw billions of dollars of foreign reserves at the speculators, trying to avoid the grim prospect of devaluation. But the market proved too strong and on 2 July 1997 Thailand was forced to withdraw from the battle, allowing the baht to float, leaving the government with depleted foreign reserves, mounting debts and a financial sector in ruins. The Thai government, which had pursued enthusiastically the policies of financial liberalization, and backed it by guaranteeing a pegged exchange rate, suddenly found that the liberalization merry-go-round goes both ways.

Just one month later, on 11 August 1997, amidst growing public pressure for decisive action and with 42 finance companies effectively in government receivership, the IMF arrived in Thailand with a US$17.2 billion line of credit and a long list of conditions. In addition to strong measures to reform the finance sector, the package included a standard stabilization and structural adjustment programme of reduced government expenditure, raised taxes, privatization, high interest rates and further trade and financial liberalization. But the IMF bailout did not restore the market's faith in the Asian miracle and the so-called contagion spread like wildfire throughout the region. South Korea and Indonesia were the worst hit and found themselves victims of speculative currency attacks and massive capital flight. By 31 October that year Indonesia had signed on to a US$43 billion IMF-brokered loan and on 3 December 1997 South Korea – which had joined the rich man's club of the OECD less than two years earlier – accepted a record-breaking US$57 billion line of credit.

THE ROLE OF THE IMF

Following its intervention in Thailand, Indonesia and South Korea, the IMF found itself under attack from all sides. Suddenly non-government organizations and the progressive left, whose criticism of the IMF dates back to the Fund's stabilization programmes of the early 1980s, found themselves in unlikely company. The criticisms came from some surprising sources, including former IMF employee and director of the Harvard Institute for International Development Jeffrey Sachs, World Bank chief economist Joseph Stiglitz, solid, conservative jour-nals such as *The Economist* and *The Financial Times*, republicans and democrats in the US Congress, and even bone-dry neoliberals such as former US president Ronald Reagan's chief economic adviser Martin Feldstein.

The debates are wide-ranging and call into question fundamentals such as the efficacy and appropriateness of the Fund's economic advice, the way the Fund operates, and its relationship with its key shareholder, the US.

The Fund sometimes gives poor advice

The public sector austerity measures imposed by the IMF, such as budget cuts, pushing up interest rates and raising taxes, were inappropriate for the circumstances of a private sector debt crisis and in fact deepened and accelerated contraction of the economies they were meant to be helping. As Jeffrey Sachs (1997) said, 'the currency crisis is not the result of Asian government profligacy. This is a crisis made mainly in the private, albeit under-regulated, financial markets.' Yet the IMF applied policy measures designed to rein in government overspending without addressing the real issue of private sector failure.

The Fund's macroeconomic requirements were meant to stabilize currencies and restore market confidence. In Thailand, South Korea and Indonesia, the currencies continued to devalue with gathering momentum even after the IMF's intervention, indicating that their economic policies were neither addressing the real problems nor having the magic effect of restoring market and investor confidence. In the year that followed the IMF's intervention, the five Asian economies spiralled into a self-perpetuating recession, and in the case of Indonesia, a depression.

The Fund's tight monetary policies, designed to control inflation, stabilize the currency and allow banks to achieve the Bank for International Settlement capital adequacy rations, are strangling the real economy. Growing unemployment, reduced exports, falling consumer demand and mounting portfolios of non-performing loans have driven the economies into deep recession.

In the past year, growth predictions have moved from a cautious region-wide growth of 2–3 per cent (predicted in November last year) to a region-wide negative growth of minus 5–7 per cent, with estimates for Indonesia as high as minus 15 per cent. In short, the IMF policy prescriptions have accelerated and deepened the crisis, and allowed it to spread from the financial sector to the real economy. And, as World Bank chief economist Joseph Stiglitz remarked in a speech to Canada's North South Institute (29 September 1998), it's much easier to get into a recession than to get out of one.

Moral hazard

The IMF also stands accused of creating the problem of 'moral hazard', whereby both creditors and debtors who make unwise investment choices are saved from the consequences of their bad decisions, thus making it more likely that they will reoffend in the future.

The Fund has also come under fire for its continued enthusiasm for freeing up capital flows. The crisis in Asia is a crisis of the private sector which engaged in excessive borrowing of easy-to-obtain foreign finance, following liberalization of capital account regimes from the 1980s onwards. Therefore the IMF's policy response of demanding further liberalization of the finance sector and financial flows is wrong and actually 'adds to financial vulnerability and renders these economies even more prone to future crisis' (Chandrasekhar and Ghosh, this volume).

Speaking in Helsinki on 7 January 1998, the World Bank's chief economist Joseph Stiglitz went even further, saying that 'financial markets do not do a good job of selecting the most productive recipients of funds or of monitoring the use of funds and must be controlled' (Hanlon 1998).

The pain of adjustment is not fairly distributed

There is a double standard at work in the treatment of 'domestic' and 'foreign' interests. Domestic firms are left to the mercy of the market (for example, the IMF insisted that numerous financial institutions in Indonesia and Thailand could not be bailed out). Foreign investors, on the other hand, are given enhanced rights to ownership, the possibility to convert debt to equity in struggling Asian enterprises and the chance of picking up others at bargain basement prices, thanks to changes in foreign ownership rules included in the IMF packages.

IMF bailouts of the private sector have also been criticized for socializing the debt, leaving the government and the taxpaying public, both in Asia and in the IMF's main contributor nations, to bear the burden of the private sector's failure.

The Fund has gone beyond its remit and should be overhauled

Critics argue that the IMF has exceeded its mandate as defined in its Articles of Agreement and has assumed the role of global economic policeman, 'forcing it into a convergence towards the reigning consensus' (Unger 1996)[1] (in this case, the Washington Consensus).

Martin Feldstein, Professor of Economics at Harvard University, President of the National Bureau of Economic Research and former adviser to US President Ronald Reagan, is sharply critical of the IMF:

> Imposing detailed economic prescriptions on legitimate governments would remain questionable even if economists were unanimous about the best way to reform the countries' economic policies. In practice, however, there are substantial disagreements about what should be done. (Feldstein 1998)

He goes on to say that the Fund should not use the opportunity of countries being 'down and out' to override national political processes or impose economic changes that 'however helpful they may be, are not necessary to deal with the balance-of-payments problem and are the proper responsibility of the country's own political system'. He continues: '[A] nation's desperate need for short-term financial help does not give the IMF the moral right to substitute its technical judgements for the outcomes of the nation's political process' (ibid.).

It is worth going back to the original Articles of Agreement of the Fund to get a rough measure of whether it is achieving its objectives, even on its own terms. The purposes of the International Monetary Fund are:

1. to promote international monetary cooperation through a permanent institution which provides the machinery for consultation and collaboration on international monetary problems;
2. to facilitate the expansion and balanced growth of trade, and to contribute thereby to the promotion and maintenance of high levels of employment and real income and to the development of productive resources of all members as primary objectives of economic policy;
3. to promote exchange stability, to maintain orderly exchange arrangements among members, and to avoid competitive exchange depreciation;
4. to assist in the establishment of a multilateral system of payments in respect of current transaction between members and in the elimination of foreign exchange restrictions which hamper the growth of world trade;
5. to give confidence to members by making the general resources of the Fund temporarily available to them under adequate safeguards, thus providing them with opportunity to correct maladjustments in their balance of payments;
6. in accordance with the above, to shorten the duration and lessen the degree of disequilibrium in the international balances of payments of members (IMF Articles of Agreement, Article 1).

In short, there is nothing about trade and investment liberalization, privatization, foreign investment or public sector austerity measures, all of which are central to the IMF's demands in Asia. Article 2, however, mentions the Fund's role in promoting 'high levels of employment and real income' – purposes which the Fund has clearly failed to achieve in South Korea, Thailand and Indonesia, with current estimates that an additional 20 million people have lost their livelihood and jobs as a result of the crisis.

While it demands greater transparency from government and financial systems, the IMF has itself been criticized for its lack of transparency and accountability. Again, Jeffrey Sachs goes straight to the point: 'Of course, one can't be sure what the IMF is advising, since the IMF programmes and supporting documents are hidden from public view. This secrecy itself gravely undermines confidence' (Sachs 1997).

The Fund has also been attacked for its intellectual arrogance in applying the same solution, regardless of the problem. According to Joseph Stiglitz, the main problem is the belief that 'political recommendations could be administered by economists using little more than simple accounting frameworks', leading to the situation where 'economists would fly into a country, look at and attempt to verify these data, and make macroeconomic recommendations for policy reforms, all in the space of a couple of weeks' (Hanlon 1998).

The IMF works in the interests of powerful nations, especially the US

Finally, there is well-founded concern about the policy and power nexus between the IMF and its major shareholder, the US. In the face of increasing resistance at home to its free-wheeling liberalization agenda,[2] the US Government is having to rely even more on bodies such as the IMF and Asia Pacific Economic Cooperation (APEC) to push its trade objectives. This became abundantly clear in the course of the recent US Congressional debate over IMF funding, where the pro-funding side argued in terms of leverage and protecting US interests. Treasury Secretary Robert Rubin put it bluntly, saying that 'failure to provide funding could reduce our leverage in the IMF' (*Far Eastern Economic Review*, 12 Febraury 1998: 14).

Interestingly, both the Congressional and Senate versions of the contested funding bill included strong trade and investment liberalization obligations as a precondition for receiving IMF funding.

The United States' Trade Representative Charlene Barshefsky, in her testimony to the House Ways & Means Subcommittee, described how US interests could be furthered by the IMF: 'Many of the structural reform components of the IMF packages will contribute directly to improvements in the trade regimes in those countries. If effectively implemented, these programmes will complement and reinforce our trade policy goals' (USTR 1998). To make it clear that the US would brook no competition, Barshefsky continued, 'Support for the IMF ... sends the important message that America will continue to lead in the world economy' (ibid.).

The IMF's first Deputy Managing Director, Stanley Fischer, reinforced this view in a speech early in 1998. Outlining the primary purpose of the IMF, he quoted first from the Articles of Agreement: 'To facilitate ... the balanced growth of international trade and to contribute thereby to ... high levels of growth and real income', and then added his own words, 'we have consistently promoted trade liberalization' (Fischer 1998). There is a seamless congruence between the IMF's worldview and that of its biggest shareholder, the US.

The US was also responsible for derailing Japan's proposal, early on in the crisis, to establish an Asian Monetary Fund capitalized at US$100 billion and designed to respond quickly to currency and market instability in the region. Japan had good reasons for putting its money on the table: Japanese banks are heavily exposed to Thailand, South Korea and Indonesia and it is in their interests to stabilize volatile currency markets. In addition the Japanese economy is deeply integrated with its neighbours so any slowdown or collapse has an immediate domestic impact.

For some time Japan has promoted an Asia-specific development model in its dealings with international institutions such as the IMF and the World Bank. Essentially, Japan has argued that the Washington Consensus of rapid deregulation, reducing the role of the state and liberalization of capital flows may not be the best path for countries such as those in Asia which have followed a state-led development model. Japan maintains that severing the links between the state and industry the one hand, and the banks on the other would be politically unpalatable and may not achieve the expected results.

In short, the Asian Monetary Fund was conceived as being more flexible, less doctrinaire and 'more Asian' than the IMF deal. It seemed like a good idea if for no other reason than to break the IMF monopoly on economic thought and open the market to new ideas and economic paradigms.

In the event, Japan was forced to back down in the face of 'heated opposition from officials at the Department of the Treasury, most notably the Deputy Secretary Lawrence Summers, and the International Monetary Fund... They instead reaffirmed the central role of the IMF in the Asian financial bailout' (Altbach 1997). The course of the economic crisis might have been quite different had the Asian Monetary Fund seen the light of day. First, the AMF would have been more flexible in its terms whereas the IMF's inflexibility deepened the economic crisis. Second, and this should not be underestimated, the IMF is seen in Asia as the instrument of Western neoliberalism and, for example, an 'Asian' approach might have proved more effective in dealing with President Suharto.

MARGINAL VOICES NOW IN THE MAINSTREAM

If we look through the list of criticisms directed at the Fund in the aftermath of the crisis, most if not all are now accepted as valid by everyone save some die-hards in the Fund itself and many of the reforms proposed since seek to address them directly. Looking at the broad clusters of criticisms in turn, we can see how each has been addressed by specific reform proposals and marked policy change.

'The Fund sometimes gives poor advice'

World Bank chief economist Joseph Stiglitz, who is leading the charge against the Washington Consensus within the international financial institutions, said:

> I do not want to enter into the debate about whether the policies which were put into place in the aftermath of the East Asia crisis exacerbated the downturn. The counterfactuals are always difficult: what would have happened if ... While not all the jury may have turned in their ballots, there is a growing consensus on the matter. (Stiglitz 1998)

Mr Stiglitz may not have entered the debate, but it's very clear which side he is on.

The IMF, however, does not admit that some of its policy advice was wrong and generally seems unwilling to debate the issues publicly. However, in the past months there have been gradual shifts on some key policy positions. Letters of intent with Thailand, South Korea and Indonesia show a decided easing of tight fiscal and monetary policy by allowing interest rates slowly to drop and allowing government deficits to expand (although given dwindling government revenues due to declining taxes and loss of export earnings, the government is being squeezed on both income and expenditure). According to IMF Asian Regional Director Hubert Neiss, 'the IMF is not preaching austerity at the moment, it's preaching fiscal expansion. We're in a different phase now' (*Bangkok Post*, 15 September 1998).

In addition, widespread support for Japan's US$30 billion Miyazawa Initiative and the US proposal to establish a quick response credit facility within the Fund which would not attract the usual IMF policy conditions,[3] recognizes the need for new, alternative and flexible responses to economic crises beyond the traditional IMF formula.

Since the early 1990s, the IMF and the World Bank have been pushing countries to open their capital accounts. Almost every analysis of the causes of the Asian financial crisis identifies rapid capital account liberalization and the subsequent uncontrolled movement of finance capital as a major contributing factor. At the September 1997 annual meetings, the IMF was pushing enthusiastically for an expansion of its remit to include mandatory capital account convertibility for all borrowing countries. However, in the past year policy advice has poured in from all directions – including the finance industry-backed Institute of International Finance – against rapid liberalization. The IMF has softened its position considerably on this count, noting in its 1998 capital markets report that 'the combination of a weak banking system and an open capital account was an accident waiting to happen.'

However, the almost universal criticism of Malaysia's decision to impose currency controls shows that there is deep hostility to nations taking these matters into their own hands, and that the *principle* of open capital accounts is still a non-negotiable item of the Washington Consensus.

'The pain of adjustment is not fairly distributed'

Criticisms about the burden of private sector failure being shifted to the public sector have also been noted. Again Joseph Stiglitz placed the question squarely on the World Bank agenda when he said:

> The situation is intolerable. We have an international economic architecture which has led to more frequent crises, and yet our means of responding have proved inadequate. While there is much talk about pain, the poor have absorbed more than their share of the pain without sharing commensurately in the promised gain. (*Bangkok Post,* 15 September 1998)

For Stiglitz, the solution lies in creating more democratic institutions 'so that these silent voices are heard'. This must be a cornerstone of the new global financial architecture, but some more immediate measures have also been proposed. For example, the US and Japan have unveiled a plan to establish a G7-funded agency to buy up debts issued by overseas creditors to private companies in Asia at a discount of 20–30 per cent (*Australian Financial Review,* 26 October 1998).

The United Nations Conference on Trade and Development's (UNCTAD) 1998 *Trade and Development Report* advocates at a global level some rules akin to Chapter 11 of the US bankruptcy code, and in particular an automatic standstill principle, to enable countries in specified circumstances to impose unilateral standstill, similar to the safeguard action allowed under the GATT. They should then be able to approach an independent international panel to justify their case and get further relief. However, the UNCTAD report warns that the IMF as presently constituted is not able to perform this task because its governance structure gives weight to the views of creditors over debtors.

Other proposals include bringing the private sector into financing bailout loans, encouraging greater private-sector risk assessment, and establishing stronger insolvency and debtor–creditor regimes. However, all of these proposals are somewhat limited in that they depend to a large extent on good will, effective domestic legislation and willingness of the private sector to assume risk.

So long as the IMF provides the ultimate guarantee against private-sector risk, the incentives are not strong. Perhaps a more compelling and simpler solution would be an international bankruptcy law to ensure the orderly workout of private sector debt in a transparent and equitable manner.

'The Fund has gone beyond its remit'

The arguments on the IMF mandate have, in fact, gone in the opposite direction, with many calls for expansion of the IMF's role to include environmental, labour, good governance and democracy conditions.

On this issue there are widely diverging opinions: on the one hand critics say that the Fund needs to take into account the social and environmental impact of its programme and therefore needs a broader mandate and better coordination with the World Bank. On the other hand, some argue that the Fund's role should be limited to preventing a breakdown in trade due to short-term balance-of-payments difficulties, and that the strictly stabilizing role of the Fund should be de-linked from the long-term development mission of the Bank and other multilateral development agencies. The thinking behind the second view is that the Fund is not a democratic, accountable or transparent institution, and therefore should not be given the authority to make judgements about issues such as good governance or democracy.

The Fund – keen to extend its purview and staunch criticism – has attempted to broaden its dialogue and discuss the social impacts of their programmes. For example, in each country the IMF has 'consulted' with the labour unions. Not that it would pass any reasonable test of 'consultation' but at least they think that they should be doing something. Or should they? This raises an important question about the IMF and its mandate: does the IMF have a right to consult with the labour sector, or vice versa? Does this undermine domestic democratic processes by sidestepping governments who should be accountable to workers? In South Korea this issue is pertinent: the IMF has agreed to meet informally with labour representatives, but the better solution would be for labour organizations to extract a commitment from their own government for workers' representation in negotiations with the Fund, or (better but even less likely) be confident that the elected government would properly represent and protect workers' interests.

Although it is tempting to see the IMF as the *deus ex machina* which can solve problems like Suharto, corruption and the *chaebol*, this is dangerous ground. The IMF is not a democratic organization and its policy interventions impinge on legitimate powers of the state and can undermine domestic political development.

'The IMF works in the interests of powerful nations'

There is no headlong move comprehensively to overhaul the IMF and so far most suggestions for institutional reform have focused on transparency and accountability. The Fund itself is completely unused to outside scrutiny and responds to most criticisms with defensive arrogance. Transparency is seen as simply making information available and accountability means making more information available (G22 1998). Democracy does not seem to be in their lexicon. Again, Joseph Stiglitz made a pertinent comment on transparency when he remarked to a group of non-governmental organizations in Washington that transparency is only meaningful if people are willing to debate different views.

However, there are some attempts to loosen the power nexus between the IMF and US Treasury.

Obviously shaken by the cataclysmic collapse of Russia (which, by the way, is never mentioned in polite company), Europe has suddenly realized that there is a crisis, that they are part of it and that the people they thought were fixing the problems are not. The French Finance Minister's proposal at the 1998 IMF World Bank annual meetings to strengthen the role of the IMF Interim Committee – a 24-member group which is equivalent to a board of governors and reflects the composition of the executive board – aims to make the Fund more directly accountable to its main shareholder governments and to break the policy stranglehold of the Board of Directors and the Washington power elite. Interestingly the proposal was supported by the IMF Managing Director Michel Camdessus, himself an elite French bureaucrat, who may be looking for a way to break free of the US Treasury and save his institution. UK Prime Minister Tony Blair has also called for 'sweeping reforms', but if Chancellor Gordon Brown's proposals for setting fiscal and financial codes of conduct are any indication, 'sweeping' can mean different things to different people.

Indeed, the Bretton Woods institutions have earned such a bad name in the current crisis that even the London *Financial Times* now refers to them as 'the gruesome twosome'.

Noticeably absent from the establishment debate, however, are calls for a complete overhaul of the IMF structure to make it more democratic and representative, or even for its abolition.

TAMED BUT NOT TIED DOWN ...

On balance it is fair to say that the International Monetary Fund has been chastened, if not yet tamed. According to *The Wall Street Journal* of 26 October 1998, the IMF is looking for a public relations firm to 'figure out why the secretive agency is most unloved just when its activities are most visible'. Frankly, that's what the Americans call a 'no-brainer' – it's not a problem being misunderstood, it's a problem of policies.

But this paper also has a sub-title: how the Asian crisis cracked the Washington Consensus. Much of the above discussion supports the claim that the Washington Consensus is starting to unravel, but there have been economic crises before, and no doubt there will be again. Why is Asia – which, excluding Japan counts for only 6 per cent of global trade – so important? Why did the collapse in Thailand, Indonesia and South Korea trigger all this soul-searching? There may be complicated answers, but there may also be a simple one.

For several decades, Southeast Asia's tiger economies were held up at the World Bank, the IMF and the US – the keepers of the Washington Consensus – as emblematic of good development, the very model of how to do things. Then everything started to spin out of control and even when the IMF applied the orthodox treatment, the standard IMF prescriptions, they came unstuck even more. It is the shattering of a dream – the dream of export-led growth, free trade and financial liberalization, in short the shattered dream of 'globalization' – that has finally cracked the Washington Consensus.

WHERE TO NOW?

The Washington Consensus is starting to unravel, but what will replace it? The set of reforms presently on offer is limited and seeks to put the train of economic globalization back on track. It includes measures such as increased surveillance, uniform reporting and accounting procedures, better risk assessment, strengthening domestic financial institutions, and more transparency in market transactions.

Many of these measures are absolutely necessary in the short term, such as opening the IMF to greater scrutiny, acknowledging that reckless capital account liberalization may not be wise and that speculative money creates instability and volatility, seeking ways of ensuring that the private sector shares an appropriate proportion of risks and loss, more coherent and better coordinated policy responses by governments and international institutions, and greater efforts to predict and prevent crisis.

But none of this actually addresses the underlying weakness of the present system. Without effective and binding mechanisms to ensure redistribution of resources and environmental sustainability, four-fifths of the world's population will continue to be excluded from the promised benefits of free trade and financial liberalization.

Reform of the global financial architecture is now on the agenda, but instead of thinking about architecture, we should be thinking about the people that we are building it for. Architects start their creative work by consulting the client, trying to understand what they want and how they live. It is a collaborative process. Designing the global financial architecture should be no different. However, the language itself limits our vision. 'Architecture' connotes institutions rather than relationships, rigid structures rather than dynamic processes. We should, instead, be thinking about the values that we want to express and promote. Only then should we think about what sort of institutions – either local, national, regional or global – that we need to do the job. When the Bretton Woods institutions were founded more than 50 years ago, there was a vision – albeit a reflection of the dominant powers – but nonetheless a vision based on shared values of a better world. There are no values in the Washington Consensus, just self-interest.

The basis for our design should be increasing political participation, economic democracy and social justice, and a desire to replenish and sustain the environment. This means pushing decisions *down* the 'food chain'. Minimally, it means stripping the IMF of its assumed power to impose policy conditions on governments. Minimally, it means allowing governments to establish whatever kinds of barriers they think are necessary to protect their domestic economies from the unpredictable global economy. Minimally, it means recognizing that there is no single solution – even though the advocates of economic globalization wish there were.

The results will be not be shiny marble-clad monuments, but eclectic and useful, sometimes idiosyncratic, constantly changing, a nightmare for transnational corporations and anathema to the zealots of economic globalization. The global economy needs to be deconstructed and built again on a sound moral basis of equity and sustainability. No amount of tinkering and reform of the existing global financial architecture will get this result. No amount of surveillance and disclosure will put economic power back into the hands of the mass of people.

Getting rid of hot money

Joseph Stiglitz has called for a 'post-Washington Consensus' which 'cannot be based on Washington'. 'One principle of the emerging consensus', he says, 'is a greater degree of humility, the frank acknowledgement that we do not have all the answers' (Hanlon 1998).

Humility notwithstanding, there are two items that must be given priority: getting rid of hot money and making sure that the 'post-Washington Consensus' does not simply reflect the views of the elite. This means actively ensuring that the silent voices – the women, farmers and day labourers, the workers and small businessmen – are heard.

There is a lot of talk about 'cooling down hot money' but we have to do a lot more than that. We have to get rid of it and discredit the whole notion that there is anything useful in speculation. The financial market, as it presently operates, serves very little useful purpose and is, for the most part, non-productive. It does not create anything that you can eat or hold or sell or use. It does not add to the public good, and it distorts our collective understanding of what is valuable and productive. And, as we have seen with the recent near-collapse of Long Term Capital Management, it can threaten the whole financial system.

One of the ways of cooling down hot money is to redirect it into productive channels. A striking contradiction of the present economic system is that the massive accumulation of finance and speculative capital is due to overproduction – which is a bewildering thought considering that we live in a world where four-fifths of the population struggle daily with poverty. Yet, this is true. The massive profits of transnational corporations and banks have nowhere 'useful' to go, so they go into speculation.

In addition corporations make such stupendous profits that they have little need for traditional banking services, so banks have found new ways of making profits by diversifying into securities and non-FDI activities. This explains – at least partly – the proliferation of incomprehensible instruments which manipulate and capitalize on the cracks in the finance market to make quick profits. In addition, the tremendous growth of pension and mutual funds – due in large part to the privatization of social security and the individualism inherent in neoliberal economics – has created an enormous pool of highly mobile capital in search of maximum return.

But the other side of overproduction is demand. A simple solution to the problem of overproduction is to expand markets – that is, to put more money in the hands of more people, so that they can buy the simple, basic, life-enhancing goods that countries like Vietnam, China, Thailand and Brazil are so good at producing.

However, creating this demand requires significant social reform in terms of asset and income distribution – it means land reform and wage and labour reform. Industrialization via cheap labour and natural resource exploitation is no longer viable. We have reached the point where further economic growth can only be achieved by expanding domestic markets and most importantly by changing our definition of what is productive to include public goods, culture, the environment and human security. We are at a moment in history where economic necessity coincides with social justice.

CRISIS OF GLOBALIZATION

After the first group of countries, the contagion spread far beyond Asia to Russia and to Latin America. Obviously, this is not an 'Asian crisis'. It is not even a global crisis, it is a crisis of 'globalization'. There is agreement that there need to be some changes, but we cannot leave this matter to the G7 or even the G22.

The logic of globalization is that as we become more interdependent and integrated, inequalities between nations will begin to disappear, which is all the more reason to bring all members of the globalized economy – not just the G7 – to the table. In addition, there must be a role for civil society groups in any discussion of alternatives.

The European Union now has a majority of members with left or quasi-left governments. These governments were elected because people are concerned about unemployment, social exclusion, security and the environment. People are tired of the economics stripped of its social and political dimensions. People will no longer accept a world where progress is measured by meeting the macroeconomic targets for Euro harmonization. These concerns – for human and environmental security and sustainability – must be injected into the international debate about the way we construct global economic relations.

The logic of economic globalization is exclusion because it is based on competition – in capitalism there are winners and losers. In Europe, we have seen that exclusion creates fear, xenophobia and hatred. Globally exclusion causes war, famine, poverty and exploitation. We cannot accept this and we have now tremendous political opportunities to create a new vision of human society and to create the institutions and mechanisms to realize our vision. This cannot be left to the global elites – the G7, the G22, the Davos Summit or the outdated and undemocratic Bretton Woods institutions. That would be like giving matches to the arsonist.

NOTES

1 This article is an interesting and constructive analysis of how the Bretton Woods institutions could be reformed, animated by the impulse that the world economy 'needs more, not less, of all the benefits Bretton Woods was designed to provide through international coordination and supranational institutions' (p. 23).

2 Late in 1997 Congress failed to renew the President's 'fast-track' trade negotiating authority responding to an all-out public campaign opposing further liberalization.

3 Eligibility for credit nonetheless depends on adherence to certain macroeconomic policies, a kind of *ante facto* conditionality.

REFERENCES

Altbach, Eric (1997) 'The Asian Monetary Fund: a case study of Japanese regional leadership', *Japan Economic Institute Report*, 47A, 19 December.

Australian Financial Review (1998) 'Corporate debt rescue for Asia', 26 October.

Bangkok Post (1998) 'IMF expects short-term capital controls in Asia', 15 September.

Chandrasekhar, C. P. and Jayati Ghosh (1998) 'Hubris, hysteria and hope: the political economy of crisis and response in East Asia', in Jomo K. S. (ed.) *Tigers in Trouble: Financial Governance, Liberalization and Crises in East Asia.* London: Zed Books.

Far Eastern Economic Review (1998) 'Dollars and sense', 12 February.

Feldstein, Martin (1998) 'Refocusing the IMF', *Foreign Affairs,* March/April.

Fischer, Stanley (1998) 'The Asian crisis: a view from the IMF'. Address to the Midwinter Conference of the Bankers' Association of Foreign Trade, Washington DC, 22 January.

G22 (1998) 'Report of the Working Group on Transparency and Accountability', October (available on the World Bank website, www.worldbank.org).

Green, Duncan (1996) *Silent Revolution: the Rise of Market Economics in Latin America.* London: Cassell.

Hanlon, Joseph (1998) 'Bank admits HIPC conditions wrong', *Debt Update,* March.

IMF Articles of Agreement, Article 1, Purposes (IMF website, www.imf.org).

Institute for International Finance, Inc. (1998) 'Capital flows to emerging market economies', 30 April.

Sachs, Jeffrey D. (1997) 'The wrong medicine for Asia', *New York Times,* 3 November.

Stiglitz, Joseph (1998) 'Responding to economic crisis: policy alternatives for equitable recovery and development'. Paper presented at the North–South Institute Seminar, Ottawa (Canada) 29 September (available from the World Bank website, www.worldbank.org).

Unger, Robert Mangabiera (1996) 'The really new Bretton Woods', in M. Uzan (ed.), *The Financial System under Stress: An Architecture for the New World Economy.* New York and London: Routledge.

USTR website (1998) 'Testimony of Ambassador Charlene Barshefsky United States Trade Representative before the House Ways & Means Trade Subcommittee', 24 February.

PART III

NATIONAL MODELS AND DEVELOPMENT STRATEGIES

EIGHT

DEVELOPMENTAL STATES AND CRONY CAPITALISTS

James Putzel

INTRODUCTION

Where not long ago the popular interpretation of East Asian success looked for explanations of the 'miracle' in terms of unique 'Asian values', after the financial crisis unleashed in July 1997 the region was condemned as the site of 'crony capitalism' and the miracle as a 'confidence trick'. Those who never were willing to accept that many Asian countries had achieved accelerated growth through constructive state intervention into their economies, in direct contradiction to neoliberal economic prescriptions, claimed vindication in light of the depth of the crisis that struck some of the region's best past performers, notably South Korea.

One of the most striking features of past discussions about Asian growth was the tendency to group all growth experiences together and attempt to find a common cause. Perhaps the most problematic attempt in this regard was the World Bank's *East Asia Miracle* report of 1993. The Bank sought to explain the success stories of eight high performing Asian economies (HPAE). In doing so the report failed to differentiate significantly between the characteristics underlying the growth experience of Japan, the 'Four Tigers' (South Korea, Taiwan, Singapore and Hong Kong) and the newly industrializing economies (NIEs) of Southeast Asia (Thailand, Malaysia and Indonesia). This was in part due to the report's implicit rejection of theories about the developmental state. In searching for common causes, there also has not been enough attention paid to distinguishing between the individual growth experiences of each of these countries.

Further, not enough attention has been accorded to the fundamental changes that have occurred *over time* in both the Northeast Asian[1] tigers and the Southeast Asian NIEs. There have been basic and far-reaching political changes within many of these countries and a sharp change in the external political environment in which they have operated. Most importantly, in the late 1980s and early 1990s there was a rapid movement towards liberalization, especially in financial markets. I argue that this move may have undermined the very basis of an earlier successful development strategy in some countries of the region and was central to the way in which the crisis unfolded.

First I shall define a 'developmental state' and recall what have been the observable accomplishments of the tigers. I shall focus especially on South Korea and Taiwan, since Singapore and Hong Kong, as city-states, are unique. South Korea and Taiwan borrowed from the even earlier experience of Japan and the growth experience in each of these three countries contributed to inform the model of a 'developmental state'. But even here, important distinctions must be made between the route followed by South Korea on the one hand and Taiwan on the other. Second, I shall look at the latecomer NIEs in Southeast Asia in an attempt to assess the extent to which they could be considered to be in the same category as the developmental states of Northeast Asia. Third, I shall examine the way in which events from the mid-1980s onwards altered practices within all the countries mentioned, and created the conditions that led to the financial crisis. It is important to situate domestic changes in the context of globalization. The particular proposition that I want to focus on is that the most salient features of the developmental state appear to be largely incompatible with financial market liberalization.

'CRONY CAPITALISM' OR DEVELOPMENTAL STATE?

The term 'crony capitalism' was coined in the Philippines in the early 1980s by some of those in the business community who had become disenchanted with Marcos's martial law regime as its shallow debt-dependent growth began to unravel.[2] It referred to the network of businessmen who gained access to wealth through their connections to the president and channelled it largely into non-productive personal fortunes at home and abroad.[3] With the charges of 'crony capitalism' now targeted at Korea, it becomes necessary to recall why Korea and Taiwan by the early 1990s were widely recognized as ruled by 'developmental states' in sharp contrast to the kinds of 'predatory states' that held sway in countries like the Philippines.[4]

A basic understanding of the developmental state grows out of the work of Johnson on Japan, Amsden on Korea and Wade on Taiwan. Robert Wade's 'governed market' theory offers the most systematic understanding of the developmental state as it emerged in Northeast Asia after the Second World War and incorporates most of the insights from other analysts of the developmental state (Wade 1990; see also Johnson 1982, 1995; Amsden 1989).[5]

Wade (1990: 26) identifies three central features that have characterized the superior performance of the developmental state:

1. very high levels of productive investment, making for the transfer of techniques into actual production;
2. more investment in certain key industries than would have occurred in the absence of government intervention;
3. exposure of many industries to international competition in foreign markets, if not at home.

These were the direct result of government policies to intervene in markets confronting private market actors with a pattern of incentives and controls to influence their decisions while spreading the risk of investment to the society at large. In Wade's model, the essential organizational feature that permitted the state to behave in this manner was its *corporatist* character combined with more or less *authoritarian* political arrangements.

Taking off from Wade, it is possible to identify six key measures taken by the developmental states that were central to their performance:

1. redistributive land reform;
2. state control over finance;
3. macroeconomic stability to foster long-term investment;
4. industrial policy fostering import substitution and export production;
5. attention to agriculture and rural livelihoods;
6. incomes policy that raised living standards while social organisations were suppressed.

Let us now look at each of these in turn.

Redistributive land reform

In Taiwan and South Korea this institutional reform whereby the state presided over a major reallocation of property rights had far-reaching effects. It brought security to a large portion of the population that resided in rural areas, providing the basis for improved income and human capital formation and sustained political support for the central government. It removed land acquisition as an important source for wealth accumulation, thus redirecting the attention of private owners of wealth towards industrial investment. Finally, it established the basis for a growing domestic market to consume the products of the import-substituting manufacturing sector.[6]

State control over finance

The state's control over finance was a central organizational mechanism that gave it leverage to influence the action of private entrepreneurs. Through this means the state was able to ensure that private financial capital was subordinate to industrial capital. In Korea the Park Chung Hee regime nationalized the banks until the 1980s and used its control of finance to direct the investment of emerging large conglomerates, the *chaebols*, into priority areas (Amsden 1989: 72–73). In Taiwan the reigning Kuomintang regime ensured that large state-owned commercial banks dominated the financial system and that state-owned firms and small and medium enterprises were allocated credit for investment in priority activities (Wade 1990: 159–172). During the formative period, state-controlled finance kept out foreign banking, prevented private firms from borrowing from abroad and together with fairly severe policing, discouraged the transfer of private funds abroad.

This relationship between government, banks and companies fostered a pattern of firm development based on high debt-to-equity ratios in the order of 2 to 1 in Taiwan and double that in Korea, as against a pattern in Western firms that rely on equity financing and usually carry a level of debt that is no more and generally less than their equity capital (see Table 8.2) (Wade 1990: 160; Wade and Veneroso 1998: 3–23). Korea relied more on government-managed borrowing from abroad to finance long-term investment, while Japan and Taiwan were able to mobilize impressive domestic savings. High levels of household savings were achieved where postal savings systems in Japan and Taiwan facilitated deposits and the lack of social security programmes provided incentives (see Table 8.3). At the same time, state-controlled finance in all three countries made most small borrowers turn to the 'curb market' or informal lending often controlled by corporations with privileged access to credit.[7]

Macroeconomic stability to foster long-term investment

The developmental state ensured stability of exchange rates, interest rates and prices over long periods of time. If anything, exchange rates were undervalued to promote exports. Borrowing rates on the whole were kept low for those who received state-directed credit. The state managed inflation – generally kept lower in Taiwan than in Korea – recognizing that fast growth required some tolerance for price rises, but ensured that real wages continued to rise, thus mitigating the social effects (Wade 1990: 42, 336; Amsden 1989: 49–50). One of the characteristics that sets off the developmental state from less effective state interventionism was the attention accorded to maintaining the fiscal integrity of the state, which allowed it to function with the long term in mind. Public sector deficits in Korea were managed (and often hidden from public view), while in Taiwan budget surpluses were generally the rule (see Table 8.3). In both countries public expenditure went mainly to investment rather than social services (Amsden 1989: 89–92; Wade 1990: 59–60 and 172–175). The overall rate of corporate taxation has been low but enforced while the state has relied on indirect taxation that had the added advantage of repressing internal consumption especially of imported luxuries.

Industrial policy fostering import substitution and export production

What differentiated the developmental states from other developing countries was not their rejection of import-substitution, but rather the timing of the introduction of export-oriented activities and the relationship established between the two processes. Unlike the claims of many who had once tried to portray Korea and Taiwan as model examples of outward-oriented open economies, a key feature of the developmental state was its use of industrial policy to promote investment in strategic industries and export-oriented industries while limiting foreign competition in the domestic market. The use of scarce foreign exchange was prioritized and the state forced investment in industries with export potential, often compelling companies to accept very low profit margins on international markets as they clawed their way to an expanding market share. In exchange, the state protected corporations in the domestic market with a system of tariffs that limited foreign competition. With its control over finance the state assisted particular industries over others. The state also systematically promoted technology acquisition from transnational corporations. As Robert Wade has argued, these states did not 'pick winners' so much as 'make winners' and the favoured enterprises had to demonstrate performance in exports in order to retain access to finance and other favours (Wade 1990: 334). In South Korea, the state fostered certain firms over others to create a capacity for production of cement, steel, shipbuilding and machinery. In Taiwan the state promoted petrochemicals, heavy metals and power generation – all of which almost certainly would not have occurred if entrepreneurs had been left to their own devices in their investment decisions (Amsden 1989; Wade 1990).

Attention to agriculture and rural livelihoods

When the achievements of Taiwan and South Korea are recognized, other than a brief mention of the political and economic impact of redistributive land reform at the outset of periods of accelerated development, few observers have underlined the particular attention paid to the agricultural sector by these rapid industrializers. The developmental states accorded a high degree of protection to local agriculture, provided credit to the sector and paid attention to rural infrastructure. When combined with earlier land redistribution, this facilitated a long period of agricultural growth and, despite significant extraction of surplus from the sector, allowed a steady improvement of income in rural areas. This contributed to the expansion of education and a steady flow of labour into the growing manufacturing sector rather than the floods of uneducated rural poor to the cities witnessed in many developing countries (Hwan 1980).

Incomes policy that raised living standards while social organizations were suppressed

Finally, while evidence on levels of inequality is extremely sketchy, the developmental states clearly achieved a more equitable pattern of income distribution than in most developing countries. Perhaps, even more important, much like the trade-offs exercised between the state and private entrepreneurs, extremely repressive labour regimes were combined with a steady growth in the standard of living for working people. However, labour had to work hard to achieve this, since for many years wage increases were kept in line with increased productivity. What is more, the increase was achieved from a very low base (after all, Korea and Taiwan relied on their low wages for a competitive edge in the international market). Workers in favoured industries and skilled *male* workers benefited more than other wage workers (Amsden 1989: 196–208).

From their commitment to redistributive land reform, through each one of the characteristics described above, the developmental states' behaviour and action sharply differ from states like the Philippines, where crony capitalism and 'predatory' state behaviour prevailed.

In sum, the developmental state ushered in a particularly profound organizational and institutional transformation. It is striking that effective corporatist authoritarian regimes were established in Taiwan and South Korea. The wealthy groups that dominated the Kuomintang when it ruled in parts of pre-1949 China and those that were behind the Syngman Rhee regime in South Korea were every bit as prone to rent-seeking and predatory behaviour as other elites in the developing world. The only way to explain why those with wealth and power allowed the emergence of such *dirigiste* states and accorded importance and resources to the training of their bureaucracies is by appreciating the extent of internal and external threats posed to the institutional foundations, survival and promotion of a system of capitalism based on private property. After the Second World War and the demise of Japanese colonial authority, mobilized rural populations in both Taiwan and South Korea could have endorsed communist movements. External threats to the survival of both South Korea and Taiwan as independent states were a very real and present danger. In countries like the Philippines, comparable threats to elite survival did not exist on anywhere near the same scale.[8]

What distinguished the developmental states was *not* the absence of corruption among public sector officials and private entrepreneurs, but rather the fact that the resources generated through corruption seemed, at least in part, to be put to productive use rather than entirely siphoned off for private consumption. Mushtaq Khan has offered the most convincing theoretical framework to understand this phenomenon. Contrasting South Asian relatively slow-growing economies to East Asian fast developers, he essentially argues that resources were channelled to capitalists in the latter and overwhelmingly to non-capitalists in the former. In South Asia clients had considerable political clout, leading to a pattern of 'growth-retarding accumulation', whereas in East Asia they did not, which allowed 'growth-enhancing accumulation' (Khan 2000).

In Korea capital flight was controlled by the state and illicit transfers of funds abroad could meet with the death penalty. But the state allowed, and some might even say encouraged, the development of the curb credit market, where ill-gotten gains could be recycled at extremely profitable interest rates to small businesses and consumers. For many years, the Korean state's guarantee of the secrecy of bank accounts encouraged the recycling of resources generated through corruption into the banking system.[9] This formula of 'productive corruption' was made possible less by the particular constellations of class power emerging from Korea's colonial experience, than by the patterns of threat facing those with command over resources, patterns of threat that led them to sanction the rise of a state with the powers and expertise to discipline capital and direct it to the most productive uses.

The achievements of the developmental states in Northeast Asia were impressive. As can be seen in Table 8.1, the structure of production was radically transformed in both Korea and Taiwan. Where agriculture contributed 38 per cent of GDP in 1965 in Korea and close to that in Taiwan, by the mid-1990s its contribution had been reduced to 6.3 and 3.5 per cent in the two countries. The share of value-added from manufacturing increased accordingly, from 18 to almost 26 per cent in Korea and from 22 to 28 per cent in Taiwan. While a significant 10 per cent of the workforce was still employed in the agricultural sector in both countries, employment in manufacturing more than doubled in both countries.

In Korea real GDP per capita jumped from US$690 in 1960, to US$10,656 by 1994, while life expectancy increased from 51 years to 71 years over the same period. Similarly, infant mortality fell from 85 per thousand births to only 10 per thousand births by 1994 (UNDP 1997: 166). Robert Wade reported that in Taiwan per capita GNP grew at an average annual rate of 6.2 per cent between 1953 and 1986 while enjoying much greater income equality than Japan, Korea or the

Table 8.1: Structure of production and employment in selected Asian countries (%)

	Korea			Taiwan			Indonesia			Thailand			Malaysia		
	1965	**1980**	**1996**	**1960**	**1980**	**1995**	**1965**	**1980**	**1996**	**1965**	**1980**	**1996**	**1965**	**1980**	**1996**
GDP by origin:															
Agriculture	38.0	14.9	6.3	n.a.	7.7	3.5	51.0	24.8	16.3	27.0	23.2	10.4	16.0	22.9	12.7
Manufacturing	18.0	29.7	25.8	22.0	36.0	28.2	8.0	11.6	25.2	19.0	21.5	29.3	14.0	19.6	34.5
	1960*	**1980**	**1996**	**1960**	**1980**	**1995**	**1960**	**1980**	**1995**	**1960**	**1980**	**1996**	**1960**	**1980**	**1996**
Employment:															
Agriculture	61.0	34.0	11.3	n.a.	19.5	10.5	75.0	55.9	44.0	84.0	70.8	40.4	63.0	37.2	16.8
Manufacturing	10.0	21.6	22.0	n.a.	32.9	27.1	8.0	9.1	12.6	4.0	7.9	16.5	12.0	15.5	27.0

Sources: Asian Development Bank, 1996, 1998, World Bank, 1992, and UNDP, 1997
*1960 data refers to Industry

United States. Life expectancy had reached 70 years for men and 75 for women by 1982 (Wade 1990: 38).

Paul Krugman argued in a celebrated article in 1994 that the achievements of the East Asian tigers were not all that extraordinary. They relied mainly on a rapid and extensive expansion of inputs into production through expanded employment, increased education and a vast expansion of investment in physical capital. Unlike in the West and in Japan, Korea and Taiwan achieved 'growth in large part through an astonishing mobilization of resources ... rather than by gains in efficiency' (Krugman 1994: 70). In other words, growth was down to 'brawn' rather than 'brains' and was not based on increases in productivity. While questioning the data that Krugman drew upon for his analysis, Joseph Stiglitz observed that, 'even in the extreme, and in my view, unlikely event that East Asia had no total factor productivity growth, the region still would have demonstrated a remarkable ability both to maintain high saving rates and to allocate that capital to productive uses' (Stiglitz 1998).[10] This is the central issue, since the challenge that has eluded so many developing countries has been precisely to mobilize labour, increase human capital formation and productively employ capital. This is what has been achieved by the developmental states, regardless of how one assesses factor productivity increases involved with the successful development of steel, auto, shipbuilding, petrochemical and computer industries.

How does Southeast Asia measure up?

The question remains, however, whether we can characterize the, until recently, fast-growing Southeast Asian followers – Thailand, Malaysia and Indonesia – as having 'developmental states'. These three countries did achieve impressive levels of growth and borrowed extensively, though to differing degrees, from the experience of Japan, Taiwan and South Korea. They adopted some of the characteristics of the developmental state, but by no means all of them, and there were sharp differences between the three in terms of what they chose to copy.

Land reform

None of these countries carried out the same kind of redistributive reforms that were formative to the Taiwan and South Korean experience. While they did not face the population pressure on the land in the same way as their Northeast Asian forerunners and while small-scale farming was ensured until recently by extensive development of agriculture, the overall distribution of land in Indonesia and Thailand, at least, remains very unequal by Asian standards.[11] Nevertheless the political changes wrought by land reform in Northeast Asia were not matched in the Southeast Asian countries, where traditional patterns of power continued to dominate in the rural areas.

In Malaysia's ethnically based political system, the ruling United Malays National Organization appealed to the rural poor population on the grounds of ethnicity, thus weakening class solidarities and preserving the privilege and power of rural elites . In Thailand, as the frontier for extensive agriculture contracted and government began to restrict access to forest lands, smallholders were increasingly replaced by tenants and wage workers and agricultural resources channelled to agribusiness (Pasuk and Baker 1995: Chapters 2–4). Provincially based business families increased their political influence and power through this process, while the rural poor have begun to engage in political organization to resist an increasing marginalization. In Indonesia, authoritarian governance reached from Jakarta right down to the village level. Intense demographic pressure on the land was responded to through transmigration programmes, with village power in the central islands of Java and Sumatra integrated into the ruling GOLKAR party (Hüsken and White 1989: 235–265).

State control of finance

The pattern of the state's involvement with finance differed between the three Southeast Asian countries, but nevertheless there was some resemblance in all three to the Northeast Asian countries in terms of privileged access to credit. In Thailand, the state was nominally the least involved in allocating credit to the private sector, but state ownership of banking assets was nevertheless significant. By the early 1990s the commercial banking sector was dominated by five banks, which controlled more than two-thirds of bank assets. The second largest bank in the country, Krung Thai Bank, was state owned; the fourth largest, Siam Commercial Bank, was owned by the royal family; and the sixth largest, the Thai Military Bank, should also be considered state-owned (Lauridsen 1998: 140).[12] Thus a small number of private conglomerates had privileged access to credit, not as a result of Thai state use of financial resources to implement a development strategy, but due to the oligopolistic structure of the banking sector.

The state in Indonesia exercised authority over the financial system largely through credit controls and during the first decade of the New Order regime state banks provided 86 per cent of all commercial credit (Robison 1986: 218–219).[13] Even after considerable liberalization of the banking industry, by 1994 state banks were still providing 48 per cent of total commercial credit, although after liberalization in 1988 each major private conglomerate opened a bank. The number of banks in the economy nearly doubled from 124 in 1988 to 244 by 1994 (Montes and Abdulsalamov 1998: 166–170). The state used its leverage over finance primarily to reduce the prominence of Chinese business in the economy by stimulating the formation of an indigenous business class, which in the end was dominated by members and associates of the Suharto family.

After independence in Malaysia, the banking sector was controlled by foreign banks and local Chinese interests, with Malay ownership at no more than 3.3 per cent as late as 1970. However, the New Economic Policy implemented subsequently led to a rapid increase in Malay ownership, particularly state ownership within the banking sector. The government controlled the two largest banks, Malayan Banking and Bank Bumiputra by 1988. The government used its increased control over finance both to promote strategic industries and to finance emergent Malay business groups close to the ruling United Malays National Organization (UMNO) (Gomez 1999: 185–197).

In Indonesia and Thailand state control of finance facilitated the formation and expansion of conglomerates that aspired to the status of the *chaebols* in South Korea. There was a mixed degree of reliance on state companies in the three countries, with Malaysia following the Taiwan experience most closely, Indonesia somewhat less reliant on state corporations and Thailand relying the

Table 8.2a: Rough estimate of corporate debt–equity ratio

	Assets	Equity	Rough long-term debt	Debt-to-equity ratio		Assets	Equity	Rough long-term debt	Debt-to-equity ratio
Korea					**Taiwan***				
Samsung Co.	7448.4	1650.4	5798.0	3.5:1	Chinese Petroleum	19079.1	9473.3	9605.8	1.0:1
Hyundai	572.6	195.0	377.6	1.9:1	Taiwan Power	34815.3	17364.9	17450.4	1.0:1
Daewoo	11500.1	2309.7	9190.4	4.0:1	Chunghwa Telecom	15076.8	11681.5	3395.3	0.3:1
Samsung Electronics	19688.6	6327.0	13361.6	2.1:1	Acer	4192	2008	2184	1.1:1
LG International	1726.0	349.1	1376.9	3.9:1	Nan Ya Plastics	4830.2	1932.9	2897.3	1.5:1
Korea Electric Power	44334.1	21010.7	23323.4	1.1:1	China Steel Corp	7382.7	4180.4	3202.3	0.8:1
Hyundai Motor	9943.0	2074.8	7868.2	3.8:1	Tatung	4202.1	1478.4	2723.7	1.8:1
Pohang Iron & Steel	19524.1	8115.8	11408.3	1.4:1	President Enterprises	2049.2	1072.1	977.1	0.9:1
Yukong Ltd.	12104.5	2671.6	9432.9	3.5:1	Hotai Motor	530.1	316.1	214	0.7:1
LG Electronics	8504.0	1854.1	6649.9	3.6:1	China Airlines	2795.4	1152	1643.4	1.4:1
Average debt/equity ratio				2.9:1	*Average debt/equity ratio*				1.1:1

Source: Reyes 1998.

*Taiwan Tobacco and Wine, no. 6, skipped as data not available.

Table 8.2b: Rough estimate of corporate debt–equity ratio – Thailand and Malaysia

	Assets	Equity	Rough long-term debt	Debt-to-equity ratio		Assets	Equity	Rough long-term debt	Debt-to-equity ratio
Thailand*					**Malaysia**				
Petroleum Authority	4583.4	1649.8	2933.6	1.8:1	Petroleum Nasional	27090.1	10857.3	16232.8	1.5:1
Elec. Generating Authority	11678.8	4609.7	7069.1	1.5:1	Sime Darby	15242.5	2286.6	12955.9	5.7:1
Siam Cement	7094.1	1295.0	5799.1	4.5:1	Tenaga Nasional	12913.1	6529.0	6384.1	1.0:1
Thai Airways Intl	5197.3	1188.3	4009.0	3.4:1	EON	3483.0	508.0	2975.0	5.9:1
Toyota Motor (Thailand)	1285.8	322.8	963.0	3.0:1	Malaysian Airline Sys	5822.0	1783.5	4038.5	2.3:1
Thai Oil	2819.9	641.8	2178.1	3.4:1	Telekom Malaysia	7946.7	4796.9	3149.8	0.7:1
Tri Petch Isuzu Sales	1392.9	119.1	1273.8	10.7:1	Berjaya Group	4954.7	772.0	4182.7	5.4:1
Telephone Organization	8064.8	5830.9	2233.9	0.4:1	Proton	1849.6	956.4	893.2	0.9:1
MMC Sittipol	1129.9	77.9	1052.0	13.5:1	Perlis Plantations	1518.7	751.1	767.6	1.0:1
Boonrawd Trading	130.9	4.1	126.8	30.9:1	Amsteel Corp	3783.3	592.4	3190.9	5.4:1
Average debt/equity ratio				4.7:1	*Average debt/equity ratio*				3.0:1

Source: Reyes 1998.
*Esso and Shell, 8th and 9th, data not available.

Table 8.2c: Rough estimate of corporate debt–equity ratio – Indonesia

	Assets	Equity	Rough long-term debt	Debt-to-equity ratio
Indonesia*				
Pertamina	14205.5	6372.2	7833.3	1.2:1
Astra Intl	7143.8	1282.2	5861.6	4.6:1
Per. Listrik Negara	22449.6	12479.8	9969.8	0.8:1
Gudang Garam	1841.9	1087.1	754.8	0.7:1
Telkom	7592.2	3785.6	3806.6	1.0:1
Indocement Tunggal	3802.6	1754.2	2048.4	1.2:1
Garuda Indonesia	1810.2	565.4	1244.8	2.2:1
Average debt/equity ratio				1.7:1

Source: Reyes 1998.

*Only these seven companies available and ratio brought down by inclusion of mainly state companies.

Debt–equity ratio here is a rough approximation based on taking the top ten publicly listed companies and estimating long term debt as the difference between reported assets and equity.

least on state-run companies. While state use of finance in all three countries appeared to be more influenced by the promotion of interests close to the regime than by the developmental goals that had informed finance policy in the Northeast Asian countries, the structure of the relationship between the state, finance and business was similar. Table 8.2 illustrates a very rough approximation of debt-to-equity ratios. The rates in Malaysia and Thailand are closer to those in Korea than Taiwan.[14] Of course, the available data illustrate only long-term debt and thus do not capture the extent of short-term debt that had such an important impact in the crisis. Nevertheless, long-term debt–equity ratios demonstrate decidedly different patterns, especially between Korea and Taiwan.[15] The data for Indonesia are incomplete and include publicly owned companies. If the major private conglomerates were shown, the pattern would probably be similar to its two Southeast Asian neighbours.

In all these countries business activity was concentrated to differing degrees in the networks of communities of Chinese descent, which infused an ethnic character to business and to relations between the state and those who possessed private wealth. This gave the state particular leverage over business as business families of Chinese descent were largely excluded from political power. At the same time, programmes ostensibly designed to redress the ethnic balance in command over wealth provided a route for indigenous interests close to the regimes in Malaysia and Indonesia to gain special privileges from the state. Thus, while the structure of state, bank and firm relations was similar to especially Korea, the dynamics of that relationship were markedly different.

Macroeconomic management

The Southeast Asian countries considered here enjoyed significant periods of sound macroeconomic management. They generally achieved strong fiscal positions, though, in Indonesia, for example, the state budget probably looked healthier than it was in reality, given its practice of 'off budget expenditures' (Crouch 1996: 44). As Table 8.3 shows, while Thailand and Malaysia operated with surpluses significantly lower than the NICs in the 1980s, these were rapidly built up in the 1990s. In fact the central government surpluses of Thailand and Indonesia skyrocketed in the 1990s.

Table 8.3: Savings and central government budget surplus, 1980–97

	Gross domestic saving as % of GDP		Budget Surplus as % of GDP	
	1980–89	1990–97	1980–89	1990–97
South Korea	31.4	35.8	3.3	4.8
Taiwan	33.4	26.4	2.9	2.3
Malaysia	33.1	38.3	2.2	5.8
Thailand	26.5	36.0	1.0	7.4
Indonesia	30.6	32.2	7.0	7.5

Source: Asian Development Bank, 1999.

The three Southeast Asian countries followed Korea in building up the rate of domestic savings in the 1990s, even as savings declined in Taiwan. Even Thailand, which had a lower rate of savings in the 1980s, sharply increased its rate in the 1990s. It is fair to say that all three countries followed the model of Northeast Asia in encouraging domestic savings to finance investment, with Malaysia achieving the highest rates.

Table 8.4: Foreign direct investment as a percentage of gross domestic capital formation

	Average 1980–89	1990	1991	1992	1993	1994	1995	1996	Average 1990–96	Average 1980–96
South Korea	-0.24	-0.28	-0.27	-0.38	-0.64	-1.20	-1.05	-1.30	-0.73	-0.46
Taiwan	-1.77	-10.60	-1.87	-2.06	-3.02	-2.20	-2.31	-3.42	-3.64	-2.87
Malaysia	10.33	17.45	22.30	25.34	22.20	15.16	17.46	13.06	18.99	13.97
Thailand	3.03	6.81	3.36	3.47	2.81	1.55	1.67	1.92	3.08	3.12
Indonesia	1.30	3.11	3.61	3.94	4.30	2.73	5.80	7.53	4.43	2.68

Source: Asian Development Bank, 1996 and 1999.

However, overall, the Southeast Asian countries relied much more heavily on foreign direct investment (FDI) to finance growth, than did their Northeast Asia predecessors. Three distinct patterns can be observed from Table 8.4, showing the role of FDI in gross domestic capital formation (GDCF). Korea and Taiwan greatly limited the role of foreign investment in their economies and by the 1980s were net investors abroad. FDI contributed about 3 per cent of Thailand's GDCF throughout the 1980s and 1990s while in Indonesia, FDI averaged only 1.3 per cent of capital formation in the 1980s, rising to almost 4.5 per cent in the 1990s.

Table 8.5: Portfolio investment as a percentage of gross domestic capital formation

	Average 1980–89	1990	1991	1992	1993	1994	1995	1996	Average 1990–96	Average 1980–96
South Korea	0.77	0.09	2.67	5.15	8.58	4.46	6.86	8.43	5.18	2.70
Taiwan	-0.79	-2.72	0.11	0.84	1.90	1.57	0.80	-1.92	0.08	-1.23
Malaysia	3.91	-7.84	-1.35	5.52	1.57	0.62	5.85	0.00	0.62	2.73
Thailand	1.58	1.30	0.11	1.19	8.25	3.28	4.98	5.75	3.55	2.48
Indonesia	0.29	-0.26	-0.03	2.49	3.88	7.06	6.35	6.74	3.75	1.80

Source: Asian Development Bank, 1996 and 1999.

Malaysia, in its effort to undermine the dominance of ethnic Chinese business, was the most reliant on FDI, where it contributed 10 per cent to GDCF in the 1980s, rising to 19 per cent in the 1990s.

Table 8.6: Other long-term and short-term foreign transfers 1980–96

As % of GDCF	Average 1980–89	Average 1990–96	Average 1980–96
South Korea:			
Other investment	5.08	2.59	2.29
Total foreign transfers	5.61	7.04	4.53
Taiwan:			
Other investment	3.45	-10.54	-2.30
Total foreign transfers	0.89	-14.09	-6.40
Malaysia:			
Other long-term	2.24	0.00	1.32
Other short-term	-1.12	8.71	2.76
Total foreign transfers	15.36	28.33	20.77
Thailand:			
Other long-term	8.41	4.16	5.87
Other short-term	2.75	4.08	3.55
Total foreign transfers	15.77	14.88	15.01
Indonesia:			
Other long-term	10.74	4.57	7.92
Other short-term	1.13	0.08	1.22
Total foreign transfers	13.46	12.80	13.46

Source: Asian Development Bank, 1996 and 1999.

Portfolio investment played a small part in the region until the 1990s, though it reached almost 4 per cent of GDCF in Malaysia in the 1980s (see Table 8.5). In the 1990s, foreign investment through the stock market played a significant role in Korea, but not in Taiwan. Portfolio investments declined in overall importance in Malaysia as direct investment increased in the1990s, but came to play an increasing role in Thailand and Indonesia. Looking at Table 8.6, overall foreign financial transfers made up a considerable proportion of gross domestic capital formation in all three Southeast Asian countries, with Indonesia and Thailand depending on foreign funds for 13 to 15 per cent of GDCF and Malaysia seeing foreign transfers counting for 28 per cent of capital formation in the 1990s. This sharply contrasts with the Northeast Asian countries, where South Korea slightly increased its reliance on foreign transfers from 5.5 per cent in the 1980s to 7 per cent in the 1990s, while Taiwan was a next exporter of capital by the 1990s.

Industrial policy

The World Bank's 1993 *East Asian Miracle* report placed these Southeast Asian countries in the same league as South Korea and Taiwan. This, I would argue, stems from a failure to appreciate fully the nature of the developmental states as described above. In fact, the World Bank report differed significantly from the analysis of South Korea and Taiwan offered by Wade and Amsden, particularly in its assessment of the effectiveness of industrial policy, which was much less coherently developed and applied in the Southeast Asian countries than in Northeast Asia (Jomo *et al.* 1997; Lall 1995). Jomo and his co-authors claim that this has been due, at least in part, to a greater influence of class and ethnic interests within the state, often employing instruments of industrial policy to redistributive goals – especially redistribution within elites (Jomo *et al.* 1997: ch. 2).

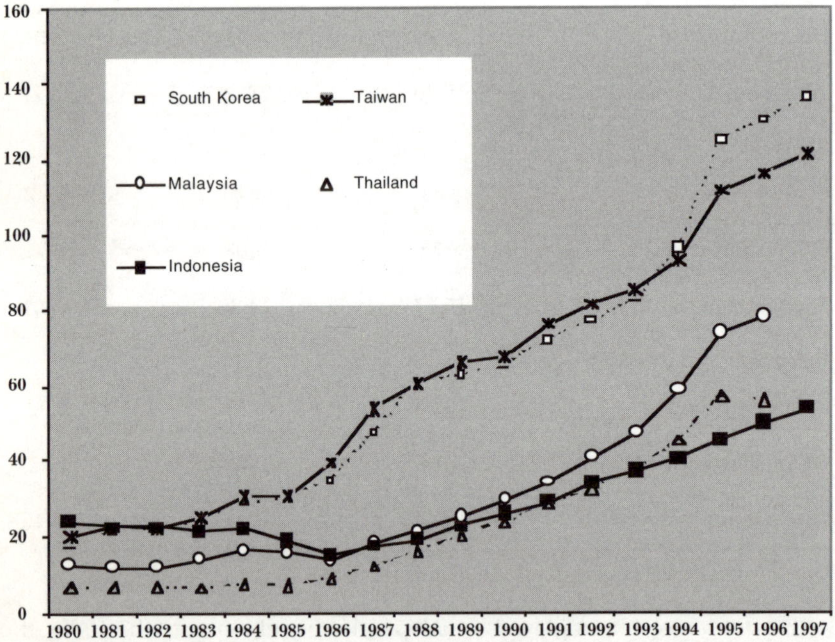

Figure 8.1: Total exports, 1980–1996/97 (in US$ billions)

All three Southeast Asian countries attempted to follow the tigers in promoting and encouraging the development of export-oriented production. As Figure 8.1 illustrates, export performance after the mid-1980s showed a consistently upward trend in the three Southeast Asian countries, mirroring – though never matching – the stellar performance of Korea and Taiwan. While manufactured goods as a percentage of total exports increased in all three countries, with Malaysia achieving the largest increases, Thailand second and Indonesia far behind (Figure 8.2), their pace of growth did not match that of overall exports. In all three Southeast Asian countries, the domestic content of manufactured exports was limited. By and large, they have remained assembly platforms, in sharp contrast to Korea and Taiwan.

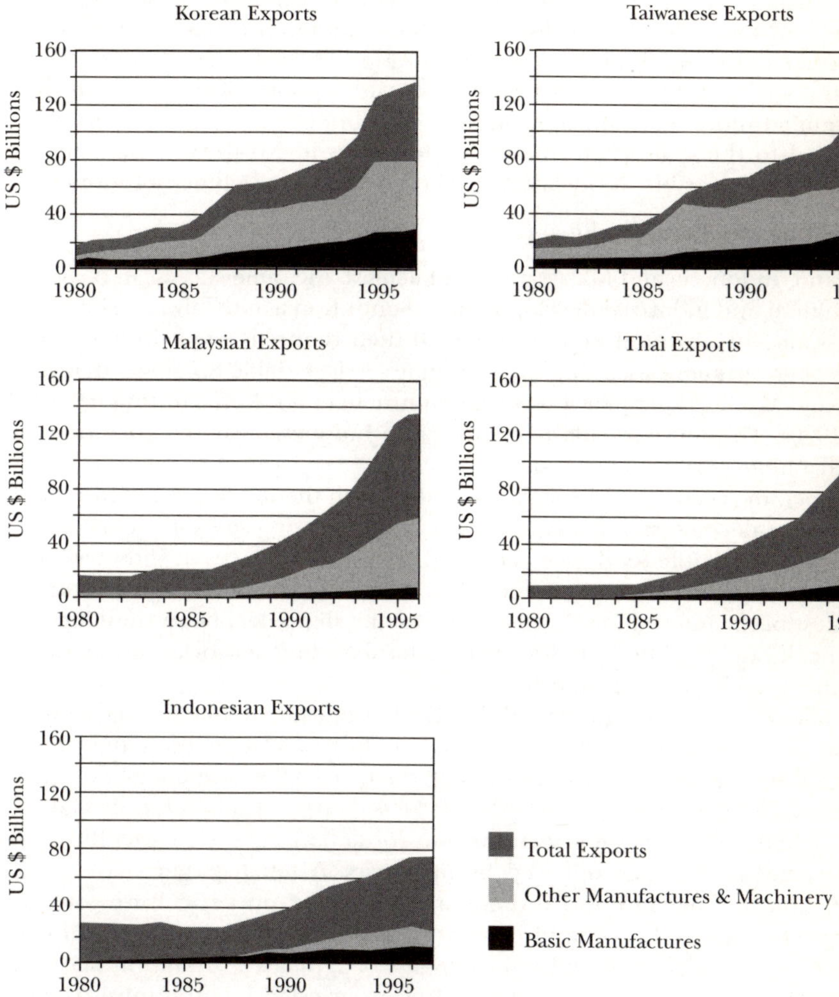

Figure 8.2: Composition of exports, 1980–1996/97

The experience of Thailand and Malaysia with industrialization differed, as demonstrated by the more shallow process of industrial development in Thailand. This can be seen most sharply in the automobile sector, where Thailand relied heavily on Japanese and other foreign investors not only for auto assembly plants but also for the network of suppliers to the industry. The Malaysian state was more attentive to ensuring the establishment of a local parts industry and used the presence of foreign investors more effectively to strengthen industrial development (Haraguchi 1997). Of the three, Indonesia had the most shallow industrialization, continuing to acquire large proportions of its export earnings through raw and semi-processed primary commodity exports. Import substitution in Southeast Asia, marked as it was by clientelism, resembled more the earlier periods of protectionism in South Korea in the 1950s and under the KMT when it was still on the mainland, than it did the later more directed protectionism in Northeast Asia. It thus contributed less to establishing the foundations for export-oriented industrialization in the three Southeast Asian countries. There was less attention placed on 'strategic' industries and the choice of state support for industry was often determined more on political grounds. State-supported industries were never subjected to the same performance standards as in Northeast Asia. This was particularly noticeable in the latter years of the Suharto regime in Indonesia.

Agriculture and rural livelihoods

Thailand, Indonesia and Malaysia did not achieve the same success in balancing agricultural and industrial development as South Korea and Taiwan. The Northeast Asian NICs invested in and protected their domestic food production. In terms of government spending on economic services, Table 8.7 shows that Indonesia and Malaysia spent far less on agriculture than did Korea during the 1980s and 1990s. This was particularly surprising in Indonesia, where agriculture still played a huge part in the economy.

In fact, in recent years in Malaysia and even in the much poorer Indonesia, there was a decided step backwards away from ensuring self-sufficiency in production of the staple food, rice. This had dire consequences in Indonesia with the onset of the crisis and its coincidence with region-wide drought. Given the tightness of the international market in rice, the sharp decline in rural incomes and the devastating impact of the crisis on local trading networks, Indonesia put its staple food supply in jeopardy.[16]

While the quest for legitimacy did lead all three states to invest in agriculture, thus achieving some of the balance between industry and agriculture that characterized Korea and Taiwan, rural people in the three NIEs have not made equivalent gains in income and security. As can be seen from Table 8.1, only Malaysia approached the extent of structural transformation between agriculture and manufacturing that was achieved by the tigers. A much larger share of the population in Thailand and Indonesia still depend on agriculture for their income. In Thailand the rapid economic growth in the late 1980s and early 1990s to some extent occurred at the expense of agriculture. In Indonesia, while a great deal of earnings from oil wealth were invested in rural infrastructure during the early period of consolidation of the New Order regime, attention to agriculture declined in later years. Malaysia relied on primary commodity exports to accumulate the resources for later industrialization and the transformation of its economy has to a larger degree provided a shift in the employment structure from agriculture to industry and services.

Table 8.7: Government spending on economic services 1980–97

Item	1980–89 % of GDP	1990–97 % of total spent on economic services
South Korea:		
Economic services	3.9	100.0
Agriculture	1.4	38.8
Industry	0.6	14.1
Electricity, gas and water	0.2	4.1
Transport and communications	0.8	21.8
Other economic services	0.8	21.2
Malaysia:		
Economic services	9.2	100.0
Agriculture	2.7	27.5
Industry	2.2	20.2
Electricity, gas and water	1.1	11.1
Transport and communications	3.1	31.0
Other economic services	0.0	0.1
Indonesia:		
Economic services	6.4	100.0
Agriculture	1.8	24.9
Industry	0.6	8.7
Electricity, gas and water	1.5	21.2
Transport and communications	1.5	20.8
Other economic services	1.0	14.4

Source: Asian Development Bank, 1996 and 1999

Incomes policy and social organization

The marked differences between Northeast and Southeast Asia in the ratio of GDP generated by a sector and employment in the sector illustrated in Table 8.1 might be said merely to mark the earlier stage of industrialization in the latter. Nevertheless, the pattern of industrialization in Thailand and Indonesia appears to have left a far greater percentage of the population dependent on agriculture than in Malaysia or the Northeast Asian countries.

Data on income distribution are notoriously difficult to compare, as there are large discrepancies between the methodologies employed in various countries. World Bank data reported in Table 8.8 suggest that Indonesia enjoyed one of the most equal patterns of income distribution in Southeast Asia, in fact more equal than that of South Korea during the late 1980s.[17] Patterns of income distribution in Malaysia, with Thailand following close behind, were far worse than those achieved in the formative periods of development in South Korea and Taiwan. Anne Booth, however, demonstrates that there are great regional disparities in inequality in Indonesia. In terms of the incidence of poverty, she places Indonesia alongside the Philippines, significantly worse off than Malaysia and Thailand (Booth 1992). Malaysia's gains in achieving a higher life expectancy at birth parallel those of Korea.

Table 8.8: Comparative indicators of income inequality and human development

	Korea	Indonesia	Thailand	Malaysia
Distribution of income:				
highest 20%	42.2 (1988)	40.7 (1993)	52.7 (1992)	53.7 (1989)
lowest 20%	7.4	8.7	5.6	4.6
Per capita GDP (PPP US$):				
1960	690	490	985	1783
1994	10656	3740	7104	8865
Life expectancy:				
1960	53.9	41.2	52.3	53.9
1994	71.5	63.5	69.5	71.2

Sources: UNDP 1997, World Development Report 1995 and 1997

'Productive corruption' or old-fashioned rent-seeking?

Perhaps the biggest question is whether or not the Southeast Asian nations have achieved the same level of 'productive corruption' as the developmental states. Mushtaq Khan places the Southeast Asian countries somewhere in between the pattern of 'growth-retarding accumulation' prevalent in South Asia and the 'growth-enhancing accumulation' that characterized the developmental states of Northeast Asia.

The starting point in answering this question is to note that the prevalence and impact of corruption in each of these countries have changed over time. This has been related to the changing legitimacy needs of state organizations and political authorities in each of the countries, as well as the changing composition and nature of the regimes in each country.

Clearly, the ethnic character of state–business relations has led to a rather different dynamic in the Southeast Asian states from that in Korea and Taiwan, and, in some cases, a pattern of perverse incentives. On the one hand, the threat of confiscation or discrimination or simply removing protection from Chinese business interests in Malaysia, Thailand and Indonesia limited the rapaciousness of rent-seeking on the side of business and ensured that its activity in some way contributed to the goals of political authorities. When those goals were motivated by demonstrating economic progress to achieve legitimacy, patterns of corruption may well have served economic progress. When threats to legitimacy had subsided, and officials could look more to their own personal enrichment, these same arrangements may have proved less productive.

In Thailand the particular form of clientelist politics in the absence of a landed oligarchy and in the context of a military-dominated regime committed to sound macroeconomic management appears to have spawned a form of rent-seeking behaviour that facilitated economic growth, if not industrial deepening, for decades (Dorner and Ramsey 2000). However, the increased strength of provincial business groups that has accompanied the democratic transition and the consequent weakening of central state management may well have undermined the possibility of channelling rents to more productive purposes (Rock 2000). In Indonesia the brutal establishment of the New Order regime provided a strong incentive for Suharto and the military to limit the more predatory aspects of rent-seeking behaviour in the interests of consolidating their power. The longer the regime stayed in power, the more rents appeared to be concentrated in the hands of the family and close associates of the president. In Malaysia, the state actively employed rent allocation as an instrument of economic policy, but often pursuing narrow political ends, which may have significantly reduced growth-promoting outcomes. The state's ability during many years to concentrate and channel the proceeds of rents could well have contributed to the country's growth, but this capacity appeared to be significantly weakened with the growing influence within the state of poorly performing business groups (Jomo and Gomez 2000).

Without the same kind of external threats as those faced in Taiwan and South Korea, there was much less incentive for those in control of state power in Southeast Asia to discipline emergent crony capitalists who enjoyed close relations with the regimes. If anything, the regimes appeared increasingly to rely on such interests to exercise their power.

INCOMPATIBILITY OF THE 'ASIAN MODEL' AND LIBERALIZATION: THE CRISIS

Wade and Veneroso (1998) argue that the model of accumulation and growth pursued by the Asian countries depended on a synergistic relationship between the state, the financial sector and the corporations. The strategy for growth was to invest heavily and increase capacity to capture market share in export markets. Conglomerates diversified to hedge against both the costs of carving out a market share in a new area of activity and falling profits in any given sector at any given point of time. Southeast Asian conglomerates mimicked the Northeast Asian countries in developing corporations with a high debt-to-equity ratio.

The model worked reasonably well when state control of finance was tight enough both to steer investment and impose penalties on corporations that failed to perform. Closed financial systems and authoritarian corporatist arrangements discouraged capital flight and provided an incentive for reinvestment of legitimate earnings as well as less legitimate sources of income into productive processes. While the states faced considerable legitimacy needs, authorities tended to be concerned with delivering on the economic front.

The financial crisis in South Korea and the Southeast Asian NIEs unfolded in a very similar fashion because of the close resemblance of their corporate structures and systems of finance. However, this was not primarily a crisis of the 'developmental state' *per se*. Interesting in this regard is the fact that Taiwan escaped the worst of the crisis. Further, the ability of the affected countries to emerge out of the crisis has differed considerably from one case to the next.

The crisis that began to unravel the economies of the region in July 1997 was actually precipitated by political and economic changes that occurred in the preceding decade. State control over the financial sector was significantly relaxed in the face of two global developments: first was the sharp increase in the availability of capital in international financial markets; and second was the pressure for liberalization of currency and financial markets.

Liberalization of the financial sector removed one of the central tools that states in the region had for ensuring that borrowed capital was invested for productive ends and it created an entirely new pattern of incentives for corporate groups. The authority of states in Korea and Thailand was further weakened by the processes of democratization in their political systems (though how important a factor this was is put in doubt by Taiwan's experience). Private groups were increasingly able to borrow on international financial markets from Japanese and Western commercial banks that were eager to lend and exercised extremely limited surveillance over their lending, sure that any defaulting loans would be covered by governments in the borrowers' countries – the now well-known problem of moral hazard. In fact, banking regulations in the West created a perverse incentive for the banking community to engage in short-term rather than long-term lending, as reserve requirements were less for the former. Combined with the reigning corporate strategy, this increased power to borrow had two effects. First, it provided an incentive to increase greatly the creation of industrial capacity. Second, with cheap finance so abundant, there was a clear incentive to engage in accelerated speculative investment. Much of these funds found their way into real estate development and a pattern of spiralling asset price inflation began.

In fact, ironically in light of much of the Western discussion of 'cronyism', liberalization of finance probably gave rise to an acceleration of crony-type activity. Private groups with cosy relations to those holding political power who were once limited by state control of finance gained virtually unlimited access to international sources of capital. Western actors were complicit in lending to those who were clearly close to the seat of political power in Asia. This was most evident in practices of Indonesian firms owned by members of the Suharto family.

These problems were not the result of a too cosy relationship between the state and enterprise, but rather the result of large private conglomerates subject to far too little regulation and supervision by the state. In South Korea, it could be argued that the *chaebols* had 'outgrown' the state. The state lost leverage over the big private conglomerates and the latter may even be seen to have come to control the state – there was a basic shift in the bargaining power between the two actors. In Khan's terms, 'new middle classes' enjoyed a significant increase in their power (Khan 2000). A lack of bank regulation allowed the *chaebols* to over-invest vastly. Access to short-term capital at cheap interest rates led to a massive increase in short-term debt.

Almost as important was the lessened sense of threat at home that emboldened, to differing degrees, both corporate interests and state officials to look less to the distributive impact of their activities and more to private profits. This was perhaps reinforced by the movement to more democratic forms of politics in South Korea and Thailand. However, Taiwan's experience is proof that democratic politics need not lead to a breakdown in sound state economic management.

It might be argued that there was actually an implicit shift in developmental strategy that affected South Korea and the Southeast NIEs. Whereas their past advantage in the international market had been built on transforming their 'comparative advantage' and promoting exports, thus undervaluing their currencies to make their products more competitive, a new strategy emerged to attract foreign capital as the principal motor of development. This was most noticeable in Indonesia, which had long managed its currency exchange rate to promote exports. All these countries effectively pegged their currencies to the US dollar. This peg was maintained despite devaluations in both Japan and Germany, thus increasingly leading to somewhat overvalued currencies. But the peg provided an incentive to international fund managers to increase their portfolio activities in the emerging markets of the region by limiting the risk of currency movements.

Furman and Stiglitz (1998: 36–42) demonstrate that the actual overvaluation of currency was not particularly significant. However, Figure 8.2 illustrates that there was a marked slowdown in growth of manufactured exports from 1995 in Korea, Thailand, Malaysia and Indonesia (interestingly, not in Taiwan). Indonesia again appears to have been most adversely affected by this. But perhaps more importantly, the instrument of devaluation, which had served countries so well in the past, was removed from their economic arsenal by the new strategy of pinning development on attracting foreign capital.

Changes in the international financial system now make capital much more mobile. One of the remarkable characteristics of the increasingly global system is the power exercised over capital movements by a relatively small group of investment ratings agencies. Based on very shallow analysis and understanding of the countries in the region, these agencies led the herd-like movements into the East and Southeast Asian markets. The problem with pinning a development strategy on the movements of foreign capital is that capital can fly away as quickly as it arrives. Far too much weight becomes placed on the 'confidence' of foreign investors that the local currency is solid and the prospects for growth are positive. Once that confidence is undermined, the whole system begins to unravel. This is precisely what happened in South Korea and the NIEs.

Interestingly, the same did not occur in Taiwan, essentially for two reasons. First, Taiwan did not rely to anywhere near the same extent on private conglomerates in its industrialization process. Consequently, as outlined above, the average debt-to-equity ratio of Taiwanese firms was half that of Korea (see Table 8.2). Second, Taiwan (Table 8.6) remained a net capital exporter. The state's bargaining power and position within the economy and influence over finance remain considerably more solid than in Korea. Clearly Taiwan, even with a process of democratization, has maintained the developmental state much more intact.

The crisis has affected the Southeast Asian NIEs in decidedly different ways. Indonesia was hardest hit because the financial crisis coincided with a political and environmental crisis. It has long been a matter of contention whether Indonesia had created the kind of state effectiveness that one could observe even in Malaysia. With each passing year that Suharto remained in power, his regime began to look more like the 'crony capitalism' of the latter days of the Marcos regime in the Philippines. Friends and family came to dominate the highest echelons of the economy in a manner unrivalled by Thailand or even Malaysia.

CONCLUSION

Understanding the sharp differences between the countries affected by the crisis is crucial to our ability to comprehend what may happen in the future. Clearly, where the financial crisis coincided with political crisis, as in Indonesia, recovery proved to be particularly complex. It is also important that the positive lessons of Asian development experience are not lost due to the sharp downturn in regional fortunes at the end of the 1990s.

The crisis in Asia demonstrated that the role of the state becomes more, rather than less, important with globalization internationally and liberalization at home. Enthusiasm for liberalization of finance should be tempered by the fact that in Southeast Asia and Korea the rapid deregulation and opening of finance appeared to vastly expand the opportunities for corruption and cronyism. Private groups close to those holding political power, who were once limited by state control of finance, had access to vastly increased sources of borrowing.

One central lesson from the crisis is that the private sector needs careful supervision and a public institutional framework that provides incentives to follow sound business practices. While developed country governments need to exercise greater surveillance and reform the regulations under which commercial banks and funds are operating, international regulation of financial transactions is always going to be problematic. A lesson from Chile's experience is that national level controls over short-term borrowing and inward investment can be extremely healthy for the local economy (Griffith-Jones 1998). It was particularly difficult to introduce this into policy debates in most of the countries after the crisis had unfolded, since cash-strapped economies were eager to attract whatever inward investment they could, just for survival purposes. The biggest danger, already evident with halting recovery in the region, remains the tendency of authorities to pin the prospects of future growth too heavily on attracting footloose capital into their markets. The time to seriously consider introducing capital controls is when the economy is strong.

Malaysia's capital controls are relevant in this regard. The Mahathir government used the breathing space created by controls, which allowed lower interest rates and increased public spending, to engage in financial restructuring. While for domestic political reasons the Mahathir government was selective in pursuing vigorous reforms, it nevertheless demonstrated that controls could be constructively employed. Some form of national controls over short-term capital flows ought to be placed on the agenda throughout the region.

It is highly likely that the strongest Asian economies will eventually re-emerge as major competitors to the developed countries in world markets. At the very first signs of recovery from the crisis, a protectionist reaction was already emerging in the developed countries. During 1998 and 1999, anti-dumping charges were levelled against South Korea in relation to its steel exports, which were threatening remaining producers in both Europe and North America. Measures were also taken against the electronic components industry in Taiwan. This will remain a worrying trend. The long-term recovery of Asia will require opposition to new protectionist pressures in the developed economies.

When the crisis began to unfold in East and Southeast Asia, the IMF reacted in what proved to be quite an erroneous manner. This stemmed from a failure to fully understand the nature of the crisis and the differential experience of the region. It is not time to discard the model of the 'developmental state', but rather to ask whether its more positive contributions in the past can be harnessed to face the challenges of the future. If nothing else, the crisis of the late 1990s should seriously put into question the wisdom of pursuing a development strategy that relies so heavily on the attraction of footloose capital. Asia needs to find new ways to harness its own savings for long-term investment. In doing so, state organizations in the region have a major role to play.

AUTHOR'S NOTE

Earlier versions of this paper were presented at the School of Oriental and African Studies and the London School of Economics. The author would like to thank Robert Wade, Pietro Masina and an anonymous reviewer for comments made on the manuscript.

NOTES

1 For the sake of clarity, it is useful to distinguish between the experiences of 'Northeast Asian' economies such as Japan, South Korea and Taiwan, and those of Southeast Asian countries.

2 The term was coined by businessman Jaime Ongpin in two devastating criticisms of the Marcos regime published in 1981 (see Putzel 1992: 173).

3 Of course the association of 'cronyism' with political corruption had been around at least since the 1950s. It was used, for instance, to describe President Truman's political appointments to the bureaucracy of the US government.

4 Outside of the liberal and neoliberal tendency to treat all states as 'predatory', the concept of a 'predatory state' has received much less rigorous definition than the developmental state. I apply the concept in the same way as Peter Evans (1995: ch. 3).

5 Of course, in many ways the model was new only to those who, under the weight of neoliberal thinking, had forgotten the pioneering work by Friedrich List (1966 [1885]) and analysis by Alexander Gerschenkron (1962) of late industrialization as it occurred in such countries as Germany.
6 A comparative assessment of reforms in Japan, Taiwan and South Korea is presented in Putzel 1992: Chapter 3.
7 In Korea, domestic savings exceeded investment only in the late 1980s (Amsden 1989: 109; Wade 1990: 61–64).
8 I make this argument in relation to the redistributive land reforms in Putzel 1992, Chapter 3, but the same argument can be advanced in relation to the developmental state as a whole.
9 For an exploration of the functional contribution of rent-seeking to development, see Myung-Ju Choi, 'Import regimes and rent seeking: the case of South Korea', D.Phil. Thesis, University of Oxford, 1992.
10 Joseph Stiglitz was chief economist of the World Bank by this time.
11 Anne Booth (1992: 101) argues that inequality of land distribution was in fact worse in Indonesia than in the Philippines, with Thailand having a distribution almost as bad as the Philippines.
12 While 14 foreign banks operated, restrictions meant that they controlled only 5 per cent of bank assets. The 15 largest banks controlled 95 per cent of assets in 1990 and were owned by no more than 16 Sino-Thai families.
13 Robison notes, though, that these figures did not include informal credit networks of the Chinese business community.
14 The Malaysian list is also dominated by state-owned enterprises and it is likely that if only private enterprises were listed the debt-to-equity ratio would be still higher.
15 One reason why Taiwan achieved a healthier debt-to-equity ratio was that the ruling party and the state were actually buying equity in firms. I thank Robert Wade for pointing this out to me.
16 This is not to say that the crisis was negative for all rural dwellers. Evidence is disputed, but it would appear that those who were earning significantly from export-oriented agricultural production actually saw their incomes rise after the onset of the crisis as agricultural exports became more competitive and increased (Thomas 1999).
17 South Korea had achieved considerably more positive results in its formative years, with Gini coefficients for income inequality in the early 1970s for rural income at 0.322, urban income, 0.259 and only business income highly unequal at 0.733 (Mason et al 1980: 411).

References

Amsden, Alice (1989) *Asia's Next Giant: South Korea and Late Industrialization.* Oxford: Oxford University Press.

Asian Development Bank (1996) *Key Indicators of Developing Asian and Pacific Countries,* Vol. 27. Manila: Asian Development Bank.

Asian Development Bank (1998, 1999) 'Country tables', Asian Development Bank website.

Booth, Anne (1992) *'Comparative Assessment of the Incidence of Poverty and its Change Over Time in Southeast Asia.'* Report for the Australian International Development Assistance Bureau, February 1992.

Choi, Myung-Ju (1992) 'Import Regimes and Rent Seeking: the Case of South Korea', D.Phil. Thesis, University of Oxford.

Crouch, Harold (1996) *Government and Society in Malaysia.* Ithaca, NY: Cornell University Press.

Dorner, Richard and Ansil Ramsey (2000) 'Rents, Collective Action, and Economic Development in Thailand', in Mushtaq Khan and Jomo K.S (eds.), *Rents and Rent-Seeking*. Cambridge: Cambridge University Press.

Evans, Peter (1995) *Embedded Autonomy: States and Industrial Transformation*. Princeton, NJ: Princeton University Press.

Furman, Jason and Joseph Stiglitz (1998) 'Economic crises: evidence and insights from East Asia', *Brookings Papers on Economic Activity*, 2.

Gerschenkron, Alexander (1962) *Economic Backwardness in Historical Perspective*. Cambridge, MA: Harvard University Press.

Gomez, Terrence (1999) *Chinese Business in Malaysia: Accumulation, Ascendance and Accommodation*. Richmond: Curzon.

Griffith-Jones, Stephany (1998) 'How to protect developing countries from volatility of capital flows?' Paper prepared for the Commonwealth Secretariat for the Expert Group Meeting, London, 15–17 June.

Haraguchi, Nobuya (1997) 'The impact of FDI on the growth of the Thai economy: study of the Thai auto industry'. M Sc dissertation in Development Studies, Development Studies Institute, LSE, September.

Hüsken, Frans and Benjamin White (1989) 'Java: social differentiation, food production, and agrarian control', in Gillian Hart, Andrew Turton and Benjamin White (eds), *Agrarian Transformations: Local Processes and the State in Southeast Asia*. Berkeley, CA: University of California Press.

Hwan, Ban Sung, Pal Yong Moon and Dwight H. Perkins (1980) *Rural Development*. Cambridge, MA: Harvard UniversityPress.

Johnson, Chalmers (1982) *MITI and the Japanese Miracle: The Growth of Industrial Policy, 1925–1975*. Stanford, CT: Stanford University Press.

—— (1995) *Japan: Who Governs? The Rise of the Developmental State*. London: W. W. Norton.

Jomo Kwame Sundaram (1988) *A Question of Class: Capital, the State and Uneven Development in Malaya*. New York: Monthly Review Press.

—— and Terence Gomez (2000) 'Rent-Seeking, Economic Diversification and Interethnic Redistribution: The Malaysian Development Dilemma', in M. Khan and Jomo K. S., *Rents and Rent-Seeking*. Cambridge: Cambridge University Press.

—— Chen Yun Chung *et al*. (1997) *Southeast Asia's Misunderstood Miracle: Industrial Policy and Economic Development in Thailand, Malaysia and Indonesia*. Oxford: Westview Press.

Khan, Mushtaq (2000) 'Rents, efficiency and growth' and 'Rent-seeking as process', in M. Khan and Jomo K. S. (eds) (2000) *Rents and Rent-Seeking*. Cambridge: Cambridge University Press, pp. 21–144.

—— and Jomo K. S. (eds) (2000) *Rents and Rent-Seeking*. Cambridge: Cambridge University Press.

Krugman, Paul (1994) 'The myth of Asia's miracle', *Foreign Affairs*, 73 (6): 62–78.

Lall, Sanjaya (ed.) (1995) 'Policy arena: the new tigers of South-East Asia', special issue, *Journal of International Development*, 7 (5): 741–800.

Lauridsen, Laurids S. (1998) 'Thailand: causes, conduct, consequences', in Jomo K. S. (ed.), *Tigers in Trouble: Financial Governance, Liberalization and Crises in East Asia*. London: Zed Books.

List, Friedrich (1966) *The National System of Political Economy*. New York: Augustus Kelly, [1885].

Mason, Edward *et al.* (1980) *The Economic and Social Modernization of the Republic of Korea.* Cambridge, MA: Harvard University Press.

Montes, Manuel and Muhammad Ali Abdusalamov, (1998) 'Indonesia: reaping the market', in Jomo K.S. (ed.), *Tigers in Trouble: Financial Governance, Liberalization and Crises in East Asia.* London: Zed Books.

Pasuk Phongpaichit and Chris Baker (1995) *Thailand: Economy and Politics.* Kuala Lumpur: Oxford University Press.

Putzel, James (1992) *A Captive Land: the Politics of Agrarian Reform in the Philippines.* London, New York and Manila: Catholic Institute for International Affairs, Monthly Review Press and Ateneo de Manila University Press.

Reyes, Alejandro (ed.) (1998) *Asiaweek: An Investor's Guide to Asia's Top 1000 Blue-Chip Companies.* Singapore: John Wiley & Sons (Asia).

Robison, Richard (1986) *Indonesia: The Rise of Capitalism.* North Sydney: Allen & Unwin.

Rock, Michael (2000) 'Thai development: if rent-seeing is so pervasive, why is development performance so good?', in M. Khan and Jomo K. S (eds), *Rents and Rent-Seeking.* Cambridge: Cambridge University Press.

Scott, James (1985) *Weapons of the Weak: Everyday Forms of Peasant Resistance.* New Haven, CT: Yale University Press.

Stiglitz, Joseph (1998) 'How did Southeast Asia measure up? Sound finance and sustainable development in Asia'. Keynote address to the Asia Development Forum, Manila, 12 March.

Thomas, Duncan (1999) 'Economic crisis and poverty: Evidence from Indonesia', RAND Corporation and UCLA, July, mimeo.

UNDP (1997) *Human Development Report.* New York: Oxford University Press.

Wade, Robert (1990) *Governing the Market: Economic Theory and the Role of Government in East Asian Industrialization.* Princeton, NJ: Princeton University Press.

Wade, Robert and Frank Veneroso (1998) 'The Asian Financial Crisis: the high debt model versus the Wall Street–Treasury–IMF complex', *New Left Review,* 228 (March-April), pp.3–23.

World Bank (1993) *The East Asian Miracle: Economic Growth and Public Policy.* New York: Oxford University Press.

NINE

South Korean Society in the IMF Era

Compressed Capitalist Development and Social Sustainability Crisis

Chang Kyung-Sup

South Korea's economic collapse of 1997 was no less dramatic than her earlier economic success for three and a half decades. Obviously, South Koreans over-stretched their economic ambitions in the 1990s, so that suicidal investment in heavy industries using short-term foreign loans was destined to cause a major balance-of-payment crisis. The economic – and, for that matter, social – crisis, however, seems rooted in many more ills of the South Korean model of development. Particularly menacing are social problems emanating from the psychological bubble concerning material betterment, the welfare-suppressive accumulation strategy, and the authoritarian treatment of labour. These practices and habits were often considered instrumental to achieving rapid industrialization and economic growth, but their social costs remained unpaid. Incidentally, various risky social conditions which had been built up under the South Korean development strategy began to hurt South Koreans at the grassroots level, with the IMF programme working as a crucial catalyst. In this sense, the IMF could (and should) have been much more careful about the local social contexts in which its economic restructuring programme would take effects (and side-effects). Does Kim Dae-Jung think differently or better than IMF supervisors? What have been alluded to by Kim and his staff concerning labour, poverty, education, housing, and other social concerns resemble Western social democracy closely. At the same time, he has not hesitated to accept and implement those programmes suggested by Western neoliberals as conservative reactions to their own social democratic past. It remains to be seen whether such inconsistencies reflect his indecisiveness or constitute a truly inventive doctrine for national development.

SOCIAL CONDITIONS OF SOUTH KOREAN DEVELOPMENT

Up until the sudden financial crisis of late 1997, South Korea's experience with economic development had served as a main arena for new theories and concepts in development studies. Neoclassical economists, political economists, sociologists, political scientists and historians joined the forum on the South Korean 'developmental miracle'. All conceivable factors for development were introduced: *laissez-faire* and free trade, state initiative, human capital formation, Confucian work ethic, state–business nexus, international product cycle, international political structure, colonial legacy, and abundant labour. Some saw the utility of the scientific tools already existing in their respective disciplines, whereas others invented new models and concepts to highlight various unique aspects of the South Korean developmental experience. Either way, the stunning speed of economic growth and industrialization in South Korea compelled these scholars to verify their ideas (and ideologies) against perhaps the most notable developmental achievement in the latter part of the twentieth century.[1]

One line of debate drawing particular attention along the economic crisis across Asia was triggered by Paul Krugman. Krugman (1994) characterized the developmental experience of South Korea (and other Asian countries) as 'input-driven' economic growth as compared to the supposedly 'efficiency-driven' growth of Western industrial economies. Many (neoclassical) economists follow Krugman's view, albeit without presenting systematic research outcomes. In Krugman's perspective, the current economic crisis in Asia may well be an inevitable outcome of what could be termed *debt-driven growth.*[2] However, there are serious case studies of South Korean industrialization – for instance, by Alice Amsden (1989), Peter Evans (1995) and John Matthews (1995) – which evince how South Korean bureaucrats and entrepreneurs successfully strove to achieve a technically advanced industrial system.[3]

I do not intend to side with either one of these opposing parties of thought. In my observation, there is no denying that South Korean *chaebol* conglomerates, under the tacit encouragement of the previous President Kim Young-Sam's *Sing-yeongje* [New Economy] administration, relied more on debt for their growth than on technological and organizational innovation. Still, these South Korean enterprises came to compete successfully with Japanese, American and European enterprises in many of the most advanced industrial sectors. Since their over-expansion was accompanied by increasing competitiveness, it was certain to create worry – if not fear – among Western and Japanese enterprises in this age of global overproduction.[4] In the 1960s and 1970s, the South Korean economy took off through the utilization of nearly 'unlimited supplies of labour' (cf. Lewis 1954). The simple fact was that the economy grew too fast to hang on continuously in the primitive labour-intensive sectors. Thus, in the late 1970s, the South Korean government decided to undertake the transition from labour-driven growth to technology and capital-driven growth, and *chaebol* leaders successfully rode on the tide to receive various preferential governmental support in building up their industrial kingdoms. In this process of ceaseless industrial transitions, South Koreans proved themselves to be exceptionally capable OJTs (on-the-job-trainees) in capitalist industrialization.

Given that the South Korean economy developed through both maximum input mobilization and substantial technological progress, my question is how South Koreans were able to drive maximum amounts of social and economic resources into the industrialization process. It has to be acknowledged that even input-driven economic development is a highly difficult task, at which only a handful of non-Western countries have had success. I do not think that South Koreans had some magical ability in this regard. Material sacrifice, political suppression and self-consoling optimism on the part of grassroots South Koreans were the basic social requirements for the economic growth strategy centred on the concentration of material and human resources in state-selected industrial enterprises.

First, the successive South Korean administrations exhausted their public budgets on economic development projects, whose benefits were immediately monopolized by private industries. They therefore had to minimize state programmes for protecting and improving the everyday lives of ordinary citizens. Until quite recently, social security had not been a significant component of national politics or government policy. Moreover, an integrative framework for social policy had not existed. Second, military-turned political leaders did not hesitate to support exploitative private industrialists, often using brutal physical violence, when workers argued for decent wages and work conditions. Labour had to be suppressed supposedly for the sake of international (price) competitiveness, and South Korean political leaders' deep confrontation with the Labour Party in North Korea intensified their hatred against the proletariat. Under such political auspices, a heavily spoiled capitalist class arose in South Korea which continued to deal with labour mainly on the basis of state-provided physical coercion.[5] Third, no South Koreans opposed the national industrialization project even when they were alienated or adversely affected by it. Even under these hostile conditions, many workers did experience increasing income, although such increases were usually far behind the profit growth of their employers. More importantly, most grassroots people motivated or hypnotized themselves to become loyal supporters of the national industrialization project. Their 'today' did look better than 'yesterday', whereas their 'tomorrow' would be even better than 'today'. Their 'yesterday', without too many exceptions, was filled with poverty, hunger, confusion and war. This mentality induced them to accept austerity measures voluntarily and to allocate all financial resources for education, savings and other future-oriented social and economic investment.

These social conditions were not exclusive to South Korea but widespread in rapidly industrializing capitalist economies. Poverty, suppression and illusion are rather typical symptoms of unfair domination, and I would not expect that South Koreans could have enjoyed an exceptionally humane capitalist economic system. However, abusive social conditions cannot, and should not, be perpetuated too long if a sustainable social and economic system is to be established. The crucial mistake made by South Korean politicians, bureaucrats and business leaders was that they clung to an unrealistic premise that such conditions could be maintained endlessly. Even at the time South Korea faltered into the current financial crisis, such problematic conditions had not been alleviated to any meaningful extent. The social pains triggered by the financial fiasco (and the

IMF regulation programme for it) are much more acutely felt because of these conditions.

Economic Bubble, Psychological Bubble

After experiencing three and a half decades of sustained and rapid income growth since the early 1960s, most South Koreans began to experience substantial reductions in or loss of income. The national economy suffered a 5.8 per cent decline in GDP in 1998 (*Hankyoreh*, 24 March 1999). In US dollars – against which the value of the Korean won nearly collapsed – the same year recorded a devastating 32.5 per cent shrinkage of the national economy. Once ranked as the eleventh largest economy in the world, the South Korean economy was demoted to the seventeenth. Likewise, per capita GNI (Gross National Income) plummeted to US$6,823 in 1998 – a 33.8 per cent decrease from the previous year, or the same level reached seven years before. South Koreans became a less-than-affluent people whose income level was only the 42nd highest in the world. Other crisis symptoms were in line. Corporate and private assets were devalued at unprecedented scales, innumerable corporations went bankrupt or liquidated, and workers in almost every industry faced massive lay-offs and pay-cuts.

The value of stocks, houses and land plummeted as a result of the national financial crisis. According to a report by Samsung Economic Research Institute (quoted in *Hankyoreh,* 18 September 1998), the total value of listed stocks decreased by 54.6 per cent between May 1997 and July 1998; the total value of houses (including apartments) shrank by 11.8 per cent between November 1997 and July 1998; and the total value of land dwindled by 20 per cent between the fourth quarter of 1997 and the second quarter of 1998. Obviously, these value depreciations far exceeded the level of economic 'bubble bursting'. It may appear rather surprising to many outside observers that most South Korean firms survived the stock price collapse. Ironically, according to the apt analysis of Robert Wade (1998), this outcome should be attributed to the fact that the financial structure of South Korean firms has been sustained by borrowing, and not by stock prices.[6] The depreciation of housing and land values and the freezing of housing and land markets effected a finishing blow to many middle-class families and small industrialists who had maintained their financial basis by investing in real estate.

Ever since the financial crisis erupted, the unemployment rate continued to climb (see Table 9.1). Even the seemingly exceptional two months of August and September 1998, were not real exceptions, because the increase in those giving up their job searches contributed to reducing the denominator of the unemployment statistic. Official figures, which count unemployment still under 10 per cent by regarding even those working a few hours per week or staying home on unwanted leave as employed, severely underrated the actual situation. The number of people under unstable and/or tentative employment has been considered even larger than the number of unemployed people. If these practically unemployed people and those who have helplessly given up on the job search are taken into account, the actual number of unemployed may well have reached 3 to 4 million, accounting for nearly 15–20 per cent of the working-age population.

Table 9.1: Changes in the official unemployment rate,* 1997–99

Month & Year	Unemployment rate (%)	No. unemployed (in millions)
Nov. 1997	2.6	574
Dec. 1997	3.1	658
Jan. 1998	4.5	934
Feb. 1998	5.9	1,235
Mar. 1998	6.5	1,378
Apr. 1998	6.7	1,434
May 1998	6.9	1,492
June 1998	7.0	1,529
July 1998	7.6	1,651
Aug. 1998	7.4	1,578
Sept. 1998	7.3	1,572
Oct. 1998	7.1	1,536
Nov. 1998	7.3	1,557
Dec. 1998	7.9	1,665
Jan. 1999	8.5	1,762
Feb. 1999	8.7	1,785

**Note:* The official unemployment rate in South Korea is calculated by assuming that one hour of work per week constitutes an employed status, and thus excludes severely underemployed workers (who are usually considered 'unemployed' in advanced industrial economies)

Source: Database of the National Statistical Office, South Korea

Because of these economic collapses, South Koreans became the second most damaged population in Asia amid the region-wide financial crisis. (The Indonesian economy suffered the greatest damage.) As shown in Table 9.2, the 'misery index' – the pressure of unemployment and inflation beyond economic growth – increased most dramatically in South Korea among all Asian countries.[7] Since the pains from an economic crisis are relative to the pre-crisis conditions of life, South Korea's difficulty appears particularly severe.

The pains, however, were not felt evenly among different classes. As shown in Table 9.3, the poorest segments of the population were hit particularly hard.

Table 9.2: Misery Index,* 1997 and 1998

Country	1997	1998
Asian countries:		
South Korea	1.5	20.9
Indonesia	6.8	96.5
Thailand	10.6	25.1
Malaysia	-2.4	10.8
China	-1.0	-0.1
Hong Kong	2.6	9.6
Taiwan	-3.2	0.7
Advanced countries:		
United States	3.4	2.8
Japan	4.3	6.7
France	11.4	10.0
Germany	10.7	10.0
England	5.4	5.8
Sweden	7.1	4.8
Italy	12.5	11.8
Spain	19.4	18.1
Canada	7.1	6.7
Australia	5.6	6.7

* *Note:* Misery index is computed as unemployment rate (in per cent) plus inflation rate (in per cent) minus GDP growth rate (in per cent); 1998 figures cover January to October

Source: Abridged from data in Daewoo Economic Research Institute, 1998, 'The Phenomenon of Pain Transfer from Advanced Countries to Asian Countries and Its Implication for the South Korean Economy' (in Korean; an unpublished report)

The richest people were clearly an exception, as they experienced a nominal income increase in the first half of 1998 (in part due to skyrocketing interest rates). These income disparities widened with time.It should be noted that these statistics omit those at the extreme ends of the economic hierarchy (i.e., urban capitalist households, on the one hand, and unemployed and underemployed persons' households, on the other), and thus cannot fully describe the actual

Table 9.3: Annual income changes among urban worker households between 1997 and 1998 (in per cent)

Income group	Quarter			1997 to 1998
	1st	2nd	3rd	
All	-2.8	-5.3	-14.4	-6.7
Highest 20%	0.9	2.3	-8.0	-0.3
2nd 20%	-3.1	-5.6	-15.2	-8.0
3rd 20%	-4.4	-6.9	-18.3	-9.9
4th 20%	-5.5	-8.8	-19.6	-11.8
Lowest 20%	-12.0	-14.9	-24.4	-17.2

Source: Compiled from the database of the National Statistical Office, South Korea

extent of the existing inequality. On average, urban worker households suffered nominal income reductions from 1997 to 1998: by 2.8 per cent between the first quarters, by 5.3 per cent between the second quarters, and by a devastating 14.4 per cent between the third quarters, and by 3.8 per cent between the fourth quarters (National Statistical Office 1999). It should also be noted that the economic crisis had already broken out in the fourth quarter of 1997, so that the comparison between the fourth quarters of 1997 and 1998 does not fully represent the effect of crisis.[8] The year 1998 as a whole showed a 6.7 per cent decrease from the previous year.

As a consequence, every household was forced to reduce consumption. The consumption expenses of urban worker households decreased between 1997 and 1998 by 8.8 per cent between the first quarters, by 13.2 per cent between the second quarters, by 16.8 per cent between the third quarters, and by 4.0 per cent between the fourth quarters (National Statistical Office 1999). The entire year of 1998 showed a 10.7 per cent decrease from the preceding year. It is quite notable that South Koreans' consumption expanded rapidly until the very moment of their country's financial collapse. That is, the third quarter of 1997 marked an 8.2 per cent increase in the consumption expenses of urban worker households over the previous year.

Reductions in consumption were relatively small among the richest and the poorest groups, however, for diametrically different reasons (Cheil Communications 1998). The most destitute people were unable to cut down on consumption any further. The most affluent people, with their cash assets bloated abruptly thanks to 'IMF-pushed' ultra-high interest rates, may have had an interest in expanding their conspicuous consumption, but social rage and political pressure against them amid the national financial fiasco forced them to feign repentance by abstaining from lavish spending.[9]

Table 9.4: Changes in monthly income and self-perceived class stratum before and after the 'IMF crisis' in the four largest South Korean cities (n=2,500)

	Pre-crisis (1997) distribution in %	Post-crisis (1998) distribution in %
Monthly income (million won):		
401 and more	6.5	3.8
301 – 400	11.2	7.5
251 – 300	16.3	13.2
201 – 250	24.3	20.0
151 – 200	21.6	22.3
101 – 150	16.5	23.0
100 and less	3.6	10.2
Self-perceived class stratum:		
Upper	1	1
Upper middle	12	6
Middle	65	60
Lower middle	19	26
Lower	3	7

Source: Compiled from data in Cheil Communications, 1998, pp. 6–7.

The figures in Table 9.4 reveal that the economic crisis induced *hahyang pyeongjunhwa* [downward levelling] of income as the proportions in the lowest income groups increased drastically. The 'collapse of the middle class', which has been talked about frequently in media articles and academic seminars, does appear to be a serious possibility for the future. It might be safe to say that a monthly household income of at least 2 million won is a prerequisite for basic human subsistence in big cities (whose cost of living has been ranked among the world highest). It was already more than a decade ago (in 1989) that Hanguknochong (the Federation of Korean Trade Unions or FKTU) estimated about 1 million won per month as the absolute household-level poverty line (as quoted in Lee *et al.* 1991: 168).

The bursting of a sort of *psychological bubble* accompanied the income reductions in South Korea. South Koreans' self-perceived class status has been falling substantially. On the eve of the current economic crisis, as shown in Table 9.4, 65 per cent of South Korean urbanites classified themselves as 'middle' class, 12 per cent as 'upper middle' class, and 19 per cent as 'lower middle' class. Six months into the economic crisis, the number of those who perceived themselves as 'upper middle' or 'middle' class had decreased notably, if not dramatically. Such a psychological downslide is far from over, as additional unemployment resulting from corporate structural adjustment and exhaustion of household savings is still on the cards for many subjectively and objectively middle-class families. According to a study in 1998 (Bae 1998), about 40 per cent of the South Korean population would lose all means of subsistence within two years, and the next 40 per cent within three years. Even if the rapid economic recovery promised by the current state leadership is realized, many of these demoted South Koreans will never be able to regain their earlier economic and social status.

In my view, this psychological dejection is what haunts South Koreans most seriously and destabilizes the social and political basis of South Korean development most critically. When the authoritarian developmentalist state denied them social rights to humane living conditions, and when greedy industrialists refused to give reasonable compensation for their work, grassroots South Koreans still remained highly motivated and optimistic about their economic future. An interesting ramification of this attitude was a sort of false middle-class consciousness. Figures in Table 9.4 illustrate that, at least before the economic crisis, almost everyone thought of themselves as middle class. A nationwide survey in 1994 by the South Korean Consumer Protection Board reported that 81.3 per cent classified themselves as 'middle class' as opposed to 7.1 per cent and 11.7 per cent who saw themselves as 'upper class' and 'lower class' respectively (as reported in *Sisa Journal*, 11 November 1998). South Koreans' 'workaholism' was largely fuelled by such psychological self-aggrandizement. The recent demoralization of grassroots South Koreans cannot but lead to a catastrophic constraint on socially sustainable development.

The precise factors generating the bloated self-perceptions of South Koreans in the social and economic hierarchy are yet to be analysed. However, I may consider the following three matters critical. First, most South Koreans were enjoying better lives, at least as compared to their miserable existence in the pre-Park Chung-Hee era, with a per capita GNP of less than US$100. In locating their class position, South Koreans seem to have used, as the basic reference category, their destitute past rather than the living standard of their contemporaries. Almost everyone felt gratified by recollecting the 'cold and hungry old days'. Second, most South Koreans were expecting even better lives in the future. Interestingly, poor late-comers in social and economic competition showed a particularly conservative attitude towards the national developmental situation. Besides hard proletarian work, educational certification, real estate speculation and small self-employed entrepreneurship were the most popular conduits for class advancement. Under a sort of *makcha* [last train] effect, those underclass individuals who had just prepared educational certificates, speculation funds or business ventures were desperately hoping that the asymmetrical economic opportunity structures would be maintained, at least until they could finally receive differential returns on their arduous investments. Third, South Koreans' material as well as psychological attachments to adult children, parents and siblings induced them to link their class status to those of their extended family members (in particular, successful ones). Poor aged parents would rank the social and economic situation of their successful children (if they had any) as more important than their own situation in evaluating their class status. Adult (as well as young) children, even when lacking educational, technical and financial resources for independent living, would identify themselves as part of their rich parents' family (if any) in evaluating class status.

For these and many other reasons, grassroots South Koreans used to maintain a highly positive and optimistic attitude about material advancement.[10] This attitude underlay the widespread political conservatism of the lower classes that was apparent in parliamentary and presidential elections. More importantly, the same attitude induced them to adopt voluntary austerity measures and to allocate all of their financial resources for education, savings and other future-oriented social and economic investments. Such future-oriented investments were customarily made on a familial basis – i.e., educational investment for children and siblings, savings pools for family business, etc. (Chang 1997b). As compared to the 'social investment state' proposed recently by Anthony Giddens (1998) for the 'renewal of social democracy' in the West, South Korea has manifested what may be called *the social investment family*. Recent statistics by the Organization for Economic Cooperation and Development (OECD) concerning educational investment reveal that South Korea was far ahead of other OECD member countries in the family-provided portion of the expenses for higher education during the 1990–95 period.[11]

Table 9.5: Percentage of agreement on the unfairness of social order in the four largest South Korean cities (n=2,500)

	Only rich people can make more money	Success is not possible with honest effort alone	Law-abiding citizens are disadvantaged
1994	75	70	39
1995	74	70	42
1996	74	71	44
1997	78	75	53
1998	80	75	56

Source: Cheil Communications, 1998, p. 18

The significance of this self-generated social and economic efficacy may be proved conversely by the fact that grassroots South Koreans have nevertheless been fully aware of the unjust and biased nature of the 'crony capitalist' order.[12]

That is, although there is an acknowledgement of the highly corrupt nature of wealth and power in their society, South Korean people strove positively to integrate their mental energy for the ongoing process of national development. As illustrated in Table 9.5, most (urban) South Koreans in the mid-1990s perceived the economic opportunity structure as skewed and unfair. Nearly half also thought that law and order had been abused for the sake of injustice. Not surprisingly, such a negative perception of social order has exacerbated since the national economic crisis of 1997. Likewise, even a 1998 survey conducted by the Free Enterprise Centre – the official ideological apparatus of *chaebol* conglomerates – revealed an embarrassing reality that ordinary citizens' perceptions of large corporations and business leaders were extremely negative (see Table 9.6). Obviously, grass-

Table 9.6: Images concerning corporations and business leaders (five most negative ones in per cent)

Images	%
Corporations:	
Voracious (*muneobalsik*) expansion	15.9
Sudden riches, greed	13.0
Exploitation of small enterprises	12.0
Government-business collusion	11.8
Insolvency	10.4
Business leaders:	
Dogmatism, authoritarianism	21.3
Government–business collusion	11.8
Only profit-seeking	8.8
Immorality	7.4
Extravagant life	5.3

Source: Survey data released to the press by the Free Enterprise Center, the Federation of Korean Industries, covering 800 ordinary people and 200 professionals in 1998, as reported in *Hankyoreh*, 25 September 1998

roots South Koreans do not have much respect for the very kind of people that they try to emulate. In the past, they tolerated these ruthless, greedy, dishonest and immoral figures and their political and bureaucratic supporters only because they thought wishfully about their own chances of joining the economic parade and sharing its perks. Now, suddenly realizing that this possibility may well be unattainable in a foreseeable future, grassroots South Korean have every reason to accumulate psychological fuel for revolt.[13]

GROWTH FIRST, DISTRIBUTION LATER AND STRUCTURAL ADJUSTMENT NOW?

What does the state offer for economically dislocated and psychologically dejected South Koreans? The immediate answer – if not from government officials – will be an emotionally charged 'Nothing!' Interviews and surveys of unemployed individuals and their dependants report unequivocally that most needy people have not received any public relief benefit, are not aware of any usable relief programme for them, and would not expect much help from the government anyway (e.g., Park 1999; Kim *et al.* 1998; Korea Institute for Health and Social Affairs and Korea Labour Institute 1998).[14] Even those who have received some assistance express very low satisfaction. For instance, according to a newspaper survey of July 1998, 19.4 per cent of the respondents expressed satisfaction with relief assistance (*Hankyoreh*, 31 July 1998). On the other hand, newspapers and television news have carried almost daily reports of fraudulent use and even embezzlement of the special unemployment programme budget by government officials and welfare contractors (e.g., *Hankyoreh*, 30 September 1998; *Sisa Journal*, 13 August 1998). It is not unusual to hear candid confessions from government officials that they are simply inexperienced and do not know what to do in this kind of situation (*Hankyoreh*, 6 August 1998).

Ironically, it is this inexperience and irresponsibility on the part of the state concerning the social conditions of people's lives that help to protect politicians and bureaucrats from critical political challenges by grassroots citizens. Simply speaking, few grassroots South Koreans have serious expectations for social protection and relief by the state against unemployment and poverty. They saw the successive authoritarian developmentalist regimes either explicitly call for 'growth first, distribution later' or channel state work implicitly in that direction. As displayed in Table 9.7, the South Korean government committed itself to social security far less than those of other late developing countries at similar levels of development, not to mention those of Western industrialized countries.[15] It is questionable whether any previous South Korean administration had an integrated conception of social policy *per se*.[16] As far as social issues were concerned, the successive South Korean administrations remained completely *laissez-faire* under the doctrine that may be called *developmental liberalism*. Supposedly for the sake of sustained rapid economic growth, the state showed a near indifference to social welfare, and thus, *the only social entitlement for grassroots South Koreans was work*.[17] As most of the available national economic resources were allocated to economic development projects and corporate subsidies, South Koreans had to find work through which they could reap some benefit from the economy-centred system. Without work, therefore, they would suffer from total social alienation. This very situation has surfaced in South Korean society. The most crucial dilemma of the incumbent South Korean administration has been that it has to persuade workers to accept such total alienation. Even if South Koreans may not complain too noisily about not receiving social security benefits from the government, they would not tolerate bureaucrats and politicians demanding their resignation from work for the sake of 'structural adjustment' in the economy. Thus, at factories, offices and other places of work, they do not hesitate to express their individual and collective anger at employers and government authorities whenever their work entitlement comes under threat.[18]

Table 9.7: Government expenditure in selected countries

Country	Year	Gov't expend. as % of GDP	% of total government expenditure			
			Social security	Education	Econ. Affairs	Defence
Australia	1995	27.9	33.8	7.6	7.1	7.6
Canada	1992	25.2	41.3	3.0	8.3	6.9
Chile	1994	19.7	33.3	13.9	15.4	8.8
Egypt	1993	35.7	11.0	12.3	8.0	8.7
France	1992	45.0	45.0	7.0	4.7	5.7
Germany	1991	32.5	45.3	0.8	9.7	6.4
Japan	1993	23.7	36.8	6.0	3.3	4.1
Kuwait	1994	56.2	16.6	10.9	8.0	22.3
Mexico	1990	17.4	12.4	13.9	13.4	2.4
South Korea	**1995**	**19.9**	**9.3**	**18.1**	**24.0**	**15.7**
Sweden	1994	48.5	48.2	5.0	13.2	5.5
Thailand	1992	15.0	3.9	21.1	26.2	17.2
United Kingdom	1992	43.1	29.6	3.3	6.6	9.9
United States	1994	22.0	29.6	1.6	6.4	18.1

Source: Social Indicators in Korea, 1997: 533

Another factor contributing to the desperate resistance of workers to lay-offs is corporate welfare. Under the slogan of 'company as family', many large companies used to offer employees such fringe benefits as housing, children's school tuition, medical protection, life insurance, childcare, leisure and vacation facilities, and even graduate study opportunities, although these benefits do not constitute corporate legal responsibilities (Song 1995). In particular, major *chaebol* conglomerates have called themselves *gajok* [family], like Samsung Gajok and Daewoo Gajok, and have provided workers with various kinds of paternalistic aid. Also, a crucial political reason has existed for bountiful corporate welfare, in particular, since 1987. The demise of Chun Doo-Hwan's military dictatorship paved the way for a sudden upsurge of workers against the government and its client industrialists. Roh Tae-Woo's next government tried to elude political confrontation with organized labour by leaving labour matters to be resolved between business and labour. At large factories and offices where organized labour was able to exercise pressure and threat, employers had to reach a compromise by offering various fringe benefits in addition to higher wages. With the government maintaining its abstinence from social welfare (even in times of a huge budget surplus), corporate welfare became a significant tool for improving living conditions, at least for those lucky workers employed in large *chaebol* companies. These days, such corporate welfare benefits evaporate as soon as workers are discharged from their companies in the process of personnel shake-ups.

As massive lay-offs have become an indispensable part of the structural adjustment programme in an overexpanded economy, the South Korean government is at last realizing the true cost of lacking a comprehensive and functioning welfare system. In this context, the so-called *sahoeanjeonmang* [social safety net] has suddenly become the key word for public discourse. Without the social safety net, a democratic government such as Kim Dae-Jung's may not be able to persuade its people to accept massive unemployment, for it would mean nothing other than a free-fall to the ground. In this context, the South Korean government is apparently struggling to reinvent itself as a *social policy state*, albeit, at a fairly rudimentary level. The tragedy is that, while political leaders and government officials use most of their time in a trial-and-error manner, thousands of grassroots South Koreans are losing their jobs and incomes every day.

Two factors in particular have intensified the anger of grassroots South Koreans. As explained in detail below, in January 1998, labour unions reached a historical agreement with government and business leaders on how to overcome the current economic crisis in a cooperative and peaceful manner. The core tenet of the historically unprecedented tripartite compromise was *gotongbundam* [pain-sharing]. As workers are supposed to accept lay-offs and pay reductions 'under certain urgent managerial situations', the government and corporations should have embarked on thorough organizational reforms, expunging their entrenched and unjust prerogatives. Neither government offices nor *chaebol* corporations have shown any meaningful initiation of such reforms. In fact, their intention to implement such reforms itself is under question.

According to a 1998 survey of 1,030 residents in the six largest South Korean cities, as many as 50.6 per cent of the respondents indicated that the occupation they most preferred for the spouses of their daughters or sisters was that of government official (see Table 9.8). *Sinbunbojang* [status guarantee] attached to these public jobs is an obvious reason for the preference.[19] Nowadays, this status guarantee is called 'the iron rice bowl' – a term borrowed, ironically, from socialist China where urban workers used to enjoy similarly secure employment conditions. In early 1998, the government announced a plan to reduce the

Table 9.8: Most favoured occupations for spouses of daughter or sister (n=1,030)

Occupation	%
Official	50.6
Big restaurant owner	11.3
Big company employee	7.7
Professor	6.0
Physician	5.5
Businessman	4.4
Professional	2.3
Prosecutor	1.9
Technician	1.8
Foreign currency dealer	1.6
Reporter/Producer	1.3
Judge	1.0

Source: A survey by *Weekly Chosun* of residents (aged 20 years and older) in the six largest cities, 28–30 September 1998 (*Weekly Chosun*, 22 October 1998)

number of administrative personnel by 10 per cent, but not many have actually been laid off. Natural retirement and some one-year-early retirement soon provided the promised 10 per cent reduction. Even the very intent of the political leadership to reform the government bureaucracy came under wide suspicion when it announced its government organizational restructuring plan on 23 March 1999 (*Hankyoreh*, 24 March 1999). Contrary to the recommendations of the special committee which had carried out base studies, President Kim Dae-Jung adopted a plan that would require the addition of one ministry and one semi-ministry to the already bulky administrative bureaucracy, omitting any significant reduction in his administrative staff. The privilege attached to public occupations is manifest even in the process of the so-called structural adjustment. When workers were discharged from state-funded and/or state-run organizations, including banks, they were offered *wirogeum* [consolation money] amounting to hundreds of thousands of US dollars. Not many private workers could have dreamt of saving that amount, even throughout their entire careers. Popular outrage was intensified further when Kim Dae-Jung remarked, ‘as far as people’s legal sentiment allows, it is necessary to generously forgive’ the petty corruption of government officials in the past (*Hankyoreh*, 26 March 1999). While this remark was intended as an offer of a ‘carrot’ to extremely resistant bureaucrats (whom Kim had not been able to discipline), the expectation held by ordinary citizens to see corrupt bureaucrats punished as part of the pain-sharing measures and to be served by a clean and efficient government evaporated.

The resistance of *chaebol* leaders to structural reforms is even more problematic. Practically no one thinks that *chaebol* conglomerates have undergone serious reforms in ownership, management or financial structure. The IMF, the World Bank, international credit appraisal companies and foreign political leaders consider the *chaebols*' sneaky disobedience as the most serious blemish on South Korea's otherwise satisfactory structural adjustment record. At the first meeting between then President-elect Kim Dae-Jung and major *chaebol* leaders in December 1997, the late Chey Jong-Hyon, then President of the Federation of Korean Industries, remarked, 'These days, we businessmen have no word to say. The economy got into this mess because of our fault. We are the worst among all sinners' (*Dong-A Ilbo*, 25 December 1997). This seemingly remorseful attitude, however, has not left any clear imprint in terms of self-limiting corporate reforms. In fact, it appears that the five largest *chaebol* conglomerates (Hyundai, Samsung, Daewoo, LG and Sunkyung) have been trying to expand their corporate bodies further, again through borrowing (Yun 1998). It was reported that these largest *chaebol* conglomerates monopolized the corporate bonds market, thereby accumulating operating funds in amounts large enough to counter governmental threats (or bluffs?) to withdraw bank loans in case of disobedience (*Hankyoreh*, 22 October 1998). In the meantime, the government, with the unexpected but inevitable encouragement of the IMF and other Western authorities, declared on 9 September 1998 that it was embarking on a programme to boost the economy through expanded public spending, lowered interest rates, etc. Even though Kim Dae-Jung would not likely agree, there is every indication that the *chaebols*' strategy of buying time has largely been effective, nullifying the governmental initiative for corporate structural reforms.[20]

Grassroots people do not have as much freedom to refuse reforms as government offices and *chaebol* corporations. As indicated above, the unemployment rate continued to climb well into 1999. Moreover, an ever increasing number of people were even giving up their job search. The mighty *chaebol* firms do not lag behind smaller firms in resorting to massive lay-offs. Between January and September 1998, about 10 per cent of the employees of the five largest *chaebol* conglomerates lost their jobs (*Chosun Ilbo*, 28 October 1998). Among about 900,000 workers employed by the 30 largest *chaebol* conglomerates as of October 1998, still one-third of them are expecting to be retrenched through the process of corporate structural adjustment in the coming months.

As a result of relentless labour reforms, South Korean companies were able to reduce the ratio of personnel expenses to total sales to 9.4 per cent in the first half of 1998, marking a 2.6 per cent point decrease from only a year before (see Table 9.9). Despite (or because of) such drastic reductions in personnel expenses, South Korean companies still enjoyed a 9.3 per cent increase in the per-worker amount of value added and a remarkable 20 per cent increase in the per-worker sales volume in the first half of 1998. Largely due to labour reform effects, the operating profit rate of South Korean companies in this turbulent economic period reached 8.8 per cent, achieving a 1.3 per cent point *increase* from a year

Table 9.9: Analysis of corporate management performance in the first halves of 1997–98 (n=2,328)

Performance item (in per cent)	1997	1998
Total sales increase rate	9.1	5.0
Sales profit ratio	7.5	8.8
Total profit ratio	1.4	-0.4
Per worker sales increase rate	13.9	20.0
Per worker value-added increase rate	11.4	9.3
Per worker expense increase rate	8.3	-4.7
Worker expenses to sales ratio	12.0	9.4
Finance costs to sales ratio	6.2	9.3
Total debt ratio (year-end for 1997)	396.3	387.0

Source: The Bank of Korea, 1998

before. The trouble, however, lay elsewhere. The burden of debt service, in terms of the ratio of finance costs (interests, etc.) to total sales, increased dramatically in the first half of 1998 to reach 9.3 per cent, recording a 3.1 per cent point increase from a year before. After paying huge finance costs which were comparable to total personnel expenses, South Korean companies had to experience a current account deficit rate of 0.4 per cent. Personnel lay-offs, pay-cuts, and increased working hours were all expended to deal with the financial mess created by the owners and managers of these companies. However, in the judgement of most South Koreans, these business owners and managers have shown scant remorse about their wrongdoings.[21]

'Development with sizeable structural unemployment' has become a new catch-phrase since the economic shock. However, though unrecognized previously, it has long been a hard reality. South Koreans now realize not only that economic depression and structural adjustment necessitate massive lay-offs at various ranks and sectors of the economy, but also that almost-full employment, unlike their perception and governmental statistics, has never been a true reality. A large proportion of the officially employed population were in effect under chronic and severe underemployment which never allowed them a secure living. Temporary workers at construction sites, sales and service workers, and part-time home service workers constituted the very first group to experience unemployment (Nam and Lee 1998). Their transitory occupational status made it difficult to institute social security programmes for them. The current economic shock hit these people most brutally as they were exposed to total unemployment with no personal or public means of relief.[22]

The newly unemployed have been trying every possible self-help measure. Some have decided to return to their home villages to switch to farming, and others have flown to foreign countries recollecting the years of the Middle East construction boom and the Vietnamese war.[23] Where possible, many workers have attempted to resurrect their bankrupt companies by taking over ownership and management. Young people about to try their luck on the job market for the first time – i.e., new graduates from colleges and high schools – have tried to avoid unemployment by applying for military service (which is already full) and higher learning.[24]

Most importantly, many unemployed people have turned to their families and kin (parents, children and siblings) for such emergency relief measures as role-switching, complementary wage-earning, cash-lending, bank payment guarantees, housing-sharing, etc. (Park 1999; Chang and Kim 1999; Korea Institute for Health and Social Affairs 1988). These familial relief arrangements have given many a breathing space to resolve their financial situation. As a consequence for many, their family relationships have been strengthened (Cheil Communications 1998). Still more people, however, are seeing their families dissolve, as extreme material destitution places them and their family members in conditions of severe stress, and induces them to neglect family support responsibilities. A 1998 government survey of unemployed people in Seoul and Pusan revealed that separation and divorce were increasing rapidly due to the material and psychological distress of unemployment (*Hankyoreh*, 26 September 1998). The numbers of children and youth in need of protection – such as deserted babies and those born out-of-wedlock, physically and mentally abused children, runaway youths, and students skipping meals – have also been increasing seriously.

The misery of the elderly, youth, children and the handicapped in poor neighbourhoods, while simply taken for granted by the government and society, is likely to worsen as scarce public attention and support tend to dwindle even further under the primacy of the unemployment issue. In the near absence of public welfare protection, needy people used to depend for their sheer survival on generous family members and relatives with regular jobs and stable incomes (Chang 1997a). Nowadays these generous family members and relatives themselves have been losing jobs and incomes with little hope of re-employment.[25] The pains of people in the poorest and most needy segments of society cannot be concealed or contained within private support networks any more; nor do they want to be institutionalized in notoriously managed (dis)welfare asylums.[26] Unemployment has induced a chain-reaction social disintegration for grassroots South Koreans.[27] It is no wonder that recent newspapers have been full of stories about the misery of these helpless groups, abandoned by the state and separated from generous but unemployed kin providers.

LABOUR–BUSINESS–GOVERNMENT COMPROMISE; LABOUR–BUSINESS BIGOTRY

South Korean workers may well take great pride in the political efficacy that has been achieved through decades of unbending struggles with ruthless employers and authoritarian governments. Their rise as a politically and economically competent class within a surprisingly short period is an outcome of the complex interplay of the labour–capital class conflict and state–society political struggle

(Koo 1993; Chang 1999). The current process of economic structural adjustment is also a complicated political economy played out by the intrusive state, aggressive monopoly capital and resolute organized labour.

Politically, the most significant achievement of Kim Dae-Jung's government is indisputably the *nosajeong* [labour–business–government] cooperation system which began in early 1998. It does attest to Kim Dae-Jung's democratic inclination to incorporate various grassroots groups in national politics under the slogan of 'participatory democracy'. However, a more fundamental condition for the landmark tripartite agreement system was derived from the fact that, merely a year before (i.e., in early 1997), labour unions had successfully defeated the attempt of the Kim Young-Sam regime to implement serious labour reforms against workers' economic and political interests in an exclusionary manner. Labour had fought its own way towards a full membership in Kim Dae-Jung's inclusionary state corporatist arrangement (Chang Hong Geun 1999; Lim 1997). However, South Korean bourgeoisie, i.e., *chaebol* heads, are not accustomed to being treated on pair with labour by state authorities. Indeed, many bureaucrats are having difficulty reforming their high-handed approach towards labour.[28] The political economic order of what may be called *exclusionary developmentalism* seems to have a strong inertia. In today's South Korean politics, however, labour unions have been much more competent than *chaebols* and bureaucracy, which are held jointly responsible for the current economic crisis.

The tripartite agreements, described in the '*Nosajeongwiweonhoe* [Labour–Business–Government Committee] Co-Declaration' of 20 January 1998, included:

1. the government's acceptance of its responsibility for the economic crisis and duty (a) to prepare serious protection measures concerning unemployment and living conditions, (b) to reform government organizations thoroughly, and (c) to supervise fundamental corporate restructuring;
2. corporations' obligation to pursue active structural adjustment, reform managerial practices, and avoid wholesale lay-offs and unfair labour practices;
3. labour unions' obligation to cooperate with corporations in improving productivity and, in urgent managerial situations, to adjust wages and working hours;
4. workers' and employers' commitment to industrial peace through dialogue and compromise;
5. the cooperation among labour unions, corporations and the government to create an attractive environment for foreign capital.

Perhaps it was this historic compromise between traditional foes that built confidence in the minds of foreign creditors and those of South Korean citizens about the possibility of an orderly economic recovery. In particular, the virtual acceptance by labour unions of lay-offs 'in extreme managerial situations was praised by foreign lenders and observers as a critical first step to an economic comeback in South Korea. South Korean employers should have felt blessed. However, a dilemma arose when employers and workers returned to their factories and offices and had to take concrete steps for economic structural reforms. When left to their own devices, little trust existed between labour and management, with each group resorting to manipulation, deception, and/or threats. The first test case concerned the Hyundai Motor Company. Ever since the company announced the plan for *jeongrihaego* [personnel shake-up], mutual accusations of breaching the labour–employer agreements prevailed, and even instances of serious physical violence were reported. Ultimately, the settlement of the feud required the intervention of major governmental and political figures, including a vice president of the ruling party and the Minister of Labour. By and large, the settlement of 24 August 1998 appeared more acceptable to labour. *Chaebols* and their client media, therefore, began to mobilize negative opinions on it (*Hankyoreh*, 3 September 1998). This tactic paid off. The next major labour dispute at Mando Machinery Company was physically quelled by police on 3 September 1998, paving the way for liberal lay-offs (*Sisa Journal*, 17 September 1998). In this manner the current administration stayed neutral between labour and *chaebols*.

As *chaebol* companies have continued to resist the national and international pressure for structural reform in management, ownership and financial structure, the rationale for the tripartite agreement system has come under serious questioning.[29] After all, the agreements reached at the tripartite meetings are not legally binding. Workers seem to have every reason for growing indignant, although they still believe in the political values of the tripartite agreement system. *Chaebol* heads have never been sincerely interested in these multiparty consultation and compromise meetings. In their experience, secret manipulation and lobbying are much more effective means for realizing their business goals. An increasing number of South Koreans now believe that the *chaebols*' attempts have been largely successful.

In the second year under the tripartite agreement, the feeling prevailed among labour leaders that the seemingly social democratic political arrangement had been (ab)used only to justify massive lay-offs supposedly for the sake of corporate structural readjustment. Minjunochong (the Korean Confederation of Trade Unions or KCTU), the progressive umbrella organization of labour unions, finally declared its withdrawal from the tripartite committee on 24 February 1999, vowing to stage street demonstrations and strikes (*Hankyoreh*, 25 February 1999). On 28 March 1999, even the more moderate Hanguknochong (the Federation of Korean Trade Unions or FKTU) announced its possible withdrawal from the committee in early April, unless the government agreed to change its unfair reform policy (*Hankyoreh*, 29 March 1999). While workers alone have difficulty mobilizing social and political support from the general public, the serious unemployment situation and the political weakness of the current administration are certain to help labour unions to exercise formidable pressure in the coming months and years.

THE IMF ENIGMA: IMPERIALIST FINANCE AND LOCAL POPULATION

The Asian economic crises have spilt over not only into Russia and Latin America but also into international financial regulators including the IMF. The IMF programme for austerity-based structural adjustments in Asia have been harshly criticized by both neoclassical economists (e.g., Paul Krugman and Jeffrey Sachs) and political economists (e.g., Robert Wade) for ignoring the unique characteristics of Asian economies. Even officials in the Organization of Economic Cooperation and Development (OECD) and, more recently, the World Bank, began to express pessimism about the outdated IMF doctrine. Ironically, even George Soros came to join the IMF-bashing by criticizing its lenient treatment of creditors (including himself?) at a recent congressional hearing in the United States (*Hankyoreh,* 17 September 1998).

In particular, the 1997–98 annual report of the OECD on the South Korean economy prepared in mid-June 1998 (in a draft version) staged an outright attack on the mistakes of the IMF and instead suggested lower interest rates and expanded public spending on welfare as indispensable requirements for economic recovery (*Chosun Ilbo,* 27 July 1998). It did not take long for the IMF to modify its position, consciously or unconsciously, in the direction suggested by the OECD. As early as 28 July 1998, the director of the Seoul office of the IMF confessed in a media interview that the high interest rate policy had devastated already troubled Asian economies and that more public spending would be necessary, in particular to establish an effective social safety net (*Sisa Journal,* 13 August 1998). At an international seminar on 14 September 1998, the director of the Asia-Pacific division of the IMF even called for the South Korean government to boost the economy by expanding deficit spending (*Hankyoreh,* 15 September 1998). Taking into account its failure to predict the Asian financial crises, the IMF seems to have bungled its mission both for prediction and prescription.

In the South Korean context, however, the IMF mandate for remedying the 'crony capitalist' structure of the South Korean economy received a heartfelt welcome from reform-minded economists. Many of them in fact claimed that the IMF regulatory system could serve as an opportunity to redress all the inefficient and corrupt practices ensuing from state–*chaebol* collusion and unnecessary state intrusion into private economic activities. Long before the IMF and Western observers began to criticize 'crony capitalism' (as the supposed cause for the economic crisis in South Korea and elsewhere), South Korea's reform-minded scholars had called for the dismantling of the government–business collusion. Without political influence, however, these scholars were frustrated by policy decisions and corporate activities that were going in the exactly opposite direction. When the 'IMF occupation' began, they welcomed, out of desperation, many of the Fund's prescriptions concerning financial, corporate and administrative reforms. Kim Dae-Jung's ready accommodation of the IMF recommendations on *chaebol* reform may be understood similarly. At least on the urgent need for *chaebol* reform, the IMF, the OECD, international credit appraisal companies and South Korea's political leadership, labour and intellectual community were all in agreement. The staunch and sly resistance of *chaebol* further reinforced this agreement.[30] In addition, the increasing emphasis of the IMF and the World Bank on the establishment of a sound social safety net has received a warm welcome from reform-minded South Koreans.[31]

Nevertheless, the liberal outlook of IMF officials (or financial liberalism based upon contradictory state-interventionist austerity principles) reflected the spirit of the times, i.e., American-dominated global economic *laissez-faire* underwritten by docile Third World states. After all, they asked to be invited in order to rescue the South Korean economy from bankruptcy and thereby ensure the payment of South Korean debts to foreign lenders. Additionally, their recent concern about the social safety net came far too late. The everyday existence of grassroots South Koreans was predicated upon paid work and occasional kin assistance, and their devotion to work was buttressed by the satisfaction and optimism generated by the prospect of continual material improvement. These basic social conditions for South Korean development have been pulverized by the austerity-based economic structural adjustment programme of the IMF, which made massive and sudden unemployment inevitable in order to ensure the repayment of South Korean debts. By ignoring the fact that the entire social system in South Korea operated on the basis of everyone's economic participation, the IMF's cherished panacea of austerity, requiring massive bankruptcy and unemployment, turned out to be disastrous.[32] As Philip Golub (1998) aptly describes, 'what was really being asked for was a radical overhaul of traditional methods of institutional working and economic and social balances that had allowed development and social cohesion to be combined'.

In sum, the IMF could (and should) have paid much more attention to the particular local social contexts in which its economic restructuring programme would take effect (and any side-effects). The initial IMF programme for structural adjustment through high interest rates, increased taxation, decreased public spending, comprehensive corporate reforms and unconstrained lay-offs may well be criticized in terms of stifling the social conditions for sustainable development. More critically, there is no denying that various potentially hazardous social conditions which had arisen under the particular development strategy of South Korea began to generate actual pains to grassroots South Koreans with the IMF programme working as a crucial catalyst.

Recasting the State: Neoliberal Social Democracy as a South Korean Alternative?

It is a truly unique phenomenon that the state corporatist arrangement of *Nosajeongwiweonhoe* [Labour–Business–Government Committee] has functioned to facilitate supposedly neoliberal economic reforms in South Korea. In European political history, state corporatism was the political mechanism for establishing and maintaining social democracy. For South Korean labour, great political significance may be attached to the fact that the tripartite committee allowed their incorporation into national politics on a stable basis for the first time in South Korean history. Kim Dae-Jung, as a globally known democracy fighter, may attach a similar political significance to this fact. More importantly, the historical utility of the so-called neoliberal economic reforms may differ between South Korea and Western social democracies.

What is being reworked and undone in South Korean reform is not a dysfunctional welfare economic system with bloated state engagement in private life, but a degenerated developmental state system with unproductive state intrusion in private economic activities. Above all, the state–*chaebol* financial nexus mediated by defunct banks and corrupt bureaucrats had been criticized by South Korean opposition politicians, intellectuals, workers and other citizens since long before Westerners suddenly identified it as the supposed cause of the current economic crisis. At least since the mid-1980s, the state-endorsed bank financing of *chaebols*' audacious business expansion has been an unquestionable failure. Thus, everyone agrees on the need to dismantle the financial linkages between the state and *chaebols*. The South Koreans' mistake in this regard is that they adopted a skewed and partial remedy, namely, liberalization according to market principles. That is, following foreign and domestic neoliberal advice, they concentrated reform efforts in rescinding state policies and regulations, leaving the *chaebols* free to overexpand into suicidal business projects and distort social and economic order through their monopolistic status. Furthermore, the rash opening of financial markets, which had been advised and sometimes coerced by the IMF and Western political leaders, allowed the *chaebols* to finance their risky projects liberally with direct foreign borrowing. If neoliberal reforms had also mandated the organizational restructuring and disciplining of *chaebols*, even workers and unions would have welcomed them with open arms. Workers want their employers to remain economically viable. The IMF and neoliberal observers suddenly discovered that *chaebol* restructuring should be a core part of neoliberal reforms and that they should encourage the South Korean government to take decisive action for it, even without being bothered by supposed 'market principles'. Thus a capable and autonomous regulatory – if not developmental – state has been called in to deal with the *chaebols*.[33]

Labour reform is an entirely different matter. The successive authoritarian developmentalist regimes in South Korea never treated labour as a dignified partner for national development and politics. The paradoxical consequence was that the political weakening of the authoritarian regimes immediately led to a revolt by indignant workers against political leadership and business. Particularly in the late 1980s and the early 1990s, organized labour was able to pressure employers to make many concessions with the softened political regime looking on. In this context, the neoliberal slogan of 'labour market flexibility' seems to have sounded quite appealing to South Korean employers. Business leaders managed to make successful efforts to persuade the Kim Young-Sam regime of the legal changes necessary for a flexible labour market. Incidentally, the Kim Young-Sam regime wanted not only a flexible labour market but also a politically contained working class. Neither was welcome on the part of workers and labour unions, who successfully fought back against the Kim Young-Sam regime's surprise attack to legalize labour market flexibility and political detainment of unions. Then, why did unions agree on liberal labour reform with Kim Dae-Jung's administration? It was because unions considered some labour reform indispensable for *chaebol* reform, particularly under this kind of national economic crisis. Workers and unions are at best inimical to such neoliberal euphemisms as labour market flexibility, especially when it is virtually synonymous with the denial of their entitlement to work.

There was an unforeseen bonus from the consent of unions and workers to liberal labour reform. In the course of implementing labour reform, it became obvious that the macro-level tripartite compromise alone would not suffice in persuading workers actually to accept lay-offs, pay-cuts, etc. These concessions would mean nothing less than an instant life crisis in the absence of any meaningful social relief programme. It did not require ideological rebirth for notoriously conservative South Korean bureaucrats to accept the urgent need to establish a comprehensive and workable social relief system as a prerequisite for sustainable economic structural adjustment. Even neoliberal supervisors from the IMF and the World Bank had encouraged the South Korean government to prepare better social relief programmes and expand public spending on them. Business leaders, even if not outspoken advocates for social security, saw the same rationale as far as new relief programmes did not require immediate increases in corporate taxes.[34] However, the direct beneficiaries of the new relief programme, i.e., workers and other grassroots people, have not been too impressed, because the inexperience, inefficiency and even corruption of government offices and officials tend to prevent the new relief programme from generating meaningful effects. Nevertheless, social security measures, as summarized under the concept of 'social safety net', now constitute the very central political agenda for the first time in South Korean history. This political agenda has an obvious political constituency (i.e., grassroots workers) whose political power may no longer be ignored. Although it may not warrant the rise of a full-fledged social policy state within a short time, a step has been taken towards social democratic transition in South Korea.

One ironic repercussion of the inexperience, inefficiency and corruption of bureaucracy in the provision of social relief has been the rapid establishment of various civil social relief efforts. These civil efforts have been provided by all types of voluntary and private organizations such as neighbourhood groups, labour unions, religious institutions, welfare movement organizations, professional associations, unemployed self-help groups, student leagues, university organizations, intellectual associations, hometown associations, media, as well as individual families.[35] Unlike governmental relief programmes, many of these civilian relief programmes have successfully assisted unemployed and other destitute people (e.g., *Sisa Journal*, 8 October 1998). Civilian social movement organizations have also taken a lead in pressuring the government and the parliament to prepare better social relief programmes as well as to implement stern measures for *chaebol*'s reform. They have also filed many *gongiksosong* [public interest suits] against *chaebol* and the government in order to protect the legal rights of grassroots citizens to basic economic justice.

On 8 November 1998, civil social movement organizations, labour unions and other grassroots interest groups held the 'People's Rally for Defending Survival Rights, Dismantling *Chaebols*, and Opposing the IMF'. At a press conference on 20 November 1998, these groups demanded ten important reforms by the Kim Dae-Jung administration:

1. an inquiry into the real cause of the economic crisis and the punishment of responsible persons;
2. the dismantling of *chaebols* and the resignation of dishonest and corrupt *chaebol* heads;
3. a revision of the IMF agreements and the writing-off of external debts;
4. the strengthening of the policies for women, job-creation, and unemployment, and the establishment of the social safety net;
5. the setting-up of comprehensive anti-corruption measures;
6. the fixing of laws and institutions for media reform;

7. the improvement in fair taxation and realization of tax justice;
8. a reconsideration of large state public projects;
9. the execution of full-scale political reform;
10. the upgrading of national competitiveness through governmental organizational reform (*Hankyoreh*, 21 November 1998).

In the long run, these civilian social movements, along with labour unions, will comprise the core force of sustainable democracy and progressive politics (cf. Rueschemeyer *et al.* 1992).

The Kim Dae-Jung regime has tried to incorporate all these changes into its political doctrine for *Jeigeonguk* [the Second Foundation of the Nation] (*Internet Hankyoreh,* 14 August 1998; also see Choi 1998). No one may be able to dig out any coherent ideological or theoretical tenet in that doctrine. Kim Dae-Jung has found himself overloaded by many mutually contradictory historical necessities and thus is juggling with them on a day-to-day basis. He has been making promises to bolster democracy, a free market economy, a responsible and efficient state, welfare rights, industrial peace, civil society, human rights and even globalism. His meetings with both neoliberal international financial supervisors and politicians and with European new left leaders have been equally congenial. Regardless of Kim Dae-Jung's own political position, the social, political and economic structures of South Korea have been reshaping in every possible direction (except state socialism) – for instance, neoliberal, state mercantilist, social democratic, nationalist and globalist lines, among others.[36] The true ingenuity of Kim Dae-Jung – and of all South Koreans – should be proved by the skilful integration of all such contradictory historical necessities.[37] This is a crucial part of the compressed modernity of South Korea (see Chang 1999).

CONCLUSION

This chapter has identified three major problems concerning the social ramifications of the current economic crisis in South Korea. First, both material and psychological conditions for the renowned hard work of grassroots South Koreans have been crumbling. Few could expect better income or maintain illusions about future material betterment when unemployment and bankruptcy, as nowadays, have left them worried daily about food and shelter. In the past, even the majority of South Koreans below the official poverty line used to classify themselves as middle class and remained optimistic about catching up with more affluent neighbours. Many of the poorer segments of society accepted a competitive and unequal economic system, at least until they finally had the opportunity to attain economic success through education, business or even speculation. Since late 1997, the dreadful everyday economic realities have been severely aggravated by the psychological distress emanating from unaccustomed expectations of a worse tomorrow. In persuading grassroots people to accept mass unemployment and poverty, the South Korean government can no longer replace immediate measures for material protection with empty propaganda for some affluent future. No sooner had South Koreans awakened from the hypnosis of future economic success than they fell into ever-deepening desperation and anger.

Second, South Koreans could not but realize the true costs and benefits of the absence of a sound and comprehensive social safety net against mass unemployment and poverty. Under the slogan of 'growth first, distribution later', the government used to maintain an extremely conservative position concerning social welfare. Officials, whether in economic or welfare bureaucracy, unequivocally viewed social welfare as unproductive. South Korean social citizenship consisted of work, not of socially protected welfare. Even the growing political power of labour since the late 1980s failed to pressure the government to change its anti-welfarist orientation, but instead forced many large business firms to implement various corporate welfare programmes for their employees. The family has been the only institution working for general welfare. It was only after the outbreak of the current economic crisis that the South Korean government came to understand the economic value of social security programme. After exhausting the abundant budget for irrational mega-size construction projects and highly questionable business subsidies, the government was no longer in a position legitimately to ask grassroots people to accept massive layoffs as part of the structural adjustment programme. In the meantime, all of the burdens of unemployment and poverty fell on individual families, so that widespread family dissolution was destined to threaten the essential fabric of this extremely familist society (Chang 1997b).

Finally, the neoliberal ethos of the non-interventionist and non-authoritarian state has been defeated not only by politicians and bureaucrats who feed on state power but also by mutual suspicion on the part of business and labour. When the South Korean government tried to mobilize grassroots resources and energies for rapid industrialization and economic growth, it neither bothered to obtain grassroots consent to unfavourable terms of economic exchange nor seriously persuaded business leaders to develop harmonious relationships with labour. Up until 1987, the military–*chaebol* alliance was politically invincible, and labour was simply disorganized. In 1998, *chaebol* heads (and numerous sympathetic bureaucrats) became extremely angry at Kim Dae-Jung for accepting labour as an equal political partner in the major decision-making process for economic restructuring. The landmark tripartite agreements among labour, business and the government in early 1998 failed to have sufficient impact when business and labour had to take concrete steps in business offices and factories. Now, Kim Dae-Jung's staff are dealing separately with (and inevitably lying to) labour and business, although the Labour–Business–Government Committee is still in formal existence. Lies, suspicion, and anger – instead of repentance and concession – tend to dominate the ongoing reform process. Once again, South Koreans (including both workers and employers) and foreign lenders seem to want decisive and determined, if not authoritarian, state leadership, although their reasons may differ diametrically.

To what extent does the IMF share responsibility for these problematic social tendencies? When IMF officials advise the South Korean government to expand public spending on social security programme, does this indicate an acknowledgment of liability for the pains of grassroots South Koreans? The obvious answer is 'No!' Their liberal outlook (or financial liberalism based upon contradictory state-interventionist principles for austerity) reflected the spirit of the times, i.e., American-dominated global economic *laissez-faire* underwritten by docile Third World states. After all, they asked to be invited in order to rescue the South Korean economy from bankruptcy and thereby ensure the repayment of South Korean debts to foreign lenders. On the other hand, the psychological bubble concerning material betterment, the welfare-suppressive accumulation strategy and the authoritarian treatment of labour were all local practices and habits that had existed in South Korea prior to the IMF intervention. Nonetheless, the IMF could (and should) have been much more careful about the particular local social contexts in which its economic restructuring programme would take effect (and create side-effects). Its programme for austerity and structural adjustment through high interest rates, increased taxation, decreased public spending, comprehensive corporate reforms, and unconstrained lay-offs have already been criticized for stifling the social conditions necessary for sustainable economic development. More seriously, there is no denying that various potentially hazardous social conditions which had accumulated under the particular development strategy of South Korea began to generate real distress to grassroots South Koreans, with the IMF programme working as a crucial catalyst. Even when South Korea eventually recovers from the current economic crisis, the question of whether the extreme material and psychological distress of grassroots South Koreans has been unavoidable will remain a fundamentally controversial issue.

This having been said, South Koreans still appear quite impressive in swiftly cleaning up the financial mess and satisfying IMF officials, Western political leaders and potential investors through the adoption of quick reform actions. Is the most successful late industrializer going to become the most successful neoliberal reformer?[38] Is that the primary motive of Kim Dae-Jung, if not of ordinary South Koreans? What of the serious concern for labour and the poor expressed by Kim throughout his political career? Of course, at least within the South Korean context, Kim's reform policy may considered socially progressive. Unemployment reductions and the alleviation of poverty receive no less emphasis than economic restructuring in policy discussions. The pronouncements of Kim and his staff concerning labour, poverty, education, housing and other social concerns closely resemble those of Western social democracy. At the same time, Kim does not hesitate to accept and implement those programmes suggested by Western neoliberals as conservative reactions to their own social democratic pasts. It remains to be seen whether these inconsistencies reflect his own indecisiveness or constitute a truly inventive doctrine for national development.

AUTHOR'S NOTE

Earlier versions of this paper were presented at the Conference on 'Current Political and Economic Issues in Korea', organized by the Centre for Pacific Asia Studies, Stockholm University, Sweden, 28–29 January 1999, at the International Conference on 'The Economic Crisis in East Asia and the Impact on the Local Population', organized by Roskilde University, Denmark, 29–30 October 1998, and at a colloquium in the Department of Sociology, Brown University, 4 November 1998. An expanded version appeared in *Development and Society*, Vol. 28, No. 1 (1999). The author is grateful to participants in these scholarly gatherings for offering me many insightful and constructive comments. Research assistance provided by Lim Chae-Yun, Park Jong-Hun, Kim Cheol-Sik, and Song In-Ju is cordially appreciated.

NOTES

1 I conceptualize these economic, social and political achievements and changes of South Korea as *compressed modernity* (Chang 1999).

2 This does not imply that Krugman attributes all responsibility for the financial fiasco to Asia alone. At least since the International Monetary Fund (IMF) rescue programme in the region caused economic aggravation and social confusion, he has been a vocal critic of international financial manipulators, including both the IMF and transnational financial speculators.

3 Moreover, in the 1960s and the 1970s, South Korea was by nature a transition economy (from family farming to capitalist industry), in which the combination of abundant village-provided migrant labour and new industrial technology led to economic growth, both input-driven and efficiency-driven. Without this condition, the Lewisian development could not have occurred (cf. Lewis 1954). Krugman's view on the efficiency-driven nature of Western economic growth takes for granted a stable, already industrialized economic system – a condition that cannot be taken for granted in non-Western, mostly transitional economies.

4 See Palat (1999) for his emphasis on this overproduction problem.

5 In addition, the owner management of *chaebol* (i.e., the direct control of corporate management by *chaebol* owners) precludes the Dahrendorfian conciliation between employee managers and workers (cf. Dahrendorf 1959). The target for workers' class struggle has always been clear – *chaebol* head and other owner-managers from his family.

6 It is this feature of the South Korean economy that IMF officials ignored in devising their supposed rescue programme based upon high interest rates, thereby aggravating the situation critically.

7 Relatedly, a survey of 15,900 people in nine Asian countries in 1998 (conducted by the South Korean branch office of FSA Sofres) revealed that among South Koreans, 70 per cent experienced income reductions, 89 per cent experienced reductions in purchasing power, and 78 per cent experienced reductions in asset values (quoted in *Hankyoreh,* 16 October 1998). These were the highest figures for the nine countries surveyed.

8 For instance, the third quarter of 1997 showed a 7 per cent increase in the urban worker household income over the previous year, whereas the fourth quarter of 1997 showed only a 0.6 per cent increase (National Statistical Office 1999).

9 Media have presented many mutually contradictory reports about lavish consumption by rich people under the economic crisis. The rich have been portrayed as unconscionable conspicuous consumers enraging unemployed workers and other troubled ordinary citizens. Their expanded consumption, however, has been called for in order to stimulate the national economy. For instance, see *Sisa Journal* (11 June 1998).

10 A similar situation is observed even in China, a much poorer but relentlessly growing economy, where a majority classify themselves as middle class in various social surveys (e.g., Korea Broadcasting System and Yonsei University 1996).

11 The figure for South Korea was around 80 per cent, and the second highest was Japan's 50–60 per cent (*Hankyoreh,* 25 November 1998).

12 As Ravi Palat (1998) points out, the term 'crony capitalism' should be qualified in regard to its different developmental consequences for different countries. Even grassroots South Koreans would not deny that some positive economic outcomes were produced by the state–business collusion. It is ironic that, confronting the boomerang effect of the Asian and Russian economic crises, even the US government had to reveal

its crony capitalist position by rescuing Long-Term Capital Management, a notoriously speculative hedge fund, from bankruptcy with astronomical amounts of public financial resources. Inevitably, this self-contradictory act caused wide criticism both within and outside the United States (*Hankyoreh*, 21 October 1998).

13 In this context, it is quite understandable that, in late 1998, the South Korean government was busy publicizing optimistic predictions for the economic situation of the coming year. Its research organs began to present predictions for economic growth in 1999 which were much more optimistic than predictions by international agencies and domestic *chaebol*-run research institutions (*Kukmin Daily*, 9 November 1998). Government officials reportedly pressured *chaebol*-run research institutions to cooperate with the government by presenting similarly rosy predictions (*Digital Chosun*, 6 November 1998).

14 According to Korea Institute for Health and Social Affairs, only about 10 per cent of unemployed people in 1998 received unemployment allowances, and most of them received benefits for no more than four months (*Hankyoreh*, 18 November 1998).

15 Simultaneously, the Confucian family ethic for mutual support was emphasized repeatedly as a fulcrum for social stability (Chang Kyung-Sup 1997a). It has been an important task for the Ministry of Health and Welfare to find out, and award special prizes to, individuals whose self-sacrificing effort for supporting aged parents, handicapped children and other needy persons under extremely destitute situations could be considered exemplary to other people.

16 Even under the Kim Young-Sam administration, ministers in charge of welfare, health, labour, and environment used to attend the Policy Meeting of Economic Ministers in order to adjust their public work according to the guidelines set by the ministers in charge of economic affairs. There was no separate meeting for ministers of social policy matters.

17 Rapid economic growth, as the core condition for supposedly full employment in South Korea, was somewhat comparable to Amartya Sen's (1981) social entitlement system.

18 In fact, once they are laid off, they cannot maintain labour union membership of any kind. Against the urgings of the ILO (International Labour Organization) and the labour-business-government agreement in early 1998, the right of unemployed workers to maintain or seek union membership at an industrial or regional level still remains legally prohibited under the strong resistance of prosecutors and other conservative bureaucrats (*Hankyoreh*, 19 November 1998). Thus, unemployment automatically leads to detachment from organized social power.

19 Owning a large restaurant was a distant second, preferred by 11.3 per cent of the respondents. The preference for large restaurant ownership is interesting, but quite understandable in that the restaurant business – a self-employed activity which carries no worry about getting fired – has become fashionable among those with certain amounts of capital.

20 It is paradoxical that Kim Dae-Jung has relied on business initiatives from *chaebols* in his most praised political work, the 'Sunshine Policy Towards North Korea'. In particular, the Hyundai Group's North Korea tour programme and other business deals with North Korea constitute the crux of Kim's 'politics–business separation' policy (*Sisa Journal*, 19 November 1998).

21 According to a 1998 survey by the Korea Development Institute (1998), of 1,000 ordinary South Koreans, 40.9 per cent of the respondents thought that business owners and managers showed no remorse whatsoever for corporate mismanagement. Another 46.4 per cent replied that the remorse of these businessmen was insufficient. Such negative perceptions were even stronger among 305 economic affairs specialists surveyed separately. According to 42 per cent of them, South Korean businessmen showed no remorse whatever for corporate mismanagement; according to 51.1 per cent of them, South Korean businessmen had only insufficient remorse.

22 According to an estimate of government-affiliated researchers in June 1998, only 6.6 per cent of the unemployed population received unemployment allowances from the

national employment insurance (*Hankyoreh,* 29 July 1998). It is suspected that a large majority of the currently unemployed people are formerly underemployed people.

23 According to figures from the Ministry of Agriculture, 4,141 urban households moved back to villages during the first six months in 1998 (*Sisa Journal,* 19 November 1998). This is more than double the figure for the entire year of 1997, i.e., 1,823 households.

24 In promoting their own material interests in this dire situation, college students have not been able to show the same effectively organized power as they commanded in their political struggle against military dictatorship in earlier decades.

25 It is paradoxical that recent legal changes and decisions encourage children to support elderly parents by allowing those providing for parents to receive larger portions of parental inheritance (*JoongAng Ilbo,* 28 July 1998; *Chosun Ilbo,* 30 September 1998). Although not many ordinary citizens would oppose such legal arrangements, provider children may ask for functioning public welfare programmes to share their burdens.

26 Incidents of human right abuse such as slave labour, physical violence and sexual abuse have been revealed in numerous welfare institutions across the country (*Hankyoreh,* 11 April 1998). But officials of the central and the local governments in supervisory positions have never taken serious measures to improve the situation fundamentally. Part of the reason, of course, lies in the rampant corruption of these officials. The most recent case was in Yangjimaeul, where accommodated homeless people were found out to have suffered from beating, sexual assault, being locked up, unpaid forced labour, and death (*Hankyoreh,* 6 August 1998). Responsible officials, not to mention managers of this institution, denied any such incident even after the media made a comprehensive report about the shocking reality. Civil organizations and activists called for the break-up of the collusion between *bokjijokbeol* [welfare mafia family] and the welfare bureaucracy as the most crucial condition for solving the problem. Incidentally, the South Korean government was then discussing the urgent need to establish numerous welfare institutions to accommodate the rapidly increasing population of homeless, runaway, and deserted persons amid the economic crisis.

27 This problem is particularly serious among female-headed families. Women have been the first to be laid off, and many of these newly unemployed women have families whose sheer survival depends on their income. For a description of the desperate situation of unemployed women and their dependent families, see Kim *et al.* (1998).

28 In 1998, a high-ranking official in the Ministry of Labour circulated into various government offices and newspapers a statement which directly criticized the conciliatory posture of the current political leadership towards labour and called for harsh measures for compelling workers' and unions' compliance with labour reform programmes. He was considered to reflect the widespread reservation of bureaucrats to the corporatist treatment of labour (*Hankyoreh,* 31 July 1998). On the other hand, many bureaucrats have attempted to sabotage the current political leadership's attempts at a thorough overhaul of *chaebol* conglomerates, among other practices, by withholding crucial information on corporate financial structures (*Hankyoreh,* 16 October 1998).

29 The two national unions, Minjunochong and Hanguknochong, claimed that only two of the 15 reform items which business leaders had agreed to implement as their responsibility in February 1998 had actually been fulfilled (*Hankyoreh,* 21 October 1998).

30 Even Bill Clinton personally remarked on the need for thorough *chaebol* reform during his meeting with Kim Dae-Jung in Seoul in late November 1998 (*Hankyoreh,* 22 November 1998).

31 According to its list of requirements for the social safety net, the World Bank suggested 17 social policy goals for South Korea, including a decent standard of living for the elderly, welfare benefits for the unemployed, the medical coverage for the sick, etc. (*Hankyoreh,* 21 September 1998).

32 In fact, the IMF had in earlier years urged South Korea to liberalize and open financial markets, with essentially the same mistake of ignoring the local context, i.e., the unrestrained propensity of South Korean companies for borrowing and the poor governmental capacity for monitoring and regulating international financial transactions. No sooner had the financial markets been liberalized and opened externally than national and corporate debts began to snowball. The ratio of the total national debt to GDP remained around the 10 per cent level in the early 1990s, and then swelled to 32.5 per cent in 1996 and 34.9 per cent in 1997 (Samsung Economic Research Institute 1998). Thanks to the near collapse of the South Korean won since late 1997, the ratio reached 50.2 per cent as of August 1998. In this respect, South Korea cannot be said to have overcome her financial crisis. Instead, the financial malady has been only anaesthetized with a much enlarged locus.

33 Mahathir's apparent success in protecting the Malaysian economy from the harassment of international financial speculators on the basis of strict foreign currency control presents an even stronger case for the necessity of active state intervention (*Sisa Journal* 17 September 1998). His strategy has drawn supporters from many regions and lines of thought. Paul Krugman's recent prescription for controlling the so-called 'hot money' presents a sympathetic account of Mahathir.

34 Most of the new budget for social relief programme is to be secured by the drastic increase in indirect taxes. Among the 3,393.9 billion won increase in taxation for 1999, indirect taxes will account for 66.4 per cent (*Hankyoreh*, 21 October 1998). This will reverse the relative weights of direct and indirect taxes in the total budget in favour of the latter, i.e., 49.3 per cent versus 50.7 per cent. As a consequence, according to a report by the Korean Institute of Public Finance, the tax burden increased disproportionately for the poorer classes. For those urban households earning 850,000 won (roughly US$700) or less a month, the combined tax burden (i.e., direct income taxes and indirect consumption taxes) literally skyrocketed from 7.1 per cent in 1997 to 14.1 per cent in 1998. For those earning 3,610,000 won (roughly US$2,970 US) or more a month, it remained unchanged at 10.3 per cent in this period (*Chosun Ilbo* 15 March 1999).

35 For instance, see various proposals for civil social relief efforts submitted to the Office of the National Movement for Overcoming Unemployment (*Hankyoreh,* 19 October 1998, 16 November 1998, 18 March 1999).

36 A popular news magazine recently branded Kim Dae-Jung as a 'neoliberal statist' (*Sisa Journal,* 26 November 1998).

37 The recent visit of Anthony Giddens – Tony Blair's mentor for his 'third way politics' – to Seoul in October 1998 left an interesting repercussion. While it is not certain if his speeches on contemporary politics gave the South Korean audience any coherent idea about the supposedly new line of politics in Tony Blair's United Kingdom, many South Korean politicians and scholars aired quite congenial expressions during their meetings with Giddens. Part of the reason may be due to the fact that Tony Blair's third way politics itself is a similarly complex mixture of various mutually contradictory goals and policies. See Anthony Giddens 1998.

38 When Bill Clinton visited South Korea in late November 1998, he offered his highest praise for Kim Dae-Jung's compliance with American economic and political policies. He was explicitly thankful for Kim's defence during the APEC summit in Malaysia of the open and free economic relationship (i.e., the American doctrine to deal with Asia). The Los Angeles Times, on 23 November 1998, explained that Kim's congenial stance towards the United States amid the rapidly spreading anti-American sentiment in Asia provided a critical support for the American influence in the region. It is no coincidence that Clinton avoided, without giving any convincing excuse, participation in the APEC summit only a week before where an unfavourable and even hostile feeling against the United States was expected.

REFERENCES

Amsden, Alice (1989) *Asia's Next Giant: South Korea and Late Industrialization.* New York: Oxford University Press.

Bae Jun-Ho (1998) 'Jeosodeukcheungui Goyong Burane Ttareun Saenghwal Byeonhwa' [Life Changes of Low Income Strata under Employment Uncertainty]. Paper presented at the National Statistical Office Seminar on 'Urinara Gagyeui Saenghwalsiltae Byeonhwa Chui' [The Changes and Trends in the Living Conditions of South Korean Households], 1 September 1998.

Bank of Korea (1998) '1998 Nyeon Sangbangi Gieop Gyeongyeong Bunseok' [The Analysis of Corporate Management in the First Half of 1998]. Unpublished survey report.

Chang Hong Geun (1999) 'Hanguk Nodongchejeui Jeonhwangwajeonge Gwanhan Yeongu, 1987–1997' [The Transformation of the 'Labour Regime' in Korea, 1987–97]. Ph.D. dissertation in the Department of Sociology, Seoul National University.

Chang Hye Kyung and Kim Yeong-Ran (1999) *Sileobe Ttareun Gajogsaenghwalgwa Yeoseongui Yeokhwalbyeonhwae Gwanhan Yeongu* [A Study of the Changes in Family Life and the Role of Women under Unemployment]. Seoul: Korea Women's Development Institute.

Chang Kyung-Sup (1997a) 'The neo-Confucian right and family politics in South Korea: The nuclear family as an ideological construct', *Economy and Society*, 26 (1): 22–42.

—— (1997b) 'Modernity through the family: familial foundations of Korean society'. *International Review of Sociology*, 7 (1): 51–63.

—— (1999) 'Compressed modernity and its discontents: South Korean society in transition'. *Economy and Society*, 28 (1): 30–55.

Cheil Communications (1998) 'IMF Bannyeon, Hanguginui Jahwasang' [IMF Half Year, Self-Portrait of South Koreans]. Unpublished survey report.

Choi Jang Jip (1998) 'D.J. Gaehyeogui bonjireul malhanda' [Speak of the fundamental nature of D.J. Reform]. *Shin Dong-A*, 41 (11): 88–98.

Daewoo Economic Research Institute (1998) 'Seonjingugui Asia Gukgaroui Gotong Jeoni Hyeonsanggwa Uri Gyeongjeeui Sisajeom' [The Phenomenon of Pain Transfer from Advanced Countries to Asian Countries and Its Implication for the South Korean Economy]. Unpublished report.

Dahrendorf, Ralf (1959) *Class and Class Conflict in Industrial Society.* Stanford: Stanford University Press.

Evans, Peter (1995) *Embedded Autonomy: States and Industrial Transformation.* Princeton, NJ: Princeton University Press.

Giddens, Anthony (1998) *The Third Way: The Renewal of Social Democracy.* Cambridge: Policy Press.

Golub, Philip S. (1998) 'Bitter fruits of a miracle: when East Asia falters', *Le Monde Diplomatique*, July 1998.

Kim Seung-Gweon, Lee Sang-Heon and Yang Hye-Gyeong (1998) *Yeoseongsireopja Mit Siljikja Gajeongui Saenghwalsiltaewa Bokjiyokgu* [Living Conditions and Welfare Needs of Unemployed Women and Their Families]. Seoul: Korea Institute for Health and Social Affairs.

Koo, Hagen (1993) 'The state, minjung, and the working class in South Korea', in Hagen Koo (ed.), *State and Society in Contemporary Korea.* Ithaca, NY: Cornell University Press, pp.131–162.

Korea Broadcasting System and Yonsei University (1996) *Hanguk Jungguk Ilbon Gukminuisikjosa Baekseo* [White Book on Citizens' Consciousness Survey in South Korea, China, and Japan].

Korea Development Institute (1998) 'Gukjetonghwagigeum Ilnyeonui Gukmin Gyeongjeuisik Byeonhwa' [Changes in People's Economic Consciousness in the One Year under the International Monetary Fund]. Unpublished survey report.

Korea Institute for Health and Social Affairs and Korea Labour Institute (1998) 'Sireop Siltae Mit Bokjiyokgujosa Bogoseo Yoyak' [Summary of the Research Report on the Unemployment Situation and Welfare Needs]. Unpublished internal report.

Krugman, Paul (1994) 'The myth of Asia's miracle', *Foreign Affairs*, 73 (6): 62–78.

Lee Du-Ho *et al.* (1991) *Bingonron* [Treatise on Poverty]. Seoul: Nanam.

Lewis, W. Arthur (1954) 'Economic development with unlimited supply of labour'. *Manchester School of Economics and Social Studies*, 22 (1): 139–191.

Lim Young Il (1997) *Hangugui Nodongundonggwa Gyegeupjeongchi, 1987–1995* [Labour Movement and Class Politics in South Korea, 1987–1995]. Masan: Kyungnam University Press.

Matthews, John (1995) *High-Technology Industrialisation in East Asia: The Case of the Semiconductor Industry in Taiwan and Korea.* Taipei: Chung-Hua Institution for Economic Research.

Nam Seong-Il and Lee Hwa-Yeong (1998) 'Choegeun Urinara Sireobui Teukseong Bunseok: Oehwanwigi Ijeongwa Bigyo' [An Analysis of the Characteristics of Recent Unemployment in South Korea: A Comparison of the Pre- and the Post-Foreign Currency Crisis]. Unpublished research report.

National Statistical Office (1999) '1998 Nyeon 4/4 Bungi Mit Yeongan Dosigeunroja Gaguui Gagyesuji Donghyang Yoyak' [Summary of the Household Financial Balance among Urban Worker Households in the Fourth Quarter and the Entire Year of 1998]. Unpublished media release.

Nosajeongwiweonhoe [Labour–Business–Government Committee] (1998) 'Nosajeong Gongdong Seoneonmun' [Nosajeong Co-Declaration]. 20 January 1998.

Palat, Ravi (1998) 'Varieties of crony capitalism', *Hindu On-Line*, 22 August 1998.

—— (1999) 'Miracles of the day before? The great Asian meltdown and the changing world-economy', *Development and Society*, 28 (1): 1–48.

Park Jong-Hun (1999) 'Hanguk Sahoe Jungsancheung Gajogui Gajang Siljige Daehan Bangeogije Yeongu' [A Study of the Protection Mechanism of Middle-Class Families against the Unemployment of Family Heads in South Korean Society]. Master thesis in the Department of Sociology, Seoul National University.

Republic of Korea, National Statistical Office (1995) *Tonggyero Bon Hangugui Baljachwi* [Footsteps of South Korea Seen through Statistics].

—— (1997) *Social Indicators in Korea, 1997.*

Rueschemeyer, Dietrich, Stephens, Evelyne and Stephens, John (1992) *Capitalist Development and Democracy.* Chicago: University of Chicago Press.

Samsung Economic Research Institute (1998) 'Gukga Oechae Jaejojeong Saryewa Sisajeom' [Cases of National Debt Rearbitration and Its Implications]. Unpublished research report.

Sen, Amartya (1981) *Poverty and Famines: An Essay on Entitlement and Deprivation.* Oxford: Oxford University Press.

Song Ho-Keun (1995) *Hangugui Gieopbokji Yeongu* [Korea's Company Welfare: An Empirical Research]. Seoul: Korea Labour Institute.

Wade, Robert (1998) 'The Asian debt-and-development crisis of 1997–? Causes and consequences', *World Development*, 26 (8): 1535–1553.

Yun Yeong-Ho (1998) 'Jijibujin, odae *chaebol* gujojojeong: "Himsen *chaebol*" D.J. gaehyeoge jeongmyeon seungbu' [Tardy and dull, the structural adjustment of the five largest *chaebols*: 'Mighty *chaebol*' head-on contest against D.J. reform]. *Shin Dong-A*, 41 (11) 160–171.

Newspapers and magazines (various issues)

Digital Chosun
Hankook Ilbo
Hankyoreh
Internet Hankyoreh
JoongAng Ilbo
Kukmin Daily
Los Angeles Times
Sisa Journal
Weekly Chosun

TEN

Dealing with the Crisis in Vietnam

The Rethinking of Development Strategies

Pietro P. Masina

Introduction

In mid-1990s Vietnam seemed to be blessed by a benign fate and was looking forward to a prosperous future. After decades of war and international isolation, the country was restoring and enhancing relations with neighbours and the rest of the world. The economy was striving with the GDP growing at more than 9 per cent per year; the flow of foreign direct investment was accelerating. The country could jump from rice importer to a position as the world's second largest exporter of the product. The poverty rate was declining. All these positive achievements were considered as a result of *doi moi* – the process of economic reform – and of the successful cooperation between the country and the international financial institutions. And Vietnam, like other countries in the region, was embracing the dream of becoming the 'fifth tiger', i.e., joining the club of the fast-growing newly industrializing economies (NIEs).

Already some months before the onset of the crisis, however, dark clouds were gathering in the Vietnamese sky. Since early 1997, in fact, it became increasingly clear that the road to prosperity was going to be full of obstacles and adversities. Foreign investments to Vietnam started to shrink and the GDP growth began to decelerate one year before the financial crisis hit the rest of the region. And the international financial institutions started to voice their criticisms and to ask for a faster pace in the process of economic reform.

The 'official wisdom' has explained recent developments in the Vietnamese economy in the following terms. Vietnam was suffering before the regional crisis because the national authorities did not implement the needed bold reforms, and because the country was plagued by inefficient bureaucracy, corruption and red tape. During the regional crisis the country was partially shielded by its scarce integration into the world economy. But in the post-crisis environment, it must implement the needed reforms rapidly to avoid been excluded from the successful recovery foreseen for other countries.

This chapter aims to challenge this official wisdom supported by mainstream economists and international financial institutions. The slowdown of Vietnamese economy before the regional crisis will be analysed against the background of the regional overproduction malaise, which reduced the need for foreign companies to invest in a 'new entry' like Vietnam. This chapter will also urge a critical reading of the measures that Vietnam should take to reshape development strategies. The country has avoided being hit too hard by the regional financial meltdown. But the future, in the aftermath of the regional crisis, is beset with challenges and risks. Therefore the adoption of a development strategy involves difficult decisions regarding the modality of integration into the world economy and the process of economic reforms.

THE REFORM AGENDA BEFORE THE CRISIS

At its Sixth Congress of December 1986, the Vietnamese Communist Party decided on a major political reform under the title of *doi moi* (renovation). Already since 1979, a number of reforms in industry and agriculture had been anticipated, especially in the South. The official adoption of *doi moi* – also a result of a change in the leadership of the VCP – added new momentum to the reform agenda. Thus, from the late 1980s Vietnam embarked on a number of policy changes, which in a few years transformed international relations, the development strategy and the socioeconomic structure of the country.

These changes derived from national and international factors, and have been explained by the analysts in different – and sometimes contradictory – ways.[1] Briefly, we can recall the two main elements behind this transformation. First, there was the need to cope with the crisis in the Soviet Union, which involved a drying-up of economic aid, the loss of the traditional export market, and a dangerous isolation in political and military terms. Second, there was the economic impasse which affected the country from the late 1970s, partially deriving from the high cost of the war in Cambodia, but also by deficiencies in the economic management and difficulties in integrating the Southern provinces into the economic system of the North.

In the field of international relations, Vietnam reached the indubitable achievement of not only avoiding being hurt by the end of the Cold War but also enhancing its strategic regional position. The withdrawal of Vietnamese troops from Cambodia (September 1989) paved the way for the re-establishment of economic and political ties with many countries in the region and beyond. In the few months following the Paris agreements on Cambodia in October 1991, Hanoi reached a full normalization of diplomatic relations with most countries, including China, with which Vietnam had a brief but intense armed clash in 1979.

The rapprochement with the nation's Southeast Asian neighbours, already initiated in 1992, was successfully concluded with formal admission into ASEAN (July 1995), which eventually opened the way for participation in the AFTA (ASEAN Free Trade Area).

The normalization of relations with the United States proved somewhat slower. Washington maintained an embargo against Vietnam until February 1994, and full diplomatic relations were not reinstated until June 1995. However, already in July 1993, the American administration removed the barrier to multilateral aid, allowing the World Bank to resume lending to the country during the following October.

The overall achievement of this global revolution in the Vietnamese international relations seems to motivate two considerations. First, this revolution was carefully managed, *improving simultaneously the relations in all directions.* While Vietnam showed great ability in playing the 'Chinese card' – i.e., letting Southeast Asian countries and the United States understand the importance of a common front with Vietnam – at the same time Hanoi was able to achieve a remarkable improvement in relations with Beijing.

Second, this enhanced international position of Vietnam proved to be a key resource for receiving financial support for economic reforms within the country. From the moment in which it again received official development assistance (ODA) until a few months before the regional economic crisis onset, Vietnam seemed to benefit from a kind of preferential treatment that some considered to be connected with its strategic position and careful foreign policy.[2]

The process of economic reform proved to be more complex and contradictory than the change in the political external relations. On this ground the debate within the Vietnamese leadership has been very intense and disagreements have surfaced at each critical juncture in the reform process. This debate has resulted in a very careful approach, which has been often depicted by foreign analysts as an excessively slow tempo in addressing the necessary reforms.

The pace of the reform process has been in fact the major criticism that international financial institutions have made to the Vietnamese authorities, while officially claiming the existence of a substantial agreement on the overall agenda and on the measures to be implemented. However, since the mid-1990s the existence of a major disagreement between the Vietnamese government and the international financial institutions has been proved by the difficulty in signing new structural adjustment programmes and by the repeated withholding of soft loans pledged on the basis of conditionalities (discussed below; 'The impact of the crisis').

The artifice of a general agreement with the international financial institutions has been maintained also by the Vietnamese side by not voicing openly an alternative development strategy, while retaining considerable autonomy in the implementation of its own national policy. This attitude can probably be traced in the traditional Vietnamese pragmatism apart from the need not to compromise relations with international donors. The nature of the Vietnamese decision-making process – based on the search for consensus within the leadership and a balancing of the different interests at stake – has also contributed to an avoidance of too binding a pronouncement and to an emphasis on a careful implementation of the agreed measures.

THE IMPACT OF THE CRISIS

The non-convertibility of the dong and the regulation of trade and exchange transactions successfully shielded Vietnam from the vagaries of international financial contagion. In the months immediately following the dramatic events of July 1997, Vietnam appeared as a serene island in the middle of a region plagued by a severe economic downturn. Though, in the course of 1998 – when the financial meltdown evolved into a crisis affecting the real economy of the region – the impact on the Vietnamese economy became increasingly evident. At the end of the year all major macroeconomic indicators revealed a rather critical situation. Vietnam did not enter into a recession but GDP growth declined sharply. During 1998 the government was forced to readjust its expectations downwards from the planned 9 per cent to about 6 per cent. The official data indicate that real GDP growth was at 5.8 per cent in 1998 and at 4.7 per cent in 1999.[3]

In the emergency situation the Vietnamese government proved quite successful in maintaining macroeconomic stability. This was recognized by the international financial institutions, which also admitted that their pessimistic forecasting had been avoided:

> In the two years of East Asian recession, Vietnam has followed a cautious economic stance, giving priority to ensuring macroeconomic stability rather than taking risks in order to achieve higher growth. This has led to some successes. Contrary to the fears of eighteen months ago, Vietnam has avoided the serious balance-of-payments, fiscal or banking crises that have been common in the region. (World Bank 1999a)

However, as the quoted report also indicated, the impact of the contraction in the growth rate has been significant in many regards. A major effect was a fall in the investment as a share of GDP: from 29 per cent in 1997 to an estimated 19 per cent in 1999, with half of this decline attributed to shrinkage in foreign investment flows (ibid.).

Another major implication of the crisis was a slump in government revenues from 23 per cent of GDP in 1996 to 17.8 per cent in 1999 (*UNDP Socioeconomic Bulletin* 2000). This decrease forced the government to cut expenditures accordingly in order to avoid fiscal instability, thus curtailing the resources for expansionary economic policy (as it was attempted, instead, by China). However, to reduce the impact of the recession on the population, the government sought to protect social expenditures (World Bank 1999a).

Shrinkage of FDI inflows became a major reason of concern for the Vietnamese authorities already months ahead of the regional crisis. Fading interest by foreign companies to invest in the country was interpreted by the international financial institutions as a sign of an impasse in the reform process: foreign entrepreneurs were put off by excessive red tape, corruption and a faltering legal system. Thus, international agencies and mainstream Western analysts pressured the government to restore confidence by addressing needed reforms. Given the country's hunger for investment capital and foreign technology, Western criticisms touched a nerve: conditions for making Vietnam more attractive to foreign investors occupied the centre-stage in the national policy debate at the height of the regional crisis. This led to the approval of a new legislation on foreign direct investment (2000) and to the simplification of administrative rules. However, there are reasons to believe that the understanding of the FDI shrinkage promoted by the international agencies was excessively one-sided and thus not able to assist policy-making adequately. The analysis of FDI commitment and disbursement to Vietnam indicates that investment shrinkage in the months before the regional crisis was essentially due to the real estate sector: i.e., reflecting a regional bubble economy malaise, which in other countries was partially concealed by short-term capital flows until July 1997. Contrary to what was normally understood, FDI disbursement to Vietnam – excluding the real estate sector – did not contract before the regional crisis. And after the regional crisis had unfolded, the sharp decline in FDI inflows to Vietnam was closely related to a decline in FDI outflows from those Asian countries who had been the major source of investment to Vietnam (Masina 2001). Thus, the analysis of data indicates that Vietnam was more closely integrated with the regional productive system than is usually reported, and was therefore vulnerable to the external economic trends. In the pre-crisis environment, Vietnam was also the object of a foreign investment rush – with the highest ratio to GDP in the region – probably disproportionate to the country's absorption capacity (ibid.). These considerations suggest that the medium- and long-term economic perspectives will largely depend on the post-crisis reorganization of the regional productive system. Therefore, an attempt to restore confidence would barely reach its goal in attracting new investment, if this is not supported by a realistic understanding of regional economic dynamics and by an effective industrial policy (we shall return to this point later).

After the onset of the regional crisis, the FDI inflows to Vietnam contracted sharply, falling from over US$2 billion US in 1997 to about 800 million in 1998, and well below that figure in the following two years.

The vulnerability of Vietnam in the midst of the regional crisis was exploited by the international financial institutions, which tried to push for a bolder implementation of pro-market reforms. Since 1993, when the US government removed its opposition to international financial institutions' lending, official development assistance (ODA) to Vietnam grew fast. Annual commitments reached US$2.4 billion in 1996 and 1997, making Vietnam one of the largest recipients of multilateral concessional loans. The rate of disbursements remained low, but on the eve of the regional crisis Vietnam improved its ODA absorption capability and implementation speed, allowing the disbursement to grow from US$430 million in 1995 to 1 billion in 1997. However, Vietnam did not succeed in attracting further aid to cope with the effects of the regional crisis.

The regional crisis unfolded at the moment when the dialogue between the Vietnamese government and the international financial institutions was characterized by deep disagreements on the reform agenda and on the time of its implementation. In 1997 the IMF withheld the instalment of roughly US$176 million, which had been agreed upon in 1994 as a third instalment of a three-year Enhanced Structural Adjustment Facility (ESAF) amounting to US$530 million. At the time of writing, negotiations for a new ESAF had proved insufficient to restore consensus, leaving Vietnam without an important support to relieve the balance-of-payment deficit. In turn, the lack of IMF agreement resulted into an obstacle for a fresh World Bank Structural Adjustment Credit (SAC), which also provides balance-of-payment support.

Official development assistance to Vietnam was discussed in Paris in December 1998 by the Consultative Group for Vietnam (CG) – the coordination meeting of international donors. The CG pledged US$2.2 billion of development aid to the country, i.e. less than the US$2.4 billion committed in 1997. The CG offered a further US$500 million package during the year, but only in case of acceleration in the reform process.

In December 1999 the annual Consultative Group meeting held in Hanoi further increased the share of ODA, subject to the condition of an enhancement of pro-market reforms. Donors pledged US$2.1 billion, and promised a further US$700 million if the government proceeded in the direction prescribed by the World Bank-coordinated report, *Vietnam: Preparing for Take-off?* (World Bank 1999a).

The shrinkage of external trade and FDI, the lower than expected ODA, and the lack of specific support from the IMF and the World Bank, all made the country more vulnerable to the risk of a shortage of foreign exchange in the midst of a regional financial crisis. Therefore, the national reserves in foreign currencies and gold were put under strong pressure, threatening the country's capacity to pay the short-term debts accumulated by state-owned and private enterprises. However, the success of the measure adopted by the Vietnamese authorities in controlling import flows and maintaining a low trade deficit prevented the most pessimistic predictions of an impending financial meltdown (UNDP 1998) or a major increase in the-balance-of payments deficit (World Bank 1997).

The positive results in the macroeconomic standing and the improved trade balance did not conceal the negative impact of the crisis. The need to curtail the fiscal deficit and to avoid an inflationary upsurge led Vietnamese authorities to adopt a strict monetary policy and to renounce anti-cyclical interventions. This was effective in containing inflation, which after rising from 3.8 in 1997 to 9.2 in 1998 went down to 0.1 in 1999 (Agence France Presse, 23 February 2000). The drastic cutback in inflation – to the verge of a deflationary drive – was largely motivated by a drop in food prices (also as a result of a record rice harvest). Proportionally, food represents the largest element in the basket of goods and services on which the price index is based. However, it also depended on a drop in the aggregated demand for investments and national consumption. News stories of stock-piling and industrial plants producing far below their potential output recurred in the national and international media throughout 1998 and 1999.

The economic slowdown had also an impact on the population's living conditions, though a precise account is limited by the scarcity of data.

In the years before the regional crisis, macroeconomic stabilization was achieved together with fast economic growth and poverty reduction. In the decade 1987–96 GDP growth was on average 7.3 per cent, increasing to over 9 per cent in 1995 and 1996. Over the decade, this result translated into an annual average per capita real income growth of about 5 per cent, increasing GDP per capita from US$100 in 1987 to over US$300 in 1996 (World Bank 1997: 17).

Some regions grew faster than others, and the gap between urban and rural areas increased to some extent, but the positive results of the economic reform were spread out all over the population. This led to outstanding results in terms of poverty reduction: no other country has recorded so sharp a decline in poverty in so short a period of time (with the possible exceptions of China and Indonesia in the 1980s) as Vietnam did between 1993 and 1998 (World Bank 1999b: iii). The proportion of people living below the poverty line dropped from 58 per cent in 1993 to 37 per cent in 1998. Reduction of poverty was confirmed not only by quantitative data on rising per capita expenditure and improving social indicators, but also by participatory poverty assessments (PPAs) which reported poor households' perception that their overall well-being had improved (World Bank 1999b). Notwithstanding these important achievements, Vietnam remained a country where a large proportion of the population live either below or slightly above the poverty line, and where poverty reduction results could be easily reversed by adverse events. Poverty was still widespread, particularly in the rural areas; but pockets of severe poverty persisted in urban areas as well, especially among poor migrant groups whose conditions are not easily reported in statistics.

How the economic downturn connected to the regional crisis affected the living conditions of the Vietnamese population is difficult to assess precisely and is still being debated among scholars and policy-makers. In urban areas some of the population had accumulated savings in the last few years of fast growth, securing them a temporary respite in a period of economic downturn. For those with savings in dollars, the currency devaluation even resulted in increased purchasing power. Some sources (e.g., ADUKI September 1998) have hinted that the urban bourgeoisie maintained its loyalty to the system (i.e., depositing the saving in dollars into Vietnamese banks instead of exporting capital abroad). This loyalty was explained by the fact that the urban bourgeoisie perceived its long-term interests protected by the Communist Party, in whose ranks it is overrepresented both among members and the leadership.

The more destitute urban population, instead, was forced to depend on the informal sector for survival in increasingly difficult conditions. However, the socioeconomic dynamics affecting the urban poor are relatively unknown for the lack of adequate investigations in the field (see Kilgour and Drakakis-Smith, Chapter 13 in this volume). Studies on poverty in Vietnam have mostly focused on rural areas; however, the ways in which the rural socioeconomic systems have absorbed the impact of the economic downturn is not very clear either. While data on urban unemployment in the formal sector do exist – and indicate that the rate grew from 6.85 per cent in 1998 to 7.4 per cent in 1999 (Reuters, 6 October 1999) – a calculation of unemployment or underemployment in rural areas is not available. Some sources have indicated a reason for optimism in the fact that Vietnamese agriculture has been only partially modernized, and therefore maintains some elasticity in employing manpower beyond limits sustainable in a fully-fledged market economy. Other scholars, however, stress that a number of workers were already redundant in agriculture before the crisis, and they have been pushed to seek seasonal or permanent employment in cities. Therefore, a reverse migration of these workers towards their home villages as a result of a deteriorating national economy would place an unbearable burden on their families and their villages.

This discussion is paralleled by a similar debate regarding other countries in the region (see Rigg and Parnwell, Chapters 11 and 12 in this volume). For Vietnam the issue is particularly dramatic because the country remains one of the poorest in the world, with about US$300 GDP per capita. The existence of informal 'coping mechanisms' able to shelter the most vulnerable in a situation of distress represents a matter of survival for many. How these informal 'coping mechanisms' are evolving in the midst of a radical process of modernization and how the state will be able to guarantee adequate levels of social protection remain major questions for an assessment of *doi moi*. Recent studies (e.g., World Bank 1999b), while confirming the important results achieved in terms of poverty reduction, have also indicated that a protracted economic downturn could compromise these results. At the same time, there is evidence that the quality of social services has been declining (e.g., health and schools) in crucial areas (World Bank 1998), while the reform process has involved the dismantling of traditional safety nets provided by family, villages and communes (Kolko 1997).

IN SEARCH OF A NEW STRATEGY?

The relation between the Vietnamese government and the international financial institutions from the early 1990s to a few months before the onset of the regional crisis has been likened to a long 'honeymoon' (Fforde 1998b). However, in 1997 this 'honeymoon' ended, with one of the two parties openly stating its discontent and the other keeping silent. A World Bank report of 1997, for instance, pointed out that 'present trends' could be 'inconsistent with long-term rapid growth with appreciable reduction in poverty and with greater equity' (World Bank 1997: iv). The criticism expressed by the agency (but also by the other multilateral institutions) was that with the current policy 'substantial inefficiencies [would] persist and growth [would be] inward looking, increasingly capital intensive and biased in favour of urban dwellers' (Ibid.). This pattern would be in contrast to the declared government objective to achieve 'significant improvement in the efficiency of the economy and promoting outward-oriented, broad-based, labour-intensive growth' (Ibid.).

Behind the World Bank (and other international agencies') declarations, there was an attempt to force Vietnam to adopt more coherently an export-led growth strategy. According to the World Bank interpretation of the 'East Asian miracle', the country was encouraged to gain from its comparative advantages, consisting of well-educated and cheap labour force. However, any element of dissent with Vietnamese authorities on long-term development strategy was concealed. The World Bank agenda was promoted as a way to avoid distortions and mistakes, in order to implement more effectively the Vietnamese authorities' own objectives of economic growth and poverty reduction. Three priorities were indicated as:

- reform of the state-owned enterprises (SOEs);
- creation of a neutral trade regime;
- development of a strong financial system.

The need for a reform (i.e., privatization) of the SOEs was supported on the basis that the existence of a large, state-owned enterprise sector – with close connections to the political leadership, non-regulated support from the state financial sector, and preferential access to FDI – was draining an excessive share of national resources. Therefore, the SOEs were an obstacle to the development of the nascent private sector and were hampering a broader-based and sustainable growth. The existence of restriction to free trade – through quotas and duties – was also considered as an impediment to the full exploitation of the country's comparative advantages. And a banking system too influenced by political constraints was considered as dangerous both for the risk of non-performing loans (especially through lending to SOEs) and for the limited access to capitals for the small and medium private enterprises.

The questions raised by the international financial institutions were not different from those raised in many other countries within and outside the region. To a large extent, they were pointing to the normal pattern of structural adjustment interventions. A number of the criticisms, however, were based on real problems, and were as such recognized by the Vietnamese authorities.

The same agenda was confirmed after the crisis by the major international agencies (e.g., World Bank 1999a; IMF 1999a; UNDP 1999), actually using the worsening of the economic conditions in order to acquire more leverage in laying down conditions to the Vietnamese government. Officially, the Vietnamese authorities subscribe to this agenda; in reality, significant resistance on key aspects of this package does exist. In the words of Tran Xuan Gia, Minister of Planning and Investment, at the donors' Consultative Group meeting in December 1999:

> We all agree on *what* reforms need to be done. The discussion is about *how*. We agree that without accelerated reforms we cannot grow rapidly and therefore the question is how best to accelerate the *doi moi* process. (World Bank 1999a, emphasis in the original)

The role of 'agenda setting' played by the international financial institutions should be considered against the backdrop of a relative impasse within the Vietnamese leadership in promoting a clear-cut reform strategy. Although the state and party leaders maintain a broad commitment to the *doi moi* policy, the complexity of this task and the existence of conflicting economic and political interests, have resulted since the early 1990s in a rather contradictory trajectory. A number of scholars (e.g., Fforde, Kokko and Ronnås) maintain that the implementation of bold reform measures in the period 1989–91 was the result of the pressure deriving from fading Soviet and Eastern European aid. The positive results of these reforms, accompanied after 1992 by increased development assistance from bilateral and multilateral donors and large flows of FDI, decreased the pressure for a furthering of *doi moi* and reduced the leadership commitment to implement sensitive measures. This interpretation led Adam Fforde (1998b) to voice openly the view that a too large ODA to Vietnam would maintain the status quo and delay needed reforms.

The belief that the Vietnamese economy was reaching a situation of impasse even before the regional crisis, led a number of scholars and the international financial institutions to take the lead in defining a new reform agenda. Ari Kokko, for instance, described the situation in the following terms:

> Even before the advent of the Asian crisis in July 1997, it had become apparent that it might not be possible to sustain the high growth rate without further reforms. The reason was that serious structural weaknesses had begun to endanger the stability of the economy. The problems included inefficient SOEs and banks, growing current account deficits, and a trade policy bias in favour of import substitution. The development of the private sector was also obstructed by unclear rules, often favouring SOEs, excessive red tape, and corruption. (Kokko 1998b: 3)

The difficulty of the Vietnamese leadership in finding a broad consensus on a policy able to give new momentum to the reform process is quite evident. Given the careful (and rather successful) macroeconomic management in the midst of the Asian crisis, it is possible to imagine that the Vietnamese authorities are maintaining a firmer control on the economic policy than might at first appear likely. It is also possible that – given the internal divergences and the need to avoid conflicts with the international donors – a cautious and pragmatic approach to policy-making is considered by leading Vietnamese forces as to be safer than embarking on highly theoretical and programmatic prescriptions.[4]

The cautious attitude of the Vietnamese leadership was confirmed after the onset of the regional crisis by avoiding major statements indicating a change of strategy. However, a number of hints indicate that the crisis has increased prudence in furthering the process of economic liberalization. The experience of neighbouring countries has signalled that liberalization – especially in a key sector like finance – would expose the country to the vagaries of international markets. Therefore, Vietnam has been reluctant to carry out unreservedly the reform agenda proposed by the international financial institutions, also considering that the prestige of these institutions has been largely undermined by the poor handling of the East Asian crisis. The implementation of reforms in the priority areas defined by the international financial institutions has been circumspect, although key issues have been addressed.

The reform of the state-owned enterprises has accelerated in the aftermath of the regional crisis. This reform started in 1989 with the merging and liquidation of about half of the more than 12,000 SOEs, reducing their number to about 6,000. In the early 1990s SOEs lost direct subsidization from the state budget, although they maintained de facto privileged access to capitals through state-owned banks. SOEs' paramount position in the national productive system made them attractive to foreign direct investment: by mid-1990s about 85 per cent of foreign invested joint-ventures were with SOEs. However, the monopolistic privileges enjoyed on the national market and the 'soft budget constraint'[5] from state banks exposed SOEs to risks of inefficiency and made many of these companies run into deficit. At the end of 1995 the aggregate debt of the SOE sector amounted to VND 279,000 billion or about 20 per cent more than the sector's aggregate turnover in the year (Kokko 1998a). This level of indebtedness represented a risk for the ailing banking system. It also undermined the efficient firms in the state sector, who were burdened by the internal debt within the SOEs sector – 'the internal debt alone was nearly seven times larger than the aggregate value of the sector's working capital' (ibid.).

To deal with this critical situation, the government embarked on a programme of restructuring and equitization. Equitization was mostly planned for small and medium firms, where it often encountered resistance from workers and managers for fear of losing state support and uncertainty about job security. By the end of 1997 only 17 enterprises had been equitized, but the number rose to 370 in 1999 according to the Vietnamese authorities (VNA, 19 February 2000). According to the government's plans the figure was to rise further, with another 500 enterprises equitized in the year 2000.[6] The goal is to reduce the number of SOEs to 3,000 in 2003 and to 2,000 in 2005 (BBC Summary of World Broadcasts, 24 May 2000). At the end of this streamlining programme, which also includes consolidation and mergers, the Vietnamese state-owned enterprises should consist of companies operating in strategic sectors and mostly organized within large corporations.

The regional crisis and the increasing pressure from the international financial institutions have certainly contributed to accelerate the process of SOE reform. However, the underlining strategy at the basis of the government plans is not easily intelligible, probably because it is based on the attempt to accommodate contradictory interests. The reorganization of a large number of enterprises operating in priority sectors within 18 General Corporations and 70 Special Corporations, realized after 1995, was largely inspired by the South Korean model. Prior to the regional economic crisis – when they came to be depicted as a case of 'crony capitalism' – the South Korean *chaebols* have been a remarkable example of successful industrialization, able to exploit national monopolies as a basis for competing in international markets. However, the Korean case – and the Taiwanese one, for that matter[7] – was based on a careful national planning able to discriminate among contrasting interests and to guide industrial strategies (for a discussion of the 'developmental state' model see Putzel, Chapter 8 in this volume). The lessons coming from the 'developmental state' experience in other countries of the region is not easily replicated in Vietnam. This would require a coherent definition of priorities and power in implementing policies that involve the sacrifice of non-strategic sectors. This is difficult to achieve in a country where political stability is constructed by cautiously balancing the different interests at stake. And this is particularly true in the process of SOE reform, given the importance of this sector in the national economy:

> [SOEs] are, in practice, sites of de facto joint ventures between various 'insiders' groups. It is the complexity and incoherence of these alliances that give the political economy its stability, as it permits for adjustments as and when resources availability shifts: insiders can co-opt outsiders (such as sources of FDI), when they wish. (Fforde 1998a: 6)

The other question regarding the implementation of 'developmental state' strategies in post-crisis East Asia is connected to a major claim made in this volume in interpreting the foundation of the regional crisis: i.e., the incompatibility between 'developmental state' policies and financial liberalization. The adoption of 'developmental state policies' demands a very careful management of the participation of the country within the world economy. Clearly, post-crisis Vietnam is under strong pressure from the international financial institutions and Western countries, and does not benefit from the same favourable conditions enjoyed by post-war Taiwan and South Korea (see Li *et al.*, Chapter 2 in this volume).

The watchful approach by the Vietnamese authorities in opening a stock market in July 2000, and the sound regulatory frame adopted, indicate that Vietnam is aware of the problem and is willing to take appropriate initiatives. However, Vietnam cannot easily resist international pressure without risking a new dangerous isolationism.

Foreign trade is another critical area in the reform process and one where the conflict with Western countries has been clearly visible. The international financial institutions have been pushing hard towards trade liberalization, pointing at the (undeniable) distortions produced on the Vietnamese market by import substitution policies. The World Bank and IMF have been indicating the need for a 'neutral trade regime', as they have done constantly in other developing countries as a precondition for financial support. Vietnam moved many steps ahead in this direction during the 1990s: exchange rate unification, elimination of export quotas, reduction of import quantitative restriction, elimination of export duties (apart from a small number of strategic products) and rationalization of import duties. However, the country has maintained a number of non-tariff barriers – especially quotas and licences – to control imports, and to discourage the import of consumer goods (this leverage proved crucial in reducing the impact of the regional crisis).

As in the case of SOEs, the process of the trade regime reform seems to reflect contradictions and ambiguities. Vietnam has formally accepted the principles of free trade, and has joined the ASEAN Free Trade Area, which is due to realize a significant trade liberalization in the region. And it has applied for membership in the WTO. At the same time, however, the government has tried to maintain a regime of import substitution. The successful experiences from the region indicate the need for the selective use of import substitution and export orientation, with a mix guided by a careful strategic planning (e.g., Wade 1990; Amsden 1989; Putzel, Chapter 8 in this volume). The Vietnamese government seems to be too dependent on revenues from import duties (up to three-quarters of state budget) and too much constrained by the need to defend contrasting interests within the system to promote a clear-cut trade policy. However, the major event in the post-crisis trade debate – the negotiation of a trade agreement with the United States – has shown a remarkable resistance by the Vietnamese leadership and the ability to achieve significant results. The story of this negotiation is very significant. In July 1999 an 'agreement in principle' for a trade pact which would have granted Vietnam Normal Trade Relations (formerly Most Favoured Nation) with the US was announced by the two countries' negotiators. But when the venue and the date for the signature had already been fixed and the negotiators were working on 'details', the Vietnamese authorities rejected the draft. Although the Clinton administration initially refused to re-open the negotiations, eventually a new trade pact was drafted – and signed in July 2000 – where Vietnam obtained improvements in key areas, namely in the protection of the national telecommunications sector.[8]

The reform of the banking system is the other major area of reform indicated by the international financial institutions. This is also an area where reforms have become more urgent following the Asian crisis, due to the high level of non-performing loans and the general fragility of the system. While there is no disagreement about the need to consolidate the financial sector, the main concern centres on the role of the banking system in supporting development strategies. The sector is dominated by four large state-owned banks; the state-owned banks account for about 80 per cent of all domestic lending and tend to take credit decisions on the basis of political rather than risk criteria, as bankers are pressured to lend to ailing state-owned enterprises.

Again, the experience from the region would indicate that loans based on political motivations are not negative *per se,* as long as they are functional to a clear industrial policy and they do not exceed a too risky threshold (see, e.g., Wade and Veneroso 1998). But this, once again, indicates the need for a clear-cut strategy, and even the ability to distinguish between a *productive* 'cosy relationship' between banks and enterprises – productive in that it supports strategic industries and is able to turn long term investment into profit – and a *backward* 'cosy relationship' supporting rent seekers and non-viable economic activities.

The role of the banking system is also pivotal for the growth of the developing private sector, which often struggles to access credit from state banks. Despite a new law to regulate and support the development of the private sector (January 2000) and an increased number of private enterprises, there is some truth in the World Bank criticism that the Vietnamese government is offering a preferential treatment to SOEs and is creating an uneven playing field for private companies (World Bank 1997: 34; see also World Bank 1999a). The private sector is still viewed with suspicion by national authorities and an excessive – and often contradictory – number of administrative regulations curtail the initiative of private entrepreneurs. Here again the experience from the region could indicate that giving priority to the state sector – as the Vietnamese authorities still intend to do – should not necessarily be in contrast with the development of an efficient private sector. On the contrary, the development of the private sector could be directed towards objectives defined by the state planning:

> To say that public enterprises [in Taiwan] have often played a central role in creating new capacities is not to say that private firms have been left alone. Incentives and pressure are brought to bear on them through such devices as import controls and tariffs, entry requirements domestic content requirements, fiscal investment incentives, and concessional credit ... And large-scale private firms are often exposed to more discretionary government influence, taking the form of what in Japan is called administrative guidance. (Wade 1990: 111)

In conclusion, post-crisis Vietnam is in search of a coherent development strategy. The traditional Vietnamese pragmatism, the need to mediate among different interests, and the will not openly to challenge international donors, have prevented the national authorities from enouncing a too-binding and elaborate strategy. The government has reacted to the crisis by maintaining firm macroeconomic management and by implementing a number of specific reforms. At the same time the government has resisted to a wholesale implementation of the reform agenda supported by the international financial institutions. Behind this resistance can be detected the desire to emulate (at least in part) the 'developmental state' model followed by other Asian countries.

However, the adoption of such a model is constrained both by conflicting interests within the system and by the external pressure coming from Western countries and from the international financial institutions.

Notes

1 An overview of current interpretations of *doi moi* is contained in Masina 1999a.
2 This interpretation has been confirmed to me by officers of the UN system in Hanoi, during informal talks in the spring of 1998.
3 The international financial institutions have suggested in several occasions that these figures should be revised downwards. They have estimated growth at about 3 or 4 per cent in 1997 and about 2 or 3 per cent in 1999 (e.g., see Yates 1999). Vietnamese authorities might have tried to adjust figures upwards for political purposes. The international financial institutions, instead, might have presented a bleak scenario in order to force the government to accept their prescriptions. The fear that 'Vietnam now faces the possibility of becoming one of the slower performers in the region' expressed by a World Bank report in December 1999 (World Bank 1999a) is not confirmed by the available data. According to Vietnam's General Statistical Office, quoted by the Chinese news agency Xinhua on 30 March 2000, GDP growth in the first three months of 2000 was at 5.6 per cent, i.e., in line with the other countries in the region.
4 The famous exhortation by Deng Xiaoping to 'cross the river by sensing the stones' would sound familiar in a Vietnamese context, although there exist important differences between China and Vietnam.
5 For a definition of the concept of 'soft budget constraint', see Kornai 1986.
6 A World Bank report released at the end of 2000 gives a lower estimate: 'Equitization has been accelerated over [the last two and one-half years] with 450 equitizations completed and half of them selling more than 65 per cent of shares (World Bank 2000: 32–33).
7 Interestingly, in the recent debate about the Vietnam economic strategy, the experience of Taiwan has been presented as opposed – and thus more successful – to the Korean one (e.g., Leung 1999: 6; Riedel 1999: 26). This does not take into account the reality of the first phase of state-led industrialization in Taiwan, when the state-owned enterprises played a central role (as demonstrated by Wade 1990).
8 For a more detailed accounting see Masina (forthcoming).

References

Amsden, A. H. (1989) *Asia's Next Giant: South Korea and Late Industrialization.* New York: Oxford University Press.

Arrighi, G., S. Ikeda and A. Irwan (1993) 'The rise of East Asia: one miracle or many?', in R. A. Palat (ed.), *Pacific-Asia and the Future of the World System.* Westport, CT: Greenwood Press.

Fforde, Adam (1998a) 'Strategic issues in Vietnamese development policy: state-owned enterprises (SOE)s, agricultural cooperatives and public administration reform (PAR)'. Seminar Paper – Political and Social Change, RSPAS, ANU.

—— (1998b) 'Handouts won't help Vietnam', *Wall Street Journal,* September 16.

—— and Stefan de Vylder (1996) *From Plan to Market: The Economic Transition in Vietnam.* Boulder, Co: Westview Press.

Fukase, Emiko and Will Martin (1999a) *A Quantitative Evaluation of Vietnam's Accesion to the ASEAN Free Trade Area (AFTA).* Washington, DC: Development Research Group, World Bank.

——— (1999b) *The Effects of the United States' Granting Most Favoured Nation Status to Vietnam.* Washington: Development Research Group, World Bank.

General Statistical Office (1999) *Vietnam's Statistical Yearbook.* Hanoi: Statistical Publishing House.

Griffin, Keith (1998a) 'Restructuring and economic reforms', in K. Griffin (ed.), *Economic Reform in Vietnam.* Basingstoke: Macmillan.

—— (1998b) 'The role of the state in the new economy', in K. Griffin (ed.), *Economic Reform in Vietnam.* Basingstoke: Macmillan.

International Monetary Fund (1999a) *Vietnam: Selected Issues.* IMF Staff Country Report no. 99/55.

—— (1999b) *Vietnam: Statistical Appendix.* IMF Staff Country Report no. 99/56.

Irvine, Reed (1999) 'A Special Report on the U.S.–Vietnam Trade Agreement', *Vietnam Business Journal,* VIII (4), October.

Jomo K. S. (ed.) (1998) *Tigers in Trouble. Financial Governance, Liberalization and Crises in East Asia.* London: Zed Books.

Khan, Azizur Rahman (1998) 'Integration into the global economy', in K. Griffin (ed.), *Economic Reform in Vietnam.* Basingstoke: Macmillan.

Kokko, Ari (1998a) *Managing the Transition to Free Trade: Vietnamese Trade Policy for the 21st Century.* Policy Discussion Paper No. 98/05, Centre for International Economic Studies, University of Adelaide.

—— (1998b) *Vietnam – Ready for Doi Moi II?* SSE/EFI Working Paper Series in Economics and Finance no. 286, December.

Kolko, Gabriel (1997) *Vietnam: Anatomy of a Peace.* New York & London: Routledge.

Kornai, János (1986) 'The soft budget constraint', *Kyklos,* 39 (1): 3–30.

Le Dang Doanh (1999) 'Vietnamese economy in 1998 and perspectives for 1999', *Vietnam Review,* January.

Leung, Suivah (1999) 'Crisis in Asia and Vietnam's Economic Policy Response', in Suivah Leung (ed.), *Vietnam and the East Asian Crisis.* Northampton, UK: Edward Elgar.

Masina, Pietro P. (1996) *Regional and International Dynamics in the Development of East Asia: The Case of Foreign Direct Investment.* Federico Caffè Centre Research Report No. 1 1996, Roskilde University.

—— (1999a) *Vietnamese Development Strategies between Tradition and Modernity.* Federico Caffè Centre Research Report No. 5 1999, Roskilde University, Roskilde 1999.

—— (1999b) *Vietnam and the Regional Economic Crisis.* Federico Caffè Centre Research Report No. 8 1999, Roskilde University.

—— (2001) 'Vietnam and the Regional Crisis: The case of a "late-late comer"', *European Journal of East Asian Studies,* 1 (2).

—— (forthcoming) 'Vietnam and the Regional Economic Crisis: an Assessment of Development Strategies'. PhD dissertation, Roskilde University.

Nørlund, Irene (1999) 'What's the impact of the Asian crisis? Economy and living conditions in joint ventures in the HO Chi Minh region and Da Nang'. Paper presented at the 4th Euroviet Conference, Universität Passau, 16–18 September 1999.

Riedel, James (1999) 'Needed: a strategic vision for setting reform priorities in Vietnam', in Suivah Leung (ed.), *Vietnam and the East Asian Crisis.* Northampton, UK: Edward Elgar.

Ronnås, Per (1998) 'The transformation of the private manufacturing sector in Vietnam in the 1990s'. Working Paper Series in Economics and Finance no. 241. Stockholm School of Economics.

Tombes, Jonathan (1999) 'Market access. The question is, "when?"', *Vietnam Business Journal*, VIII, (4), October.

UNCTAD (1999) *World Investment Report.* Geneva: UN.

UNDP in Vietnam (1998) *East Asia: from Miracle to Crisis. Lessons for Vietnam.* UNDP Staff Paper.

—— (2000) *Socioeconomic Bulletin.* www.undp.org.vn.

Wade, Robert (1990) *Governing the Market. Economic Theory and the Role of Government in East Asian Industrialization.* Princeton, NJ: Princeton University Press.

—— and Frank Veneroso (1998) 'The Asian Crisis: the High Debt Model Versus the Wall Street–Treasury–IMF Complex', *New Left Review,* 228: 3–23.

World Bank (1997) *Vietnam: Deepening Reform for Growth.* Washington, DC: World Bank.

—— (1998) *Poverty, Social Services, and Safety Nets in Vietnam.* Washington, DC: World Bank.

—— (1999a) *Vietnam: Preparing for Take-off?* An Informal Economic Report of the World Bank. Consultative Group Meeting for Vietnam. Hanoi, December 14–15.

—— (1999b) *Vietnam Development Report: Attacking Poverty.* Hanoi: World Bank.

—— (2000) *Vietnam 2010: Pillars of Development.* Hanoi: World Bank.

Part IV

Socioeconomic Implications of East Asian Development – between Miracles and Crises

ELEVEN

Rural Areas, Rural People and the Asian Crisis

Ordinary People in a Globalizing World

Jonathan Rigg

Introduction: From Financiers to Farmers

This chapter does not concern itself with the macroeconomic and macro-political perspectives on the Asian crisis. There are scores of such assessments – and many more, no doubt, in the pipeline – ranging from the journalistic (e.g. *The Economist* 1998a, 1998b), to the radical (e.g. Bello 1998; Bullard *et al.* 1998; Beeson 1998), the mainstream (EUROSEAS 1998), and the more reactionary (Krugman 1998; *Finance & Development* 1998).[1] Three things are evident in this fast-expanding collection of literature. First, the disjuncture between how people viewed the East and Southeast Asian regions before the collapse of the Thai baht in early July 1997, and how they view it now. Almost everyone, it seems, is wise after the event, and yet almost no one predicted the collapse of Asia. Paul Krugman might have challenged the basis of the 'miracle' thesis (Krugman 1994; 1998), and scholars like Walden Bello and Stephanie Rosenfield (1992), Alice Amsden (1994), Peter Bell (1996) and Mike Parnwell (1996) might have questioned the negative effects of fast-track industrialization on peoples, cultures and environments, but no one envisaged a meltdown of this type, or on this scale.[2] The second striking feature of the literature is the absence of people, or at least ordinary people, from the analyses. This is a crisis where currencies, stock markets, business tycoons, political leaders and the IMF take centre stage (see, for example, Nouriel Roubini's website: www.stern.nyu.edu/global macro/). It is a crisis with abstraction; a crisis where the so-called 'real economy' makes only a fleeting appearance. Even those publications that claim to examine the social effects of the crisis do so from afar and in a strangely disengaged fashion (e.g. ILO 1998).[3] The third facet of the literature is the degree to which not just the origins of the crisis, but the progress of events throughout the crisis, have confounded predictions.

On reflection, these features of the great bulk of the literature on the Asian crisis – at least at the time of writing – are not surprising. The crisis began with the collapse of currencies and stock markets, a reflection of a massive loss of confidence in Asia and the Asian economic 'miracle'. This then fed into widespread private sector bankruptcy and, in turn, into the real economy. It was only at this point that 'ordinary' people began to be drawn into the crisis.

THE ASIAN CRISIS AND RURAL CHANGE

> The present financial crisis is like a nuclear explosion. At first it kills the financial sector ... Afterwards, very slowly, it kills various other companies, the construction industry, then people, families, communities. (Srisuwan Kuankachorn 1998: 38)

There is no doubt that the Asian economic crisis was an important event in the region's economic fortunes. It burst the Asian bubble. It ended the triumphalism associated with talk of the Asian/Pacific twenty-first century. It challenged the World Bank's Asian miracle thesis. It undermined established political dynasties. It bankrupted many of the region's most successful companies. It put people out of work. And it drove many households into poverty. It may, with hindsight, prove to be a turning point. But, and as I shall argue below, the evidence emerging is that people, families and villages have been more resilient and adaptable than most people expected during the depths of the crisis. Many of the worst predictions – massive declines in the health and educational status of vulnerable groups – have not come to pass. It is still uncertain whether Asia is truly out of the woods (and Indonesia's special problems and challenges must be noted here). But this chapter tentatively suggests that the most remarkable feature of the crisis is the fact that the great majority of people have managed to keep their lives on track, even during a period of massive economic contraction. In the optimistic belief that the crisis has passed, the following discussion is couched in the past tense.

The sectors of the economy most profoundly hit by the crisis were the low-skilled and labour-intensive, and within these sectors especially those domestically invested industries dependent on the local market. Construction suffered more than any other. These industries were also those that hitherto had absorbed most migrants from rural areas. In September 1998 the Thai government estimated that unemployment had reached 2 million and that 1.3 million of these unemployed were rural villagers working in Bangkok and other cities. The same study suggested that at least 1 million had returned home to their rural communities (Richburg 1998).[4] Unemployment rates in Indonesia, Malaysia, the Philippines and Thailand doubled during the course of 1998 (Table 11.1).

The countries of Southeast Asia, with the exceptions of Singapore and Brunei, lack a welfare system that provides any social safety net to speak of. Those being laid off, as the ILO pointed out in a report in March 1998, had to fend for themselves (ILO 1998: 12). At the same time, the 'moral' economy of old had been fractured by years of modernization.[5] Some people and households had built up savings during the years of 'feast', and others received (usually very modest, around three months' salary) severance payments. But many of those most at risk had

Table 11.1 Unemployment forecasts

	Unemployment*		
	% of Labour Force		No.
	1990–96 (avg.)	1998 (forecast)	(millions, end 1998)
Indonesia	2.2	15	15–20 million
Malaysia	-	7	-
Philippines	-	13	-
South Korea	2.1	7.5	2 million
Thailand	2.5	9	2.0–2.8 million

Sources: various

* *Note:* The forecasts of numbers unemployed and percentage of labour force unemployed are from different sources and are not necessarily compatible.

neither savings nor redundancy payments to fall back on. These households, with their incomes fast disappearing, were forced to pawn their motorbikes, bicycles and televisions to meet their immediate, essential needs. More worryingly, some analysts described (or predicted) that increasing numbers of children would be taken out of secondary school to save on fees, undermining their future employment prospects, while the old, the infirm and the sick would be denied medical care because of a lack of financial resources and the increasing costs of drugs.

In Negara Jaya, a transmigration settlement in Lampung, South Sumatra, 10 per cent of sampled households reported having to withdraw a child from school because they were unable to pay the fees and were unwilling to take the risk of borrowing money (Elmhirst 1998a: 5). Other families had sold nearly all the contents of their houses – even land – to keep their children in school, while still more were economizing by turning to cheaper non-rice staples, gathering non-timber forest products, foregoing on luxuries like soap – or going hungry (ibid.: 12–14).[6] These are, it should be said, classic responses to crisis which are all too familiar in structural adjustment-prone Africa and Latin America (see Marshall 1998).

In terms of key indicators such as poverty, real wages and unemployment, Southeast and East Asia experienced an economic crisis in 1997–99 of the same level of intensity as those that hit Latin American in the 1980s and 1990s. There was an almost 40 per cent decline in real wages in Argentina and Mexico in the 1980s leading to a rise of almost 33 per cent in levels of poverty. During the 1995–96 Latin American crisis, real wages fell by over 30 per cent in Mexico while in Argentina poverty increased by over 50 per cent as levels of unemployment hit 18 per cent (World Bank 1998b: 24). These figures match those reported for Southeast Asia.

The social impacts of the crisis have been multi-dimensional: 'falling incomes, rising absolute poverty and malnutrition, declining public services, threats to educational and health status, increased pressure on women, and increased crime and violence' (World Bank 1998a: 14). But while, in this way, we can generalize about the effects of the crisis in the region, when it comes to measuring the impacts of the region's economic meltdown at the level of the individual household, the picture is much more complicated. Not only is there considerable variation in terms of the severity of impacts, but also in the mix of effects. Furthermore – and in writing this I would not wish to minimize the effects of the crisis – people have managed and dealt with the crisis significantly better than was imagined.

RETREATING INTO (SUBSISTENCE) AGRICULTURE?

A common theme that emerged in the literature during the crisis – we might call it the populist response – was that those workers who were laid off as industries closed or scaled down have taken refuge in the countryside. Articles appeared in the regional press with titles like 'The countryside will save the day' (Chang Noi 1997) and 'Farmers come to the rescue' (Bullard *et al.* 1998: p. 554, fn. 73). It seems that some people viewed the crisis as offering an opportunity to move away from the so-styled destructive policies associated with fast-track industrialization. The Forum of the Poor, an umbrella organization representing Thai farmers' groups, for example, saw the crisis as 'an opportunity to go "back to the village" and slow the seemingly irreversible pattern of urbanization and industrialization, bridging the gap between urban and rural populations and re-establishing the traditional values associated with village and agricultural life' (ibid.: 22). Nor were these feelings expressed only by pressure groups and populist journalists. In 1998, during the depths of the crisis, Chatthip Nartsupha (one of Thailand's most prominent scholars) argued that the country's economic malaise offered an opportunity to 'look again at the local peasant community as the basis of the economic life and culture of the people, and to support a new direction in national development, beginning with strengthening from the bottom up, from the level of the family, the local community, and the agrarian economy' (quoted in Baker and Pasuk 1999: 129).

This 'retreat to the village' is sometimes painted as the traditional Southeast Asian response to crisis. Individuals who may have spent several years away, living and working in the city – it is argued – never relinquished their associations with 'home', and economic retrenchment led them back to their roots. Rural areas, in short, acted as an economic, social and political safety-valve. Certainly, there is ample evidence from before the crisis of income being remitted on a regular basis, and of periodic returns home whether to meet agricultural needs or to attend festivals or ceremonies. Furthermore, there is evidence that, to coin a phrase, 'home is where the heart is', and the hearts of many urban workers remain rooted in the countryside.[7] With jobs in the formal non-farm economy evaporating, people, it was repeatedly stated, were retreating into agriculture. Sometimes this was described as a retreat into subsistence agriculture. The King of Thailand, on the occasion of his 70th birthday at the end of 1997, suggested that returning to a self-sufficient, farm-based economy might offer a way out of the crisis (*Bangkok Post* 1998). 'Whether or not we are a tiger is unimportant', he said, '[t]he important thing is for the economy to be able to support our people', adding, in populist vein, 'We need to go back so that we can go forward' (TDN 1997: 12).[8]

This vision of what occurred as the crisis deepened begs a number of important questions that the rest of this chapter will address:

1. Was there a significant shift of population back to rural areas during the crisis?
2. How permanent is this shift (if indeed it occurred) likely to be?
3. How did different groups in rural and urban society respond to the crisis?
4. What was the impact on agriculture of this influx of returnees?
5. Will the crisis lead to a fundamental, long-term change in Southeast Asia's trajectory of development?

A shift of people back to rural areas?

In January 1998, a Thai government survey estimated that 188,000 urban-based workers in the kingdom had returned to rural areas (ILO 1998). An NGO estimate at about the same time put the figure at around 300,000 (Bullard *et al.* 1998: 19). In September 1998 another official estimate (noted above) suggested a figure of 'at least' 1 million (Richburg 1998). While in March 1999 some commentators were writing of an estimated 2 million urban unemployed having left Bangkok for rural areas (Prangtip and Tasker 1999: 53).

The sheer range of estimates illustrates the difficulty of knowing quite what was happening. A large part of the reason for this is that there has long been a strong circulation of people between rural and urban locations. The question, then, was how far this established stream was augmented and amplified during the crisis. Significantly, the data available for the region on where people live and what they do, are of dubious accuracy (see Rigg 1997) and cannot be used as a baseline to determine shifts back into rural areas and agriculture.[9] Much of the evidence used to support the 'back to the village' thesis is anecdotal (see Bullard *et al.* 1998: 19).[10] Nonetheless, there are good reasons to believe that the reverse flow of migrants back to rural areas was less than the scale of redundancies in urban-based formal work might indicate, and also less than many newspaper and other 'populist' articles suggested.[11] Moreover, there is some evidence that those who left for the countryside at the beginning of the crisis fairly quickly drifted back to urban areas (Prangtip and Tasker 1999: 53).

Drawing on this perspective – that growing levels of redundancy would encourage a shift of people back to rural areas – the Indonesian government provided funds in early 1998 to assist the new urban unemployed return to their presumed rural homes by providing discount travel tickets. At the same time the authorities tried to limit the flows of new migrants from the countryside to urban areas (Elmhirst 1998c: 2). Some commentators saw this move on the part of the government as largely political: a means of removing the potentially volatile unemployed from urban areas and dispersing them to the countryside. Nonetheless, in a report on the discount fare initiative, Margot Cohen observed that 'the preliminary passenger count fell far short of official expectations – and few travellers were laid off factory workers' (1998: 17).

Patterns of response

In order to understand in a more nuanced manner the pattern of response to the crisis, it is useful, at least to begin with, to think in terms of age cohorts. It is suggested here that the young unemployed are the least likely to have returned to rural areas, and less likely still to have been re-absorbed within agriculture. For many young Asians, agriculture has become a low-status occupation to be avoided. In her work among the Batak of Sumatra, Rodenburg emphasizes that Batak youth 'despise' work in agriculture, and writes that farming is held in 'increasingly low esteem' (Rodenburg 1997: 201). This perspective resonates across the region. Wherever and whenever feasible, young people have remained in urban areas, possibly meeting their needs through recourse to the informal sector. Further, those that returned home because opportunities in urban areas simply evaporated, found their reincorporation difficult on both economic and social grounds. It has been suggested that returning migrants brought, as well as themselves, 'a host of new problems and urban pathologies [spousal and child abuse, crime, drug abuse, AIDS] previously unknown, or at least rare, in these remote villages' (Richburg 1998). For older cohorts there may have been a more pronounced movement back to rural areas (although this is largely based on conjecture). These older generations are less committed to modern, urban lifestyles and livelihoods and have better established links with rural areas. In the short term at least, then, this group may have been able, and willing, to take refuge in the countryside.

There is also some sketchy evidence that the crisis affected men and women differentially, and that they also responded in different ways. Those sectors most severely hit by the crisis, especially construction and construction-related industries, are male-dominated. Women have a higher representation in export-oriented sectors that weathered the crisis rather better. Indeed, with the competitive devaluation of most currencies in the region, many such industries remained buoyant, even during the depths of the crisis. For example in Lamphun, a province in Northern Thailand with a large concentration of foreign-invested factories, there was no sharp decline in foreign investment and employment during 1998 and 1999.[12] It has also been suggested that women are more reliable remitters of money. This is partly because women are said to be more dutiful (see Mills 1997) and partly because they are thought to be more frugal and resilient and better at managing and saving money. The result is that rural households sometimes prefer to have daughters working in the city, rather than sons.

While rural people showed great agility when it came to shifting from farm into non-farm work, it does not follow that any shift back was likely to be equally rapid or easy. Coxhead and Jiraporn Plangpraphan argued in the Thai case that having made a commitment – and an investment – in urban work and life, migrants would be unwilling to give this up, especially if they believed that a 'recovery is imminent and therefore they should remain "in line"' (1998: 21). This is partly because urban wages are considerably higher than rural wages. Therefore a period of unemployment, if it could be financed, was attractive if there was a realistic possibility of re-employment. In the case of Indonesia it is less certain whether urban/non-farm work offers much of a premium over agricultural work (see

Rigg 1997 for a discussion), although those with skills to sell remained surprisingly committed to urban areas even in the face of the crisis.

The 'back to the farm' hypothesis makes two heroic assumptions. First, that people had a bolt hole to retreat to in the countryside; and second, that agriculture could be made sufficiently productive to support this influx of people. (The second of these assumptions will be dealt with in the following section.) It is true that many – perhaps most – people in Southeast Asia have a rural 'home'. Some though do not, and this 'some' is probably larger than the official figures indicate.[13] Juliette Koning's village study in Central Java reveals that almost half of households have access to no land, and another quarter have access to less than 0.25 ha (Koning 1998: 11). For these households, rural livelihoods have little or nothing to do with agriculture. She writes: 'Labour migration provided those staying behind [in the village] with social and economic security, although at the same time it also made them more dependent on external sources of income' (ibid.).

Along with these landless and land poor rural households, there are those who have been displaced entirely from the countryside because of the concentrating effects of agricultural modernization. They, too, were not in a position to exploit the safety-net of agriculture. They were forced to 'trade down' and scratch a living in the increasingly tough urban employment environment. There were reports during the crisis, for example, of many more people ('thousands') scavenging through the municipal rubbish mountains of Jakarta (Matt Frei, BBC News, 21.00, 19 August 1998). Even in Thailand, which is usually presented as the example *par excellence* of a country where urban workers can take refuge in the countryside, there is a question mark over how pronounced the flow of urban unemployed turned out to be. 'The government expects unemployed workers to return to the agricultural sector, but they don't realize this sector has long been abandoned. ... Many in Bangkok no longer [have] access to rural communities' (Anjira 1998: 2; see also Vatikiotis 1998: 10).[14] The ability of the farm sector productively to absorb the new urban unemployed was also undermined in Thailand by a serious drought. Perhaps partially driven by the effects of the drought, some commentators reported a significant drift back to urban areas of those who left during the depths of the crisis in 1998 (Prangtip and Tasker 1999: 53).

The absorption capacity of agriculture

There is no question that some people who formerly worked in urban areas returned to rural areas during the crisis. But, to return to the second heroic assumption: was there ever the scope to make agriculture sufficiently productive to support this influx of people? To understand this we need to look more closely at the inequalities that exist in rural society and the nature of the changes that have, it is suggested, profoundly reshaped production in the countryside. In other words, we need to move from examining likely patterns of response in demographic terms (in terms of age cohorts and gender), to adopting a class/wealth-based perspective.

How did those households with sub-livelihood landholdings fare? Scholars, particularly those working in Java, suggested – at least until the crisis – that non-farm work subsidized agriculture. This has been used to explain the remarkable tenacity of small holders in the face of modernization (see for e.g. Cederroth 1995; Hart 1994; Maurer 1991; White and Wiradi 1989). For this group there was, we can surmise, little scope to absorb displaced workers from urban areas. Indeed, the loss of urban earnings may well have pushed some members of this group below subsistence level, and probably into poverty. In such circumstances there was considerable pressure for individuals to stay in urban areas, finding work where they could. Without remittances from family members working in urban areas, some farm families will have found it hard to survive (see Prangtip and Tasker 1999: 53). Indeed, some very small rural landowners will have sold their only significant asset – their land – and moved to urban areas. Should this pattern of response have revealed itself to any significant extent, then it would have had profound implications for longer-term trajectories of development in those rural areas affected (see below). Fortunately, it seems that for the crisis-affected countries of Asia – with the possible exception of Indonesia – recovery has occurred quickly enough for most households to survive without the distress sale of their land.

There are also farmers who were drawn into non-farm work, not so much because their landholdings were too small to support their families, but because of environmental marginality (clearly there is a link here). Elmhirst, for example, writes of Negara Jaya, a village in the southern Sumatran province of Lampung where 'poor soil fertility, pest invasions and drought mean returns from land are uncertain in the extreme ... [and] all households are dependent to a greater or lesser degree on income obtained away from their own farms' (Elmhirst 1998a: 6). Like those with sub-livelihood holdings, farmers operating in environmentally marginal areas were also constrained in their ability to exploit farming as a safety-net.

What, though, of those households better endowed with land who embraced non-farm, urban-based work not as a strategy of survival, but as one of consolidation or accumulation? Here the possibilities for reabsorption were rather brighter. Nonetheless, the implications for rural livelihoods and agricultural methods remain significant. The effect of people returning to rural areas shifted many households that were formerly in labour deficit, into labour surplus. In such cases, one might have expected the agricultural changes initiated in the 1980s as people moved into non-farm work – the shift from transplanting to broadcasting, the mechanization of production, the use of wage labour, and the move into labour-saving crops for instance – to be reversed. Mike Parnwell in chapter 12 of this volume notes, for example, farmers in Northeastern Thailand reverting to transplanting their rice.

However, this notion that the processes of agricultural change that were such a feature of the region in the 1980s and much of the 1990s could simply be thrown into reverse, assumes that change was both easy and desirable. It also smacks of permanency. It is too easy to forget that for many farmers their crisis responses were, in many instances, short-term coping strategies to be reversed – or revised – just as soon as conditions allowed. Permanent changes involving considerable cost, whether in terms of labour or cash, were avoided. In those areas where land had been allowed to fall into disuse and there was a deterioration in the productive base, resurrecting it posed considerable challenges and significant investment. An extreme example might be the case of the rice terraces of the Ifugao of Banaue in Luzon which have been neglected over many years.

It is also hard to imagine the process of mechanization of production being easily reversed. Many farmers sold their buffalo during the boom years and invested in labour-saving technologies. In the central region of Thailand, the number of buffalo declined from 534,000 in 1980 to 274,000 by 1995. Over the same period the number of two-wheeled Rotavators rose from 141,000 to 376,000, and large tractors from 11,000 to 88,000 (figures from assorted Ministry of Agriculture and Cooperatives (MDAC) statistical yearbooks). Writing of Thailand, Coxhead and Jiraporn Plangpraphan argue that 'even if labor were to return to the farm, fixed investments in labor-replacing machinery may mean that the creation of new farm jobs occurs only with a long lag – too long, perhaps, to motivate any labor transfer in the short run' (1998: 21). Likewise, those farmers who planted labour-saving tree crops during the years of labour shortage would only have resorted to uprooting them and moving back to the cultivation of annuals in extreme circumstances.

Assuming, though, that there was sufficient flexibility in the agricultural system, then we can speculate that at least some people will have been reincorporated back into farming. However even this will have had significant implications. To begin with, and as the ILO pointed out in a report produced at the beginning of 1998, it will have been 'at the cost of reduced labour productivity and returns per capita' (ILO 1998). Furthermore, if people really have been reabsorbed into family farming, there is likely to have been a knock-on effect for the land poor who formerly benefited from the growth in wage labouring opportunities on the farms of the land rich. With returning urban workers taking their jobs, these landless rural poor will have found themselves displaced into urban areas. This also raises questions about international labour migrants, particularly in Malaysia and Thailand. During the boom years, hundreds of thousands of Burmese took up poorly paid jobs in Thailand, and rather more Indonesians in Malaysia. There was a widespread assumption that many of these migrants would be displaced as unemployed Thai and Malaysian nationals traded down and took their jobs.

Fortunately, for the reasons outlined above, the balance of evidence currently shows that that kind of poverty-driven, knock-on effect has not occurred, or at least not to any significant extent (although see Arghiros 1998). With respect to international labour migrants, Thailand and Malaysia had become dependent on cheap imported labour and many Thais and Malaysians proved unwilling to trade down except in the most dire of circumstances. In June 1998 the Thai government amended its decision to repatriate 500,000 illegal aliens, allowing 95,000 to remain for another 12 months. This decision was said to have been influenced by pressure from Thai rice millers who could not find sufficient local workers to fill the vacuum created by the departing Burmese, even in the face of the economic downturn (*Far Eastern Economic Review* 1998: 54).

Rethinking the relationship between rural and urban areas in the light of the crisis

The question of the productivity and viability of the agricultural sector is important. In Wolpe's well-known analysis (1980) of migrant labour and the links between the capitalist industrial sector in South Africa and the pre-capitalist rural economy in southern Africa, he suggested that there was a delicate balance between production and reproduction, or between work and renewal. In summary, rural areas had to remain sufficiently viable so that they could reproduce – or renew – labour for work in South Africa's industrial and mining sectors. At the same time, however, returns to rural work had to be sufficiently unattractive to maintain the flow of young workers to the mines and factories where they could be paid at an equivalent wage less than the full cost of their reproduction.

Clearly, Southeast Asia is no southern Africa but there are parallels and contrasts worth pursuing. In particular, there is a case for arguing that agriculture in Southeast Asia has been progressively undermined by its articulation with the industrial sector. In Central Thailand (Chantana Banpasirichote 1993), Peninsula Malaysia (Kato 1994), Luzon in the Philippines (Kelly 1998; 1999), even in Java (Preston 1989), a process of disintensification and in some cases land abandonment has been underway for some years as emerging tensions between farm and non-farm have worked their way out to the detriment of agriculture. With this in mind, whether agriculture could have been reinvigorated to absorb large numbers of laid-off workers was always questionable. Moreover, this could only have been achieved by reversing some of the important trends of the past couple of decades.

The belief that somehow Southeast Asia 'can go back, to go forward' rests, in part, on the idea that in the past the village was a closed system. As a great deal of historical work indicates, extra-village links were, in all likelihood, much more developed than this agrarian ideal allows and, importantly, pre-dated by many decades the recent period of modernization (see, for example, Bowie 1992; Hoadley and Gunnarsson 1996; Kemp 1988; Rigg 1994; Pincus 1996: 30–32). Another facet of the 'back to the countryside' perspective is that the 'family farm' will save the day. However, the family farm has been a fiction for some time – if, by 'family farm', it is meant a farm that draws on family labour. Southeast Asian farmers have long been involved in the labour market.

What of the 'rural' poor?

Until now, occupational multiplicity – allying urban with rural livelihoods – has been used to explain the persistence of small landholdings. White and Wiradi, working in nine villages in Java, for example, have argued that non-farm activities permitted small landowners, with 'sub-livelihood' holdings, 'to achieve subsistence incomes without the distress sale of their ... plots' (White and Wiradi 1989: 299). With this in mind, I wrote before (but published during) the crisis, that:

> Modernization, far from elbowing these people out of the countryside and displacing them into urban areas as a disenfranchised proletariat, has allowed them to persist and in some cases to prosper ... In a sense, and ironically, the intrusion of the modern (non-farm) economy into rural people's lives has allowed some aspects of traditional life to persist (Rigg 1998: 506–507)

So, and to return to a theme introduced above, how have people in this group – the 'rural' poor – responded when faced with the drying-up of their non-farm working opportunities? It always seemed unlikely to me, for the reasons already outlined, that many people would or could have retreated to the countryside – or at least not in the numbers and proportions imagined. But there is an alternative scenario to this one of rural abandonment, namely that of rural retrenchment. Indeed, the available evidence would seem to favour this second perspective.

In this schema, rural people metaphorically battened down the hatches. They did not retreat into subsistence agriculture, but they adjusted their spending behaviour to take account of the sharp drop in incomes. With respect to education, families were willing to pay the price of meeting school fees and other costs even in sharply constrained circumstances. Those most at risk were also supported by government action. This is true, for example, of Thailand, where scholarships were made available to children from the poorest families, and of Indonesia, where primary level fees were waived and scholarships also extended to those most at risk (Booth 1999). Local communities also acted to keep children in school. There have been reports, for example, of teachers paying for school meals and of head teachers encouraging the cultivation of vegetables on school land. For these reasons, the '*severity of impacts [in Thailand] expected at the outset of the crisis [did] not materialize*' (World Bank 1999: 2 [emphasis in original]). While there is more evidence still to appear, the social impacts of the crisis in Thailand and Malaysia were rather less severe than expected. The Bangkok office of the World Bank's report (1999) into the health and education effects of the crisis in Thailand concludes:

> In those dark days [of the crisis], many feared, with some justification, that the economic and financial reversals would impose severe hardship on the social welfare of Thai families. ... [But] over the last two years [since the beginning of the crisis in mid-1997], a growing body of evidence is showing that families and government programmes acted to cushion impacts in health and education: *health and education outcomes have shown little or no discernible declines from past positive trends.* (World Bank 1999: 1 [emphasis added])

Even in Indonesia, some of the more dire predictions have so far failed to materialize. With regard to primary level schooling, for example, enrolment rates have been – overall – surprisingly resilient. A survey carried out in October 1998 found no significant fall in primary level enrolment rates for the country as a whole, and a 1.6 per cent fall in lower secondary school enrolment. This fall was concentrated in poorer areas of Jakarta (quoted in Booth 1999: 23–24). By the end of 1999 preliminary official data appeared to indicate a marginal increase in enrolment (Booth 1999: 24).

In urban areas there is some reason to suppose that the urban informal sector expanded just as jobs and the size of the formal sector shrank (see Griffith-Jones *et al.* 1998: 13–14). Many of the workers who kept their jobs found their wages in decline. For example, the per diem payments to civil servants were cut while factory workers had to forego their traditional bonuses. For Indonesia, Chris Manning estimated that real incomes for those workers who kept their primary jobs fell by at least 20–30 per cent (Manning 1998: 19). In addition to this cut in wages there were also substantial increases in the cost of some essentials. This meant that those workers fortunate enough to remain in employment nonetheless found their real incomes falling. Looking for ways to economize, they turned to the informal sector for transport, food or other services.

Some evidence to support this view that the informal sector acted as a safety-net is provided by the World Bank Director for Indonesia, Dennis de Tray. He suggested at the end of 1998, based on the Bank's research, that women and young people especially were being drawn into informal sector activities to make up for the drop in urban household earnings associated with the decline in formal sector work (Thoenes 1998). Sarah Turner, too, in her PhD thesis on small-scale manufacturing in Sulawesi, Indonesia, suggests that 'workers displaced from large companies are entering the small scale enterprise sector to eke out an existence' rather than resorting to the traditional 'shock absorber' of rural areas and the rural sector (Turner 1998: 484). The informal sector, therefore, provided both an important alternative to the formal sector for those who faced a squeeze on their incomes, and also an important alternative range of activities for those deprived of their livelihoods. Nonetheless, it seems that earnings in the informal sector were depressed as new entrants displaced from the formal sector or ejected from rural areas increased competition (Manning 1998; Ranis and Stewart 1998: 15). In addition, some of the increase in informal sector work can be seen to have been undesirable: prostitution and child labour, for example (see Griffith-Jones *et al.* 1998: 13; Robb 1998).

It is also important to emphasize that the crisis did not lead to a total collapse of formal sector jobs. Take, for example, the response of factory workers from the Lampungese village of Tiuh Baru in South Sumatra to redundancy (Elmhirst 1998b). Some young women did, indeed, take up the Indonesian government's exhortation and money, and returned home.[15] But many more 'remained in the city, using the *ikatan*[16] as an important information source for tracking down factory jobs, which still exist, but with factories recruiting when orders come in, and laying workers off when there are no orders' (Elmhirst 1998b). Nor, for that matter, was it just a case of the rural unemployed staying in urban areas in the hope of tracking down a job of some kind, whether in the formal or informal sectors. Negara Jaya, another village studied by Elmhirst in Lampung, provides further evidence to support the view that 'off-farm work outside the area has become more important as [rural] livelihoods have come under pressure'. Elmhirst continues: '[T]emporary and permanent migration from Negara Jaya in search for work has increased considerably over the past 12 months [i.e. during the crisis]' and 'scores of women have gone to Jakarta to work as domestic servants' (1998a: 15). While some households used domestic work as a means to ease the subsistence burden at home, others abandoned the village of Negara Jaya entirely and moved to Java.[17] On the basis of this evidence from one village in Southern Sumatra, Elmhirst argues that 'it would be misleading to suggest that rural areas, where subsistence food cropping may support farm families, provide a buffer for people experiencing the knock-on effects of the monetary crisis' (ibid.: 19).

There is no question that people responded to the crisis in a variety of ways, reflecting their own positions, inclinations, skills, contacts and resource constraints. Some people remained in urban areas because they had nowhere else to turn while others stayed either because they had no wish to return to their village roots or because they hoped a job might materialize. Some people left rural areas for urban centres because they perceived them to offer more opportunities, while others were displaced as they were forced to sell their sub-livelihood plots or lost their jobs. But far more rural people during the crisis did none of these things. Instead they prioritized their outlays, cut back on luxuries, economized on necessities, and drew on savings. They hunkered down.

UNEVEN IMPACTS

From afar it can sometimes seem that the effects of the crisis were homogeneous and all-pervasive. Indeed this chapter may have reinforced the fiction of an undifferentiated crisis affecting a largely undifferentiated Southeast Asian population. And yet it is clear that not only were differences between countries highly significant in mapping out the effects of the crisis, but that even within regions in the same country there were some industries and some people who were much more severely affected than others. Indeed, there are people who have done very well. While some unevenness of impact was predictable, there were also some surprises.

Perhaps most predictable was the collapse of activities connected with the construction industry. Daniel Arghiros has been studying the brick industry in Ayutthaya province in Central Thailand since the late 1980s (see Arghiros 1997a, 1997b, 1998; Arghiros and Wathana Wongsekiarttirat 1996). By the early 1990s such was the demand for bricks that tensions had emerged between the brickyards and agriculturalists in their search for labour. Wages in the brickyards doubled from 50–60 baht in 1990 to 100–120 baht in 1996 and severe shortages of labour in both agriculture and brick-making were beginning to manifest themselves. Non-local and even non-Thai labour had to be sourced to fill an intensifying labour shortage. By the summer of 1998 this situation had been turned on its head. The price of bricks had plummeted from 0.75 baht each in 1996 to 0.17 baht in 1998 as demand contracted. In contrast to the situation just 18 months earlier, entrepreneurs faced 'a situation in which labour is abundant but there is no demand for their product' (Arghiros 1998: 11).

However, the situation in Thailand's export-oriented industries in the summer of 1998 was much more buoyant. Indeed, many companies were recruiting workers as the depreciation of the baht made their exports highly competitive in the international market. Anne Booth notes much the same with respect to Indonesia. She also suggests that this applied to smallholders, mostly in the Outer Islands, who were growing export estate crops like coffee, rubber, pepper and cocoa (Booth 1998).

WHAT DO THE PRESENT AND FUTURE HOLD?

In order to tell a story with some consistency, this chapter has sometimes papered over the evident diversity that exists in Asia. Not only do countries in the region face different sets of problems but so too do households and individuals. Furthermore, even when similarly resourced households in the same village face apparently the same predicament, there is no guarantee that their responses will be the same. Social networks, force of will, initiative, patterns of expectation, it is these kinds of unknowable, unmeasurable and therefore unaccountable factors which are often deterministic when it comes to understanding patterns of response.

A major challenge facing accounts of the Asian crisis is that it is still too close – too near at hand – to get any sense of perspective. For example, of the responses outlined above, it is hard to know for certain which are short-term crisis responses and which are longer-term developments that may have a marked impact on the trajectory of development in rural areas. This is a point that Wetterberg *et al.* make in their 'snapshot' of the social effects of the crisis in Indonesia. 'The present data', they write, 'are silent on whether the crisis has changed fundamental dynamics' (1999: 151). Currently we can only guess at the direction of change based on largely anecdotal evidence, quick-and-dirty surveys, and a handful of more thorough studies. The result is that the significance of the crisis in the *longue durée* is far from clear.

The economic crisis in Asia has been used as a pretext to do many things:

- To challenge the Asian miracle;
- to suggest that there is some Occidental conspiracy at root;
- to argue the case for farm-based, traditional economic systems;
- to highlight the dangers of dependent development;
- to further the case for globalization;
- to emphasize the weaknesses in Asia's crony capitalist tendencies; and
- to undermine entrenched political dynasties.

This chapter has focused on the effects of the Asian crisis on 'ordinary' people and in particular those with their roots and hearts in rural areas but with their livelihoods dependent on urban work. The media and some analysts and academics in the region have argued, quite strongly, the case for a rural revival. 'There is growing realization', Chang Noi wrote in the *Thai Development Newsletter*, 'that the countryside contains some assets which are more solid and more bankable in the long term than the electronic illusions in the balance sheets of finance companies or the concrete dreams in the ambitions of property developers' (Chang Noi 1997).

However, the view that laid-off urban workers could return to the farm, as they have previously done at times of crisis, overlooks some important technological, economic and social changes that have occurred over the last decade or so. Such a view is based on a series of assumption which are open to challenge. It assumes:

- that rural areas have the productive capacity to meet the needs of the urban unemployed;
- that urban-based workers will jump at the chance to retreat to the countryside;
- that agriculture is sufficiently flexible to adapt to the new conditions imposed upon it;
- that most people have a productive base in the countryside; and
- that urban work has evaporated, leaving few alternatives to 'going home'.

As Elmhirst writes with reference to Indonesia, this belief 'is based on a set of assumptions that are naïve and fundamentally flawed ...[and] it ignores the realities for most poor people' (Elmhirst 1998c: 3).

AUTHOR'S NOTE

This paper was initially written for the Southeast Asian Geographers' Association (SEAGA) conference held in Singapore in November–December 1998. My attendance at that conference was generously supported by the British Academy. In its first guise this chapter benefited greatly from the detailed comments of Mike Parnwell, who has also contributed to the present volume. His view of how events in rural areas of the region have, and are likely to evolve, are different from my own – although we do agree on much. Finally, I would also like to thank Becky Elmhirst for allowing me to refer to her unpublished papers on the crisis in Indonesia.

Notes

1 A good selection of papers from a conference on the crisis held at the Institute of Development Studies in Sussex in July 1998 can be found at http://www.ids.ac.uk/ids/research/easwkshp.html.

2 Though Paul Krugman may have been crowned with the title of the man who 'forecast East Asia's crisis' (see *THES*, 4 Sept. 1998: 17) he is the first to admit that he was '90 per cent wrong'. However, and as Jomo K. S. recently observed, other economists were '150 per cent wrong' (Jomo 1998).

3 The World Bank's (1998a) 'Social consequences of the East Asian financial crisis' (Sept. 1998) is better but still thin in terms of the human impacts of the crisis.

4 The difficulty of estimating the numbers of unemployed is reflected in the fact that the World Bank, a few months earlier, suggested that 800,000 workers in Thailand would have lost their jobs by the end of 1998 (World Bank 1998b).

5 Mike Parnwell, in Chapter 12 of this volume, suggests that some elements of Thailand's moral economy have been reactivated quite quickly and easily. There is certainly a rich tradition the world over of community structures re-emerging during times of adversity. However there is also evidence of a breakdown in social mores and community trust as the crisis has exerted intolerable pressures on livelihoods. In a slum settlement in Khon Kaen province in Northeast Thailand, an NGO study revealed an increase in theft, violence and other crimes, and a decline in community cooperation as the exigencies of survival forced families to compete for scarce jobs (quoted in World Bank 1998b: 38). Crime, drug dealing and prostitution are also said to have increased markedly in Bangkok (Vatikiotis 1998: 11).

6 It should be emphasized that Negara Jaya was facing not one but a series of crises. In particular, the impact of the monetary crisis (*krismon*) was compounded by the effects of an extremely long dry season.

7 Writing of circulation as a way of life among the Wosera Abelam of Papua New Guinea, Curry and Koczberski argue that '[i]n many ways, a migrant never really leaves the village in a spiritual and cultural sense, and hence there is no clear distinction between source and destination sites when examining the lived experience of Wosera migration' (1998: 36).

8 Later, the King said that his comments had been 'misunderstood' and that he had not called for Thailand to embark on a path to self-sufficiency (*Nation* 1998).

9 This also applies to other Asian countries. Recent work by Rawski and Mead (1998) on China suggests that official figures consistently and systematically overstate the size of the country's agricultural workforce. Their calculations show that there may be more than 100 million 'phantom farmers'.

10 Bullard *et al.* quote a social researcher in Pichit, in Northern Thailand: 'To my surprise I was talking to field labourers who had recently been laid off from construction jobs in Bangkok. They were dispirited and they were hungry' (1998: 19).

Prangtip and Tasker note that in Thailand there are 'no official forecasts or accurate figures' on the number of former urban workers now living in rural communities (1999: 53).

11 This is also something that Coxhead and Jiraporn Plangpraphan conclude in their analysis of the crisis in Thailand (1998: 20–21).

12 Investment increased in Lamphun from 2.8 billion baht in 1997 to 5.3 billion in 1998 and 4.3 billion in 1999.

13 Once again we come up against the problem of making assumptions based on dubious statistics.

14 Anjira does not discuss the additional point that some people, even though they may have lost their jobs and have a rural base to retreat to, will have remained in the city.

15 While they returned home these young women, who were prevented from working in the fields for cultural reasons, became a burden rather than an asset to their families at a time of economic difficulty. There is also the question of the permanency of their return home.

16 An *ikatan* is a club or association offering support to its members, in this case people from the village of Tiuh Baru working in Tangerang, outside Jakarta.

17 Of the original sample of households surveyed in 1994/95, 30 per cent had sold up and left Negara Jaya by the time of the second survey in 1998 (Elmhirst 1998a: 16).

References

Amsden, Alice H. (1994) 'Why isn't the whole world experimenting with the East Asian model to develop?: Review of *The East Asian Miracle*', *World Development* 22 (4): 627–633.

Anjira Assavanonda (1998) 'Unemployment rate at its highest level', *Bangkok Post,* 19 August: 2.

Arghiros, Daniel (1997a) 'Rural industry and development in Central Thailand', *The Journal of Entrepreneurship,* 6 (1): 1–18.

—— (1997b) 'The rise of indigenous capitalists in rural Thailand: profile of brickmakers in the Central Plains', in Mario Rutten and Carol Upadhya (eds), *Small Business Entrepreneurs in Asia and Europe: Towards a Comparative Perspective,* New Delhi: Sage, pp. 115–145.

—— (1998) 'Mutual obligation and work: changing labour relations in provincial Thai industrial enterprises'. Paper presented at the Second EUROSEAS Conference, University of Hamburg, 3–6 September.

—— and Wathana Wongsekiarttirat (1996) 'Development in Thailand's extended metropolitan region: the socioeconomic and political implications of rapid change in an Ayutthaya district, central Thailand', in Michael J. G. Parnwell (ed.), *Thailand: Uneven Development,* Aldershot: Avebury, pp. 125–145.

Baker, Chris and Pasuk Phongpaichit (1999) 'Afterword: Chatthip and the Thai village', in Chatthip Nartsupha, *The Thai Village Economy in the Past* (translation by Chris Baker and Pasuk Phongpaichit). Chiang Mai: Silkworm Books, pp. 114–131.

Bangkok Post (1998) 'Back to relying on basics', *Bangkok Post Year End Review,* 15th January: 8–9.

Beeson, Mark (1998) 'Capital offence', *Inside Indonesia* 55 (July–September): 17–18.

Bell, Peter F. (1996) 'Development or maldevelopment? The contradictions of Thailand's economic growth', in Michael J. G. Parnwell (ed.), *Thailand: Uneven Development*. Aldershot: Avebury, pp. 49–62.

Bello, Walden (1998) 'The Asian financial crisis: causes, dynamics, and prospects'. Paper presented at the ASEASUK annual conference, April 1998, London.

—— and Rosenfield, Stephanie (1992) *Dragons in Distress: Asia's Miracle Economies in Crisis*. London: Penguin.

Booth, Anne (1998) 'Round table discussion: Asia after the crisis'. Second EUROSEAS Conference, University of Hamburg, 3–6 September.

—— (1999) 'Survey of recent developments', *Bulletin of Indonesian Economic Studies*, 35 (3): 3–38.

Bowie, Katherine A. (1992) 'Unraveling the myth of the subsistence economy: textile production in nineteenth century Northern Thailand', *Journal of Asian Studies* 51(4): 797–823.

Bullard, Nicola, Walden Bello and Kamal Malhotra (1998) 'Taming the tigers: the IMF and the Asian crisis', *Third World Quarterly*, 19 (3): 505–555.

Cederroth, Sven (1995) *Survival and Profit in Rural Java: the Case of an East Javanese Village*. Richmond, UK: Curzon Press.

Chang Noi (1997) 'The countryside will save the day', *Thai Development Newsletter* 33 (July–December): 43–45.

Chantana Banpasirichote (1993) *Community Integration into Regional Industrial Development: a Case Study of Klong Ban Pho, Chachoengsao*. Bangkok: TDRI.

Cohen, Margot (1998) 'Easing labour's pain: fearing unrest, Jakarta tries to soften job losses', *Far Eastern Economic Review*, 29 January: 17.

Coxhead, Ian and Jiraporn Plangpraphan (1998) 'Thailand's economic boom and bust, and the fate of agriculture', *TDRI Quarterly Review*, 13 (2): 15–24.

Curry, George and Gina Koczberski (1998) 'Migration and circulation as a way of life for the Wosera Abelam of Papua New Guinea', *Asia Pacific Viewpoint*, 39 (1): 29–52.

The Economist (1998a) 'Frozen miracle: a survey of East Asian economies', 7 March.

——(1998b) 'The perils of global capital', 11 April: 76–78.

Elmhirst, Rebecca (1998a) '*Kismon* and *kemarau*: a downward sustainability spiral in North Lampung tanslok settlement'. Report to the International Centre for Agroforestry Research (ICRAF). Bogor, Indonesia, May.

—— (1998b) 'Daughters and displacement: migration dynamics in an Indonesian transmigration area'. Paper presented at the workshop on Migration and Sustainable Livelihoods, University of Sussex, Brighton. June.

—— (1998c) 'Crisis in rural Indonesia: the politics of poverty in a North Lampung transmigration settlement', unpublished paper.

EUROSEAS (1998) 'Asia after the crisis'. Round table discussion, EUROSEAS 98, University of Hamburg, 3 September.

Far Eastern Economic Review (1998) 'Business briefing', 30 July: 54.

Finance & Development (1998) 'The Asian crisis' (special issue), June 1998.

Griffith-Jones, Stephanie with Jacques Cailloux and Stephan Pfaffenzeller (1998) *The East Asian Financial Crisis: a Reflection on its Causes, Consequences and Policy Implications*. Institute of Development Studies discussion paper no. 367, Brighton, Sussex: IDS.

Hart, Gillian (1994) 'The dynamics of diversification in an Asian rice region', in Bruce Koppel, John Hawkins and William James (eds), *Development or Deterioration: Work in Rural Asia*, Boulder, CO, and London: Lynne Rienner, pp. 47–71.

Hoadley, Mason C. and Christer Gunnarsson (eds) (1996) *The Village Concept in the Transformation of Rural Southeast Asia*, Copenhagen: NIAS and London: Curzon.

ILO (1998) 'The social impact of the Asian financial crisis'. Technical report for discussion at the high-level tripartite meeting on social responses to the financial crisis in East and Southeast Asian countries, Bangkok (22–24 April 1998), http://www.ilo.org/public/english/60empfor/cdart/bangkok/index. html.

Jomo Kwame Sundaram (1998) 'Southeast Asia: from miracle to débâcle? The financial crisis in Southeast Asia and its effects'. Keynote address to EUROSEAS 98, University of Hamburg, 3 September.

Kato, Tsuyoshi (1994) 'The emergence of abandoned paddy fields in Negeri Sembilan, Malaysia', *Southeast Asian Studies* (*Tonan Ajia Kenky*), 32 (2): 145–172.

Kelly, Philip (1998) 'The politics of urban–rural relations: land use conversion in the Philippines', *Environment and Urbanization,* 10 (1): 35–54.

—— (1999) 'Everyday urbanization: the social dynamics of development in Manila's extended metropolitan region', *International Journal of Urban and Regional Research,* 23 (2): 283–303.

Kemp, Jeremy (1988) *Seductive Mirage: the Search for the Village Community in Southeast Asia.* Dordrecht: Foris.

Koning, Juliette (1998) 'Rural social security in Java', *Indonesian Environmental History Newsletter* 11 (June): 10–12.

Krugman, Paul (1994) 'The myth of Asia's miracle', *Foreign Affairs,* 73 (6): 62–78.

—— (1998) What happened to Asia?', http://www.mit.edu/krugman/www.DISINTER.html.

Manning, Chris (1998) 'The employment crisis', *Inside Indonesia,* 55 (July–September): 19.

Marshall, Katherine (1998) 'Social dimensions of the East Asia crisis – some reflections on experience from the adjustment eras in Africa and Latin America'. Paper prepared for the IDS seminar on the Asian crisis, July, http://www.ids.ac.uk/ids/research/easwkshp.html.

Maurer, Jean-Luc (1991) 'Beyond the *sawah*: economic diversification in four Bantul villages, 1972–1987', in Paul Alexander, Peter Boomgaard and Ben White (eds), *In the Shadow of Agriculture: Non-farm Activities in the Javanese Economy, Past and Present.* Amsterdam: Royal Tropical Institute, pp. 92–112.

MDAC (n.d.) *Agricultural Statistics of Thailand* (assorted years). Bangkok: Ministry of Agriculture and Cooperatives.

Mills, Mary Beth (1997) 'Contesting the margins of modernity: women, migration, and consumption in Thailand', *American Ethnologist,* 24 (1): 37–61.

The Nation, (1998) 'HM clarifies call for "self-sufficiency"', 5 December: A1.

Parnwell, Michael J. G. (ed.) (1996) *Thailand: Uneven Development,* Aldershot: Avebury.

—— and Daniel A. Arghiros (1996) 'Uneven development in Thailand', in Michael J. G. Parnwell (ed.) *Thailand: Uneven Development,* Aldershot: Avebury, pp.1–27.

Pincus, Jonathan (1996) *Class Power and Agrarian Change: Land and Labour in Rural West Java.* Basingstoke: Macmillan.

Prangtip Daorueng and Tasker, Rodney (1999) 'Fear on the farm: drought and falling prices put farmers on the edge', *Far Eastern Economic Review*, 11 March: 53.

Preston, David (1989) 'Too busy to farm: under-utilization of farmland in Central Java', *Journal of Development Studies*, 26 (1): 43–57.

Ranis, Gustav and Frances Stewart (1998) 'The Asian crisis and human development'. Paper prepared for the IDS seminar on the Asian crisis, July, http://www.ids.ac.uk/ids/research/easwkshp.html.

Rawski, Thomas G. and Robert W. Mead, (1998) 'On the trail of China's phantom farmers', *World Development*, 26 (5): 767–781.

Richburg, Keith B. (1998) 'Asia's migrant workers forced home', *Washington Post* reprinted in *Guardian Weekly*, 20 September.

Rigg, Jonathan (1994) 'Redefining the village and rural life: lessons from Southeast Asia', *The Geographical Journal*, 160 (2): 123–135.

—— (1997) *Southeast Asia: the Human Landscape of Modernization and Development*. London: Routledge.

—— (1998) 'Rural–urban interactions, agriculture and wealth: a Southeast Asian perspective', *Progress in Human Geography*, 22 (4): 497–522.

Robb, Caroline M. (1998) 'Social aspects of the East Asian financial crisis: perceptions of poor communities'. Paper prepared for the IDS seminar on the Asian crisis, July. http://www.ids.ac.uk/ids/research/easwkshp.html.

Rodenburg, Janet (1997) *In the Shadow of Migration: Rural Women and their Households in North Tapanuli, Indonesia*. Leiden: KITLV Press.

Srisuwan Kuankachorn (1998) 'The roots of the Thai crisis: a failure of development', *Watershed*, 3 (3): 37–40.

Thai Development Newsletter (1997) 'IFCT sees poor economic growth', No. 33 (July–December): 12–13.

The Times Higher Education Supplement (1998) 'Stylish theory kind of guy', 4 September: 17.

Thoenes, Sander (1998) 'Indonesian rupiah shrugs off unrest', *Financial Times* 20 November: 4.

Turner, Sarah (1998) 'An applicable paradigm? Flexible specialisation and small scale enterprises in Ujung Pandang, Indonesia', unpublished PhD thesis, University of Hull.

Vatikiotis, Michael (1998) 'No safety net', *Far Eastern Economic Review*, 8 October: 10–13.

Wetterberg, Anna, Sudarno Sumarto and Lant Pritchett (1999) 'A national snapshot of the social impact of Indonesia's crisis', *Bulletin of Indonesian Economic Studies*, 35 (3): 145–152.

White, Benjamin and Gunawan Wiradi (1989) 'Agrarian and nonagrarian bases of inequality in nine Javanese villages', in Gillian Hart, Andrew Turton and Benjamin White (eds), *Agrarian Transformations: Local Processes and the State in Southeast Asia*. Berkeley: University of California Press, pp. 266–302.

Wolpe, Harold (ed.) (1980) *The Articulation of Modes of Production: Essays from Economy and Society*. London: Routledge.

World Bank (1998a) 'Social consequences of the East Asian financial crisis', http://www.worldbank.org/poverty/eacrisis/partners/library/socconsq/index. html.

—— (1998b) 'Responding to the crisis: backing East Asia's social and economic reforms', http://www.worldbank.org/html/extdr/asian_crisis/backingreform. html.

—— (1999) *Thailand Social Monitor: Coping with the Crisis in Education and Health.* Bangkok: World Bank.

Yongyuth Chalamwong (1998) 'Economic crisis, international migration and the labor market in Thailand', *TDRI Quarterly Review,* 13 (1): 12–21.

TWELVE

Coping with Crisis and 'Migration Reversal' in Thailand

Michael J. G. Parnwell

Introduction

As the Asian crisis spread rapidly from the financial sector to the real economy, one of the most immediate, prominent and politically urgent problems centred upon the spiralling level of unemployment, as construction projects were halted, investment dried up, purchasing power was severely constrained, and demand for products and services was dramatically curtailed. Alarming projections surfaced which pointed, *inter alia*, to a dramatic process of 'migration reversal', with floods of rural–urban migrants returning to their villages, and waves of international migrants facing forcible repatriation. On the surface it would appear that these projections proved to be relatively accurate. There were reports of hundreds of thousands, indeed millions, of internal migrants having to return to their rural homes, or seek solace and survival in the urban informal sector (ILO 1998). Partly as a consequence, the economic crisis rapidly spread into the social and political realms, creating a great deal of volatility and uncertainty about the capacity to cope with the crisis (ibid.). Meanwhile, the international migrant workforces in several East and Southeast Asian countries – only recently an essential and thus tolerated component of their dynamic economies and affluent lifestyles – suddenly became a massive, unwanted economic and political liability (*Migration News*, February 1998; Yoshimura 1997, 1998).

This chapter aims to explore some of the consequences and implications of 'migration reversal' as seen from the perspective of one of the pivotal countries in the regional labour migration system, Thailand. Using empirical case material from a field visit in 1998 to Northeast Thailand, the chapter seeks to reveal how not only reverse migrants from urban areas but also the rural communities to which they returned were affected by the economic crisis. The chapter reveals that people have managed to 'cope with crisis' to a remarkable and unexpected degree, and suggests that this is at least partly attributable to some of the long-established, functional characteristics of the migration process itself. Migration (particularly from the impoverished Northeast) has historically represented a response to difficulties, and is also a process that is often beset by difficulties: the mechanisms that migrants have developed to help them to cope with these difficult situations have placed them in a relatively advantageous position in terms of helping them to cope with the economic crisis.

The chapter forces us to take a closer and much more critical look at the notion of 'crisis' and also, by continuation, the wider notion of 'development'. It suggests that the notion of 'crisis' is very much a relative one, with the current situation taking on crisis proportions principally when viewed against a backdrop of more than two decades of economic achievement, and when seen from the perspective of those who have lost the most. It is, in relative terms, much less of a crisis when viewed through the lens of those who had been largely 'excluded' from the economic boom and the orthodox development process (Rigg 1997), whose under-rewarded sweat and toil provided its foundation, and whose daily lives have habitually been mapped out by an everyday crisis of survival. For these people, the post-1997 situation has simply compounded a constant crisis of precarious existence; of 'maldevelopment' (Bell 1996: 49). The hyperbolic use of the term 'crisis' serves to obscure this fact, portraying these people as victims of economic meltdown rather than of the development process itself.

The following discussion will highlight the versatility and dexterity that people on the margins of the economic boom have displayed in using migration as a strategy for coping with and confronting their exclusion from mainstream development. The mechanisms that they have developed and employed in this regard appear to have been cranked up as a means of coping with the additional burdens imposed by the economic downturn. As part of this post-crisis reassessment of development, it is hoped that more attention can be drawn to the failings of orthodox development in respect of those who have been excluded from its spoils, and that lessons can be learned from both the existence and the effective functioning of the coping mechanisms that the migrant population in particular has carefully honed.

MIGRATION: COPING WITH CRISIS

When I travelled to the Northeast of Thailand in the summer of 1998, it was in anticipation of detailing the myriad negative consequences of the involuntary mass return of migrants to their home communities from Bangkok and its extensive hinterland. Banner headlines such as 'Misery for Migrant Millions' (Guardian, 7 January 1998), set against the hyperbolic use of the words 'crisis' and 'meltdown', had helped to form such an expectation. But there was also a strong sense of the rural Northeast being powerless to resist the contagion of what initially had been essentially an urban, industrial and modern sector problem, because of the degree to which the Northeast had been drawn into, and thus had become dependent upon, the Bangkok-centred spatial economy, most particularly through migration. Jonathan Rigg's recent volume on development and modernization in Southeast Asia (Rigg 1997) had suggested, *inter alia,* that many 'rural' people had become 'too busy to farm' as a result of their heavy involvement in the non-farm and metropolitan economies. Whilst the apparently decaying rural and agricultural 'safety net' may not have been of any great consequence while the region's economies were booming, the sudden loss of urban-derived livelihoods on the one hand and the need (because of mass return migration) to support more people from the rather limited fruits of the land on the other, suggested a potentially quite disastrous outcome.

The actual situation, revealed through field visits to 25 villages in four northeastern provinces, was startlingly different to that which had been anticipated. There was no doubting the scale of return migration, with quite possibly more than 1 million migrants having returned at some stage to their home villages in the Northeast. Circumstances had become a lot harder for many rural households. But crisis: what crisis? Many of the study villages had demonstrated a remarkable capacity for absorbing and supporting returning migrants, finding little niches here and there which helped to generate a bit of income. The vast majority of returnees had also apparently managed to slip relatively painlessly back into the rural roles they had previously played. Moreover, the villages were not teeming with reverse migrants, as I had been led to expect: many had subsequently returned to Bangkok and other parts of Thailand to look for work, to take up new jobs as information flowed back as to their availability, or even (accompanied by rather large helpings of humble pie) to return to jobs that they had earlier left because incomes had fallen below levels that were deemed by migrants to be adequate or acceptable. There was no great sense of anxiety or concern about how these rural households were going to manage to cope in the short- to medium-term in the face of the country's wider economic predicament. The overall picture, whilst quite serious and perhaps downplayed by respondents whose lives have regularly centred on coping with crises and difficult circumstances, was nonetheless far from being as bleak as had been expected. It quickly became apparent that a clearer understanding of the rural and migration impacts of the economic crisis requires a deeper exploration of the migration process and the circumstances of those involved. A generic, universal and somewhat exaggerated notion of 'crisis' was not sufficient for this purpose.

The following section will introduce in conceptual terms how the maintenance of rural–urban linkages, particularly through the institution of return migration, has helped to sustain a rural 'safety valve' which has played a crucially important role during the current economic crisis, and in face of the resultant phenomenon of 'migration reversal'. The subsequent discussion will then add some empirical meat to these bare conceptual bones, in the process hopefully adding some depth and insight to our understanding of the social impact of the Asian economic crisis.

RETURN-MIGRATION AND 'MIGRATION REVERSAL'

The first quite obvious point to make here is that the return of rural migrants to their villages of origin is not exclusively related to the current economic crisis. *Return-migration* and *circulation*[1] are long-established and integral features of the movement of *khon isaan* [northeasterners] between the region and their employment destinations, predominantly Bangkok (Lightfoot *et al.* 1983). Initially (i.e., up until about the early 1970s), this was due to the fact that a significant proportion of migratory movements from the Northeast was timed to coincide with the peaks and troughs in the agricultural cycle, with migrants taking mostly temporary jobs (such as *samlor* [pedicab] driving [Textor 1961], casual labouring, etc.) during the long and agriculturally unproductive dry season, and returning to their home villages for the main farming season as soon as the rains arrived, and when the harvest was ready to gather. Even as recently as the early 1990s the population of Bangkok was some 9 per cent larger in the dry season than in the wet season, implying an inflow of up to one million seasonal migrants (Chamratrithirong 1995, cited in Rigg 1997: 182).

As the shape of Thailand's economy began to change in the 1970s, and especially the 1980s, with an increasingly buoyant urban-industrial sector, the country underwent a 'mobility transition' (Zelinsky 1971), with the balance between temporary/circular and permanent/linear movement shifting significantly in favour of the latter. This was particularly associated with the economic situation: as Thailand rapidly industrialized, more factory jobs became available which were readily filled by migrant workers (women especially) but which required a year-round commitment of labour. Thus, a genuinely seasonal pattern of migration did not adequately match the labour needs of an industrializing economy. However, there was also a socio-psychological dimension to this mobility transition: in very general terms, 'rural' northeasterners increasingly came to aspire (either for themselves or for their offspring) towards lives, livelihoods and lifestyles which were more 'urban' than they were 'rural'; if you like, more 'modern' than 'traditional'; and which were supported to an increasingly significant extent by the non-agricultural economy.

Accordingly, while the Thai economy was buoyant, more and more people spent more and more time in and around Bangkok and, to a much lesser extent, elsewhere in Thailand's spatial economy. The pattern of 'circulation' changed dramatically but – of considerable significance to the current discussion – not completely. As we have seen, a fair proportion of migrants would squeeze their farming responsibilities into their urban-industrial itineraries. With few exceptions, migrants would also return home for Songkhran – the Thai New Year – partly out of filial duty, partly because this is a time of considerable fun and joyfulness, and partly to maintain their profile and 'stake' in the village community; partly also, perhaps, as an opportunity for them to recharge their 'rurality' or, paradoxically, emphasize their 'urbanity'.

Where means, time and inclination allowed, migrants might also return at other times of the year (e.g. during festivals and ceremonies). But, in general, migratory movements were for all intents and purposes no longer 'seasonal' and to a significant extent no longer 'circular' in nature. For many, factory (and other) jobs in the modern sector were seen as preferable to farming, urban life as more exciting than rurality, urban incomes and facilities as infinitely better than those available in the countryside, and at least until the crisis hit hard, the prospects of life in the capital region seemed significantly brighter than in the Northeast.

It is largely for these reasons that many rural northeasterners became 'too busy to farm' (Rigg 1997). This does not mean that the farming sector started slowly to shut down – far from it. But a number of adjustments took place which allowed the mobility transition to progress whilst keeping the 'rural' motor ticking over, and not entirely on 'idle'. Thus, where family labour was scarce because of out-migration, farm labour would increasingly be hired in, either from elsewhere in the village or from villages (or even other regions or countries, especially Laos) lying further afield. Whereas in the past the reciprocal tradition of *long khaek* (where villagers would take it in turns to help, and be helped by, others – without payment – during the peak farming seasons) was very widely practised, today this has almost completely disappeared from many parts of the Northeast, either because migration has made it increasingly difficult for households to fulfil their labour obligations to others, or because it has become more convenient and dependable to rely on commercial labour transactions. Significantly, therefore, migration has created opportunities and rewards for non-migrants (often constituting the poorer, landless or land-hungry, and more marginal members of the village community) as well as the migrant population, thereby helping to spread more widely the spoils of rural areas' engagement with Thailand's booming urban-industrial economy. Labour shortages have also pushed up local wage rates. Landless people have often been given access to the land of households where migration has reduced either their ability or inclination to farm it themselves (in line with Rigg's argument: thus, although some people have undoubtedly become 'too busy to farm' this does not mean that the land is not being worked). Mechanization has been another very widespread response, with buffaloes (*khwaay*) being widely replaced by two-wheeled tractors (*khwaay lek*, lit. 'iron buffalo') where means allow. There is also evidence of a shift away from labour-intensive production methods, most particularly the replacement of transplanting of rice seedlings by seed broadcasting (see the case of Ban Don Daeng in the following section). Migration has also been accompanied by significant changes in the demographic and social make-up of villages in the Northeast, with entire cohorts of people (typically those aged between 15 and 35) missing, sometimes for years on end, and with parents or grandparents frequently being required to look after very young children where young married couples are employed in Bangkok but have neither the means nor the opportunity to look after their young children in the metropolis (a process figuratively referred to as *kaan thing luuk*, literally 'throwing away one's children'). Consumption patterns have also changed, both in the village and amongst households that have exposure to the incomes and lifestyles of Bangkok.

The significance of the above as far as the current discussion is concerned is that the characteristics of circulation and return-migration have changed greatly over the last 15 to 20 years – but, crucially, *not* completely. So, the migrant population, in general, has been spending steadily more time away from the village to the extent that migration flows have taken on a very long term, if not 'permanent' character. Thailand's mobility transition seemed to be nearing completion. However, do migrants from the Northeast constitute the 'new urbanites' of today and tomorrow, or do they remain 'rural' sojourners at heart (Nelson 1976)? This question obviously creates a false dichotomy between the city and the countryside, and forces an impossible judgement as to whether people 'belong to' or 'identify with' one realm or the other. The reality is (a) that the two have become increasingly integrated, inseparable and indistinguishable, and (b) that people can, and indeed do, consider themselves as belonging simultaneously to both realms. Return-migration may thus be seen as an important mechanism whereby migrants can enjoy whatever opportunities and rewards (but, of course, also suffer many of the disadvantages) that the city offers, whilst forming a 'bridge' that allows them also to maintain a presence, profile, connection and, possibly, a stake in their home community. This may be because of a long-term intention to return, or because their extended family remains rooted to the village, or because of the felt need for a security back-up where a migrant feels a little bewildered or overawed by the city. Significantly, it may also constitute a rather more conservative measure in case the wheels fall off the urban economy and thus the bottom falls out of their urban world. In the specific case of the *khon isaan*, there is also an ethnic dimension which overlaps with, and confuses, this urban–rural dichotomy: migration to Bangkok also takes them away from their (generally preferred) sociocultural setting into a very different (although by now very familiar) urban world. Return-migration thus constitutes one of several means (see Parnwell and Rigg 1996) whereby *khon isaan* may remain in touch with their ethnic roots.

As we now know, the wheels did indeed fall off the Thai economy. The main point of this chapter is to emphasize that the remaining connections with migrants' home areas, however tenuous they may have become, have played a crucial role in helping a significant proportion of the migrant population to cope with the economic crisis, albeit to a quite variable extent. But, before developing this point, it is necessary briefly to consider the differences between return-migration and what we shall call here 'migration reversal' or 'reverse migration'.

To a significant extent, return-migration is a largely voluntary phenomenon. Migrants and/or those who have an influence on migration decisions will often make a conscious and premeditated decision (for the migrant) to return to their home village at some stage during their 'sojourn' in town, be this for a few days, weeks or even months or years. Less certain, but usually an option (provided a 'stake' is retained in the village, and connections are not severed), is a more or less 'permanent' return to the village at the end of the urban 'sojourn' – be this after a certain savings or consumption (or educational) 'target' has been reached, for marriage and/or child-rearing, rest and recuperation, retirement or whatever. For quite a significant proportion of migrants, this may represent the 'myth of return' – an intention which is never actually realized, although the hope/expectation of return may have a significant influence on a migrant's behaviour (e.g., in respect of sending remittances, returning to visit, use/investment of city earnings, psychological attachments, etc.). People do also, of course, return to their villages at times of personal crisis – when they are made redundant, if they suffer anomie or illness when in the city, if they become HIV positive or contract AIDS, and so on. In this sense, the village (provided a stake is retained, and a familial infrastructure remains) will often be seen and sometimes used as a 'safety net' should things go wrong in town and expectations not be realized. So, whilst the macro-level tendency in Thailand may have taken the form of a mobility transition, with a strong underlying trend towards relentless urbanization and industrialization and associated changes in values, attitudes and expectations, in the Northeast context at least, the general trend will continue to hold considerable scope for a return movement as well as continued out-movement, and failure as well as success. To a significant extent, however, the migrant population retains a reasonable degree of choice over whether or not to move and whether or not to return (even though this is Hobson's Choice in many instances).

'Migration reversal' represents a situation where the element of choice is removed or significantly constrained. It is also used here to signify a situation which affects a mass of the migrant community rather than a smattering of individuals. At its heart is likely to be a significant change in the economic (but also potentially the political, social and even environmental) status quo. A classic example of migration reversal in the past, as far as Thailand is concerned, was the huge volume of return-migration which occurred during and as a consequence of the 'Gulf Crisis' and 'Gulf War' from August 1990 and January 1991 respectively (Stern 1998). The Gulf States – Saudi Arabia in particular – had become a hugely important destination for contract migrant workers from Thailand and several other Asian countries (see Rigg 1989). The build-up to, and eventuality of, hostilities led to the enforced evacuation/deportation and repatriation of tens of thousands of Thai workers, and more than a million workers overall. For few if any of these migrant workers was their premature departure from the Gulf a voluntary or intentional move: many had the greater proportion of their labour contracts still to run, which meant (a) that they had been unable to pay off the sometimes massive debts they had incurred in order to finance their travel and work contracts, and (b) that their savings/consumption ambitions/aspirations had not been realized. Some were able to return to the Gulf after the end of the War, not least to help in the postwar reconstruction of Kuwait and other Gulf states, but others were left hugely indebted and impoverished as a consequence of the enforced mass 'migration reversal'.

In the context of internal population movements, however, reverse migration is neither an option that is necessarily open to everyone, nor an option taken by all to whom it is open. Much clearly depends on the extent to which people are individually affected by changing economic (and other) circumstances, the range of options open to them *in situ*, and the extent to which a return to the rural sector is both a realistic proposition and a desirable option given the alternatives. Often, this is not a straightforward matter, as a certain amount of inertia has also to be accounted for: migrants will tend to stay in the destination area longer than would objectively appear rational, either because they are reluctant to lose the niche they have carved out for themselves there, or because they are reluctant to return to their home areas as 'failures', or because they want to be in the right place when economic recovery finally arrives. There may thus be a noticeable time-lag between the onset and deepening of an economic crisis and the reactionary phenomenon of reverse migration.

In general, rural return is a realistic proposition only for those who have maintained firm connections (e.g. through remittances, return visits, occasional help with farming) with their villages of origin, although even this may not provide a guarantee that reverse migrants would be able to slip easily back into rural society. Thus, reverse migration may involve socio-cultural and socio-psychological as well as economic determinants and variables. In the Thai context, rural people increasingly *prefer* to live in town, irrespective of the economic rationality of doing so. As such, reverse migration will be seen and treated by most as a temporary setback on their long-term journey through life. It is too early for us to be able to assess whether reverse migration in response to the economic crisis in Thailand constitutes a 'blip' or a 'trend', although the former is much more likely than the latter. People will continue to look to the city as their passport to the future; the countryside, just as now, will always be perceived to be there to bail them out, so the risk will continue to appear worthwhile. As we shall see later, in spite of the massive volume of reverse migration, networks of information and contact between the village and the city remain intact and, indeed, have been working overtime in order to help people cope with the current crisis. A more important question in the short term, therefore, concerns the extent to which reverse migration may be responsible for transferring the keenest effects of the economic crisis from urban areas to the countryside, where its effects had hitherto been less strongly felt.

Coping with crisis in Northeast Thailand

The following discussion presents some of the findings of a field investigation into the impact of the economic crisis in rural Northeast Thailand. The field study was conducted during July and August 1998, and incorporated 25 villages in four northeastern Thai provinces (see Figure 12.1): Roi-et and Mahasarakham, two of the poorest provinces in Thailand's poorest geographical region; Buri Ram, because it allowed the opportunity to look at international migration networks; and Khon Kaen, which was intended to represent one of the Northeast's more dynamic and prosperous provinces. The methodology focused upon identifying provinces and villages that official data and anecdotal evidence had suggested contained a fairly significant number of reverse migrants. The study villages may therefore not be considered 'representative' of all types of villages and situations, although various data sources suggested that most villages in the study provinces had been affected to a similar degree, making the following findings broadly indicative of the situation in the region as a whole.

The general situation

Before looking at some of the rates and differential effects of reverse migration, we need to understand why people returned to their home areas in very large numbers. This requires a brief examination of the situation before the economic crisis, and an assessment of how the crisis initially affected the migrant population.

With the exception of the villages in Khon Kaen province which, because of its general level of prosperity pre-crisis, was able to support a quite high level of intra-provincial migration, all other villages had a remarkably high level of migration to Bangkok.[2] In almost every village virtually all households have currently or recently had at least one member who has been working in the capital metropolitan region (Ban Ka Haat, Ban Kheen and Ban Nong Tae, in Buri Ram, had virtually a 100 per cent migration participation rate on a household basis). This may appear to be a remarkably high level of movement, but past work on migration in the Northeast has shown this to be quite typical. None of the study villages (outside Khon Kaen) had fewer than 50 per cent of households involved in migration, and very often this meant that up to half of the entire adult (15 years and above) population of these villages was actively involved in migration at the time the economic crisis broke.

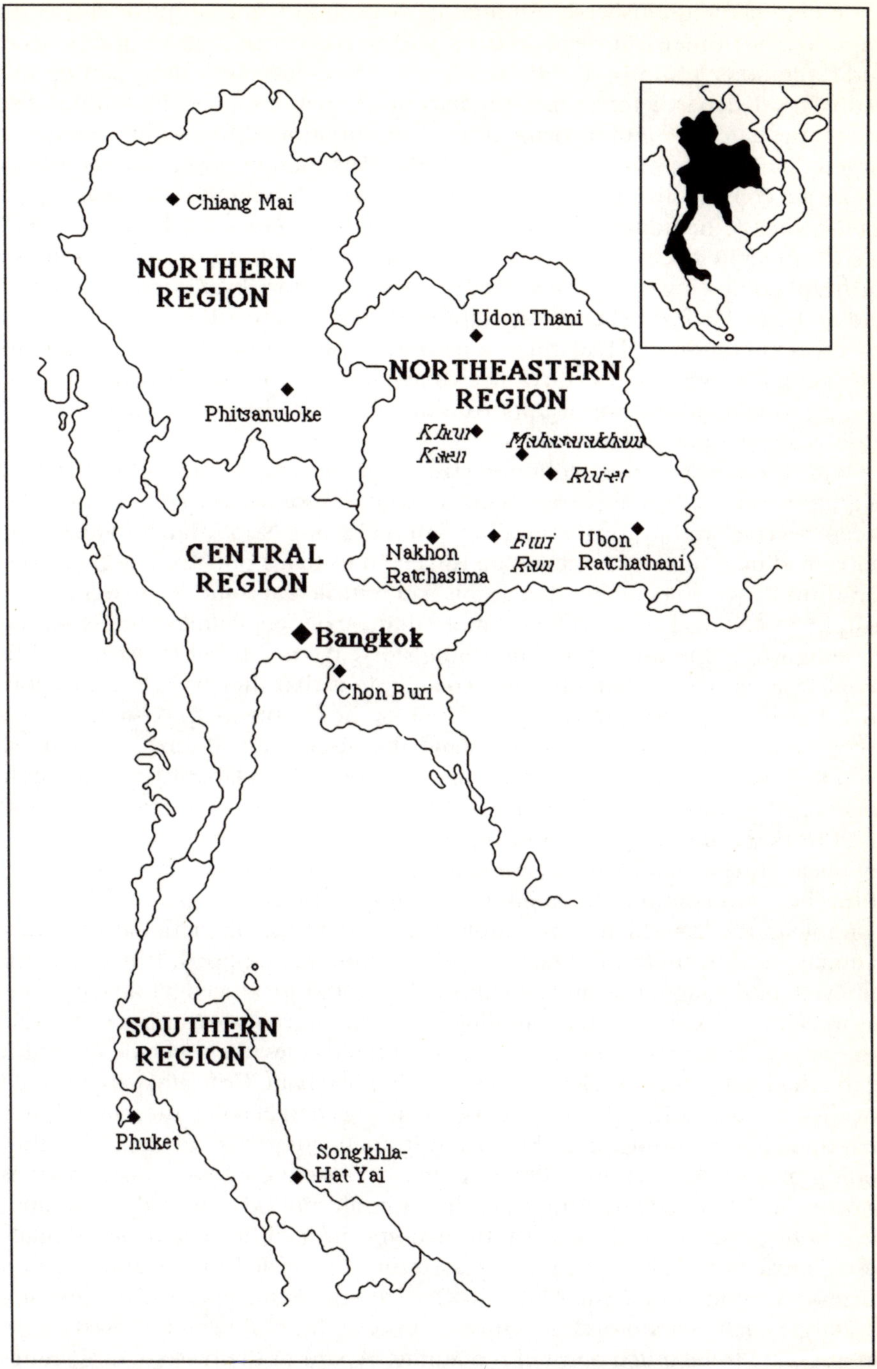

Figure 12.1: Map of Thailand, showing the main geographical regions, principal regional centres and the study locations

In general, migrants were responding to a combination of 'push' and 'pull' impulses: the former (shortages of land, work, income; rising consumption needs and aspirations; growing dissatisfaction with 'rural life' etc.) determining that people needed to look for a supplementary or alternative source of livelihood elsewhere; the latter (economic dynamism, modernization, different lifestyles, etc.) largely determining where in Thailand's spatial economy people would move to. There is a considerable degree of differentiation within migration streams from the Northeast, including both those for whom out-migration is little more than a 'survival strategy' and those who opportunistically aim to use migration as a means of enhancing their already stable and satisfactory livelihoods (McDowell and de Haan 1997; de Haan 1999; Lipton 1980). In general, it is helpful to see pre-crisis migration in Thailand as a natural response to uneven development, with people seeking to leave relatively backward and impoverished areas and moving to take advantage of opportunities that have become available in the country's economic heartland.

With the onset of the economic crisis, equally remarkable rates of reverse migration were reported (care was taken to get respondents to differentiate between 'reverse' and 'return' migration). In Ban Nong Noo (Mahasarakham) 40 per cent of migrants returned; in Ban Kheen (Buri Ram) one-third; in Ban Nong Yen (Buri Ram), 80 per cent of migrants had returned at some stage over the last year; in Ban Nong Tae (Buri Ram), more than 50 per cent; and so on. However, these figures alone do not tell the whole story. We need first to ascertain why people are returning. The obvious explanation is that they have lost their jobs but, in reality, a quite significant proportion of the people we spoke to had effectively given up their jobs. To understand this apparently absurd situation, we need to look at the process of 'redundancy'. Under Thai labour law, employers are obliged to make redundancy payments (equivalent to 5–6 months' earnings) to all workers whom they lay off, regardless of whether or not the firm is experiencing financial difficulties, as many clearly were. However, if a person leaves of his/her own volition, the employer has no such legal obligation. This left a loophole in the law which many employers, large and small, national and international, used to their advantage. Thus, overtime was stopped, fringe benefits removed, basic wages cut, and sometimes factories introduced a four- or three-day working week. This had a crippling effect on migrants' earnings: in general these were at least halved, although we encountered cases where people's monthly salaries had fallen from 12,000–18,000 to only 4,000 baht. Crucially, people could not afford to live in Bangkok where their earnings had become substantially less than their previous outgoings. Significantly, many migrants indicated that they would not work for such low salaries, either because their pay-cuts were seen as an insult which, to avoid losing face, simply could not be tolerated, or because the whole point of working away from home in a difficult and occasionally hostile environment had been the opportunity it provided to save and accumulate money, either for parents or families back home, or for a particular consumption target such as a motorcycle. Once that possibility had been removed, there did not seem to be much point in remaining. Whatever the reasons, large numbers of our respondents had given up their jobs in Bangkok, waiving their rights to redundancy payments, and most had taken the first bus home. Perhaps, at this stage, life in the village looked a lot more attractive than striving to scrape by in the noisy, busy and dirty atmosphere of Bangkok. Possibly, also, people were not yet fully aware of either the depth or the likely longevity of the economic situation.

Not everyone returned, of course, and indeed not everyone was affected in the same way. Construction workers and other unskilled labourers were the first to be affected, followed in time by factory workers. Meanwhile, those who were working in export-oriented firms, where demand for products had actually increased as a result of the baht depreciation, and in agro-industrial enterprises, were largely insulated from the effects of the crisis being felt elsewhere. Many of those who were directly affected sought to struggle on. Those who were living with their families in Bangkok sent spouses and children back to the village in order to reduce their urban expenditure; younger migrants turned to more fortunate friends or relatives in Bangkok to help tide them over until their circumstances improved. Alternatively, where their parents preferred them to stay in town, they depended on reverse remittances from the village. There was, however, virtually no evidence of people turning to the 'informal sector' as a means of surviving in the city.[3]

Having returned to their home villages, however, not everyone stayed. This, in turn, tells us a great deal both about the relative severity of the impact of the crisis on the migrant population, and about the ability of the countryside to provide a safety net for reverse migrants. We shall return to the situation in the village shortly, but first we shall look at the phenomenon of *re-migration.* Given the extent and depth of the economic crisis, and the reasons why people had returned to their home villages in the first place, this is quite an interesting development. There are three overlapping reasons for this, all of which will be examined in more detail later. First, some found that the opportunities and means in the village to support them in unemployment were not adequate. Second, returnees were very active in mobilizing networks of communication, information and support in order to secure alternative employment opportunities in Bangkok and elsewhere.

Third, unemployment and a subsequent return to the home village had caused many migrants to reconsider their earlier reaction when faced with dwindling earnings in Bangkok. Where their rural households could not adequately support one or several unemployed members, or where returnees simply did not fancy a return to their former roles as farmers and villagers, it was considered preferable for these people to return to Bangkok where they could at least earn enough money to support themselves. Thus, attitudes towards migration changed (at least in the short term) from it being a strategy for accumulation to it representing a means of ensuring economic survival. So, salaries of 3,000–5,000 baht per month, at which migrant workers were turning their noses up only a few months previously, were now reluctantly, even resentfully, but certainly resignedly considered to be better than nothing. In the process, several migrants have actually returned to the same factories that they had left only a few months earlier. The general feeling is that migrant workers can no longer afford to be quite so choosy; as such, any complacency which may have crept in during the times of economic boom quite quickly evaporated.

Agriculture and local employment opportunities

We shall now turn to consider what opportunities were available to migrants once they returned to their home communities, and how readily these communities have been able to cope both with the sudden influx of substantial numbers of reverse migrants and the loss of their supplementary income from Bangkok. The following discussion therefore helps to inform our understanding of the local impact of and response to the current economic crisis.

The study villages are quite diverse in terms of their 'normal' degree of self-reliance, and this is clearly likely to have an influence on how people have been able to cope with the migration response to the economic crisis. Thus the villages in Khon Kaen province, most particularly Ban Don Daeng, have long benefited from their close proximity to a dynamic regional centre and the myriad employment opportunities this has provided. As a consequence, these villages have been much less dependent on the Bangkok-centred economy than has been the case with most of the others. Elsewhere, although there have generally been fewer non-agricultural opportunities available locally (hence the quite high levels of out-migration), the villages have generally managed to retain a high degree of self-reliance in terms of agricultural production, in the process creating a quite steady demand for agricultural labour. During the migration boom, labour was often drawn in from other villages and areas to compensate for local labour shortages. Only Ban Nong Noo in Mahasarakham province could be considered not to be self-reliant, and to be very heavily dependent upon the income received from Bangkok. The headman there claimed that some 30 per cent of the households were not self-reliant, and suggested that this figure was likely to increase to 40–45 per cent during the course of 1998 as a consequence of the agricultural crisis. Elsewhere, headmen were of the opinion that the increased engagement with and thus dependence upon the Bangkok economy had not eroded the degree of self-sufficiency/reliance in the study villages; it had simply provided the opportunity to make the 'best of both worlds'. In this way, the economic crisis is seen more as an inconvenience than a disaster. The greatest problem that many farmers faced as a result of the economic crisis was a quite serious cost/price ratio squeeze, where the costs of farming inputs had increased very rapidly whilst the prices they received for their products had been falling.

Given the general lack of alternative employment opportunities, it is the agricultural sector which has come under particular pressure as a means of accommodating the large volume of reverse migrants. In general, migrants have managed to slip back into the local farming system relatively easily, although there have of course been exceptions: in some villages, work teams had become so long-established that, unless one was related to a member of one of these teams, it was extremely difficult for returnees to find work. We should also emphasize that the field visit coincided with the ploughing and transplanting season, and therefore there was a surfeit of short-term work available locally, both in rice cultivation and in harvesting and planting cassava. Nonetheless, reverse migrants were observed to be picking and choosing whether or not they wanted to work on any particular day, and very few people were seen to be working any longer than was dictated by their immediate needs. The same applied to local government construction projects (*Or Gor Chor*; *Or Por Tor*), which effectively constituted part of the government's long-standing rural job-creation programme. People would work for one to two days as the need for cash arose, but few would work every day that work was available as a means of accumulating savings. This take-it-or-leave-it attitude was partly explained by the extremely arduous work that was involved, but it also possibly reflected the fact that people were not as badly off as one might have expected, given the prevailing circumstances. If the crisis had been affecting them more seriously, they would surely have been more likely to have worked at every opportunity available. There were, however, signs of tension where returnees had been rather unwilling to get involved in farm work.

Few of the 100 or so farmers that we spoke to expressed any real sense of desperation and anxiety about their ability to feed themselves. Belts had been tightened and horizons lowered in respect of people's hopes and aspirations for the coming year, but the general view was that, provided there was enough food to eat, the crisis would be manageable. Accordingly, the highest priority was afforded to agricultural production. A respondent in Khon Kaen summarized the situation thus:

> This year, the economic problem is heavy, but at least we can survive – we should have enough food to eat, and we can find enough *rap jaang* [casual work] to get by. But next year, who knows? We can survive in the short term, but if this economic problem continues we will increasingly struggle. Still, as long as we have rice, we can survive.

One widely observed response was that farmers were selling less and consuming more of their agricultural produce, where they were able to produce a surplus.

Sugar cane cutting

An interesting case study regarding alternative non-urban employment opportunities concerned the long-established tradition whereby migrant farmers from the Northeast travel to provinces in the south-central, central and west-central parts of Thailand (e.g. Kanchanaburi, Suphan Buri, Ratchaburi, Pitsanuloke and Petchabun) to cut sugar cane on large farms and estates. This tradition can be traced back at least to the early postwar period, and has long represented a means by which *khon isaan* could supplement their farming incomes by spending two to four weeks in these regions, often earning as much as 300–400 baht per day and saving up to 20,000 baht per trip.

Every year, most typically towards the end of the dry season when farmers' rice reserves and incomes are at their lowest, and thus when they are most prone to financial inducements, agents would come to the villages and offer contracts for cane-cutting in the following season, giving them an advance on their wages if they agreed to sign. The work is very arduous, but the combination of reasonably good wages with high savings potential (there is little opportunity to spend one's wages) and cash up-front when it was most needed, determined that the labour recruitment agents seldom returned without securing the services of all the workers they required. Most have brokers within the village who contact people in advance of the agents' visits to ascertain people's availability and willingness (and possibly also their level of financial desperation). These brokers subsequently liaise with the recruitment agents to facilitate the transportation of the workers to their destinations, and help oversee the workers while on site. Very often the same workers would undertake this kind of work for several years running – these people were always given first-refusal – and many of the villages we visited yielded up to 100 workers each year.

It appears, however, that in 1998 for the first time in recent memory the recruitment agents had not arrived in the Northeast in any real force. The explanation given by local brokers was that the *towkay* (Sino-Thai entrepreneurs) in the destination provinces did not have the requisite capital (*tun*) because of liquidity and banking constraints caused by the current economic crisis (one broker reported that he had been given 170,000 baht last year to use as down-payment money for his villagers; this year he had been given only 80,000 baht). An alternative explanation was that the agents and their brokers were holding back on the downpayments (typically 6,000–7,000 baht per household) in anticipation that there would be no shortage of demand for cane-cutting work as a result of the economic crisis, so there was no need to indenture workers by making down-payments.

Once again, however, no one that we spoke to seemed to be particularly alarmed about the prospect of having no cane-cutting work available later in the year, in spite of the financial squeeze caused by the economic crisis. Given the opportunity that sugar cane-cutting provides for substantial accumulation, it was surprising that people appeared not to be unduly alarmed by the possibility of losing this supplementary income source at a time when they would presumably be desperate for it. This attitude was possibly influenced by a rather complacent feeling that there was adequate farming work available locally, although this was unlikely to last very far beyond the planting season, and could rarely yield the sums of money available from cane-cutting. One respondent gave us a very interesting and insightful explanation: 'many people will not cut cane in spite of its good earnings and savings potential, because it does not suit their preferred way of life.'

Gender

An interesting gender dimension emerged during the course of the field visits. It was already quite well known that the gender composition of the flow of migration from the Northeast had changed rather dramatically as Thailand had undergone an economic (and social) transformation from the late 1970s onwards. Before then, migration flows had traditionally consisted mostly of men linked, to some extent, to the earlier established tradition of *pay thiaw* [literally, to go travelling] which, some argue, represented something of a *rite de passage* for male *isaan* adolescents (Klausner 1981). By contrast, there were major sociocultural barriers to female migration: in simple terms, the daughter's responsibility was to stay at home and look after the house and her parents, whereas sons were pretty much free to do as they pleased – in part they were expected to act as a bread-winner for the family, but in part they were quite at liberty to travel for their own personal experience and economic benefit. From the late-1970s onwards, a pendulum swing occurred in the gender make-up of migratory movements, with women coming to dominate labour flows from the Northeast to Bangkok. It is difficult to know whether the changing structure of the Thai economy, with more factory jobs for which female workers were often preferred, caused some of the traditional sociocultural barriers to female migration to break down, or whether wider processes of modernization and social change had this effect, allowing many more women to apply for jobs in the modern industrial sector. Whatever the reason, female migrants have come to dominate the migration picture in Thailand over the last 15 to 20 years.

In general (although, of course, there are many exceptions to this 'rule'), women are considered to be much more skilful or careful savers, and much more dependable remitters than men – which partly reflects a continuing sociocultural influence on the gender characteristics of migration behaviour. Either because they have historically and traditionally been allowed a much freer rein, it is often seen as perfectly acceptable for a young man to migrate, say, to Bangkok and to fritter away all of his earnings on alcohol, women and other forms of expenditure. Apparently, according to one respondent, the association between male labour migration and the tradition of *pay thiaw* is still very strong in the minds of many young males. An amusing case we encountered was of a young lad who had, in his words, 'taken a long time to learn how to spend money' while in Bangkok, which reflects both the thrift which is generally expected of people living under difficult circumstances in the village, and the need for him to fit in with his male peers when in Bangkok. Women are expected to act much more responsibly in terms of looking after parents and siblings who remain in the village, hence their more dependable remittance behaviour.

Field visits revealed that many more men than women had returned to the village, even though females now constitute up to three-quarters of the migrant community. This was explained by the fact that (in line with the above discussion) women were better able than men to 'tighten their belts' when economic pressures started to build up. Although the economic crisis had made it much more difficult for female migrants to save and remit, they nonetheless were better able to survive in the city than men (we should also bear in mind that women often earn less than men, even if they are doing effectively the same work tasks). It is possible, however, that gender differentials in reverse migration may have been influenced by the different employment characteristics of migrant males and females, with more of the former found in unskilled occupations such as construction, and more of the latter in semi-skilled jobs such as in factories, or working as domestic workers where living costs are provided by the employer. On the other hand, more men than women have the opportunity to move into casual employment, such as *samlor* or taxi driving.[4]

Given the above, it was remarkable to hear the parents of migrants frequently stating that they would prefer, given the choice, the *female* migrants to return from Bangkok and the male migrants to remain there. Although this may appear irrational from a purely economic perspective, mothers in particular expressed the opinion that the young women would be better able to look after their parents and the home than their sons, many of whom became quite a financial burden on their parents the moment they returned to the village.

Social networks and social tensions

A central focus of the conceptual discussion in this chapter was the way that very strong connections have been established and maintained as a consequence of the considerable volume of circulation which occurs between migrants' origin and destination areas (essentially, the Northeast and Bangkok). There is no need to retrace this discussion here, but it is useful to emphasize just how important networks of contact and communication between the two areas have been, both in the ordinary course of migration and as a response to the current economic crisis. Migrants from relatively impoverished households have rarely been able to jump on a bus to Bangkok in the hope of finding a job in the metropolis. The cost of living in Bangkok while looking for work would usually be prohibitive relative to the migrant's economic means. Accordingly, and to a much greater extent than is the case for migrants from other regions in Thailand, especially the Central Region, potential migrants tend to make strenuous efforts to ensure that they have a job to go to before they leave the village. Indeed, a more common scenario is for a job to become available in town, and for migration to be initiated by and for this reason. In the above instances, the communication of information about job opportunities by fellow villagers who are already established in the city plays a crucial role in initiating and, more particularly, facilitating out-migration (see Lightfoot *et al.* 1983). This is also another indication of the continuing connection and commitment of migrants to their home communities.

These networks have played a crucial role in enabling reverse migrants to re-establish themselves in Bangkok after a short period in the village. Even where a very high proportion of migrants have returned to the village, these networks continue to function very effectively, as they incorporate not only people from the same community but also the friends and associates that migrants have established during their sojourn in Bangkok (and also very wide extended family networks – especially the ubiquitous 'uncles' and 'aunties' – which may consist of former migrants who are now long-established 'urbanites'). The existence, persistence, efficiency and sophistication (the mobile phone is now an indispensable tool) of these networks not only constitutes a crucially important factor in helping reverse migrants and their dependants to 'cope with crisis', but also represents a means whereby rural areas may be expected to bounce back quite rapidly as the crisis begins to recede. Almost all of the migrants we interviewed, and their parents, indicated that their return to Bangkok was the first priority once economic conditions started to improve.

Although social relations thus continued to be very strong in this regard, if only for largely functional reasons, there was some limited evidence that social tensions were also beginning to increase as a result of the economic crisis. In most instances these related to a very small number of reverse migrants who had no intention or inclination to help out on the farm, perhaps because they considered themselves to be 'above' and 'beyond' such a menial task. In general, these people constituted sons (rarely daughters) who were not particularly close to their parents, had seldom shown much responsibility *vis à vis* the household economy, and who had been subject to the 'bad influences' of the capital city. One might argue that the social tensions which resulted from these cases were quite well established before the onset of the crisis, to which they could not easily be attributed.

Villages in the Northeast have historically displayed myriad sociocultural mechanisms which have offered a local 'safety net' for, say, the poor/destitute, landless, aged, infirm and disabled. In general, these mechanisms have functioned less effectively as modernization and development have proceeded apace in Thailand, and as a greater degree of individualism has come to characterize rural social relations. It would be nice to speculate that the economic crisis would lead to a renaissance of these communal mechanisms of social support, but at present there are no signs of this being the case. The reintroduction of *long khaek*, for instance, would significantly reduce the financial burden of farming for cash-strapped households (even though it would also lead to a reduction in local paid employment opportunities). Most farmers interviewed indicated that the most important criterion for them today is *convenience*, which the commercial labour market is better able to provide than traditional forms of labour relations. Other traditional forms of sharing, as opposed to selling, also seem destined to remain as historical recollections, as the following short case study of how market relations have replaced social obligations (*bun khun*) illustrates.

Case study

In Ban Nong Noo (Mahasarakham province) there live two old women, aged in their seventies and eighties, who in the past had been traditional midwives. Between them they had delivered most of the middle-aged people in the village, but not many of the young ones who had been able to take advantage of improvements in formal, modern medical provision. Because of their respect for these women, the older villagers would always go to their houses at *Songkhran* (the Thai New Year) to pay respect and to give alms – these women could no longer support themselves financially, so this constituted a form of charity.

The women were also regularly employed by villagers to do tasks which appeared (in rational economic terms) to be unnecessary and meaningless, but in fact constituted a way of the villagers giving them money without it looking like charity. The headman suggested that next year these women would face much greater problems as there was less money available in the village for such forms of charitable giving, with priority quite naturally being given to kin under such circumstances. Also, a dwindling proportion of the village population felt any form of social 'obligation' to these women.

Education

Over the last 10–15 years, more and more households in the Northeast have been both aspiring to and have possessed the means to keep their children on at school. Whereas in the past it was quite uncommon to encounter households where sons and daughters had gone on to secondary and especially tertiary education, today both practices are commonplace. This is consistent with the widely held belief in the Northeast, as elsewhere in Thailand, that education holds the key to a successful and satisfactory economic future.

With the onset of the economic crisis, families responded in two quite different ways influenced, to a large extent, by the means available to them and/or the extent to which they had been directly affected by the economic downturn. Where it was possible, some parents indicated that they planned to keep their children on at school for as long as the economic crisis continued, rationalizing that there was no (appropriate) work available, either in the village or in town.

More typically and less progressively, however, a greater number of respondents indicated that they had taken, or would shortly take, their child(ren) out of school both because they could no longer afford to pay the school fees and other associated forms of expenditure, and because they needed their children to go out to work to help see them through the current crisis. Such a short-term coping mechanism would inevitably have longer-term developmental consequences.

Overseas migration

International migration became a very important issue in Thailand in the immediate aftermath of the crisis, with perhaps a million or so foreign workers facing imminent deportation and repatriation and, simultaneously, the Thai government looking to labour export as a means of clawing the country out of the current crisis. In relation to the current discussion, it also constitutes a major story in its own right, which we can only touch on very briefly at this stage.

A large number of reverse migrants were seriously considering the possibility of international migration as a means of coping with some of the effects of the current economic downturn. Thailand is particularly fortunate in that the countries to which it is currently exporting labour – especially Taiwan, but also Singapore and Brunei (less so Japan and Hong Kong) – have remained largely insulated from the Asian financial crisis. However, international migration is an avenue that is open to only a relatively limited proportion of rural north-easterners. This is primarily because prospective international migrants must find a sizeable capital sum in order to pay for work contracts, agents' fees, travel costs and so on. Initial payments range from around 50,000 baht for a job in Singapore, Brunei and Israel, to a reputed 120,000 baht for a job in Taiwan (up from around 60–70,000 baht only a few years ago). Work contracts are usually for two years and, depending upon the cost of the contract and the migrant's salary, it can take anything from 4 to 15 months before the migrant worker realizes a 'profit' on his/her initial investment. In spite of the social and psychological hardship that many experience as a result of being away from home and in a foreign land for an extended period, international contract labour migration offers rural migrants an opportunity to accumulate savings in excess of 100,000–200,000 baht, which migration to Bangkok could not rival even in the best of times; hence its attractiveness, particularly when the wheels have fallen off the domestic economy.

Although overseas migration is thus a highly attractive proposition in the present circumstances, it is not a realistic option for the vast majority of reverse migrants. Generally speaking, only migrants who have returned from a period of work overseas can afford the outlay for a further contract from their savings. All other prospective overseas migrants must borrow, and to borrow they require collateral: usually land, typically between 10–15 *rai* of land as collateral for a loan of 60,000–90,000 baht. This therefore excludes quite a significant proportion of prospective migrants, particularly the younger ones. Before the economic crisis, loans could be secured from a number of Thai public or private banks, at reasonable rates of interest. As a result of the financial crisis, the banks have ceased to be an important actor in this regard, and the void has been taken over by commercial moneylenders who may charge very high rates of interest – 3–5 per cent per *month* for a secured loan, and 5–7 per cent per month for a partially-secured or non-secured loan.

Middlemen have thus been able to cash in quite strongly on the weakness and desperation of rural people in the aftermath of the crisis. Some of the money-lenders and agents are quite unscrupulous, whereas many of the prospective workers are very poorly informed about prospects and procedures: we encountered many instances where people had been cheated out of their deposits, where promised jobs had not materialized, and where working conditions and salaries did not match the recruitment agents' earlier descriptions. Labour-receiving countries are also now becoming much more selective in the workers they will accept, in terms of age, gender, skills and experience. The Taiwanese government will not accept Thais back on a second contract, so there were many instances where villagers had changed their names in order to return. Prospective migrants complained that, although the Thai government wishes to promote overseas migration as a means of earning much-needed foreign exchange, and to ease the pressure of unemployment at home, very little effective support is being given to the many thousands of returnees in the Northeast who would like to explore this option.

When asked whether, on balance, they would prefer to migrate overseas or to Bangkok, the majority of respondents indicated the latter because there was no need for capital down-payments, whereas others preferred the former because it offered better prospects for short-term capital accumulation. Although going abroad meant separation from one's family for an extended period, it was also considered by some to represent a better means of providing for one's family, and thus the personal sacrifice was considered worthwhile. There was also a generational difference in this regard, with younger migrants expressing a preference for Bangkok, partly because the opportunities for *sanuk* [fun] were perceived to be greater in the capital city than in the more cloistered and alien environment overseas, but also because many were aware of the very hard work and difficult circumstances that they faced in working overseas. There was a general sense that younger male migrants were less burdened by family 'responsibility' than older (typically married) migrants, and thus they were more at liberty to enjoy themselves and less obliged to make personal sacrifices in the course of their migration (Pinit Lapthananon personal communication).

Discussion

This chapter has examined some of the ways in which rural migrants and their home communities in the Northeast region have been affected by Thailand's current economic crisis, and how they have responded. The chapter has generally shown these communities to be coping quite well, not because they have been insulated from the worst effects of the crisis, but because they have become more adept than others at coping with regular crisis situations borne of their exclusion from, or peripherality to, mainstream development. The migration process – most particularly the networks of contact, information and support that help it to function – has over time developed an efficiency and sophistication which has allowed rural northeasterners not only to take opportunistic advantage of the Bangkok/EBMR-centred economic boom, but also to cope quite effectively with the sharp economic downturn, at least in the short term. However, none of this should be construed as indicating that migrants and their home communities have been unaffected by the economic crisis: they have simply managed to cope rather better than many others. The discussion has also shown how vulnerable these individuals and communities will become if the economic situation does not improve quite quickly.

It is to be hoped that the post-crisis 'rethinking of development' will focus not so much on people as victims of crisis, so much as on people as victims of 'development'. The fact that, for some people at least, the economic downturn is more an inconvenience than a crisis is a reflection of their established response to prevailing developmental realities, rather than an indication of their development achievement. The social response to the economic crisis has shown how strong the rural sector has remained in spite of its serious neglect as a consequence of growth-oriented, urban-industry prioritized, centralized, top-down and market-driven development paradigms and policies in Thailand. The countryside and the periphery have played the role of labour source to oil the wheels of industrialization, and now of safety net, as these wheels have ground to a halt. People's resourcefulness has been an important resource for the country. When the economic 'bubble' burst, the attention of millions of people shifted to the countryside: migrants looking for a means of coping; politicians and bureaucrats looking for a sustainable foundation upon which to base the recovery process. It was still there. But when it has fulfilled its function, and the country's economy starts to return to 'normality', will any serious lessons have been learned about the importance of integrated and complementary development? Or will the notions of 'grassroots', 'bottom-up' and 'appropriate' development return once more to the lexicons of speech-writers and plan-drafters – the people who readily spout rhetoric but who largely remain out of touch with reality?

It is certain that the migration system will very rapidly re-establish itself, which is only proper: set against the prevailing development orthodoxy, migration represents the most realistic means whereby poor farmers from the Northeast can claim for themselves a share of the spoils of 'development'. However, unless serious lessons are learned from the developmental causes, consequences and implications of the economic crisis, migration is likely to continue to function as a means of coping, and not as a source of development.

AUTHOR'S NOTE

The period of field research in Thailand was supported by a grant from the Research Support Fund of the Faculty of Social Sciences, University of Hull, which I gratefully acknowledge. I am grateful to Ajaan Pinit Lapthananon for accompanying me during the field visits, to Ajaan Suranart Khamanarong and Ajaan Pitundorn Nityasuddhi in Khon Kaen, and to the people of the Northeast for participating so willingly and helpfully in the study. I would also like to thank the staff of the Asia Research Centre for Migration, at Chulalongkorn University in Bangkok, for the observations and suggestions that they contributed following the presentation of a seminar to the Research Centre on this topic in August 1998.

NOTES

1 Effectively 'circular migration', although the duration of the 'circle' (often, multiple circles/cycles) can be anything from a few days to the entire working lifetime of a migrant.

2 Bangkok here refers not only to the capital city but also the Extended Bangkok Metropolitan Region – the hinterland area of Bangkok into which a great deal of economic activity has spread during the course of the last 20 years (see Ginsburg *et al.* 1991, and McGee and Greenberg 1992, for more details).

3 It is important to emphasize that this study's methodological focus on villages to which migrants have returned from their urban jobs is likely to have significantly under-reported '*in situ*' coping responses in Bangkok, such as turning to the 'informal sector'. Involvement of migrants from the study villages in the urban informal sector was nonetheless found to be negligible, even before the economic crisis.

4 This occupation, according to the many taxi drivers that I spoke with, has been used as a significant source of refuge from the economic crisis, with a consequence that there are many more taxis on the roads now at a time when people are switching to cheaper modes of transport (buses), resulting in seriously restricted earnings for Bangkok's 90,000–120,000 taxi drivers.

REFERENCES

Bell, Peter M. (1996) 'Development or maldevelopment? The contradictions of Thailand's economic growth', in Michael J. G. Parnwell (ed.), *Uneven Development in Thailand.* Aldershot: Avebury, pp. 49–62.

Chamratrithirong, Apichat *et al.* (1995) *National Migration Survey of Thailand.* Bangkok: Institute for Population and Social Research, Mahidol University.

Ginsburg, Norton, Bruce Koppell and Terry McGee (eds) (1991) *The Extended Metropolis: Settlement Transition in Asia.* Honolulu: University of Hawaii Press.

de Haan, Arjan (1999) 'Livelihoods and poverty: The role of migration – A critical review of the migration literature', *The Journal of Development Studies,* 36 (2): 1–47.

International Labour Organization (1998) *The Social Impact of the Asian Financial Crisis,* Technical Report. Bangkok: ILO Regional Office for Asia and the Pacific, Cross-Departmental Analysis and Reports Team.

Jones, Huw and Allan Findlay (1998) 'Regional economic integration and the emergence of the East Asian international migration system'. *Geoforum,* 29 (1): 87–104.

Klausner, William J. (1981) *Reflections on Thai Culture.* Bangkok: Suksit Siam.

Lightfoot, Paul, Theodore Fuller and Peerasit Kamnuansilpa (1983) *Circulation and Interpersonal Networks Linking Rural and Urban Areas: The Case of Roi-Et, Northeastern Thailand.* Honolulu: East–West Center, Papers of the East–West Population Institute, no. 84.

Lipton, Michael (1980) 'Migration from rural areas of poor countries: the impact on rural productivity and income distribution'. *World Development,* 8 (1): 1–24.

McDowell, Christopher and Arjan de Haan (1997) *Migration and Sustainable Livelihoods: A Critical Review of the Literature.* IDS Working Paper no. 65. Sussex: Institute of Development Studies.

McGee, Terry and Charles Greenberg (1992) 'The emergence of extended metropolitan regions in ASEAN: towards the year 2000'. *ASEAN Economic Bulletin,* 9 (1): 22–44.

Nelson, Joan (1976) 'Sojourners versus new urbanites: causes and consequences of temporary versus permanent cityward migration in developing countries'. *Economic Development and Cultural Change,* 24: 721–757.

Parnwell, Michael J. G. (1993) *Population Movements and the Third World.* London: Routledge.

—— (ed.) (1996) *Uneven Development in Thailand.* Aldershot: Avebury.

—— (1998) 'The extended metropolitan region as postcolonialist/orientalist space? musings about Bangkok'. Paper presented to the panel on 'Urban Development in Southeast Asia: City and Countryside' at the Second EUROSEAS Conference, Hamburg, 3–6 September 1998.

—— and Jonathan Rigg (1996) 'The people of Isan, Thailand: missing out on the economic boom', in Denis Dwyer and David Drakakis-Smith (eds), *Ethnicity and Development: Geographical Perspectives.* Chichester: John Wiley, pp. 215–248.

—— and Sarah E. Turner (1998) 'Sustaining the unsustainable? City and society in Indonesia', *Third World Planning Review,* 20 (2): 147–163.

Potts, Deborah (1995) 'Shall we go home? Increasing urban poverty in African cities and migration processes', *The Geographical Journal,* 161 (3): 245–264.

Rigg, Jonathan (1989) *International Contract Labour Migration and the Village Economy: The Case of Tambon Don Han, Northeastern Thailand.* Honolulu: East–West Center, Papers of the East–West Population Institute, no. 112.

—— (1997) *Southeast Asia: The Human Landscape of Modernization and Development.* London: Routledge.

Stern, Aaron (1998) *Thailand's Migration Situation and its Relations with APEC Members and Other Countries in Southeast Asia.* Bangkok: Asian Research Center for Migration.

Textor, Robert (1961) *From Peasant to Pedicab Driver: A Social Study of Northeastern Thai Farmers.* New Haven: Yale University, Southeast Asian Studies Cultural Report Series, no. 9.

Yoshimura, Mako (1997) 'Economic development and foreign labour in Malaysia: Indonesian workers on estates', *Journal of International Economic Studies,* 11: 109–120.

—— (1998) 'Economic development and labour structure in Malaysia in the 1990's', *Journal of International Economic Studies,* 12: 87–99.

Zelinsky, Wilbur (1971) 'The hypothesis of the mobility transition', *Geographical Review,* 61: 219–249.

Newspapers and magazines

Asian Migration News (various issues)

Guardian, 7 January 1998.

Migration News (various issues)

THIRTEEN

The Changing Economic and Urban Situation in Vietnam

Andrea Kilgour and David Drakakis-Smith[1]

Introduction

Vietnam has once again started to make a steady recovery after the economic turmoil of the late 1990s. The Asian crisis has had repercussions and has been blamed for a number of the present problems of the nation, together with socialist inexperience and indecision since transition to a market-oriented economy. This chapter will investigate whether the problems encountered in Vietnam have been predominantly created by domestic practices or are the result of the economic decline in Southeast Asia. The evidence is based on primary research undertaken in Vietnam before, during and after the economic crisis. Although at times contradictory to the views of bilateral and multilateral organizations, this chapter reflects the situation in urban areas at the ground level. This is currently an area where international sponsors and NGOs have limited access.

Background

Vietnam had a population of some 75 million people in the mid-1990s (the current population stands at around 79 million) with one-fifth of these classified as urban (authorities still claim this to be the case at present) by official Vietnamese statistics (GSO 2000).[2] This urban population is heavily concentrated around the two major centres of Ho Chi Minh City and Hanoi, with the two city primacy index of 0.33 being high by international standards (Drakakis-Smith and Dixon 1997). Such high densities have allowed McGee (1995a) to suggest that the areas can be recognized as incipient mega-cities which attract and provide the majority of economic growth and urbanization within the country and allow some comparisons to be drawn with countries including Thailand, within the Southeast Asian region (see Dixon and Drakakis-Smith 1995; McGee 1995b).

Vietnam's later introduction, through the policy of *doi moi*, into the Southeast Asian and global markets, allowed formulation of economic programmes which, in theory, could benefit from the experiences of other Asian countries. The phenomenal rates of growth being achieved by the 'Four Tigers' and ASEAN four provided the perfect opportunity for Vietnam to 'ride on the tiger's back' (see Drakakis-Smith 1999). Most socialist systems of the 'Second World' were in the process of disintegration, removing from Vietnam trading partners, aid and ideological influence. In China reform that increased foreign economic cooperation but retained control over social and political change had proved fruitful and suggested that there were opportunities to maintain some principles of socialist ideology whilst taking advantage of market forces. This was subsequently adopted by the Vietnamese bureaucracy.

Limited reforms had been enforced internally since 1979 (Forbes 1996); however, these had been predominantly directed towards agricultural and rural development. The official introduction of *doi moi* (meaning renovation or transformation) in 1986, opened the economy to global exchange whilst remaining under state control; offering the opportunity for regional cooperation and participation in the Asian growth phenomenon. The reforms were aimed at reducing disparities between rural and urban dwellers by encouraging investment in rural enterprises and, in particular, in agriculture, in the process removing the 'universal poverty that the system [had] produced' (Doanh and McCarty 1996: 68). However, those providing foreign capital preferred investments yielding harder economic returns in urban centres. The admission of Vietnam to ASEAN in 1992, the removal of the US trade embargo in 1993 and the improved US/Vietnamese relations as a result of the Clinton visit have greatly benefited domestic growth. However, the style of growth adopted, and the new reliance on exchange with partners predominantly in Pacific Asia, have meant that Vietnam has been affected by the economic downturn in the region in the late 1990s. The country has been hit in a somewhat sporadic fashion, with the urban centres and those areas linked directly to foreign trade and investment feeling the greatest pressure. Conversely, it might be argued, many of those in the 'universal poverty' of the pre-*doi moi* period, who had not benefited greatly from economic liberalization, were 'shielded' from the problems of the recession and simply continued to cope with the daily difficulties of life as they always had.

VIETNAM IN THE 1990S

Vietnam entered the 1990s hailed as the 'next Asian tiger'; the country was engaged in a process of complete turnaround (Schiffrin 1998a, 1998b), a transformation from hyper-inflation and alleged widespread starvation, to a real growth rate of 7 per cent increased domestic and export markets, and prosperity. Reports produced by academics, the state and various donors focused on growth in incomes, improvements in infrastructure and advancements in communications. It was heavily predicted that Vietnam would take over the low-cost manufacturing mantle within the region, enticing garment and footwear production, monopolized in the recent past by her Asian neighbours, particularly Thailand and Indonesia.

Since this period, Vietnam has indeed experienced rapid economic growth which has been correlated with a re-engagement with global economies and a reduction in control exercised by the state. Vietnam has, as a result of 'opening to the West', attracted eager investors and secured close to US$30 billion in approved foreign investment, although progress was limited prior to 1990 (Vokes and Palmer 1993). Investment, like trade, has come predominantly from the Pacific Asian region, and has been dominated by Taiwan, Hong Kong, Singapore, South Korea and Japan. Whilst the largest shares of foreign investment have been in the primary sector, particularly in oil and gas, rapid growth continued in manufacturing until 1996. Investments in tertiary activities, however, have become more lucrative since 1995, with real estate speculation featuring high on the agenda of new investors in Hanoi and Ho Chi Minh City.

The influx of investment, in particular into labour-intensive manufacturing, from the Asian NIEs and Japan, together with reorientation of trade towards these countries, is a reflection of the continued deepening and widening of the regional division of labour within Pacific Asia (Dixon and Drakakis-Smith 1995), so that patterns of growth and structural change found in Vietnam would appear to be widely related to, and influenced by, broader regional developments. According to the official statistics published by the Ministry of Planning, foreign investment projects have accounted for between 10 and 30 per cent of Vietnam's GDP annually since 1986, remaining the fastest-growing and most influential contributor. Foreign investment, moreover, has sustained Vietnam's current account deficit with capital inflows accounting for 84 per cent (Hornstein 1998). Although figures within this sector have fluctuated as a result of the Asian crisis, foreign direct investment is still regarded as fundamental to Vietnam's development.

The initial vision of the state was to increase foreign investment in rural development. Indeed, Doanh and McCarty (1996) claim that crises in the agricultural sector 'precipitated' liberalization. However, the distribution of foreign investment has focussed closely on the urban centres of Hanoi–Haiphong, Ho Chi Minh City, and to a lesser extent Danang–Hue. By the late 1990s for example, almost 90 per cent of foreign investment was still located in Hanoi and Ho Chi Minh City. The parallel expansion of overseas trade has also become heavily dominated by Pacific Asian countries. In contrast to historical links, where the majority of exports were for Soviet provision, by 1994 the country's Pacific Asian neighbours represented over 75 per cent of Vietnamese trade (Drakakis-Smith and Dixon 1997).

The pace and nature of change in Vietnam in the 1990s have been remarkable, if somewhat uneven; serious institutional and regulatory shortcomings remain, particularly in the financial system, which are contributing to the country's problems. It is possible that the domestic financing of reforms for the first eight years of *doi moi,* prior to the lifting of the US trade embargo and exclusion from broader forms of international finance and development, is now taking its toll. Since the normalization of relations with the IMF and World Bank in 1993, the nature and scope of reforms have been influenced by the conditionalities attached to membership of and loans from international agencies. In this respect, Vietnam has much in common with other developing, in particular Southeast Asian, economies that have been subjected to formal IMF and World Bank Structural Adjustment Policies (SAP) (Drakakis-Smith and Dixon 1997) which have had serious repercussions on social programmes.

URBAN DEVELOPMENT

Historically, the patterns of urbanization within Vietnam have been fundamentally different between North and South and this has contributed to some of the economic and social problems witnessed today. For example, the North followed policies similar to those of the Soviet Union, which aimed to restrict the size of cities, increase manufacturing bases and encourage population movement to sparsely populated regions (McGee 1995a), particularly during the 1954–75 period. Successful agriculture collectivization, too, encouraged people to stay in the rural areas. In contrast, in the South the state concentrated heavily on increasing levels of infrastructure and communications, lost control over population and saw the continued rapid growth in particular of Ho Chi Minh City (formerly Saigon). The country developed an uneven population distribution, always said to resemble a pole with a rice basket at each end; this has to a large extent continued. Since *doi moi*, and the introduction of comprehensive strategies designed to permit the growth of market relations, freer movement of people and wider range of goods have been forthcoming. However, this has increased movement to the two major urban areas and has accelerated urban problems.

The United Nations has estimated that the urban population of Vietnam will rise to 33.8 million by 2010, with shifts of population taken into account (McGee 1995a). This dramatic change from a predominantly rural to a rapidly urbanizing society has been recognized and has affected policies designed by the state and developers. However, the extent to which the change is understood cannot be anticipated. Much of this movement is not accounted for in official statistics and although the Vietnamese changed their definition of urbanization to introduce a new hierarchy of urban settlements to ease administration, they still regard places as either urban or rural, failing to take into account that in areas of rapid growth, urban activities may sprawl beyond urban boundaries (McGee 1995b). In Vietnam as a whole, agriculture is still by far the most important economic activity, a factor which contradicts the usual definition of a country engulfed in a process of rapid urbanization. Indeed, as Oudin (1998) states, between 1987 and 1994 more than three times as many jobs were created in agriculture than in commerce and service, and more than eight times as many as were created in manufacturing and construction.

While it is the case that the principal beneficiaries of recent growth are urban-based and that most poverty is still rural in its location, there is evidence of change within those rural areas with links to the city and/or to export industries. Thus agricultural production of foodstuffs has increased, particularly with the shift towards tenure rights in the mid-1990s, and there is evidence of entrepreneurial activity in rural areas (see for example Meyer-Tran 1998). However, for the bulk of the rural population life remains a hard struggle for survival (Hiebert 1994), barely affected by export-oriented industrialization and more related to the pressures on social services, such as education or healthcare, to become increasingly self-funding. As one report has pointed out, hunger is as widespread in the 1990s as it was in the 1950s, affecting some 25–30 per cent of the population (Centre for Population and Human Resource Studies 1995).

As the financial downturn has progressed, it is assumed that it is those within the export-oriented urban centres who have suffered most from global or regional economic changes. And yet as problems increase in the countryside and exports of agricultural commodities become less important, it is likely that more people will be encouraged to find a livelihood in the urban centres, which will continue to fuel urban population expansion. The Vietnamese have always maintained that this can be controlled. The country's Master Plan includes the containment of population sizes in the major cities and the encouragement of development in secondary towns to prevent population influxes in the urban areas (Tran Dinh Gian 1991), and yet infrastructural improvement advocated by international donors, particularly to transport facilities, serves only to accelerate the shift to the big cities. Add to this rural in-migration, demobilized army personnel, returnees from Eastern Europe or the old Soviet Union, and the 1990s saw the build-up of urban populations from several sources often unaccounted for in official statistics.

In reality, the urban structure has been loosely controlled and the largest cities are already bursting at the seams. An estimate for the population size expected by the Master Plan in Hanoi by 2010 is 4.75 million, yet many have suggested that this population size has already been met and is increasingly rapidly. Peripheral growth, an expansion of squatter settlements, increasing signs of people living on the streets, together with a growing volume of traffic, movement of people and goods, all imply dynamic changes and continuing growth. The spread of industrial, commercial and residential developments along routeways has engulfed already densely populated rural areas and connected smaller centres, tending to confirm McGee's (1995a) opinion that the growth of Hanoi and Ho Chi Minh City is giving rise to rapidly emergent Extended Metropolitan Regions (EMRs) similar to those observable elsewhere in Pacific Asia (Drakakis-Smith and Dixon 1997). Within these EMRs serious problems of congestion, pollution, inadequate drainage, water supply, power and communications have emerged. Urban expansion and redevelopment have been largely uncontrolled, resulting in chaotic patterns of land use. Infrastructure deteriorates rapidly in the wake of the demands placed upon it, and upgrading and maintenance are limited if they exist at all. Provisions supplied by donors do not meet the needs of all, particularly those in the cities without civic registration. In Vietnam, removal of state subsidies and the decision of the bureaucracy to direct economic development towards industrial growth has left the major cities facing these problems. How have their residents coped with these problems?

URBAN ISSUES

The urban employment opportunities and the economic boom provided by foreign investment and entrepreneurial activities in the early 1990s now appear to have stagnated, being heavily linked to the changing fortunes in the Vietnamese economy. In the past the emergence of new manufacturing plants, in particular, has increased the work opportunities and improved the income and lifestyle of some urban dwellers. Today, however, unemployment is rising as those who continue to migrate to the cities fail to find work in the manufacturing sector. The usual response in Vietnam, as elsewhere in Asia, is for these new arrivals to find work in what is often termed the informal sector, frequently in service activities on the street, such as retailing, bicycle repairs or as barbers. However, even this alternative is becoming saturated and migrants are turning to other coping mechanisms to make ends meet. One such mechanism is daily commuting from nearby villages to places where casual labour is hired, primarily in the construction industry. Another alternative is circular migration in which the migrants retain their rural base but stay in the city for weeks or months at a time, as long as work is available, in cheap guest houses, spending less than VND 7,500 on accommodation and food in order to remit money to their rural families (Khan, M. 1997).

The UNDP (1997: 1) suggests that the Vietnamese experience illustrates how 'well-managed market liberalization measures can provide high returns and expand socioeconomic choices so that the poor can better manage themselves in a sustainable manner'. Quite what this means is debatable, and few of the policies devised by the UNDP or similar organizations have provided assistance for the lowest income groups in the cities in the form of self-help programmes or credit schemes. Financial assistance has tended to be directed towards infrastructural improvements and road construction which do not provide relief for the poorest members of society. Other initiatives supposedly directed towards the poor (including the new agreements signed in October 1998 by the British government), fail to acknowledge urban poverty and designate funding for predominantly rural infrastructural projects. Much of this is due to government reports of international organizations which suggest that poverty, and in particular urban poverty, has declined since the introduction of *doi moi*. Much official Vietnamese documentation has suggested that extreme poverty is below 4 per cent in Vietnam's major cities (see UNDP 1997; MOC reports 1995–97; Phan Tam 1997), whilst Dong To Tuan has suggested that only 210,000 persons in Hanoi can be classified as poor (see Drakakis-Smith 1997 for further discussion). Khan (1994) alleges, however, that income disparity between rich and poor widened 3–4 times in the 1970s, 6–7 times in the 1980s, 20 times in rural areas in the 1990s, and forty times in urban areas again during the same period. Many fail to recognize that there is a higher cost of living in the city, raising the poverty datum line considerably higher than for the country as a whole. Padmini (1995) suggests that in general 70 per cent of income in urban areas is spent on food, yet a quarter still remain undernourished. He maintains that as inflation and food prices increase, as they have continued to do, the people in extreme poverty will suffer most. As Table 13.1 indicates, the extent of poverty is greater amongst the urban poor, and fully one-third of urban dwellers in Vietnam have monthly incomes that are below the rural average.

In contrast to reports of international donors, these figures may appear rather disconcerting. Again, this is the result of the methods of coordination between state, NGOs and donors who produce projects for areas approved by the state. The residents of these areas have civil registration and formal employment, even if this is low paid. There remain, however, people who are unaccounted for within census data, without registration and employed in casual, informal employment, who live in houses without even the most basic of services. The introduction of IMF and World Bank development strategies has exacerbated this problem as the Vietnamese government is forced to follow guidelines leading to the readjustment of policies and the reduction of subsidies

Table 13.1: Vietnam: average monthly income in VND 1000s, 1995

	Total		Urban		Rural		Hanoi	HMC†
Rich	530.2	(4.1)*	615.0	(12.4)	429.8	(2.3)	-	-
of which: very rich	743.7	(1.8)	834.2	(6.3)	607.1	(0.9)	-	-
Upper middle	188.9	(17.2)	218.4	(33.2)	173.5	(13.7)		
Middle	100.7	(36.4)	130.0	(26.3)	96.3	(38.7)	-	-
Lower middle	65.8	(22.3)	92.0	(18.0)	61.4	(23.2)	-	-
Poor	40.9	(20.0)	56.9	(10.1)	39.3	(22.1)	-	-
of which: very poor	27.5	(4.4)	42.1	(3.3)	25.2	(4.6)	-	-
All	119.0	(100.0)	220.3	(100.0)	94.4	(100.0)	163.4	315.6

†HMC = Ho Chi Minh City

*Figures indicate the average monthly income of each group, presented in thousands of VND. Figures in parentheses indicate the percentage of the population group in question which earns the given income.

Source: GSO (1995)

for many basic needs, including food, education and housing. The poorest levels of society are forced into marginalized, environmentally hazardous areas, with increased chances of ill-health and with fewer opportunities to earn a living. Pham Tan (1997), has suggested that this encourages more promiscuous forms of employment in order to compensate for the lack of official work. In contrast, the better educated, particularly men, tend to be absorbed into the state sector, creating a socialist middle class whose quality of life is not only better than most but is well protected by the system (see Nørlund *et al.* 1995; Oudin 1998).

The rapidly growing urban population has, therefore, increasingly affected the position of planners and residents alike in response to the increasing housing and environmental problems witnessed in Vietnam during the early 1990s (see Kilgour 2000). Even in the 1980s squatters were beginning to appear, despite the regulations governing migration, and by the mid-1990s these movement controls had broken down almost completely. New migrants to Hanoi often relied on families or friends rather than the state to provide assistance in finding work and shelter, and this has continued. Added to this is an increasing 'floating population' with no permanent residence in the capital. These tend either to sleep in the rough or pay small rents to share rooms with up to 20 others in similar situations, often working harder and for smaller salaries than previously earned in the countryside. However, the growing urban population is only one factor affecting housing development. Administrative mechanisms for housing have for many years discouraged state employees from developing their own housing or adding new buildings to the housing stock. Land-use administration has followed a top-down approach and policies have become accountable only since the implementation of *doi moi* (Drakakis-Smith and Kilgour 1998). The impact of the population growth alone has also been enormous for the environmental prospects of the cities. Most green spaces have been built over and in some districts of Hanoi construction densities cover as much as 85 per cent of the land surface. Moreover, most of the existing housing stock and related services are in poor condition – creating health and environmental problems. Those built by the state have not been maintained for decades, because revenues from rents were too low, whilst tenants were prevented from making their own improvements. For those with privately constructed homes, they often cannot afford to repair them or keep them well maintained owing to the increasing costs of living in urban areas and the need for earnings to be spent on necessities. In all, some 55 per cent of Hanoi's housing is classified as 'needing repair' or 'not safe' (Drakakis-Smith and Dixon 1997).

Discussion of affordable housing broadens the debate on coping strategies into environmental issues, particularly those related to the 'brown agenda'. Thus, pressure on water supply from both residential and industrial sources has meant that aquifer reserves have fallen, in addition to becoming more polluted, with growing consequences for consumer health. FINNIDA (Finnish International Development Cooperation Agency, at this writing no longer in existence as such, but now subsumed under the Finnish Ministry of Foreign Affairs), the World Bank and the city authorities optimistically planned to provide water to all households in the city centre area of Hanoi by the end of 1999 within a meter system. This has caused many problems both in implementation and operation, as in areas of the city where water is shared from a community pipe there is presently no charge (HWBC 1998). Residents resent the fact that their supply will now be accountable.

Meanwhile, the discharge of waste water, which in Hanoi is combined with sewage and industrial liquid waste, uses a system built in the 1930s and services only 60 per cent of the city. Much of this is in poor condition and is built dangerously close to drinking water pipes. Leakages and run-off from illegal connections create mixes of the two and may be attributable to an increase in the number of water-borne diseases in areas where illegal tapping is present. Furthermore, approximately 25 per cent of the waste water is discharged directly onto the ground or into water bodies which, together with leakages from pipes, results in considerable pollution of aquifers (Drakakis-Smith and Dixon 1997). In the suburban areas of the city where newer sub-standard settlement has occurred, the situation is even worse, with some 65 per cent of waste water going directly into the ground. The four main rivers that drain Hanoi are all seriously polluted, as are most of its lakes. This is caused largely by the discharge of domestic and industrial waste water and solid waste. Not surprisingly, water-borne diseases, such as malaria and diarrhoea, are widespread, affecting labour force capacity and attendance, particularly as ability to pay for healthcare has decreased. In addition, poor drainage also results in frequent flooding. Hanoi's flat topography, together with poor dyke maintenance, results in about one-third of households suffering annual floods in the rainy season, further contaminating water supplies and highlighting the inadequacies of the outdated drainage system.

Other infrastructural service problems which affect the urban environment relate to refuse collection. Half of Hanoi's refuse is organic, so that fermentation and decay occur rapidly and daily collection is necessary. Significant improvements in collection have been made by URENCO (state-owned waste removal company), but estimates continue to suggest that only 60 per cent of the waste of the central city is collected each day (Viet Le Hung 2000). This has been noted by interviewees as a significant improvement which has occurred during the last few years. The majority of the clearance, however, is done manually rather than mechanically, by women who are allocated streets to be cleaned daily. In the suburban areas such services are more scarce, resulting in some 44 per cent of waste being disposed casually onto the ground or into a water body. Most waste is simply dumped, untreated, at three landfill sites, which support the scavenging activities of a number of people (di Gregorio 1994). Interestingly, many of these scavengers are themselves circular migrants, seeking to use both rural and urban activities to support their families.

Air pollution too has worsened, but although industrialization has contributed to situations where two-thirds of the households surveyed by the Ministry of Construction complained about noxious smells, most complaints relate to the immediate environment of decaying wastes and inadequate sewerage. Another air pollution problem affecting Hanoi is dust, with levels ranging from two to seven times permitted levels (Khien 1996). Much of this relates to increased motorized transport and the continued use of coal and charcoal for cooking and heating in many households. The increase in the number of motorbikes is also a source of pollution emission. Low-quality Chinese and Russian bikes, although being replaced by up-to-date Japanese models by the urban bourgeoisie, continue to be used and prized by the lower classes. As a result, highly polluting vehicles are still used as transport by the majority of people. Post-crisis, it is anticipated that an increase in lower quality transport will occur, as people still try to maintain new individualist aspirations (see Fforde 1998).

Quite clearly the growth of industry has also been an important factor in increased pollution levels, but the sheer increase of population and inadequate infrastructural framework existing in the city are of equal significance. Indeed, domestic pollution is suggested to outweigh that of industry at present (Mol and Frijns 1997), although primary research has revealed this is not the principal concern of all city residents (Kilgour 2000). This would appear to imply that domestic environmental problems, such as improved water supply, sanitation and rubbish collection, ought to receive greater priority than industrial pollution controls, or at least equal priority. There are few signs that this is occurring as, although guidelines have been issued, in reality both national and municipal concerns appear to relate more to industry and the work of international donors occurs only in the most visible areas of the city. As Satterthwaite (1997) notes, this is not an unusual situation in the context of developing countries, where elite and foreign concerns, which improve the country's economic position, receive much greater priority than the day-to-day problems of the urban poor.

The Worsening Urban Situation

With foreign-owned factories laying off employees as export orders tumble and with the already growing problem of underemployment in the countryside, many additional people are seeking work in the cities. Almost inevitably this adds to the burden on urban resources because of the numbers who fail to find work. Soaring unemployment has been witnessed in the late 1990s, possibly as both a direct and indirect response to the Asian crisis, but, nevertheless, causing problems within the capital in particular. Unemployment figures, although unreliable, set the official number of jobless for Vietnam at around 6 per cent and in Hanoi at approximately 9 per cent (up from 7 per cent for 1996) (GSO 1999). This would be the highest since reforms began (Marshall 1998), but is likely to be an underestimation as even in 1994 when Vietnam was enjoying economic growth, T. Khan (1994) and Hiebert (1994) suggested that the actual levels were around 15–20 per cent. The problem could worsen soon as the State is being encouraged to streamline the labour used in government enterprises. Economists have suggested that at least half of those employed in the state sector are unnecessary, threatening further increases in the numbers of urban unemployed (Schiffrin 1998a). The already buoyant informal sector in the cities, as noted earlier, may find it difficult to absorb such pressures, so that new forms of migration may be the eventual response.

Reductions in stable employment affect other social issues and exacerbate poverty. Lack of stable employment affects the sustainability of the household in a deteriorating economic situation. Problems related to food sufficiency, health, education and welfare are consequently more apparent (Kilgour 2000).[3] Wider social issues emerging from this include crime and prostitution (as the informal sector expands into less desirable areas) and the growing number of homeless, with both legal and illegal migrants often selling homes in order to subsidize falling wages and increasing their susceptibility to health risks by moving to more marginal, environmentally unsafe areas. Families are being left in poverty as there are few social benefits to soften the blow of unemployment. After tasting a more comfortable life, it is possible that city dwellers may react more strongly to a downturn than will the Vietnamese rural poor, who have seen fewer benefits since *doi moi*. Some have predicted that the results of the downturn could produce enough serious unrest to cause concern for the government, but as yet this has not happened to any great extent – a possible legacy of socialist societal structure. Uprisings have admittedly been curtailed in rural provinces, but it is unlikely that trouble in the cities could be hidden as effectively from the public eye. And yet the possibility of tension is growing. Consumer prices in Vietnam rose by as much as 1 per cent in one month according to the official GSO data, with a yearly rise of 9 per cent over 1997, and were predicted to worsen subsequently, largely due to the rising price of rice. Further protests against the construction of additional landfill sites in Dong Anh, Hanoi, disrupted the city for three days in October 1999 (see Kilgour 2000).

The housing situation too continues to show few signs of improvement. Some recent private NGO and state projects have tried to improve the quality of housing for slum dwellers in Ho Chi Minh City, but this has helped only a minority

(Coit 1998). As migrants continue to swarm into the major cities and the middle classes face the threat of redundancy, more are becoming marginalized in the search for accommodation or land. The situation is likely to worsen despite recent efforts by the state and international sponsors. The resulting environmental pressures can only be detrimental to the efforts of organizations aiming to provide cities with services, including clean water and waste removal. If residents cannot afford to pay the new charges, they will illegally tap resources once again in order to survive. Thus, although on paper the situation is officially reported to be improving, in reality the situation is improving for only a number.

Conclusion

Vietnam has to a large extent been shielded from the worst effects of the Asian crisis because its associations with the global economy are not as strong as those of neighbouring countries. Reductions in export growth and the withdrawal of foreign investment, however, indicate that the crisis may yet still affect the country in a more dramatic fashion than has been previously anticipated. Undoubtedly the regional economic downturn has both directly and indirectly affected growth and development within the country, but Vietnam cannot blame the Asian crisis entirely for the problems it faces. Much financial support has come from the regional market, and Asian investors are now choosing to close or stay away en masse as they gradually try to gradually recover from the crisis themselves (Hornstein 1998). However, events from as early as 1996 indicate that reductions in investment and curtailment of growth were likely to occur anyway, as the Vietnamese government failed to relax certain regulations related to foreign corporations. In fact, the value of newly pledged foreign capital has declined in real terms each year since 1994, and utilization of foreign capital has also decreased. Therefore, although the Asian crisis is clearly preventing the arrival of new foreign initiatives, persistent inefficiencies mean that the Vietnamese themselves have done little to ensure that previous levels of FDI were maintained. It is likely that FDI would have slowed regardless of the regional economic crisis, but possibly not to the extent currently seen in Vietnam, particularly regarding export growth. This cannot be blamed entirely on the state. Their desire to meet the demands of IMF regulations (see Kolko 1997) encourages the blame to be placed at the door of Vietnam's global reformers. In spite of this, international agencies are keen to overlook these major issues and imply that neoliberal reform and economic transition have proved a resounding success.

So how do we relate the regional economic crisis to the escalating problems of poverty that are evident in both rural and urban areas? The response must be that uneven development has been present in Vietnam for the last ten years and that much of the distress evident in the country has been affecting those not incorporated into the economic boom. Those directly affected by stagnating economic investment and growth are relatively few in number compared to the millions in the rural areas still facing threats to their subsistence, and to those who have migrated to the cities in search of work only to be trapped in their informal sectors, in terms of housing, work and meeting basic needs. Of course, in a way, those in the urban informal sector are affected by what happens to the urban industrial economy, since many are engaged in activities that filter through to its support. However, there are signs that the ability of the urban informal sector to absorb ever-increasing numbers is being affected by stagnation in the economy as a whole.

In this sense the coping strategies of the rural and urban poor in Hanoi and Ho Chi Minh City are no different from those practised by similar groups in Mexico City or Lagos. Their situation is the result of economic development, not political ideology. More children are kept out of education and put to work in the informal sector (school attendance rates are down, particularly in the later age groups (T. Khan, 1994). Fewer can afford to pay for healthcare services and turn to traditional herbalists. Circular migration and daily commuting have increased in order to minimize living expenses in the city. Families eat less – malnutrition rates are still too high in a country whose food exports are increasing. Official reports may suggest the situation is improving, and it may be for some. However, the situation is not improving fast enough and the economic downturn and removal of FDI are further reducing the opportunities for others to climb on the development ladder. The greatest problems are likely to occur not in the most impoverished circles, but for those who have started to benefit from economic transition and who lack in social safety nets.

It is these coping strategies which need to guide future policy directions in poverty alleviation. Simply stating that maintaining growth will reduce poverty, as the DFID (Department for International Development) Country Strategy Paper for Vietnam does (DFID 1998), is not an adequate response if the societal impact of hitherto spectacular national economic change has been so shallow. The implementation of much stronger social and spatial redistribution policies is required if this is to be achieved.

Notes

1 David Drakakis-Smith participated in writing the early drafts of this chapter, but unfortunately died of a serious illness several months before publication of the volume became a reality.

2 The Vietnamese definition of urban does not include those partaking in agricultural practices in or around the urban centre, or those living in the city without legal residence.

3 For more detailed discussion on urban sustainability see Drakakis-Smith (1995–97).

References

Centre for Population and Human Resource Studies (1995) *Analysis, Evaluation of the Relation between Population, Migration, Human Resources and Employment.* Project VIE/93/P02, Hanoi.

Coit, K. (1998) 'Housing policy and slum upgrading in Ho Chi Minh City', *Habitat International,* 22 (3): 223–280.

Dang To Tuan (1996) 'Housing for the poor in Hanoi, Vietnam', *Ambio,* 2 (25): 113–114.

DFID (1998) *Vietnam: Country Strategy Paper.* London: Department for International Development.

di Gregorio, M. (1994) *Urban Harvest: Recycling as a Peasant Industry in North Vietnam.* Occasional Paper no. 17, East–West Center, Honolulu.

Dixon, C. and D.W. Drakakis-Smith (1995) 'The Pacific Asian region: myth or reality?', *Geografiska Annaler*, 77: 75–91.

Doanh, L. D. and McCarty, A. (1996) 'Economic reform in Vietnam', in SF Naya and J.L.H. Tan (eds) *Asian Transitional Economies.* Singapore: ISEAS, pp. 99–153.

Drakakis-Smith, D. W. (1995–97) 'Third World Cities: sustainable urban development, I–III', *Urban Studies*, vol. 32 (4–5), vol. 33 (4–5) and vol. 34 (5–6).

—— (1999) 'Cities in the Pacific Rim', in R. Paddison and W. Lever (eds), *Handbook of Urban Studies.* London: Sage.

—— and C. Dixon (1997) 'Sustainable urbanisation in Vietnam', *Geoforum*, 1: 21–38.

—— and Kilgour, A. L. (1998) 'Poverty, housing and the environment in Hanoi'. Paper presented at the Second EUROSEAS Conference, September 3–6, Hamburg.

Fforde, A. (1998) 'Handouts won't help Vietnam', *Asian Wall Street Journal*, 16 September.

Forbes, D. (1996) *Asian Metropolis – Urbanisation and the Southeast Asian City.* Melbourne: Oxford University Press.

GSO (1995) *Statistical Yearbook 1994.* Hanoi: Statistical Publishing House.

—— (1997) *Social Indicators in Vietnam.* Hanoi: Statistical Publishing House.

—— (1999) *Social Indicators in Vietnam.* Hanoi: Statistical Publishing House.

—— (2000) *Social Indicators in Vietnam.* Hanoi: Statistical Publishing House.

Hiebert, M. (1994) 'Stuck at the bottom', *Far Eastern Economic Review*, 13 January: 70–71.

Hornstein, A. (1998) 'Vietnam is feeling the pressure', *Bridge News*, (Hong Kong) 21 August.

HWBC (1998) personal communication with Nguyen Hung Vy, Deputy Director Hanoi Water Business Company, Hanoi.

Jamieson, N. (1993) *Understanding Vietnam.* Berkeley, CA: California Press.

Khan, M. (1997) 'Following the yellow brick road', *Vietnam Economic News*, 36: 47–48.

Khan, T. (1994) 'Social disparity in Vietnam', *Business Times*, 24 September.

Khien, N. D. (1996) 'Current environmental condition in Vietnam'. Paper presented to the Euroviet III workshop, University of Amsterdam.

Kilgour, A. L. (2000) 'A Study of Low-Income households and their Perceptions of Environmental Problems during Rapid Urbanisation in Hanoi'. Unpublished thesis, University of Liverpool, UK.

Kolko, Gabriel (1997) *Vietnam: Anatomy of a Peace.* New York & London: Routledge.

Marshall, S. (1998) 'With layoffs soaring, Vietnam braces for unemployment crisis', *Asian Wall Street Journal*, 22 September.

McGee, T.G. (1995a) 'The urban future of Vietnam', *Third World Planning Review*, 17 (3): 253–277.

—— (1995b) *The Mega-urban Regions of Asia.* Vancouver: UBC Press.

Meyer-Tran, E. (1998) 'Emerging capitalism: new entrepreneurship in rural Vietnam'. Paper presented at the Second EUROSEAS Conference, Hamburg, Sept. 3–6.

Ministry of Construction (1995) *Urban Sector Strategy Report* (draft), Hanoi.

Mol, A. P. J. and J. Frijns (1997) 'Ecological restructuring in industrial Vietnam: The Ho Chi Minh City region'. Paper presented to the Euroviet III workshop, University of Amsterdam.

Nørlund, I. (1993) 'The labour market in Vietnam: between state incorporation and autonomy', in J. D. Schmidt, J. Hersh and N. Fold (eds), *Social Change in Southeast Asia.* Harlow: Longman, pp. 155–182.

—— Gates, C. and Vu Cao Dam (1995) *Vietnam in a Changing Word.* Richmond: Curzon Press.

Oudin, X. (1998) 'Labour restructuring in Vietnam since economic reform'. Paper presented at a NIAS workshop on 'Asia's Changing Labour Laws', NIAS, Copenhagen.

Padmini, R. (1995) Report on Social Aspects, *Vietnam Urban Sector Strategy Review.* TA 2148–VIE, Manila: ADB.

Phan Tam (1997) *Shelter and environmental improvement for the urban poor.* Hanoi: International Development Research Centre and Hanoi Architectural University.

Sattertwaite, D. 'Sustainable cities or cities that contribute to sustainable development', *Urban Studies,* 34 (10): 1667–1679.

Schiffrin, A. (1998a) 'IMF: Vietnam balance of payments under significant pressure'. 23 September, Agence-Presse, Hanoi.

—— (1998b) 'Vietnam faces hurdles in restructuring commercial banks'. 9 September, Agence-Presse, Hanoi.

Tran Dinh Gian (1991) *The National Urban Development Strategy.* Hanoi: Hanoi Publishing House.

UNDP (1997) *Some Lessons Learned in Supporting the Transition from Poverty to Prosperity.* UNDP Staff Paper, September. Hanoi.

Viet Le Hung (2000) *Pollution Analysis of Hanoi Urban Centre.* Hanoi: Department of Chemistry, University of Hanoi.

Vietnam News (1998) Press Highlights: 9 September – 16 October.

Vokes, R. and Palmer, L. (1993) 'Transition in a centrally planned economy: the impact and potential of economic reform in Vietnam', in C. Dixon and D. Drakakis-Smith (eds), *Economic and Social Development in Pacific Asia.* London: Routledge, pp. 169–196.

FOURTEEN

Pastoral Adaptation and Subsistence in Mongolia's 'Age of the Market'

David Sneath

In the 1990s the Mongolian state rapidly implemented a series of reforms designed to create a competitive market economy based on private property. At that time a bright economic future was predicted for Mongolia – the government talked of it becoming the fifth Asian tiger within five years (Odgaard 1996: 113). The reforms included the wholesale privatization of the economy, including the dissolution of the collective and state farms. The reality, however, proved to be a bitter disappointment for most Mongolians, who saw a collapse in their living standards, declining public services and rising levels of unemployment and crime.

This chapter will outline the economic reality facing rural Mongolians in the 1990s, and the impact of the 1998 Asian crisis on the national economy. This is the background for an examination of the coping strategies pastoralists employ, based on a study of two localities in the Northern province of Hövsgöl in 1996. The ability of herding families to cope with the economic crisis varies widely, even within remote rural districts, as differences in wealth between rich and poor have widened. But most families continue to rely on social networks, particularly kinship relations, and long-standing methods of self-provisioning to survive amid worsening economic conditions. However, the dissolution of the state and collective farms did not represent a straightforward return to some timeless 'traditional' form of pastoralism. The collectives had also organized large-scale pastoral operations, which in some ways resembled those conducted by pre-revolutionary authorities and elites in the past. Indeed, the inextricable linkages between the political and economic spheres long pre-dates the state socialist era of pastoral Mongolia, and the disappointing results of reform force a re-examination of the thinking behind the privatization campaign.

The Doctrine of Reform

As Nolan (1995: 75) points out, the economic advice that Western experts gave to former Soviet-bloc nations was similar to the stabilization and structural reform packages recommended for poor countries by the IMF and the World Bank in the 1970s and 1980s. It including price liberalization, cutting state subsidies and expenditure, currency convertibility, privatization of public assets and the rapid introduction of markets.

The central theme of this new discourse was the idea of a 'transition' from what was seen as an inefficient and wasteful socialist system to the presumed dynamism of a market economy. Central to this thinking was the more or less explicit assumption that the economic sphere could and should be emancipated from the political structure, and furthermore, that the economy has a latent 'natural' form, composed of private property coupled to the market, which would tend to generate growth if given the chance. In this discourse the economy was cast as an object upon which the political system acted; in particular it could act negatively so as to distort the economy's natural form. In Asian Development Bank literature, for example, the description of pre-revolutionary Mongolian society was based upon the notion that the economy was being prevented from attaining its true potential because it lacked certain features found in market economies – such as the private ownership of land.[1] The state socialist system was also seen as preventing the growth and development of an embryonic market economy. Much of the development economics literature of the time reflects this sort of imagery. The World Bank (1994: 12) notes that state controls on foreign exchange had created 'pervasive distortions'. The 'nascent private markets' and small enterprises would 'emerge', almost like natural forms, when state policy provided them with a conducive climate (see Asian Development Bank 1992: 103; World Bank 1994: 23; Nolan 1995: 82). The basis of the market was conceived of as private property, so privatization was considered the key to economic reform.

In 1991, acting on the advice of western development agencies, Mongolia began a huge programme to privatize state and collective enterprises through the issue of share coupons (*tasalbar*) (Asian Development Bank 1992: 86–88; World Bank 1994: 9). The government was also urged to withdraw from the economic sphere, so as to allow it to develop properly in line with the market forces that were well understood by neoclassical economists. In 1992 the Asian Development Bank complained that

> the Government continues to issue mandatory state orders under which various public agencies procure at a fixed price established by the Government. Local price commissions also continue to interfere with market forces. The Government should, therefore, abolish these commissions and phase-out the system of mandatory state orders (Asian Development Bank 1992: 88).[2]

The Asian Development Bank and World Bank also called for the privatization of land, and throughout the 1990s they urged the Mongolian government to pass a highly controversial law to this effect.

The results of economic reform

The period of 'transition' saw Mongolia plunge into economic crisis. The worst disruption occurred in the early 1990s when incomes plummeted. The World Bank estimated that real wages halved between 1990 and 1992, and then declined by a further third in 1993 (see World Bank 1994: 19).[3] The percentage of the population living below the poverty line at that time shot up. Official figures showed that income-poverty increased from zero per cent in 1989 to 27 per cent in 1994, and this figure may well be an underestimate (see Griffin 1995: 31–33; World Bank 1994: 35). Social services were slashed; real expenditure on health services decreased by 43 per cent from 1990 to 1992, the education budget was cut by 56 per cent (World Bank 1994: 41; Robinson 1995: 4). Further reductions followed and social service spending has remained low since that time (UN Systems in Mongolia 1999: 5).

The official figures for unemployment increased rapidly in the early 1990s, from 10,300 in 1989 to reach 72,000 in 1994 – over 8 per cent of the labour force. These figures were probably an underestimate, however, and the actual level has been estimated at 10–12 per cent (Asian Development Bank 1994: 14; von Ginneken 1995: 47). By 1996 the official total had risen to over 80,000, and actual unemployment was estimated at 15 per cent in 1997.[4] The rate of inflation shot up and stayed in triple figures from 1991 to 1993, only gradually falling since then.

In part this economic crisis was due to what Griffin described as three external shocks – the aid shock, the trade shock and macroeconomic management shock. The huge flow of Soviet aid (which is thought to have amounted to as much as a third of the GDP or more)[5] was reduced in 1989 and stopped altogether in 1991. At this time the Soviet trading bloc, the Council for Mutual Economic Assistance, also collapsed and Mongolian trade fell accordingly (exports declined from US$832 million in 1989 to 370 million in 1991). Soviet advisors also withdrew from Mongolia at this time, and the government had to manage with fewer experienced planners and administrators. However, the place of Russia as an aid donor and economic advisor was taken over, to some extent, by Western nations, Japan and international financial institutions, which between them provided support equivalent to about 15 per cent of GDP in 1991 and 1992, about half the shortfall (Griffin 1995: 6). By 1996 this aid had risen to around 25 per cent of GDP (Bruun and Odgaard 1996: 26). The three external shocks can only be held partially responsible for Mongolia's crisis. As Griffin argues, one of the reasons for the severity of the economic collapse was the inappropriate nature of the reform policies carried out at the time – in particular the rapid privatization programme, which raised unemployment, reduced saving and investment and generated a series of negative effects (Griffin 1995: 12–13).

After this savage economic contraction, the situation stabilized to some extent, with GDP seeing some positive growth in 1994 and reaching 6 per cent in 1995, largely as a result of a boom in the price of copper, one of Mongolia's main exports. However, this growth stalled in 1996 when the prices of copper and cashmere fell and a newly elected government embarked on an aggressive programme of economic 'shock treatment' to remove the last vestiges of the centrally planned economy, including liberalizing fuel prices and a campaign to privatize housing (United States Embassy 1999). Growth slowed to an estimated 2.6 per cent, little more than the rate of population growth (*Mongol Messenger*, 9 July 1997).

Growth in GDP crept up to 3.3 per cent in 1997, but the country's economic difficulties were exacerbated again in 1998 by the Asian economic crisis. The main effect was to drive down the prices of its major exports: copper, gold and cashmere. Mongolian exports, which had included a range of livestock-related products in the 1980s, had become heavily dependent on the copper and molybdenum mine in Erdenet, which now accounts for around 60 per cent of the country's exports (Bruun and Odgaard 1996: 25). The reduction in the price of these commodities reduced the value of exports by 30 per cent to US$317 million (United States Embassy 1999), even lower than the level of 370 million reached in 1991, and less than half the 1989 level.[6] Government income from corporate taxation declined accordingly (42 per cent), but the state made up some of the loss by increasing the tax burden on Mongolian citizens, including a 30-per-cent increase in individual income tax collections. Despite these measures, however, government income could not match spending, and the budget deficit widened. The government budget for 1999 has a deficit of US$122 million, which is more than 11 per cent of GDP.

The Asian crisis also affected the Mongolian stock market: the index of the top 75 shares declined by 35 per cent during 1998. The financial sector was beset with problems, the banks had accumulated a great deal of bad debt and stopped providing much in the way of new credit for business. Many Mongolians either have no savings or will not trust them to banks even if they do.

Nevertheless, some economic growth was reported in 1998 – around 3 per cent of GDP. This apparent growth was largely due to the increase in the livestock herd by over one million head and assessments of growth in the informal and service sectors, particularly in the capital city of Ulaanbaatar. The official figures of unemployed have dropped, with the 1998 total at just under 50,000 (about 5 per cent), but it is still unclear what the actual rate really is. Employment in industry and construction has continued to decline, however, so the new jobs have presumably been recorded, or estimated, in the informal, self-employed and pastoral sectors.

Livestock numbers have risen steadily since 1994 as many pastoralists have come to rely upon their herds for subsistence. However, this has not meant an increase in the associated manufacturing or processing industries, quite the reverse – the collapse of livestock product processing industries has been dramatic. From 1993–98 carpet production fell by 64 per cent, felt production declined by 31 per cent, camel wool blankets fell by 46 per cent, and felt boots by 19 per cent. Leather goods have been particularly badly affected: leather shoe, coat and jacket production have fallen to a fraction of their earlier levels.[7] Only cashmere production has increased, but the fall in prices meant that in 1998 cashmere exports were worth slightly less than in 1997, despite an increase in their volume.

What has emerged from a decade of market-oriented reform is a national economy that is heavily dependent on a handful of export commodities – copper from the remaining Russian-Mongolian joint mining venture at Erdenet, gold and cashmere. The pastoral sector is now largely devoted to subsistence production, and poverty has increased throughout the 1990s. A survey of living standards conducted in late 1998 suggests that at least one-third of Mongolia's population is now living below the poverty line (UN Systems in Mongolia 1999: 5). The real transition that Mongolia has experienced has been from a middle-income to a poor country, as if the process of development had been put into reverse. This is certainly how some pastoralists saw it, describing the country as having lost decades of improvement with conditions beginning to resemble the 1940s!

PASTORALISTS AND THE 'AGE OF THE MARKET'

Before the 'age of the market' (*zah zeeliin üye*), as Mongolians call it, most of the nation's 310 rural districts (*sum*) supported a single collective farm (*negdel*) which raised livestock in line with state planning. Some 50 districts had state farms instead (*sangiin aj ahui*), including the regions that carried out large-scale crop production.[8] The *sum* generally consisted of a central settlement of a few hundred households and a large area of grassland in which something like the same number of pastoral households kept livestock, most of them living in mobile felt yurts (*ger*) and moving to different seasonal pastures in an annual cycle. These families herded the collective or state-farm livestock alongside a smaller number of their personal animals. The collectives also owned machinery for transportation and hay-cutting services that were used to support pastoralism. The dissolution of the collectives began in 1991 and was complete by 1993, with most of the livestock and other agricultural resources becoming the private property of the members of the collectives. The surviving state farms and collectives became companies (*kompan*). In some rural areas these companies have been dissolved or collapsed since that time, although in some districts they remain – largely as marketing organizations.

As the formally collective assets were divided, some enterprises termed 'cooperatives' (*horshoo* or *horshoolol*) were formed by members pooling their shares to gain joint ownership of some section of the old *negdel*. These cooperatives either attempted to operate a former collective resource – such as a small vegetable-growing operation – or acted as a marketing organization to sell the produce of pastoral families and deliver the goods they ordered in return. Most of these have gone bankrupt in the last few years, or have become inoperative as a result of financial difficulties. The result is that most pastoral households have to manage independently, relying on their own livestock and labour, selling their products as best as they can.

Although pastoralists gained livestock, the dissolution of the old system has meant the loss of a number of important benefits that the collectives had supplied. The collectives had provided pastoralists with a guaranteed income, trucks to support pastoral movement, and deliveries of winter fodder for the animals. One of the most important aspects was the security of basic food provision. The price of flour and other staple foods has increased, in relative terms, much more quickly than the prices paid to pastoralists for their products (wool, meat and milk) and supplies are often unreliable in remote pastoral districts. This is of central importance to pastoral households, who need carbohydrates to balance their meat-rich diet, and have few alternatives to flour. Mongolia used to be self-sufficient in grain production, but the grain harvest has declined steadily since reforms began, from 718 thousand tonnes in 1990 to less than 240 thousand tonnes in 1996. The 1997 harvest was a little higher, but in 1998 the total fell to 195 thousand tonnes (*Mongol Messenger*, 18 September 1996; Ministry of Agriculture and Industry of Mongolia 1998; United States Embassy 1999). The shortfall has to be filled with imported flour, and prices have risen accordingly.

In the past the cheap fuel that the Soviet Union supplied to Mongolia meant that mechanical transport, a key factor in such a huge and thinly populated country, was affordable and widely available to local government, national services and productive enterprises alike. As the price of petrol increased rapidly in the 1990s, transportation became more expensive and medical and veterinary treatment less accessible for most pastoralists. Basic medicines werer in short supply, and fewer and fewer people could afford to go to the capital for the treatment of serious ailments. There was a slow collapse of effective state social security. People could, all too easily, become destitute in a way that was unthinkable in the late 1980s.

In 1996 the newly elected government yielded to IMF and Asian Development Bank pressure and removed the remaining subsidy on fuels, as part of its aim to liberalize the economy more fully.[9] In September the cost of petrol rose by 46 per cent, from 130 to 190 tögrögs (US$0.24 to 0.35)[10] per litre. This had the immediate effect of increasing the prices of all the items required by pastoral families, and depressing the prices they could expect to get for their animal products, as traders faced dramatically higher transportation costs.

The results of these changes were immediately felt in the districts of Renchinlhümbe and Hanh, two *sums* in Hövsgöl, the northern region of Mongolia were I was conducting fieldwork in summer and autumn 1996. Hövsgöl is a relatively long way from the large markets of Ulaanbaatar, and so its pastoralists faced more severe economic hardships than those nearer to the capital, who were better placed to sell their produce at higher prices, and obtain consumer goods more cheaply. The price of commodities reflects the increased transportation costs to remote areas. The price of flour rose from 280–300 tögrög (US$0.53) in August 1996 to 450 tögrög (US$0.82) a kilo in September after the rises in fuel price. (In comparison, the price of flour was still 380 tögrögs at that time in better-connected rural areas such as Ih Tamir *sum* in the Arhangai region of central Mongolia.) Since that time the cost of food has risen further, and it should not be assumed that one can always find flour even if one has the money to buy it. In Hanh *sum* there simply was no flour for sale for much of 1996, families and organizations having made private arrangements to buy it for themselves, but not for local resale. Disappointingly, if pastoralists could find buyers for their produce, the prices obtainable for animal products remained low: 250–300 tögrög (US$0.50) per kilo for wool; cashmere generally sold for less than 3,000 tögrög (US$5.45) at that time, and a sheep for 12,000 tögrög (US$21.82) or less.

As the government reduced education funding, teachers' salaries and morale dropped. In Hanh *sum*, for example, the secondary school was forced to stop teaching the final year of school education (the 10th grade) to reduce its costs. Schooling the children of mobile pastoral families had posed some difficulties for the state socialist regime, but these had been largely overcome by the provision of boarding facilities for children to stay at the school during term time. By 1996 this system was in crisis, and where school boarding facilities still operated, it had become usual for herding families to be charged a sheep for each child staying in the dormitories. This livestock was sold to finance the food and fuel necessary to feed the children while they are away from their families. Conditions have declined and a local administrator, 43-year-old Gereltsetseg, complained to me about the miserable food that the schoolchildren had to eat.

In rural areas the shortages of goods and services have promoted the tendency for produce to be obtained through personal contacts of one sort or another. Of course, this is by no means a new phenomenon. In the state socialist period this practice was widespread, and as a wide range of goods and services were accessed through the bureaucracy, links with those in positions of authority proved to be of prime importance. Despite decollectivization and reform, some of the old networks remain. In rural districts the economic dislocation of reform (particularly the problems of distribution) has led to shortages and a general sense of economic insecurity. In this situation many local officials retain effective control of much of the distribution process, because they remain part of old networks that have access to what is left by way of goods and resources. In Renchinlhümbe, for example, the only person to have obtained a large supply of rice and flour was one of the local government officials, who had managed to arrange a shipment and kept a large stockpile of grain in a sturdy lock-up from which he sold it to local households at prices considered outrageously high.

The response of many normal Mongolians is to rely to an even greater degree on family and friends – these people are the resources that you can count upon. Through such networks they still hope to gain access to the wide range of goods and services that are expensive or otherwise difficult to obtain. Furthermore, the insecurity faced by many pastoralists who are now having to worry about maintaining basic food supplies for their families, makes many of them unwilling to sell more than a minimum number of livestock, in case they need them for food in the future. High inflation had damaged pastoralists' confidence in the security of cash savings, so that accumulating livestock remains the goal of most livestock owners. This is one reason for the continuing increase in livestock numbers. From 1990 to 1998 the national herd had increased by over 20 per cent from 25.9 to 31.9 million heads (Statistical Office of Mongolia 1993: 28; Ministry of Agriculture and Industry of Mongolia 1998: 2).

Far from being able to market and purchase more than in the past, many pastoral households are increasingly subsisting on their own produce and marketing only their surplus (if they have any) – particularly wool and cashmere, which they can collect without losing livestock.

Another aspect of the recent changes has been a process of deurbanization. The old regime had promoted a form of urbanization, fostering the rapid growth of cities and towns, and establishing settlements in the *sum* centres. The economic crisis was particularly destructive for activities associated with urban lifestyles, such as office and industrial employment, health and educational services. The collapse of formerly state-run enterprises and the dissolution of the pastoral collectives threw thousands of employees out of work, forcing many of them to herd livestock to make a living. This helped create a flow of people from urban centres into rural districts. From 1992 to 1995 the urban population declined by around 4 per cent (50,000 people), while the rural population increased by over 15 per cent (150,000) (UNDP 1997: 63; Statistical Office of Mongolia 1993: 3). However, the capital city of Ulaanbaatar still attracts people from rural districts, and there has also been a flow of people into the city which still offers some economic opportunities, particularly in the informal sector. Between 1991–98, nearly 70,000 people moved to Ulaanbaatar, so that about 10 per cent of the city's present population migrated there during this time.[11]

Decollectivization and Reduced Mechanization

The dissolution of the collectives made large numbers of the service sector employees unemployed and has forced them to rely upon their livestock holdings for subsistence. This is affecting the patterns of pastoralism as many of these 'new' herders still have dwellings in the *sum* centre and so tend to be much less mobile that the established herding households who were part of specialized herding brigades in the collective (such brigades have now generally been renamed *bag*, the pre-revolutionary name for the subdistricts of a *sum*). A common coping strategy is for such households from the *sum* centre to pasture their livestock quite close to the centre during the summer months, and then have some or all of their livestock herded by relatives or friends among the pastoral families in more distant pastures for the rest of the year. The collectives used to cut hay mechanically, using tractors, and then distribute it for use as winter fodder to pastoral households by truck. Since decollectivization, individual households have had to cut hay by hand in late summer and early autumn, and transport it themselves – often using animal carts. This hay-making is exhausting and physically demanding work. Those households without active adult members or the money to buy hay can find it difficult to collect sufficient winter fodder for their animals.

In the collective period each production brigade moved to seasonal pastures, and for the longest legs of this annual migration they were usually relocated using a collective truck, which greatly eased the difficulty of these distant movements. The motor pools of the collectives have been privatized and today almost all the annual movements in both Renchinlhümbe and Hanh are done using animal transport. Along with the need to cut their own hay by hand, this has greatly increased the overall burden that households face.

Many of the mechanical assets of the collectives have now ceased to be productively used. Livestock gained from privatization could be relied upon to provide some sort of income, even when divided into small herds owned by individual families. But machinery like tractors and welding equipment, on the other hand, were largely used as part of the collective's overall operation, and are now seldom used. The lack of hay reserves and collective motor pools that could have been used to deliver fodder and move livestock is one of the principal reasons for the catastophic losses of livestock in the disastrous winters of 1999–2001 (*zud*) in which more than 5 million animals have died at the time of writing. These have been entirely predictable disasters for Mongolian pastoralists, and the scale of losses was a direct result of the collapse of the state and collective transportation and fodder-supply systems.

Case study

A typical example of the results of decollectivization was the case of one of the families that recently had become pastoralists in Renchinlhümbe. Batbayar[12] was a 34-year-old welder who relied upon his herd of 200 animals to make a living. He was the youngest of three brothers, and the two others, Pürev and Bat-Erdene, were tractor drivers for the collective. They, too, had begun to herd livestock to make ends meet. Batbayar learnt his trade in the army, where he welded for three years before leaving to work for the local collective for the next seven years. He lost his job, like his brothers, in 1993 when the collective was dissolved.

All three brothers managed to secure their equipment from the collective during the privatization process. Batbayar had his welding equipment and his brothers had a tractor each – a remarkable set of expensive assets which should have made them relatively wealthy men.

In fact the tractors stood idle, outside their *gers*, and were hardly ever used. When I got to know the brothers in August 1996, they were preparing to cut hay by hand, despite the fact that they also had the grass-cutting machinery needed to do this by tractor. The main obstacle, they explained, was the expense and difficulty of running their tractors. The fuel was very expensive, as were spare parts (if they were obtainable at all). I asked why they could not cut enough hay to sell to local families to cover their costs. Pürev laughed at this suggestion. The really good hay fields were a long way from where they were, he explained, and the ones used by local families were smallish patches of rather sparse hay, spread out over a large area. This meant that it would be very expensive to cut a lot of hay by tractor and transport it, and very few local families were wealthy enough to be able to afford such costly hay. Instead, local men spend an exhausting fortnight or so in late August, working dawn to dusk to cut hay by hand. Some of this hand-cut hay was sold by those families who most badly needed cash. A full truck-load of hay (around 2 tons) sold for about 30,000 tögrögs (about US$50).

Since the collective had closed, most of the residents of Renchinlhümbe *sum* had become directly dependent on livestock for their subsistence. 1,207 people (over 70 per cent of the total *sum* population of 1,724) were officially classed as *malchid* [herders] by the local government in Renchinlhümbe in 1996, for example, and a further 405 were unemployed and likely to be indirectly dependent on the livestock sector. Indeed, only 6.5 per cent of the *sum* population (112 people) were employed in non-pastoral sectors. Most households had found that ownership of animals had not provided sufficient income to compensate them for the loss of salaried employment in collective and government sectors.

Pastoral households faced a cash shortage, because selling their animal products was far from easy, and inflation was still high. Herding families were understandably reluctant to retain large amounts of cash, and preferred to have the products that they required instead – flour, cloth, candles, tea and salt. This led to the spread of barter trade, whereby traders took livestock directly in exchange for the consumer goods that they brought with them. Local families complained that opportunities to obtain consumer goods were so rare that they ended up paying very high prices (in livestock) for the traded goods.

WEALTH DISTRIBUTION

Although pastoralists in Hövsgöl and elsewhere all face severe economic difficulties, the poor face the gravest problems. An idea of the differences in wealth that have emerged can be seen from a detailed examination of the economic situation of one pastoral subdistrict (*bag*) of the *sum*. The number of livestock owned by every household in the fifth *bag* of Renchinlhümbe *sum* is shown in Figures 14.1 and 14.2.

The figures show a now typically unequal pattern of wealth distribution, with the wealthiest 25 per cent owning over 40 per cent of the total wealth in the *bag*. It should be remembered, however, that this *bag* does not contain many of the

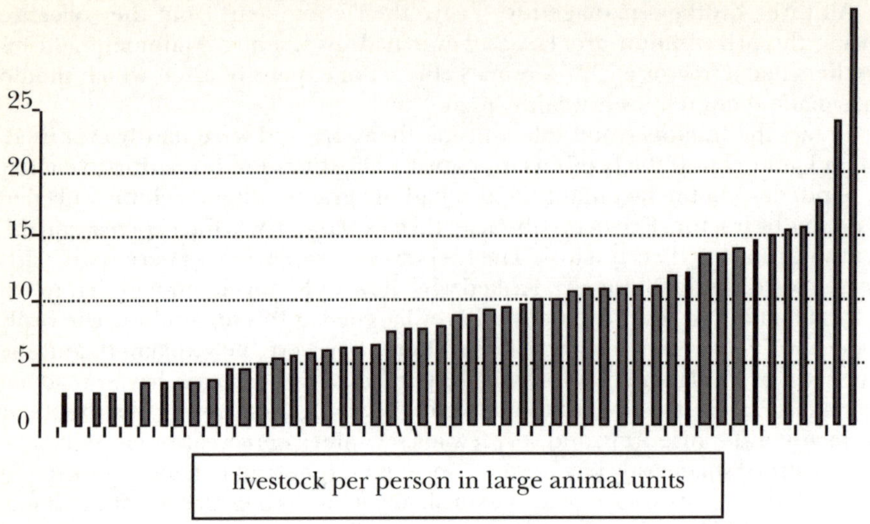

Figure 14.1: Wealth distribution – livestock per person (Renchinlhümbe, *bag* 5)

households with the fewest livestock in the district, who are pensioners in or near the *sum* centre, and are often poorer still. Networks also connect these and other households, so that there is still some support for many of the old and poor. Still, in the current economic situation those households that have very low numbers of animals – some have just two or three large animals – face severe problems with basic food supplies. One of the households that I knew in Hanh *sum* was unable to buy any flour or rice at all, and the children's health was already suffering as a result of their poor diet.

Figure 14.1 shows the number of large animal units per person in the households of the fifth *bag*, as a simple comparison of household ownership would not take account of the number of mouths to feed in each unit. (The large animal units used here are *bod* – one of the traditional Mongolian methods of reckoning livestock of different species by calculating them in large animal equivalents).[13] Figure 14.2 shows the percentage of total livestock in the *bag* owned by different sections of the population, calculated by *household*.

As Figure 14.2 shows, the poorest ten households own only 5.9 per cent of the total *bag* livestock, whereas the richest ten households own over 43 per cent. Within a few years of privatization, then, significant inequalities in wealth have emerged, even within the 51 families of this remote rural district which itself has suffered from impoverishment, both in absolute terms and in relation to urban centres such as Ulaanbaatar.

Social Networks

Mongolian rural households supply and receive goods and services from relatives and friends on a regular basis. Within these social networks, the help people provide one another ranges from gifts of consumer goods like alcohol and tobacco, to animals and the use of motor vehicles.

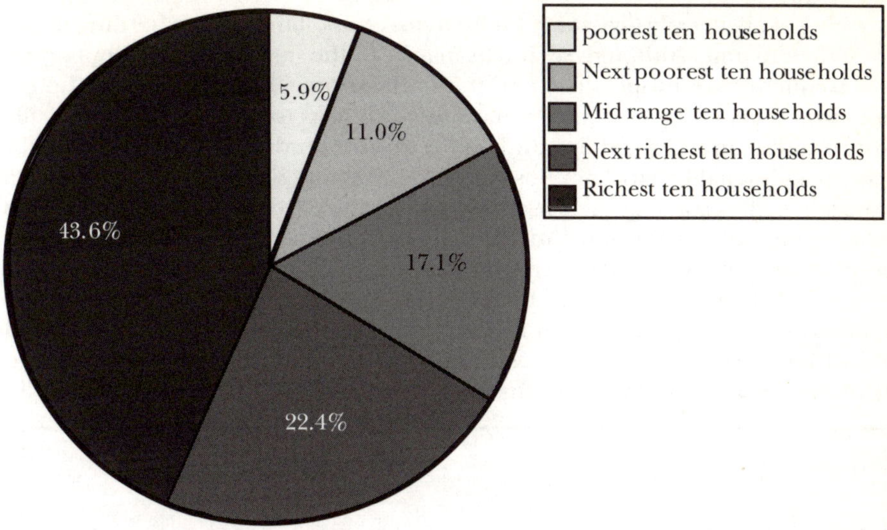

Figure 14.2: Proportion of total livestock owned by sections of the population of *Bag* 5 (*bod* units per person)

In general, relations with kin (*hamaatan* or *töröl sadan*) provide the most important strands in these networks.[14] Mongolians tend to have large families, and kin networks are generally large and well-extended. The strongest links are usually between close kin, particularly those who were once members of the same household, such as one's children, siblings, parents, and grandparents. However, kinship is generally traced bilaterally to a depth of at least three generations. The expectations that relatives have of one another differs somewhat, depending upon their relative ages. In general, elder kin are expected to provide assistance such as advice, influence and material goods or money, while juniors are expected to provide respect, obedience and labour. Connections with affines seem to be no less important than those to cognates.

After close kin, the strongest bonds of obligation tend to be between good friends, particularly schoolmates and those who carried out military service together. The strong obligations that kin should feel for one another are also expected in close friendship, and many Mongolian terms apply to both types of relationship. A common term for good friends is *ah düü* (literally – 'elder and younger siblings'), and this explicitly draws upon the idiom of kinship. In many cases gifts between such friends will be associated with recreation, such as presents of alcohol and tobacco, but they are also entail obligations to provide services or goods that one partner may need from time to time. For example, help with obtaining transport or local government authorization are typical favours that friends will expect from those able to provide them.

Networks are also of importance when it comes to the ownership of livestock and their pasturing arrangements. The livestock belonging to the former employees of the collective living in the *sum* centre are frequently herded for them by relatives and friends, outside formal economic relations, so that if they give anything at all, people give some useful items or assistance to the herding family from time to time. Although such gifts may be in the form of cash, their amount and frequency are unspecified, and left to the owner to decide. A poor household would generally welcome animals to herd, so as to make use of their milk, wool or other animal products, and even a well-off herding household generally accepts additional livestock for this reason. The family owning the livestock would expect to collect some of their livestock and produce from time to time. This is a vital coping strategy for non-pastoral families in the settlements, who could not properly keep livestock all year-round themselves.

Most of the pastoralists that I knew in Hövsgöl and elsewhere were herding animals in this way for relatives or friends.[15] The figures below show data gathered from 13 of the 51 households in *bag* number five of Renchinlhümbe *sum*,[16] and 21 of the 208 households in the first and third *bags* of Hanh *sum*.

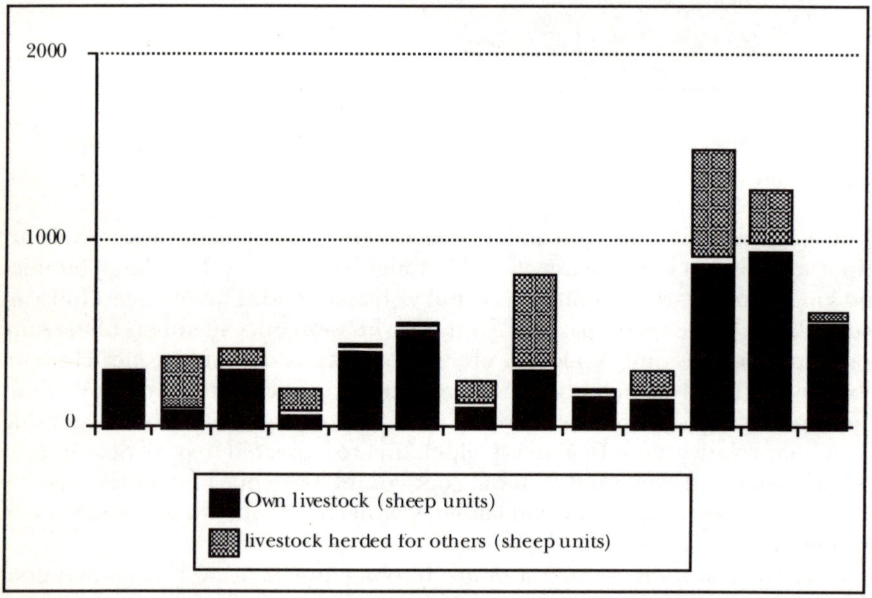

Figure 14.3: Livestock herded by interviewed households (Renchinlhümbe, *bag* 5)

The high proportion of livestock belonging to others (38 per cent of the total in this sample) reflects the fact that the fifth *bag* was still largely composed of relatively specialized pastoral households who moved to distant pastures, and were therefore more likely to be asked to herd other people's domestic animals. In the interviewed *ails* in Hanh, the proportion of livestock belonging to other households that were being herded in this way was rather less, as shown in Figure 14.4, although still significant (17.5 per cent of the total). In one case the household concerned was herding livestock belonging to a branch of the local government under a more formal contract arrangement, but for all the other households that herded for others, the animals were owned by kin or friends, and not subject to any formal economic contract.

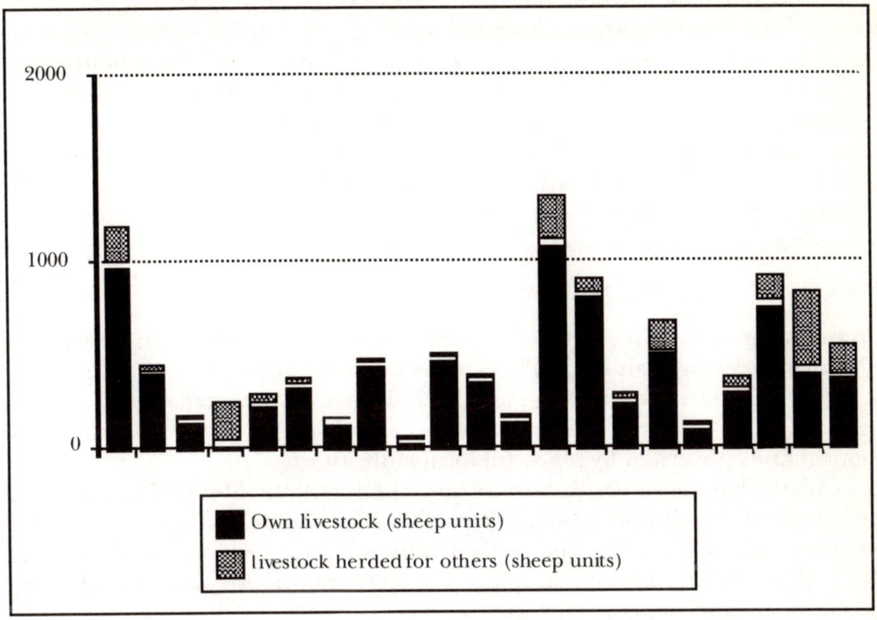

Figure 14.4: Livestock herded by interviewed households (Hanh *sum*)

Mongolian pastoral households[17] generally camp in small groups of one or more yurts (*ger*), forming an encampment or residential group. This is known as the *ail*. (If there are several dwellings it may be called a *hot-ail*, although this term is not widely used in some regions, including Hövsgöl.) The households composing an *ail* or *hot-ail* usually herd their livestock jointly, and help one another in numerous everyday tasks.

In fact, the encampments are flexible groupings based on underlying patterns of kinship and other social relations. Residence is used strategically to take advantage of whatever opportunities can be found in the current crisis. Where circumstances permit, families may have both settled and mobile sections. Older family members, and children of school-going age for example, may remain in the settlement, while the more active adult population carry out mobile pastoralism.

Most pastoral encampments are composed of a number of component parts (usually nuclear and stem families)[18] which are brought together for some reason – often by kinship, sometimes by friendship or convenience. These not only change from year to year, in line with changing interpersonal relations of the members, but in many cases they vary from season to season, so that those making up an encampment at the summer pastures are often different from those at the autumn, winter or spring pastures. In Hanh, 12 of the 21 encampments that I studied changed their composition during the year, and the other nine retained a constant composition all year round. About half the encampments that I studied in Renchinlhümbe also varied throughout the year. Often it is only the component parts of encampments (generally nuclear or stem families) that remain constant units throughout the pastoral year.

Mobile and settled households are connected by social networks so that products and personnel (particularly children) move between the settlements and the mobile pastoral encampments, creating a social matrix that includes both mobile and settled life. These flexible residence patterns and the social networks that underpin them allow families to adapt in the face of change. If there is an opportunity – such as the chance to sell milk at the *sum* centre – a family may detach a component nuclear family with the milk cows to stay close enough to the centre to make the sales. Unfortunately there are, at present, few such ways of earning a cash income in pastoral districts, and often a shortage of goods to buy in any case.

PRE-COLLECTIVE PASTORALISM

Although the collectives were clearly exogenous, bureaucratic structures that transformed Mongolian rural life in many ways, it would be misleading to suggest that since decollectivization pastoralism has simply reverted to its traditional form. For many centuries pastoral families raised livestock as part of larger socio-political units governed by powerful local authorities.

From the late seventeenth century until the twentieth, Mongolia was ruled by the Manchu Qing dynasty, which collapsed in 1911. Communist power was established in 1921 in Mongolia, and collectivization was carried out in the 1950s and 1960s. If we wish to describe 'traditions' of pastoralism, we must study the pre-revolutionary and pre-collective periods.

In the Manchu period the people and territory of Mongolia were ruled by the Emperor, and were administered on his behalf by nobles and officials.[19] The principal administrative district was the *hoshuu* ('banner') administered by the *Zasag* – the aristocratic prince of a secular *hoshuu,* or the *Hubilgan* (reincarnate senior lama) of an ecclesiastic one (Bawden 1968: 88). Within the *hoshuu,* the herdsmen were assigned to sub-units called *sum,* and within these to smaller units called *bag.*[20] Each of these units had officials responsible for them, and the herdsmen were usually required to use pastures allocated to these sub-units.

Large numbers of the animals of a district were typically owned by the nobles or monasteries, and herded for them by their subjects. Most of these commoners also owned their own livestock, although there were some poor households with little or no livestock who worked for wealthier families. Although most households owned a range of livestock breeds, there were also specialists who would look after large herds of certain breeds (particularly horses) for their noble or monastic masters.

This pattern of pastoral management continued well into the twentieth century, until the nobility and Church were stripped of their power and wealth in the 1920s and 1930s. The Mongolian state increased its direct control of the pastoral economy, introducing compulsory state delivery quotas in 1941, and incorporating pastoralists into the new collectives and state farms in the 1950s.

THE POLITICAL ECONOMY OF PASTORALISM

In a complex and stratified society such as Mongolia, pastoralism has long had to fulfil two types of requirements. The first was to provide produce for pastoral households themselves – the 'domestic subsistence' role. The second was to provide good levels of return in terms of produce on the herds belonging to pastoral elites – the 'yield–focused' role. These two roles overlapped and supported each other, to some extent.

Domestic subsistence activities were oriented towards satisfying household requirements, and as such were characterized by each pastoral family owning and herding relatively small numbers of several species of domestic livestock. The various species provided different necessities for the pastoralist: sheep and goats for meat and winter clothing; cattle for milk; horses for riding; and camels for transportation. As these were the personal livestock of the family, not herded for others under contractual obligation – the produce went directly to the working household.

The yield-focused activities were based on the ownership of large numbers of animals by a single agency – usually a noble family, ecclesiastical institution, local government office, or a rich commoner. It was characterized by the owner having his herds cared for by other pastoral households, and often involved the specialized herding of large, single-species herds. The subordinate herders had contractual obligations to supply a certain quota of produce and retained only the surplus for themselves. This system (called *süreg tavih*) generally made use of certain economies of scale in that large herds could be herded with little more labour than small ones.

By the nineteenth century most of the Mongolian elite was in debt to Chinese merchant firms. In the pre-revolutionary period much of the produce of the districts ruled by the princes and senior lamas was expended on servicing this debt (see Sanjdorj 1980: 80).[21] The orientation of such herd-owners was towards the Chinese market, mediated by their debts to merchants, and rich herd-owners had every reason to extract the maximum surplus from the livestock economy. When this neo-feudal social order[22] was abolished in the 1920s, some of the livestock was redistributed among herding households and the surplus animals extracted by the old elite could be accumulated by pastoralists. The total number of livestock increased from 10 million in 1918 to over 25 million in 1940.

It should not be assumed, however, that subsistence pastoralists and wealthy yield-focused herd-owners necessarily had conflicting interests. The existence of specialist herding seems to have allowed smaller producers to place some of their stock with these larger herds, so benefiting from economies of scale. Furthermore, the feudal district authorities also organized other specialist activities of benefit to the whole community, such as the cultivation of wheat. This agriculture was often an assigned feudal duty for specialist households.[23]

The period following the abolition of the neo-feudal order and before collectivization saw a decline in the large-scale and specialist production and high herd offtake organized by the neo-feudal elite, and an increase in the domestic subsistence sphere and livestock totals. With the introduction of the collectives, it was as if the yield-focused specialist mode, with its large herds of 'official/duty animals' (*alban mal*), had expanded to include all of the pastoralists and most of the livestock. The small remaining sector devoted to domestic consumption was represented by the small numbers of private animals that herders were allowed to keep.

Both neo-feudal and collective systems managed to export large amounts of livestock. By the end of the nineteenth century, Outer Mongolia was probably exporting at least 1 million sheep units of livestock to China each year – about 5 per cent of the total national herd.[24] In the collective era the Mongolian state was also able to procure and export large numbers of animals. State procurement in 1985, for example, was almost 207 thousand tons (live weight) of meat and livestock, and 87.4 thousand head of horses. Of this 63.1 thousand horses and 61.5 thousand tons of livestock and meat were exported – 4.7 per cent of the national herd, by my estimate, rather close to the pre-revolutionary figure given above.[25] Exports of meat and livestock fell rapidly with the dissolution of the collectives – by 1992 the total had dropped to one-fifth of the 1985 figure.

In some respects the conceptual shift from neo-feudal to collective notions of property was not a very radical change. In both feudal and collective periods there were centralized, commandist politico-economic units that regulated residence and the use of pasture, and extracted a surplus through rights to livestock. Normal citizens, in both periods, had legal duties to their leaders. In the feudal period this consisted of providing livestock and produce, and might include acting as servants, or performing military service. In the collectives the duty of members was to fulfil the 'norm' set by the farm (as well as performing military service).

It is significant that the everyday term used for collective or state animals was *alban mal* ('official' or 'duty' animals) and the root of this term is *alba* – the feudal obligation owed by pre-revolutionary subjects to their lord. Indeed, the term for a common citizen or serf was *albat* – meaning one with duty. In both collective and feudal pastoral economies, common herders were tied members of an administrative district and owed politico-economic obligations to the central authorities of that district. When the collectives were introduced to Mongolia, they were widely perceived by local pastoralists as being a new form of local government, and their combination of political and economic functions was a familiar organizational form.[26]

Other Mongolian concepts reveal the inextricable linkage between political and economic spheres, and their roots in a unitary form of social order. The term for government, for example, is *zasag*. This is the same term that was used for the lord of the patrimonial fief. In Mongolian the very term for the 'economy' rests upon this notion of government – *ediin zasag* – composed of the word *zasag*, and the term *ed* – which means both 'possessions', 'property' and 'thing,' 'article' or 'item'. 'Economy' in Mongolian literally means something like the 'governance of property' or 'possessions authority'.[27] We can see here that the very definition of the economic sphere depends upon the notion of political authority. This was no Soviet import, this linkage was a long-standing one.

In both the feudal and collective period the large-scale pastoral operations of the district authorities (be they lords, monasteries or collectives) were official activities – obligations that subjects owed their political masters. The personal herds of animals were allotted and allowed to them for their domestic needs. In the Mongolian context, pastoral privatization, then, meant dismantling the collectives and increasing the personal allocation of the members and subsistence production oriented to the needs of the household. It has also resulted (in the short term at least) in a decline in the economies of scale of the larger politico-economic units upon which pastoralism had hitherto been based.

Quite early in the reform process it was seen that 'freeing' the markets was not having the desired effects on the pastoral economy. In 1991, for example, Western economic advice led to the Mongolian government introducing a policy of 'freeing' the price of milk. Liberalizing the prices, it was thought, would increase the rewards to the producer for selling more milk and increase the supply. However, after letting milk prices float for six months, the price of milk in the cities had increased to nine times the original cost, but the amount of available milk had been halved (Campi 1994: 240–241). The dramatic increase in meat prices in 1991 also failed to improve the supply of that commodity.[28] The pastoral economy that had been generated by the reforms was composed of thousands of scattered households providing themselves with animal produce, only a fraction of which were in a position to supply highly perishable produce to the urban markets. The reform policies were simultaneously dismantling the state procurement system and the institutions primarily oriented towards providing milk and meat for the cities. Without the transportation arrangements of the official procurement system, selling milk and meat represents a good deal of effort for hard-pressed pastoral families, and there was no longer any official obligation for them to do so. In rural Mongolia the reality of institutional settings and their associated methods of operation and transportation had a greater influence on pastoralists than the prices for commodities paid in distant urban markets.

CONCLUSION

In retrospect, the notion that by privatizing state property and removing political controls (seen as suppressing market behaviour) Mongolia could join the Asian tiger economies, seems entirely unrealistic, and based on an unreasonable faith in the existence and potency of a latent, untapped economic potential, which would be released by free market reforms.

In the pastoral sector the large-scale pastoralism of the collectives had formed part of a politico-economic structure that supported manufacturing and processing industries. Unsurprisingly, perhaps, these declined together, leaving pastoral households to fall back on long-standing domestic systems of self-provisioning and subsistence. The conceptual separation between the economic and the political – and in particular the notion of a latent but highly productive market economy that could be rapidly emancipated from a restrictive politico-economic system, made little sense in the pastoral context. In this context dismantling the political framework of the large-scale pastoral institutions led to the collapse of their district-wide operations, and expanded the domestic subsistence operations of individual families that were poorly adapted to supply livestock products to commerce and manufacturing industry.

Mongolia's 'age of the market' has seen a retreat to subsistence for many pastoral families, a reduction in the circulation of their produce, the development of inequalities of wealth, and a loss of mechanization. In the face of economic crisis, pastoralists have continued to rely on networks of family and friends, parts of which may be manifested in the residential form of the encampment.

State socialism in Mongolia had adapted older notions of a hierarchical politico-economic order, which was well adapted to the organization of pastoral life. Pastoralists had long made flexible use of pasture land that was held by the large political unit of which they were members, changing the operation and composition of the herding unit as necessary to fulfil their obligations. Local authorities have long represented the unity of political and economic spheres. It is increasingly clear that importing the market economy into Mongolia was not an uncomplicated matter of enacting some new laws. The efficient market depends upon a whole series of institutions, concepts and conventions which were not indigenous to this region, and in the short term at least, decollectivization has disrupted the large-scale, semi-mechanized, politico-economic pastoral system that had been developed in the past. Experience may yet show that the particular characteristics of Mongolian pastoralism make it inappropriate to attempt analysis and reform by treating it like the livestock sector of a Western market economy.

NOTES

1 'Mongolia entered the twentieth century as an impoverished country ... an inadequate financial system hampered mobilization of savings and financial intermediation. Private wealth was stored mostly in domestic animals, and since peasants [*sic*] did not own the land under the prevailing system of land tenure, there was little incentive for agricultural investment and development' (Asian Development Bank 1992: 13).

2 The government provides substantial hidden subsidies through controlled rents on public housing. 'These subsidies need also to be removed gradually, paving the way for the privatization of the housing sector' (World Bank 1994: 27).

3 Griffin (1995: viii) estimates the decline in average incomes at around 30 per cent over that period. IMF data suggest a smaller decline in average incomes of about 25 per cent (Griffin 1995: 5). UNDP and Asian Development Bank estimates suggested a decline of 34 per cent in GNP per capita from 1989–92 (Griffin 1995: 25).

4 The CIA *World Factbook 1998* entry on Mongolia (http://www.odci.gov/cia/publications/factbook/mg.html). A 1996 article in the Mongolian daily *Ardyn Erh* suggested that the concealed unemployment total approached 90,000 (*Ardyn Erh*, 27 September 1996).

5 The UN Systems in Mongolia (1999: 6) estimates that this assistance represented, on average, 37 per cent of annual GDP.

6 Exports were US$832 million in 1989 and 493 million in 1990 (World Bank 1994: table 4.1).

7 Leather shoe, coat and jacket production showed a 24, 33 and a 160-fold decrease respectively. Sheep skin processing also declined by 55 times and the production of processed goat-skin by 14 times (Ministry of Agriculture and Industry of Mongolia 1998).

8 In some districts state farms have survived as companies, usually much reduced in size after large parts of their assets were privatized. Where such companies continue to hold large numbers of animals, these are herded by households under 'lease' arrangements that are similar to the old 'norm' by which the collective members were given production plans.

9 The IMF and Asian Development Bank had actually made some new loans conditional on energy price liberalization (*Mongol Messenger*, 4 September 1996).

10 The exchange rate was around 550 tögrög to the dollar at this time.

11 President Bagabandi mentioned these figures in a public speech in March 1999.

12 The names and certain details of the informants have been changed to protect their anonymity.

13 The *bod* unit is equivalent to one horse, cow or yak; two-thirds of a camel; seven sheep or ten goats.

14 Social networks are not stable groups or institutions; rather they are social fields 'defined by an intense flow of reciprocal exchange' (Lomnitz 1977: 209).
15 Ih Tamir *sum* in Arhangai *aimag* and Sumber *sum* in Gov'sumber *aimag* where I also worked in autumn and winter 1996, for example.
16 There are two Mongolian 'Standard Stocking Units' that can be used to evaluate the overall number of livestock in a herd of several species. One is the large animal (*bod*) unit, the other commonly used stocking unit is in sheep equivalents (*bog*). In terms of small animals, goats are worth 0.9, cattle (including yaks) 5, and horses 6 sheep units (Mongolian Academy of Sciences 1990: 108).
17 I use 'household' to mean a hearth-group that shares one dwelling, and whose members consume meals together regularly.
18 A nuclear family is a conjugal pair and their unmarried children, whereas a stem family is a nuclear family living with the parents of one of the spouses.
19 Sanjdorj (1980: 1) takes a Marxist line and states that in the sixteenth and seventeenth centuries 'the land ... was the property of the feudal classes' and this may obscure the way in which the ultimate rights over land were vested in the Emperor, and the *hoshuu* was administered in his name by the *Zasag noyan.*
20 The *bag* was the usual secular sub-division, the subunit used in the ecclesiastical districts had a different term – *otog.*
21 Sanjdorj suggests that in effect Mongolia had virtually become an economic periphery of China. Huge numbers of animals were exported to China, probably much more than 1 million sheep units a year (Sanjdorj 1980: 91).
22 Although doubts have been raised as to the applicability of the term 'feudal' (Gellner 1988), there can be little disputing the many ways in which pre-revolutionary Mongolian society resembled a feudal system (enfiefment, the division between commoners and nobility, and a legal system which tied commoners to land administered by the enfiefed lord). Rather than debate the vocabulary, I follow Bawden (1968) in using the term 'feudal' as a useful shorthand to describe the stratified social order.
23 Simukov (1933: 55–56) describes grain production organized by a monastery.
24 Sanjdorj (1980: 91) notes that in the late nineteenth century Chinese traders were taking 25,000 horses, 10,000 cows and 250,000 sheep from the area of Ih Hüree alone every year. This represents about 0.45 million sheep units. Considering that Uliastai and Hovd would have probably been engaged in comparable but smaller amounts of export trade, and southerly regions are unlikely to have traded with China via Ih Hüree, I think it safe to assume that the total export was more than twice that of the Ih Hüree figure. In 1917 the total herd wealth of Outer Mongolia was just over 20 million sheep units.
25 I estimate the total exports as equivalent to 2.1 million sheep units out of a total national herd of 45 million sheep units (see Statistical Office of Mongolia 1993: 45, 82). I estimate the total state procurement to be 6.3 million sheep units using the average live weight of each species of livestock procured by the state in 1980 (see State Statistical Office of the MPR 1981: 221). Using the same average ratio between tons of meat and sheep units, I estimate that 1985 exports represented 1.72 million sheep units of cattle, sheep and goats; adding the 0.38 million sheep units for the exported horses gives the 2.1 million figure.
26 There was a long history of local authorities owning large numbers of livestock, and requiring the district's residents to herd them. The pre-revolutionary monasteries, for example, could own more than 60 per cent of the total livestock in a district (Lattimore 1940: 97, footnote 50).
27 Another term, *aj ahui,* means 'living' or livelihood.
28 The Asian Development Bank (1992: 103) notes, as a rather unimportant detail, that the increase in meat prices in January 1991 did 'not improve the supply'.

References

Asian Development Bank (1992) *Mongolia: A Centrally Planned Economy in Transition.* Oxford: Oxford University Press.

—— (1994) 'Agricultural Sector Study of Mongolia', Division 1, Agricultural Department, February 1994.

Bawden, C. R. (1968) *The Modern History of Mongolia.* London: Weidenfeld & Nicolson.

Bruun, O. and O. Odgaard (1996) 'A society and economy in transition', in O. Bruun and O. Odgaard (eds), *Mongolia in Transition: New Patterns, New Challenges.* Nordic Institute of Asian Studies, Studies in Asian Topics, no. 22. Richmond, Surrey: Curzon Press.

Campi, A. J. (1994) 'The special cultural and social challenges involved in modernizing Mongolia's nomadic socialist economy', in E. H. Kaplan and D. W. Whisenhunt, D.W. (eds), *Opuscula Altaica: Essays Presented in Honour of Henry Schwarz.* Centre for East Asian Studies. Washington: Western Washington University.

CIA (1998) *World Factbook 1998*, entry on Mongolia, http://www.odci.gov/ciapublications/factbook/mg.html.

Gellner, E. (1988) *State and Society in Soviet Thought.* Oxford: Oxford University Press.

Griffin, K. (1995) 'Economic strategy during the transition', in K. Griffin (ed.), *Poverty and the Transition to a Market Economy in Mongolia.* New York: St Martin's Press.

Lattimore, O. (1940) *Inner Asian Frontiers of China.* American Geographical Society, Research Series no. 21. London and New York: Oxford University Press.

Lomnitz, L. A. (1977) *Networks and Marginality: Life in a Mexican Shantytown.* New York: Academic Press.

Ministry of Agriculture and Industry of Mongolia (1998), *Mongolian Agriculture and Agro-industry*, Report published on the Internet. http://www.agriculture.mnagro industry.htm#2.

Mongolian Academy of Sciences (1990) *Bügd Nairamdah Mongol Ard Uls: Ündesnii Atlas* [Mongolian People's Republic: Basic Atlas]. Ulaanbaatar: Mongolian Academy of Sciences Publications.

Nolan, P. (1995) *China's Rise, Russia's Fall: Poitics, Economics and Planning in the Transition from Stalinism.* London and Basingstoke: Macmillan.

Odgaard, O. (1996) 'Living standards and poverty', in O. Bruun, and O. Odgaard (eds), *Mongolia in Transition: new patterns, new challenges.* Nordic Institute of Asian Studies, Studies in Asian Topics, no. 22. Richmond, Surrey: Curzon Press.

Robinson, B. (1995) 'Mongalia in transition: a role for distance learning?', *Open Learning*, Nov., pp. 3–15.

Sanjdorj, M. (1980) *Manchu Chinese Colonial Rule in Northern Mongolia.* London: C. Hurst.

Simukov, A. D. (1933) 'Hotoni' [Hotons], *Sovrennaya Mongoliya* [Contemporary Mongolia], 3: 19–32.

State Statistical Office of the MPR (1981) *National Economy MPR for 60 Years 1921–81.* Ulaanbaatar: State Publishing House.

Statistical Office of Mongolia (1993) *Mongolyn Ediin Zasag, Niigem 1992* [Mongolian Economy and Society in 1992]. Ulaanbaatar: J. L. D. Gurval.

UNDP (1997) *Human Development Report, Mongolia 1997.* Ulaanbaatar.

United Nations Systems in Mongolia (1999) *Annual Report 1998.* Report published on the Internet (http://www.un-mongolia.mn/publications/anrep98.pdf).

United States Embassy (1999) *Embassy cable, subject: IMI: Mongolia shows signs of economic growth: 1998 Statistics Compiled.* Report published on the Internet. http://us-mongolia.com/general/economy.html.

von Ginneken, W. (1995) 'Employment promotion and the social safety-net,' in K. Griffin (ed.), *Poverty and the Transition to a Market Economy in Mongolia.* New York: St Martin's Press.

World Bank (1994) *Mongolia: Country Economic Memorandum; priorities in macroeconomic management.* Report no. 13612-MOG, Country Operations Division, China and Mongolia Department, Asia and Pacific Regional Office.

Newspapers and magazines

Ardyn Erh, 27 September 1996

Mongol Messenger, 9 July 1997

FIFTEEN

Conclusion

Pietro P. Masina

The aim of the studies presented in the present volume is to look at the dramatic circumstances of the East Asian economic crisis as an opportunity to reconsider the recent developmental experiences of the region. The events connected with the crisis – both its economic foundations and the social patterns of response – allow a better understanding of the economic trajectories and the process of modernization in East and Southeast Asian countries. At the same time, however, the crisis might potentially represent an important watershed in the region's recent history. East Asia entered the new millennium in the midst of a painful process of reassessment of national development strategies and the region's role within the international economic and political system. This ongoing process of transformation requires further investigation. A raft of analyses of the economic causes and consequences of the Asian economic crisis has already been launched, of course, but there is also a need for new research agendas to be drawn up to assess some of the wider dynamics of East Asian development as a precursor to, and victim of, the crisis. New issues need to be addressed and new directions are opening up for future research.

This volume has interpreted the crisis as the end of a cycle where East Asia's export-oriented growth strategies and Japan-led regional economic integration had been consistent with Western geopolitical interests. The increasing level of conflict within and over the international trade regime and the rapid growth of China as an economic power have definitively closed that cycle. This book has also presented the rather more controversial hypothesis that the crisis might have been used by Anglo-American capital to regain control over the region and prevent the advent of the so-called 'Pacific Century'. Nonetheless, the outcomes of these conflicts within the international system are not easily predictable. Since the collapse of the Soviet Union, the United States has tried to reinforce its role as the world's only superpower, although neo-isolationism at home and resistance abroad have resulted in contradictory achievements. The United States maintains a lead in technological innovation, and its economic forces retain a dominant influence on the world economy. However, the role of the United States as a hegemonic centre, able to regulate the international regime, is visibly eroded. In the aftermath of the Asian crisis, the world economy appears to be 'de-synchronized': i.e., business cycles in the major economic centres diverge and contrast. Multilateral institutions such as the WTO are in a clear impasse, challenging the optimistic prediction of an integrated global market.

The international system seems affected by such deep contradictions that the current conditions are often likened to those existing in the late 1920s in the wake of the 'Great Depression'. At present it is possible to analyse the forces of change and the conflicts ahead in the world economy, but not to anticipate the ultimate consequences. Some scenarios, however, can be depicted. One prospect is that Anglo-American capital will regain hegemonic control over the international regime, in association with Western countries (the United States in particular). An alternative prediction is the development of 'triadic capital' – less rooted within national boundaries – which is able to push ahead the globalization agenda of the 'borderless state' or of the neoliberalist agenda which sees the decline of the nation state. A third thesis foresees the reorganization of the world economy into competing regional economic blocs, with different regions struggling for a hegemonic position. Associated with this last scenario, some scholars have anticipated that East Asia could emerge as the new hegemonic centre of the world capitalist system. Interestingly, one of them – Giovanni Arrighi – in anticipating this eventual outcome *before* the Asian crisis, has noted that the transition from one system of hegemony to another historically has always been announced by *a financial crisis in the new centre* (Arrighi 1994).

Whatever scenario proves to be true, the economic crisis signals the end of a decisive phase in East Asia's development. The participation of the region in the world economy will go through readjustments and changes in the years to come. The integration of China into the capitalist international regime will unavoidably produce a shift in the world political and economic equilibrium. The conduct of Japan in this context seems still open to different strategies, either emphasizing its role as a 'triadic' centre or its regional roots. The process of sub-regional integration of ASEAN countries is also open to different outcomes: as a tool for protecting Southeast Asia from the vagaries of international markets; as a political counterweight in dealing with China (maybe in close association with the United States); or as an articulation of wider East Asian regional cooperation.

In the aftermath of the crisis, East Asian countries are in search of new development strategies. Recovery has been attempted through a closer integration into the world economy, further embarking on a process of liberalization and deregulation. Thus, national governments face increasing obstacles in returning to traditional 'developmental state' models, whose incompatibility with financial liberalization has emerged during the crisis. National growth strategies, therefore, will depend either on attempts to adapt to the process of internationalization (for instance, by exploiting regional synergies), or on an at least partial reversal of liberalization policies, through new forms of regulation and protection of national and regional economies. These different options will depend on the dynamics prevailing in the international system together with the national consensus and interest representation within the countries of East Asia.

A rethinking of the 'developmental state' is also emerging, basing the possibility of success in a more liberal world order on the ability to build knowledge-based assets, as suggested by Alice Amsden (Amsden 2001). The present volume has explored post-crisis social and political change in a 'first tier' Asian country – i.e., South Korea – where a phase of 'development' under traditional 'developmental state' policies has been concluded both by the country's admission into the OECD and the onset of the regional crisis. The results of the South Korean transition, however, are still unclear. Questions regarding the possibility of resuming growth strategies based on classical 'developmental state' policies, in the context of the new international setting, have also been raised for Southeast Asia. 'Second tier' countries such as Thailand, Malaysia and Indonesia have seen in the past only a partial implementation of the development pattern adopted by their Northeast Asian neighbours. In the aftermath of the crisis, these countries might choose to look again at the Asian 'developmental state' for inspiration; or they might opt for more (neo-)liberal recipes. The question also applies to late-late-comers like Vietnam, where the post-crisis search for development strategies is very much influenced by the experience of other Asian countries.

The growth strategies that post-crisis East Asian countries adopt, and the conditions connected with the evolving international regime, will obviously affect the lives of ordinary people. In the aftermath of the crisis, people in the region have striven to cope with the effects of 'uneven development' and the hardships deriving from the economic meltdown. The experience of the crisis has confirmed that the impact of economic distress and patterns of response are widely divergent, and are strongly connected to the way in which people have been integrated into the process of 'uneven development'. East Asian societies are in the midst of a rapid transformation, with growing urbanization and industrialization challenging traditional cultures and traditional livelihoods. Forms of resistance to these transformations, however, have played a significant role. The persistence of traditional 'safety nets' has been visible during the crisis, helping at least a part of the population to 'cope'. But the erosion of the traditional forms of village corporate solidarity is progressing, while the emergence of 'modern' safety nets through welfare systems is scarce. How 'modernization' will change East Asia in the years to come is still uncertain, in that 'modernization' is not a linear process. Forms of resistance to 'development' are emerging, sometimes on the basis of a surprising mixture between traditional and post-modernist forces (i.e., environmental movements composed of NGOs, indigenous populations, Buddhist monks, etc.). Industrialization is resulting in new labour conflicts. Urbanization is already accompanied by a 'rediscovery' of the countryside among the middle classes.

The crisis has contributed to the unveiling of the disparities that have underlain East Asia's economic success. But there is no guarantee that the path to recovery will address these inequalities, or will reform the process of 'uneven development'. After the rhetoric of the 'miracle', a new rhetoric of 'successful recovery' is already emerging. In concluding this volume, therefore, we express the wish that future research will help to provide a more realistic explanation of the process of socioeconomic transformation in East Asia, without concealing its contradictions and its forms of exclusion.

References

A. Amsden (2001) *The Rise of the Rest: Late Industrialization Outside the North Atlantic Economies.* New York: Oxford University Press.

G. Arrighi (1994) *The Long Twentieth Century: Money, Power, and the Origins of Our Time.* London: Verso.

INDEX

The Nordic Institute of Asian Studies (NIAS) is funded by the governments of Denmark, Finland, Iceland, Norway and Sweden via the Nordic Council of Ministers, and works to encourage and support Asian studies in the Nordic countries. In so doing, NIAS has published well in excess of one hundred books over the last three decades, most of them in cooperation with Curzon Press.